SIR JOHN LAWRENCE, born in England and educated at Eton and Oxford, first visited Russia in 1934. During World War II he lived in the Soviet Union for more than three years as British Press Attaché and editor of the *British Ally,* an uncensored weekly newspaper with a readership of a half-million. Since 1955 he has revisited Russia many times and was for many years chairman of the semigovernmental Great Britain–USSR Association. He is currently president of Keston College, formerly the Centre for the Study of Religion and Communism.

A HISTORY OF RUSSIA

JOHN LAWRENCE

7TH REVISED EDITION

A MERIDIAN BOOK

To My Wife, Audrey

MERIDIAN
Published by the Penguin Group
Penguin Books USA Inc., 375 Hudson Street,
New York, New York 10014, U.S.A.
Penguin Books Ltd, 27 Wrights Lane,
London W8 5TZ, England
Penguin Books Australia Ltd, Ringwood,
Victoria, Australia
Penguin Books Canada Ltd, 10 Alcorn Avenue,
Toronto, Ontario, Canada m4V 3B2
Penguin Books)n.Z.) Ltd, 182–190 Wairau road,
Auckland 10, New Zealand

Penguin Books Ltd, Registered Offices:
Harmondsworth, Middlesex, England

Published by Meridian, an imprint of New American Library,
a division of Penguin Books USA Inc.
Published by arrangement with the author. Originally appeared in
a Mentor paperback edition.

Twelfth Meridian Printing (Seventh Revised Edition), May, 1993

11 13 15 14 12 10

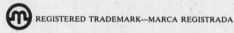 REGISTERED TRADEMARK—MARCA REGISTRADA

LIBRARY OF CONGRESS CATALOGING-IN-PUBLICATION DATA
Lawrence, John, Sir, 1907–
A history of Russia / John Lawrence.—7th rev. ed.
p. cm.
ISBN 0-452-01084-5
1. Russia—History. 2. Soviet Union—History. I. Title.
DK40.L38 1993   92-44548
947—dc20   CIP

Printed in the United States of America

foreword

by Lord Runcie of Cuddeston,
Archbishop of Canterbury
from 1978 to 1991

The speed and the convulsive nature of recent changes in the Soviet Union have taken many people by surprise. The readers of previous editions of this *History of Russia* have been equipped to understand some of the dynamics of the present turbulence. Now the author has put us further in his debt by bringing his history up to the era of "glasnost" and "perestroika."

During the Second World War, John Lawrence was resident in Moscow as the editor of an uncensored weekly newspaper of British news, *The British Ally*. He has remained an "ally" in the best sense. His love for Russia is deep, but his knowledge of the country is so considerable and extends over so many years that he has been able to penetrate the propaganda barrage which has obscured Soviet affairs in recent decades.

In particular, he has been tireless in drawing attention to the significance of the churches in Russian life and the sufferings of Christians of all denominations during the Soviet period.

The vital role played by the churches in the democratic movements in contemporary Eastern Europe has astonished many self-styled experts. They should have read John Lawrence's book and I hope that they will take advantage of this new edition to do so.

preface

1991 is not an easy year in which to prepare a new edition of my *History of Russia,* no doubt the last edition that I shall live to write. Russia is in turmoil and no one can see the end of it. But my purpose in writing this book has been to emphasize those elements in history that have made Russia what she is and will make her what she will be. Indeed, the first edition was called *Russia in the Making,* in order to emphasize that history is both continuous and open-ended. Moreover, it is not really harder to write contemporary history than it is to write of "old, forgotten, far off things and battles long ago," but if you go wrong you will be found out. So I take my courage in both hands and write on.

In preparing the seventh edition of this book there is nothing that I wish had been unsaid in previous editions. But there is much that I would like to have added had there been space. I would like to have said more about Lenin's fanatical hatred of all religion. And in the light of hindsight, I wish that I had emphasized that the plans of Stalin and his successors for "changing nature" laid the groundwork for an appalling ecological catastrophe and that the over rapid development of industrial resources was at the cost of pouring pollution into the environment. I also would have given more attention to Ukrainian nationalism, which is bound up with the tangled problems of the varied Ukrainian churches.

When the Soviet Union took over the Western Ukraine in 1939, they acquired provinces which had never been subject to any Russian state since the days of Kiev. During much of the intervening period they had been Polish and had acquired a hybrid character. In this region, as in Ireland, political allegiance is largely determined by churchmanship; so it is necessary to go into some tangled problems of ecclesiastical history.

In 1595 the Poles had established a branch of the Church which acknowledged Papal supremacy while retaining the Eastern Orthodox rite. This act of potential statesmanship had at its beginning more than an element of cynicism, but over the centuries good priests had given their parishioners a deep devotion to their Uniat, or Greek Catholic, or Eastern Rite Catholic religion, as their branch of the Church was variously described. In a region where religion was the test of national allegiance, this failed to make them fully accepted as Poles, while making it doubtful whether they were Russians. They were forcibly absorbed into the Orthodox Church after the Second World War. But they have stoutly, if clandestinely, maintained their allegiance to Rome and now number at least four million. Their movement is strongly opposed by some Orthodox hierarchs and has, until recently, been rigidly suppressed by the Communist authorities. It was legalized in December 1989, but the Communists made no arrangement whatever for the division of Churches and other property. Since then, however, this branch of the Catholic Church has attracted Ukrainian worshippers from outside the western Ukraine among those who feel that the Orthodox Church has compromised too much with the Communists. They may forget that this branch of the Catholics, being altogether illegal, had no opportunity for compromise.

To make the situation even more confused, there is also a branch of the Orthodox who proffer allegiance, not to Moscow, but to the Ecumenical Patriarch in Constantinople. this branch of the Orthodox Church has now been legalized and is making rapid progress. It too could not compromise with the Communists because it was totally illegal. It shares with the Uniates a further advantage, that its services are conducted in Ukrainian, while the "official" Russian Orthodox Church sticks to the old Church Slavonic.

In this confused situation there are, of course, secular influences working for separation, as well as many Great Russians in the Ukraine who naturally pull the other way.

When I started to write this book I did not foresee that it would have quite such a long life. Reference to "contemporary" events should therefore be interpreted as referring to events at any time between the fifties and seventies of the present century.

contents

acknowledgments

In preparing this edition of *A History of Russia* I have received valuable advice from Leonid Finkelstein, Martin Dewhirst, Alec Nove, Peter Reddaway, John Roberts, and Michael Boudeaux and his colleagues at Keston College. I am very grateful for their advice and encouragement but none of them has seen the book in its final stages and thus they are not responsible for any mistakes or misjudgements which remain.

J. W. Lawrence

PART I

forest and steppe

From the year of
   the Lord-out-of-Ur
about two millennia.
Two thousand lents again
   since the first barleymow.
Twenty millennia (and what millennia more?)
Since he became
   man master-of-plastic.
         David Jones, THE ANATHEMATA

CHAPTER I

in the beginning

*Дела давно минувших дней
Преданья старины глубокой.*

(*Deeds of days long vanished
Traditions of deep antiquity.*)

Pushkin

1. The Great Plain

IN England visitors to Cambridge looking eastward from the low Gog Magog Hills are told with pardonable exaggeration that no higher ground lies between them and the Ural Mountains. The unending fields, forests and marshes of eastern Europe lie flat and steady upon a most ancient thickness of crystalline rock, which has remained as a solid "continental platform" throughout all changes in the earth's surface. For long ages distance and slowness set the tone for human life on the Russian plain. It has been said that you may jump on your horse and ride for three months without reaching the edge of Russia. Even the transition from Europe to Asia is no barrier to movement. The Ural Mountains were formed many ages ago by a violent folding of the earth's surface against the eastern edge of the Russian continental platform. But the Himalayan peaks of the pristine Urals have long since been worn away until now the boundary mark between Asia and Europe on the Trans-Siberian railway stands on a gentle wooded slope. Beyond this the flat lands of western Siberia stretch without a break to the mountains on the confines of China. You may sit for many days in a Russian train moving at a steady, leisurely pace, and perhaps after a week you will only have crossed one corner of a large map. Russia is a world of her own, containing so much that it is hard for her people to imagine any other life.

The cradle of Russia is the broad strip of rich land that lies between the northern forest and the southern steppe or prairie. Here the famous Russian black earth lies deeper than a plow can reach and the forests supply both building material and fuel. This would have been an earthly paradise for the first Russian farmers, had they had no neighbors. But southward the wooded country soon shades into open steppe; and for countless centuries the steppe was the home of nomad peoples whose chief pleasure and profit was to raid their settled neighbors. Describing the steppe lands of the Ukraine as they were in the great days of the Cossacks in the seventeenth century, Gogol writes:

"The whole of the country was a vast green wilderness. Never a plough had passed over its measureless waves of wild grass. Only the horses, which were hidden in it as though in a wood, trampled it down. Nothing in nature could be more beautiful than this grass. The whole of the surface of the earth was like a gold and green sea, on which millions of flowers of different colors were sprinkled. Through the high and delicate stems of grass the cornflowers twinkled—light blue, dark blue and lilac. The yellow broom pushed upward its pointed crests; the white milfoil, with its flowers like fairy umbrellas, dappled the surface of the grass; an ear of wheat, which had come heaven knows whence, was ripening."

The incredible fertility of the soil is such that, where the land is not plowed, the grass grows tall enough to hide not only herds of horses, but men on horseback.

Still farther south a broad strip of poorer, waterless land covered with wormwood separates the black earth from the lively ports of the Euxine and from the traffic and civilization of the Levant. Eastward the poorer soil shades off imperceptibly into the deserts of central Asia, a teeming haunt of homeless land pirates who came raiding every year, mounted on lean but tireless nags.

The nomadic life had a unity which crosses national boundaries, for a man can ride through desert and steppe from China to the Carpathians without meeting any natural obstacle. Having no fixed cities, every tribe wandered seasonally in search of grass. Where there were too many mouths to feed the choice was to starve or to seize fresh grazing from neighbors. For countless ages nomadic tribes drawn by the magnet of the black earth pastures contended and drove each other on from the east until at last they reached the south of Russia.

2. The Scyths

Russia, but not the Russians, first comes into the stream of world history in the seventh century B.C. when the nomadic Cimmerians and Scythians broke out from the south Russian steppe to ravage Hither Asia for a full generation. Our first written account of the cruel but brave and generous life of the steppe comes from Herodotus, who visited southern Russia in the fifth century B.C., and learned much from the traders of the Greek cities round the Black Sea. He tells us that

"The Scythian soldier drinks the blood of the first man he overthrows in battle. Whatever number he slays, he cuts off all their heads, and carries them to the king; since he is thus entitled to a share of the booty, whereto he forfeits all claim if he does not produce a head. In order to strip the skull of its covering, he makes a cut round the head above the ears, and, laying hold of the scalp, shakes the skull out; then with the rib of an ox he scrapes the scalp clean of flesh, and softening it by rubbing between the hands, uses it thenceforth as a napkin. The Scyth is proud of these scalps, and hangs them from his bridle-rein; the greater the number of such napkins that a man can show, the more highly he is esteemed among them. Many make themselves cloaks, like the capotes of our peasants, by sewing a quantity of these scalps together. Others flay the right arms of their dead enemies, and make of the skin, which is stripped off with the nails hanging to it, a covering for their quivers. Now the skin of a man is thick and glossy, and would in whiteness surpass almost all other hides. Some even flay the entire body of their enemy, and stretching it upon a frame carry it about with them wherever they ride. Such are the Scythian customs with respect to scalps and skins."

Among much other information about the warlike customs of the Scyths, Herodotus describes their habit of taking vapor baths:

"First they well soap and wash their heads; then, in order to cleanse their bodies, they act as follows: they make a booth by fixing in the ground three sticks inclined toward one another, and stretching around them woolen felts, which they arrange so as to fit as close as possible; inside the booth a dish is placed upon the ground, into which they put a number of red-hot stones; . . .

"The Scythians take some hemp seed and creeping under the felt coverings, throw it upon the red-hot stones; immediately it smokes, and gives out such a vapor that no Grecian vapor bath can exceed; the Scyths, delighted, shout for joy, and this vapor serves them instead of a water bath; for they never by any chance wash their bodies with water."

The Arab geographer, Ibn Dast, writing in the tenth century A.D., describes a variant of this custom. Russian winter huts were, he says, a kind of cellar dug in the ground with a pointed roof like a Christian church covered with turf and heated by stones made red-hot in the fire, upon which water was poured till the hut was filled with steam and the whole family could take off their clothes and sit in friendly comfortable nakedness. For many centuries now the "bath house" has been a separate building, but the Russian peasant still likes to "steam himself." And sometimes strong beer or even vodka is poured on hot stones in order to charge the atmosphere of the bath house with alcohol.

The Scythians were barbarous, but they were not mere savages. Herodotus tells of a city of Gelonus in the Russian forest "surrounded with a lofty wall thirty furlongs each way, built entirely of wood" where the people had blue eyes and red hair and pidgin Greek was spoken in the marketplace. Some tribes cultivated the land and sold corn for export; the builders of the Parthenon would have gone hungry without Russian wheat; but the ruling element remained nomads, living in tents, yet not altogether eschewing the arts of civilization. The Scythian kings and nobles bought the best Greek gold and silver ware and as patrons were responsible for a new and beautiful variation from Greek art, which is now the glory of the Hermitage Museum in Leningrad. There were also native goldsmiths who worked in a vigorous barbaric style which persisted for many centuries and has influenced the art of both Europe and China. But the Scythians were suspicious of undue contact with foreigners. Herodotus records the cases of two famous Scythians who were murdered by their own people for adopting Greek customs. When the xenophobic side of their nature rises to the surface, modern Russians sometimes call themselves Scythians.

No doubt some Scythian influences went to the making of Russia. Traditional Russian dress owes much to Scythia, and no one can tell how much Scythian blood flows in Russian veins, but those ruling tribes of Scythians, whom Herodotus chiefly describes and who have left us the finest gold and silver, must be counted among the wandering peoples of the steppe; these have ever been the fiercest enemies of those more peaceful cultivators of the forest who created the Russian way of life.

3. Life in the Forest

For many centuries such neighbors as the Scythians drove the cultivators of the soil to escape by moving into the depth of the forest where no horseman could follow. There was space for all in that great forest, which stretches from Norway to the Pacific. Here the chief enemy was nature, not man. The important question to decide was how far north was it desirable to go.

The farthest north of Russia is Arctic tundra, the haunt of reindeer and primitive hunters who remained outside the stream of history until yesterday. South of the tundra lies a continuous forest of pine and birch. The thick growth shuts out daylight, and moss grows everywhere, but the hard and long winter is healthy and invigorating for, as a rule, there is neither damp nor wind. In the short, hot summer, plants grow fast, but pine needles and moss keep the grass down, so that humus forms very slowly and the soils are acid, cold, infertile, badly aerated and poorly drained. Here the challenge of nature has called forth a sturdy response from lonely hamlets of independent men and women, but the land will not support a large population. South of Leningrad oak, lime, maple, ash and other broad-leaved trees are mixed with the endless pine and birch, and the warmer summers encourage life-giving decomposition. Here the cultivators of the land might hope to live in comfort and even prosperity, so long as they did not come so far south as to invite attack from the steppe.

Well within living memory the primitive pattern of Russian forest life was still followed in the province of Archangel. Every few years each family chose a new site near water but high enough to stand above the spring floods. Here they would make their home for the time being. The trees were cut and the best timber used to make dwellings. The rest was burned on the ground and the ash made manure, which secured good crops for a few years, till the ground was exhausted, whereupon the family moved on to repeat the same laborious process elsewhere.

Bread was the main food of these tillers of the soil, but there was game in the forest and an abundance of fish from the rivers and lakes. There were plenty of berries and mushrooms in the summer, and men soon learned to pickle food in salt for the winter. The taste of salted vegetables and salted fish must have been as homely to early Russians as it is to their descendants. Timber was everywhere and the forest dwellers became expert carpenters, contriving to do everything with their short two-handed axes.

The earliest houses were pits in the ground, with a roof of reeds or straw. By degrees, people learned to line the walls with wood and to raise them above the ground. But to this day if a Russian peasant lacks a house, he digs a rectangular hole about four feet deep, lines it with shaped logs, puts a wooden roof on and lives in it until the emergency passes. Innumerable families lived in such dugouts when their villages were burned by the Germans in the last war. Before chimneys and windows were invented, the smoke from the hearth used to eddy through the door or find its way out through chinks; in the long winter evenings the only light was from the fire and from torches. Outside the air was crisp and invigorating, inside it was dark, dirty and snug. Virgil has left us in the 3rd Georgic (lines 376-80) a poetical description of winter life in a primitive Russian dugout:

Ipsi in defossis specubus secura sub alta
Otia agunt terra, congestaque robora totasque

Advolvere focis ulmos, ignique dedere.
Hic noctem ludo ducunt, et pocula laeti
Fermento atque acidis imitantur vitea sorbis.

The men to subterranean caves retire,
Secure from cold, and crowd the cheerful fire;
With trunks of elms and oaks the hearth they load,
Nor tempt the inclemency of heaven abroad.
Their jovial nights in frolics and in play
They pass, to drive the tedious hours away,
And their cold stomachs with crowned goblets cheer
Of windy cider and of foaming beer.

(Tr. Dryden.)

The Dutch stove, gradually perfected over the centuries,
has taken the place of the open fire, but the taste of life in a
Russian winter has scarcely changed.

In April the snow melts, flooding the whole countryside.
The days vacillate treacherously between heat and cold, and
no field work is possible in the waterlogged ground. May is
cold and rainy, and no trees are in leaf till toward the middle
of the month. Then very suddenly the birch are out and next
the larch, with the others hard on their heels. The countrymen look out anxiously for the floods to subside so that they
can begin to plow, for the summer is short and treacherous,
and ten days' delay may spoil the harvest.

In June outdoor work is well under way in hot weather,
and the long days bring long hours of work. In August the
harvest has to be gathered in, with a touch of autumn already
in the air. This is by tradition the Russian peasants' "time of
suffering," when young and old, men and women, work
their utmost, sustaining themselves with fabulous quantities
of bread.

Light frosts begin at the end of September, and the slanting sun strikes on stubble fields and birch thickets already
golden. In the autumn heavy rain turns the countryside into a
sea of mud and isolates every village, but there are some
bright clear days, a hushed pause before the winter storms.

In November or December it snows and the rivers freeze;
coughs and colds vanish in an instant, driven away by lung-
fuls of cold air, and the sledges come out. Winter was the
season of fairs, for there is no field work and the frozen
"winter road" makes travel easy. In early days the men took

life easy and kept their stomachs full throughout the winter,
if the harvest had been good. But there was always work
for the women; home spinning was the rule until living memory. Fish were caught through holes in the ice, but toward
the end of the season the bread might begin to run out; then
everyone went short.

In March it still freezes hard at night, but the middle of
the day becomes warmer, and toward the end of the month
the migratory rooks, returning to build their nests, announce
that another season of hard labor is not far off.

4. Marshes, Rivers and Towns

Dwellers in central and northern Russia are kept
apart from each other by forest and marsh. Every visitor who
penetrates into the Russian countryside is astonished by the
extent of the marshes and bogs. The reason is to be found in
events which are recent, as the geologists count time.

In the ice ages broad rivers of ice, hundreds of feet thick,
worked their way slowly from the north, grinding down the
granite hills of Finland until there was left nothing but
smooth and rounded stumps of rocks. Where the ground was
softer the glaciers plowed out new channels, and when the ice
retreated these valleys filled with the melting water and remained as countless lakes, which are now slowly silting up to
become marshes and eventually dry land. To this day a great
part of northern Russia remains marsh or bog, for the new
rivers and streams which have been born since the last ice
age have not yet had time to scoop out for themselves beds
deep enough to carry off the marsh waters. But in the present
age man has begun to hasten the work of geology by artificial
drainage.

During the summer months the Volga and other great rivers provide natural roads which trade has followed from the
beginning. At an early date trade in furs, wax, honey and
amber from the Baltic began to draw the scattered hamlets of
the forest into touch with a wider world. The great water
road which eventually became the backbone of early Russia
led from the Black Sea up the Dnieper and then, after an
easy portage, to Great Novgorod on the Volkhov, in reach of
the Gulf of Finland. Herodotus calls the Dnieper—

"the most productive river, not merely in Scythia, but in the whole world, excepting only the Nile with which no stream can possibly compare. It has upon its banks the loveliest and most excellent pasturage for cattle; it contains abundance of the most delicious fish; its water is most pleasant to the taste; its stream is limpid, while all the other rivers near it are muddy; the richest harvests spring up along its course and, where the ground is not sown, the heaviest crops of grass; while salt forms in great plenty about its mouth without human aid and large fish are taken in it of the sort called antacaei (or sturgeon), without any prickly bones and good for pickling. Nor are these the whole of its marvels."

The Scythians were a people whom we should have recognized as Europeans, and it seems that most of them spoke dialects of an Indo-European language akin to Persian. There was no great difference in appearance between the peoples of the steppe and the forest dwellers, until the advent of the Huns, who swept into Europe in the fifth century A.D. to terrify our ancestors by their unheard-of flattened faces and slanting eyes. Henceforward, peoples of Mongolian appearance, and speaking for the most part Turkish dialects, succeeded each other under various names. No doubt some of the old Scythian stock was absorbed, others were killed and the rest fled west and north to amalgamate with the cultivators of the forest fringe, some of whom were already known as Slavs.

The Romans fought many wars in the attempt to set up a frontier between the peaceful inhabitants of the empire and the nomads. The theme is as old as Horace's:

Intraque praescriptis Gelonos
Exiguis equitare campis.

And if we may believe an obscure hint in the *Lay of the Host of Igor* (see pages 31 and 40), the Emperor Trajan's expedition to the Black Sea lived in the Slavonic memory for a thousand years. But there was trade as well as warfare for, though the nomads produced little themselves, they acted as middlemen between the forested north and the Roman empire. By degrees little trading settlements grew up along the great rivers and artisans learned to supply the needs of each surrounding district, while finds of Roman coins of the second and third centuries A.D. upon the banks of the Dnieper testify to a wider commerce. And the strange coincidence of Roman and Russian measures of capacity suggests that the contact between Russia and the classical world may have been closer than we could have inferred from the literary evidence by itself.

As the Dark Ages drew on and passed away, town life began to grow faster. No writing has survived from these days and the wooden buildings have vanished, leaving no trace aboveground; but the Vikings called Russia Gardaric or the "land of cities" and recent excavations have given substance to the name. These first Russian towns, which served both as markets and as general refuges in time of peril, were protected by earth ramparts and by stockades cut from the giant forest timber which abounded everywhere. It is not hard to imagine the scene on a market day in summer at one of these wooden fortresses perched on a hill or rising from the marsh, like Ely from the fens. The men were dressed like traditional Russian peasants in large Turkish trousers with brightly embroidered linen shirts, under a long gown. "Russian boots" were already known but they were a luxury. The rich wore barbaric jewelry of gold, gilt and amber or perhaps some piece of gorgeous Oriental silk or Byzantine needlework. The crowd went barefoot or wore shoes plaited from bast, while the well-to-do wore long Russian boots of leather carefully greased for market day. No money was minted in Russia, but coins from Baghdad and at a later date from Byzantium changed hands for the larger purchases. The rich rode on horseback, while the poor trudged to market or rode on little carts, which each man would fashion with his ax from the trees cleared for this year's plowing. In the summer evenings there would be dancing, and Russian men had already learned to dance squatting on their haunches in the way that is still characteristic of them.

The neighbors of the ancient Slavs to west, south and southeast all agree that in war they were cruel as well as brave, but yet friendly and hospitable to strangers even beyond the custom of that age. Their humane treatment of slaves struck both Arabs and Byzantines. To this day visitors to Russia are equally struck by the unthinking cruelty of many public actions and by the overflowing kindness which they see around them in ordinary life.

At the dawn of written history the northern forest was inhabited by Finnish tribes, whose slow and peaceful absorption by their Slavonic neighbors is not yet complete. A member of one of these tribes, the Mari, was my chauffeur in Moscow in the year 1945. But already in the Dark Ages most of central Russia and the northern Ukraine was settled by people speaking a language far nearer to modern Russian than Anglo-Saxon is to English. The middle Volga, however, was held by a Turkish tribe, the Bulgars, another branch of whom gave their name to Bulgaria. The southern steppe was dominated by another Turkish tribe, the Khazars, who dwelt in walled cities and encouraged transit trade with Byzantium and with the Arab Caliphate, though they had little or no manufactures of their own. The ruling element of this remarkable people became converted to Jewry and established a relative security, under which the great trade routes of the Dnieper and the Volga began to thrive. Furs, wax, honey and slaves from the northern forest were exchanged for the fine textiles, glass and wine, gold and spices of the south, and the peoples of Russia were brought into commercial relations with the most civilized peoples of the known world, while the luxuries of the East began to reach the growing commercial centers of the Baltic through Russian intermediaries. Landowning soon became an important source of wealth, but trade was the cement of the composite Khazar state and of its Russian successor. Every part of the long trade routes depended on every other. Any power that controlled the whole length could call upon the powerful influence of trade to support the maintenance of political unity.

The conditions for a unified state thus grew up spontaneously along the Dnieper-Volkhov route, but national union was accomplished by a stimulus which came from outside. In the ninth century the Scandinavian pirates and traders known as Vikings broke upon western and eastern Europe alike. As King Alfred was hiding from the Danes among the reeds of Athelney, other Viking or "Varangian" adventurers were seeking wealth and honor in the "land of cities." One Rorik of Jutland plundered the coasts of France, Britain and Germany between 845 and 850. According to tradition the Viking Rurik established himself at Novgorod on the Volkhov in 862. It may be the same person. We shall never know. However that may be, 862 is the date from which the foundation of the Russian state has been reckoned, although two years earlier the Greeks record a fierce Russian attack on Constantinople. For 700 years all rulers claimed descent from Rurik.

5. Trade, Piracy and Taxgathering

Among the Vikings, as in every "heroic" society, trade, piracy and war were scarcely distinguishable. Adventurous men banded together with a ship and merchandise for a long voyage. When violence was profitable, they robbed and murdered, but, if resistance was effective, they behaved as peaceful traders. There might be little difference between the exaction of Danegeld and the collection of tribute. Many hundreds of years later the ballad cycle of Vassily Buslaev shows memories of this confusion. Vassily is a sort of Robin Hood, a heroic buccaneer of the Russian rivers, who admits no control save that of his widowed mother. Being at enmity with a rival gang of "peasants," he challenges them to a free fight on condition that the losing side is to pay tribute to the other at the rate of 3,000 roubles a year.

With reckless skill the Northmen traveled regularly in their open boats as far as Iceland and on to Greenland and America in the west, while to the east the magnets of Greek and Arab wealth drew them down the Russian rivers and on to Baghdad and to "Micklegarth" or Constantinople. The island of Gotland was the metropolis of northern trade, and in the museum at Visby row upon row of Arab coins is shown side by side with the Danegeld minted by Ethelred the Unready, a visible reminder of vanished links.

By the second generation the house of Rurik had imposed upon the basins of the Volkhov and the upper and middle Dnieper a rough unity based upon a yearly routine of trade and taxcollecting. In November, when the hard frosts set in, the prince with his armed bodyguard set out to travel his domains collecting tribute and living off the country. These taxgathering expeditions may not have been very different from other visits of the Vikings, except that the victims knew when to expect them and knew also that on payment of the prince's demands they would probably be left in peace. In return the prince imposed a rough semblance of law and order and protected his people from external enemies. During the first vigor of this system, the nomads were kept at bay and cultivation extended far into the black earth steppe.

While the prince was engaged in his winter taxgathering, carpenters were busy making boats for him and for lesser merchant-warriors. When the ice melted, great flotillas laden with merchandise and manned with warriors and slaves assembled at the chief towns and, above all, at Kiev, where the armada was fitted out, often with rudders and other gear from last year's boats. In June everything was ready and the expedition sailed down the Dnieper bound for Constantinople.

During its passage through the steppe, the convoy had to run the gauntlet of nomad attacks, a hazard which was made greater by a geological accident. The "continental platform" on which Russia stands has been forced down in the middle like a gigantic basin so that no surface rock appears over a vast area. But the rocky southern rim of this basin peeps above ground just at the bend of the Dnieper, forming rapids which prevented navigation for many miles. At frequent intervals the boats had to be put on land and dragged past the rocks. At every portage the peoples of the steppe lay in ambush. Only a strong force could keep the way to the south open. When it was cut, Russia was shut off from the light of Mediterranean civilization.

From the mouth of the Dnieper the ships coasted along to the mouth of the Danube, while the nomad forces rode along the shore, ready to attack if bad weather forced the Russians to land. At Constantinople the Byzantines allowed their turbulent guests to enter the city by one gate only, and on condition that they came unarmed and in parties of less than fifty. The slaves and other merchandise were soon sold and the fleet returned by the same route laden with a return cargo in time for next winter's tribute collection and boat building.

The Byzantines called their visitors Varangians, and at first the Scandinavians were the majority among them, but from the first there were Slavs too and soon the Slavonic element predominated. For the last hundred years and more these facts have been the subject of embittered controversy. The depreciators of Russia seek to prove that the Russian state owes its origin to Nordic Scandinavians or to Byzantine Christianity and that the very word "Rus" is Scandinavian. This may well be the case, but it scarcely matters. England and France are called after German invaders and Scotland takes its name from an Irish tribe. But some of those who dislike Russia have argued from this uncertain evidence that the Russian people are by nature incapable of governing themselves, and with equal inconsequence some Russians have retaliated by insisting on the originality and superiority of everything Russian.

Byzantium, indeed, gave Russia her religion, some of her statecraft and much of her arts and her esthetic feeling, and the Scandinavians gave a vital impetus to the birth of the Russian state. "By their military skill and organization into standing garrisons, they enabled the more advanced Russians . . . to maintain themselves against waves of aggression from the steppe" (N. K. Chadwick, *The Beginning of Russian History*, p. x.). Names such as Olga, Oleg, Igor and Vladimir are the Scandinavian Helga, Helgi, Ingvar and Waldemar under another guise, but the Viking aristocracy was a cosmopolitan society which could be joined by anyone with a strong arm who accepted the Viking code of conduct. The third in descent from Rurik bore a pure Slavonic name—Svyatoslav (reigned 964-977).

A fragment of saga preserved in the earliest Russian chronicle gives a picture of this prince at the head of his chosen bodyguard of adventurers.

"When Prince Svyatoslav grew up and came to man's estate, he began to gather together many valiant warriors. Stepping light as a leopard he undertook many warlike expeditions. On campaign he took with him neither baggage wagons nor pots for cooking; he boiled no meat but cutting slices from the flesh of wild beasts or horses or beeves, he roasted them upon the coals and did eat. He had no tent but spread out a saddle cloth with a saddle at his head. And such were all his warriors."

In one campaign he broke the power of the Khazars. Their ruin was completed by the Byzantines in the next generation and the Black Sea steppe was left without a civilized master.

Having finished with the Khazars, Svyatoslav invaded Bulgaria and began to carve out a new empire with its capital on the Danube. But from here he could not defend his old possessions and in his absence the nomads nearly took Kiev. Undeterred, Svyatoslav invaded Macedonia, slaughtering and burning with such ferocity that the land did not recover for many decades. For the first time a Russian land army had come within striking distance of Constantinople. It was to be 900 years before another Russian army would approach the second Rome, but the dome of St. Sophia and the shipping of the Golden Horn have never ceased to haunt the Russian imagination, sometimes a distant prospect and sometimes almost within reach but always eluding the grasp of outstretched hands.

At the first onset Svyatoslav seemed invincible, but the Byzantines rallied and the imperial forces won victories which surprised even themselves. The Russians were finally defeated on the Danube, and Svyatoslav with the remnant of his army withdrew on terms, but first he sought an interview with the emperor. Leo the Deacon describes the scene.

"Wearing armor chased in gold, the emperor rode to the bank of the Danube at the head of a vast multitude of horsemen, shining in gold and armor. But Sphedosthlavos (Svyatoslav) came upon a kind of Scythian bark, that ran down the stream, and he pulled at an oar, rowing with the others like one of the rest. And his appearance was thus: he was of medium stature, neither excessively tall nor inclining to shortness; his eyebrows were thick and his eyes gray blue, he had a snub nose and his chin was bare but on his upper lip grew very long, bushy mustaches. And his head was shaved bare, except that a long forelock hung on either side, as a mark of noble birth. His neck was massive, his chest broad and his other members well formed, but he seemed to be somehow dour and fierce. An earring adorned with a carbuncle between two pearls hung from one ear. His dress was white, differing from that of the others in nothing but cleanliness. He discussed the peace shortly with the emperor, sitting on a thwart of his boat and then departed."

Svyatoslav tried to return to Kiev by boat but his end was already approaching. The nomad tribes barred the rapids and he was forced to winter at the mouth of the Danube, where his force was stricken by famine. In the spring he was slain trying to force the rapids, and his skull was made into a drinking cup which bore, it is said, the following inscription:

Seeking what belonged to others, he ruined his own.

These words had a tragic sense which may have eluded the chronicler who records them, for the vacuum left by the destruction of the Khazars was soon filled by the Kipchak, a powerful tribe drawn from the desert's reserve of fierceness who had no use for the sophistication of trade. The Kipchak set a barrier of savagery between Kiev and that late Greek civilization which Svyatoslav and his Russian Vikings had glimpsed from a distance. While Kiev was strong, an annual battle at the rapids reopened the "road to the Greeks" every summer, but two or three generations after Svyatoslav the Kipchak began to get the upper hand.

For the most part, the peoples of the steppe come before us with the unsmiling faces of those who are remembered only by their deeds of violence. The Russian chroniclers generally looked on the raiders who burned their towns and villages much as the Old Testament writers regarded the Ishmaelites and other Bedouin. But the medieval *Chronicle of Galicia and Volhynia* gives one a glimpse of the world as it was seen from a nomad's saddle. It tells us that Vladimir Monomakh (see Chap. II, pp. 40–41)

". . . seized all their land and drove out the accursed sons of Hagar; he drove Otrok to the land of Obez, beyond the Gates of Iron, but Syrchan, his brother, remained by the Don, feeding upon fish. When Vladimir died, there was abiding with Syrchan a musician called Orevi; Syrchan sent him to the land of Obez and charged him to say: 'Vladimir is dead, return, O my brother, and come into thine own land. Speak unto him words and sing unto him the songs of Kipchak; if he still will not return, give him to smell the herb which is called yemshan or wormwood.' When Otrok would not return or listen, Orevi gave him to smell. When he smelt it, he wept and said: 'It is better for me to lay my bones in mine own land than to win fame in a strange land.' So Otrok came into his own country and begat Konchak." *

* The Kipchak are the Polovtsians of Borodin's opera *Prince Igor*. The opera is founded on the old *Lay of the Host of Igor* which records an unsuccessful attempt to reopen the trade route down the river Don in the year 1185. Konchak is Igor's chivalrous captor.

CHAPTER II

the age of Kiev

Stat magni nominis umbra.

Lucan

1. Russian Religion

The Russian state was already one of the largest kingdoms in the world, covering most of Russia in Europe, but the Russians were still pagan and lacked the arts of civilization, though Greek missionaries had invented an alphabet for Slavonic writing. The southern and western Slavs were already Christian, with a growing literature in their own language. At this early time the Slavonic languages were much less different from each other than they are now. Therefore any Russian who learned to read would have access to the new Slavonic literature. It was high time for Russia to adopt a monotheistic religion and to become part of the civilized world.

The choice lay between the religions and cultures of Christianity, of Islam and of Judaism represented by the Khazars. The difference between Roman Catholicism and Greek Orthodoxy had not yet hardened into schism, but differences in custom, ethos and language had already produced a profound antagonism. So far as the Russians were concerned, the issue was hardly in doubt. For them all roads led to Byzantium, the second Rome, still at the height of its splendor. Baghdad was civilized but distant, and the West was both distant and barbarous.

However, the first Russian chronicle, written before the memory of these events had faded, tells us that ambassadors were first sent to neighboring lands. The law of Islam practiced by the Bulgarians of the Volga was judged "not good," and those who were sent to the Holy Roman Empire reported —so we are told—that they "saw no beauty" in the Latin Mass. But the ambassadors who attended church in Constantinople said:

"We do not know whether we were in heaven or earth; upon earth there is no such sight or beauty, we do not know what to say; we only know that there God is present among men and that their service is the best of all lands. We cannot forget that beauty: every man, if he taste of sweetness, will not then partake of bitterness; even so we cannot live here."

That is a picturesque way of describing the most fateful decision in the life of Russia, but it embodies an important truth. The Liturgy of the Orthodox Church has scarcely changed since the Russian ambassadors attended the Eucharist in Constantinople and for Eastern Christians this service is the all in all of their religion.

In taking their Christianity from Greece, not Rome, the Russians threw their lot in with that part of Europe which was then the most civilized. But the future lay with the West and their association with Greek Christianity excluded them from any share in Western achievement for many centuries to come. In the past the differences between the Latin and Greek churches had not broken the communion between the two halves of Christendom. No one could foresee that the Crusades would take place in the next two centuries. Still less could it be foreseen that the resulting friction between peoples and their churches would become so fierce that at the end deep hatred and incomprehension would have put an impassable gulf between Eastern and Western Christians. But so it was. We are still paying for the lack of balance, both moral and material, which this dispute has brought into the life of Europe. The present antagonism between East and West takes a different form, but its animosity is nourished by antipathies that come from the earlier quarrel.

The Roman Empire had contained three streams of civilization—the Greek, the Semitic and the Latin. Greek culture set the tone for the eastern half of the Empire, and Latin for the western. The Semitic peoples had free access to Greek and Latin civilization, but their own traditions were never made at home in the Greco-Roman world. The early Church followed the pattern of the Empire. The West was Latin, the East was Greek; and in spite of its own Semitic origins the Church found it hard to give their rightful place to Semitic ways of thought. Latin Christianity was more active and more disposed to think in legal terms. Greek Christianity was more philosophical and more contemplative. The Latin West, following St. Augustine, stresses the inability of fallen humanity to rise without the help of grace freely and mysteriously given by God. The Greek East stresses God's power to raise man to himself and speaks boldly of the "divinization" of man in a way that can be shocking to Western Christians. Eastern Christians love to quote the saying of St. Athanasius that Jesus became what we are so that we might become what He is. If Western theology, both Catholic and Protestant, puts a special emphasis on the Fall, the Transfiguration is at the heart of Eastern theology.

Latin and Greek Christianity were incomplete without each other. While the Roman Empire had even a vestige of unity, each complemented the other. But in the political divisions of the Dark Ages the two halves of the Church began to go their separate ways. In the West the collapse of the previous political order placed political responsibility upon the hierarchy, and the collapse of culture placed the priesthood apart as the sole interpreters of the word of God, for it was written in a language which they alone could understand. In the East the continuance of the Empire made the clergy dependent upon the civil power, and the existence of educated laymen helped to preserve the influence which the laity had exercised up till then. In the East continuity of language (and translation when necessary) made it possible for the people to fulfill their traditional part in the worship of the Church.

The early Christians stressed the corporate nature of Eucharistic worship. They believed that in the Eucharist God gives himself to the faithful, that in some mysterious way he joins the worshipers to himself and to each other. The Eastern Church has never lost the experience which lies behind this belief. But in the West the Latin of the Mass had become a foreign language. The people began to forget their part in the responses and in congregational singing. Moreover, the Roman priests had begun to turn their backs to the congregation during the Mass, instead of facing the congregation across the altar, as had been the custom in the early Church. So during a considerable part of the service the people could not see the priest's face and might not be able to hear his words. Henceforth the Mass seemed to be something performed by the priest for the people rather than a corporate action in which all had their necessary part.

The West lost something which the Eastern Church, following the original Christian tradition, has considered essential, but the loss in corporate understanding was partly made up by the growth in individuality. The faithful had a perfect occasion for private devotions while the priest celebrated Mass on their behalf. At such times the human soul was brought before its maker in naked individual responsibility. Many were inspired by this to serve God in new ways with all the gifts of their individuality and, above all, with their intellectual gifts.

The philosophers of antiquity were rediscovered and medieval thinkers applied Aristotelian logic with a sustained passion to the material provided by the Christian revelation. Never before or since, not even in Greek antiquity, have men thought so much, so long and so clearly about philosophical problems. Experimental science lay in the future, but without the medieval belief that the nature of the universe can be investigated by reason we westerners could never have conceived the scientific view of the world. Without our medieval schooling in exact thought we would never have discovered or applied the modern scientific method, but all this passed Russia by and she entered on the modern age utterly unprepared. Those continual challenges, which have revived the Western Church from the early Middle Ages until today, did not touch the Russian Church until the last century.

In their prosperous days the Greek Christians loved theological argument and contributed their full share to the Church's common stock of intellectual understanding, but during the last five centuries the Orthodox world has received many heavy blows. The climate has not been favorable to thought, and energy has been concentrated on preserving the Orthodox inheritance unchanged. So in Russia there has been little intellectual Christianity. Have not the problems of belief been solved by the great councils of the Church many centuries ago? Is not all sound tradition embodied in the writings of the early Fathers and in the incomparable Orthodox Liturgy?

Eastern Christians often suspect that the West has trusted the reasoning powers of the individual too far. Orthodoxy is inclined to accept the mysteries of Christian belief without trying to give them a rational expression, while the West never tires in the search for philosophical understanding. The Latin Church has very typically expressed the mystery of the Eucharist in the technical language of Aristotelian philosophy, asserting that the accidents of the bread and wine remain unchanged but that the substance of the elements is changed into the body and blood of our Lord. When the Or-

thodox reject the doctrine of transubstantiation, they probably do not intend to deny what the Roman Catholics assert,
but rather to protest at the meticulous way in which the medieval West tried to define these mysteries. In denying the
Roman doctrine of purgatory, the Orthodox are more concerned to protest against the logical and almost legal elabora-
tion of the hidden mysteries of judgment than to deny the
possibility of a middle state where the souls of the departed
are secure from damnation but not yet admitted to beatitude.
The Orthodox Church has been more ready than the Roman
Church to put up with theological disagreements.

Orthodox thinkers say that the Catholic philosophy of the
Middle Ages leads straight to what they regard as the excessive rationalism and fragmentation of Protestantism. To
them, Catholic and Protestant are two sides of the same
medal and they do not like one better than the other. These
criticisms go deeper than most Catholics or Protestants will
admit. But some Western Christians have shown themselves
aware of some of those weaknesses in their worship to which
the Orthodox point. The Protestant reformers of the sixteenth
century and the leaders of the Catholic Liturgical revival of
the present age, to mention no others, have both tried to restore the corporate character of Eucharistic worship. An Orthodox critic might say that these efforts cannot succeed until
Western Christians see the connection between the weaknesses of their devotional life and the one-sided rationalism
and individualism of the West.

Russian strength and weakness are often the converse of
ours. If Russia has never had much of the benefits of our
bustling, individual, rational Western world, if Russian thinkers do not rival the greatest logicians and speculative philosophers of the West, the Russians have never tried to keep the
heart and the mind separate. The Communists inherited this
from Orthodoxy, and that was part of their strength.

At a very early stage Russian religion began to put a special stress on the humanity of our Lord. Longing to identify
themselves with Christ's humility and poverty, some of the
Russian saints shared voluntarily in the life of the poor in a
way that was not altogether usual in the ascetic tradition of
the East. St. Theodosius, a monk of Kiev who died in 1074,
insisted on making "coarse and patched garments and when
his parents tried to make him put on fresh clothing and play
with other children he would not obey, for he wanted to be
identified with the poor." His father died when Theodosius

was about thirteen. From that time on he "went into the fields with his serfs where he did the humblest work. To prevent this his mother used to keep him indoors. She also tried to prevail upon him to put on good clothes, and go out to play with boys of his own age, for she said that if he were so poorly dressed, he would expose himself and his family to disgrace. But he would not obey her, and often she beat him in her vexation. She was robust of body, and if you could not see her but could hear her voice, you might well have mistaken her for a man." (From Nestor's *Contemporary Life of Theodosius*, translated by Fedotov.) Theodosius kept these peculiarities to the end. He became the counsellor of princes but would not dress the part, a circumstance which led to some amusing misunderstandings. He would have understood the later Russian revolutionaries who "went to the people" and made a cult of untidy clothes.

Less institutional than the Western churches, the Russian Church is at the same time more Erastian. For while Papacy grew upon the decaying remnants of the Western Roman Empire which it supplanted, Orthodoxy grew under the shadow of the mighty Eastern Empire and the patriarchs of Constantinople became accustomed to take orders from the Byzantine Caesar. This tradition passed to Russia. In general, but with some notable exceptions, the Russian Church has been very ready to reach an accommodation with the powers that be, under every system of government, including the Soviet.

From the beginning the language of the Russian Church was intelligible to the people. Old Slavonic is not a rich language, but it is strong and warm. An English admirer has written "in the full vigor and perfection of its youth" Old Slavonic was "as subtle and flexible as Greek, as vigorous and terse as Latin and as clear and precise as either of them" (Birkbeck, Vol. II). When new words were needed, they were formed from a Slavonic stem but on a close analogy with the corresponding Greek word. To this day those who know both Greek and Russian are struck by certain strange similarities between the two languages. As modern Russian diverged from Old Slavonic, the language of the Liturgy was modernized to a certain extent. Nowadays the liturgical language is an artificial mixture known as Church Slavonic. It is only half intelligible to those who know nothing but modern Russian, but it is easy for them to pick up. Any lay man or woman can become a member of the choir and take a full part in the Liturgy without difficulty. In the Russian middle ages all books were written in Old Slavonic or old Russian. In many ways this was an advantage, but it removed most of the impetus to learn Greek. Without classical studies medieval Russia became an intellectual backwater.

Yet there were some characteristically original elements in the Russian view of their place in the divine economy. They regarded themselves in a concrete, historical manner, as the last comers to the heavenly feast. God had acted through particular nations, first through his ancient chosen people, the Jews, then, after the conversion of Constantine, through the Roman Empire, and now finally through the late-converted Slavs. So, in a sense, the conversion of Russia set a seal on God's work and it is in this way that the first seed of Russian Messianism was planted. These things being so, medieval Russians took an intense interest in the historical books of the Old Testament, but they knew them almost entirely through epitomes; old Slavonic literature was so meager that it is even doubtful if there was a complete Slavonic translation of the Old Testament before the end of the Middle Ages.

It would seem that the new religion was not at first welcomed by the common people. The country was large and the peasants lived in scattered hamlets so that evangelization was slow, but in the end the Russians have been as deeply affected by Christianity as any people in the world. Their faith is simple, but it is rich in fellowship. It has brought beauty into drab lives, and it has broken down those invisible barriers between man and man. The Russians have an unaffected way of accepting their own and other people's sinfulness which gives them a brotherly sympathy for all sorts and conditions of men. These lovable qualities have touched many who would deny the name of Christian, and they lie at the root of that magnetic power which Russia has for all who have lived among her people.

2. The Empire of Kiev

Primitive Russian law, like the early Saxon and other Germanic codes, did not distinguish clearly between crimes and private injuries. Murder could be expiated by the payment of wergeld. But the Greek ecclesiastics, who generally held the highest offices in the Russian Church, brought with them the Roman conception of the state and some of the principles of Roman law. By this time, however, the Byzantine administrators took their Roman law from abbreviated handbooks. So at a time when rediscovery of the great sources of Roman jurisprudence gave to the West a renewed hope in the possibilities of civilized life, Russia had nothing but third-hand epitomes of Justinian. Moreover, the Greek churchmen, for good or ill, lacked the legal training and inclinations of so many Roman ecclesiastics. Nonetheless, the influence of Byzantine ideas taught the Russians by degrees to look for their political ideal in a mighty unified state under an absolute ruler served by a faithful bureaucracy. Russian rulers gradually came to exercise a Byzantine ruthlessness against wrongdoers and rivals for power, but for many centuries the Byzantine and the older Russian or Scandinavian ideas of law contended and intertwined with each other.

In the eleventh century all European countries were rough and lawless to the verge of anarchy. In Russia, as elsewhere, murder and robbery were very common. The sack of cities often came near to massacre and the beaten side was often sold into slavery, but savage floggings, torture and maiming were not the instruments of rule until in the name of efficiency first Byzantium and then the Tartars brought a crueler conception of government.

All in all, Russia in the great age of Kiev was about as civilized as western Europe. In the West no state so vast had endured so long. No Western city could compare in size and splendor with Kiev. In the great fire of 1124 six hundred churches were destroyed. Nowhere else was there such a far-flung network of trading cities. The few monuments of architecture that have survived show a mastery of form and splendor of color which are subtler if less strong than the rude grandeur of the earlier Romanesque. Even in pagan days Olga, the mother of Svyatoslav, had lived in a palace decorated with mosaics and frescoes. Later, antique statues looted from the Crimea were erected in the center of Kiev, where four bronze horses stood, as in Venice, by the Cathedral of the Blessed Virgin.

The princes of Kiev were connected by marriage both with Byzantium and with the leading states of western Europe. Harold Hardrada, who ended an adventurous career in 1066 fighting against King Harold at Stamford, was married to

Elizabeth, daughter of Yaroslav the Wise, grand prince of Kiev. By a curious coincidence, Gytha, the daughter of Harold of England, was married to Vladimir Monomakh, the greatest statesman of early Russia. Many of the princes fostered learning, some practiced what they preached, and Vladimir records that "without having quitted his country, my father learned five foreign languages, a thing which won for him the admiration of foreigners."

The first Russian chronicle, *The Story of the Passing Years*, was written at Kiev in the eleventh century. It sketches the history of the Slavs from the earliest times, drawing upon oral tradition, saga and the Russian state archives as well as on Byzantine sources. The author or authors weigh their evidence to the best of their ability. They often use vivid eyewitness accounts for contemporary events and sometimes they weave stirring fragments of old poetry into their narrative. Almost the only complete poem that has survived the calamities of succeeding centuries is *The Lay of the Host of Igor* (see note to p. 31 above). Those who enjoy *Beowulf* and the *Nibelungenlied* will probably like the *Lay of the Host of Igor*, which has moments of beauty and has been pronounced a masterpiece by good judges.

In the great days of Kiev the word of the grand prince was generally effective in major issues throughout his domains. Trade held the empire together so long as the trade routes were open to the south, but pressure from the nomads was increasing, and in the course of the eleventh and twelfth centuries the Dnieper route was first interrupted and then severed. Hard upon this the Crusades opened more direct routes between Europe and the Levant, and the "road from the Varangians to the Greeks" was altogether forgotten. In the year 1000 Russia was the mistress and organizer of a great artery of commerce which was vital to the most active part of the West. By the year 1200 she had become a distant land, hard of access and leading to nowhere.

As the eleventh century drew on, the land became more settled so that the local aristocracy began to draw more wealth from landowning at the very time when their gains from trade began to fall off. This weakened their ties with the center. The ramshackle empire of the house of Rurik was visibly falling to pieces, but the dissolution was stayed for a whole generation by the work of one great ruler, Vladimir Monomakh, who was born in 1053 and reigned in Kiev from

1113 to 1125. His father was a younger son of Yaroslav the Wise, grand prince of Kiev, his mother was the daughter of the Byzantine Emperor Constantine Monomakhos, from whom Vladimir took his second name, and his sister was married to the Holy Roman Emperor, Henry IV. His imperial descent gave Vladimir added prestige among his contemporaries, but this would have availed little in a stormy age if he had not possessed strength of will combined with a realistic judgment of what was possible. Perhaps his not very Russian sense of moderation came from Greek blood.

When his father, who had succeeded to the throne of Kiev, died, Vladimir not only resisted the temptation to bid for the succession but he helped to place his cousin Svyatopolk on the throne. Until Svyatopolk died Vladimir remained his faithful ally, using his influence, not to increase his own domains, but to induce his brother princes to unite against the Kipchak.

The first great battle, fought against Vladimir's advice, was a terrible defeat. Everything up to the walls of Kiev was opened to the enemy. A contemporary describes how those who remained outside the city of refuge were driven into slavery.

"Downcast, tormented, exhausted with hunger and thirst, naked and barefoot, black from dust, with bleeding feet and melancholy faces, they trudged into captivity and one said to another: 'I am from such a town,' 'I am from such a village'; they told of their families and with tears raised their eyes to heaven to the All Highest Who knows every secret."

For ten years more Russia was engaged in civil wars, and the Kipchak rejoiced, until in 1103 Vladimir Monomakh, though not yet grand prince, had composed all differences and led a united Russian army far into the Don steppe. The Russians won a mighty victory and the tide was turned back for thirty years. In 1113, at the age of sixty, Vladimir succeeded peacefully to the throne of Kiev, where he reigned for twelve years.

Vladimir Monomakh lived honorably by the best standards he knew, but he was the creature of a rough age. If he both preached and practiced the keeping of oaths given by one Christian prince to another, this did not prevent him from treacherously murdering two hostages given by the pagan Kipchak. He admonished his own sons to do no wrong to the widows and the fatherless nor to peasants, but this did not prevent him taking part in the massacre of Minsk when neither man nor beast was left alive.

He has left a famous open letter to his children which gives a vivid insight into his own character and the ideals of his time. Writing, as he says, on the very edge of the tomb, he expresses himself with a human mixture of pride and diffidence. Almost beseeching the reader to take nothing amiss, he writes: "Listen to me and, if you do not accept the whole of my words, then take half."

Vladimir Monomakh had a warm heart and loved his family. He was religious and would be moved to tears by the church service, but he bids his sons not to seek salvation by becoming monks or hermits or by fasting, but rather by "repentance, tears and almsgiving."

He wants his descendants to take joy in the world as it is:

"Diverse beasts and birds and fishes are given bright hues by Thy providence, O God. And we admire this wonder, that man is made from earth yet the countenances of men are each of diverse forms. . . . The birds of heaven come from warm lands, even first into our lands, yet they do not stay in one land but strong and weak fly throughout all lands, according to the commandment of God; yea the fields and forests are full of them; and God has given all for the use of man, yea and for his delight."

A tireless hunter, he describes with exultation his fearful encounters with wild beasts and admonishes his children to live dangerously. He reminds them that he himself made eighty-three long and strenuous journeys across Russia, and he warns them not to delegate power but to rule and to judge in person.

Vladimir Monomakh held the center of the stage throughout a long lifetime, and many generations looked back on him as an ideal ruler; the difference between him and Svyatoslav is the measure of Russian progress in little over a hundred years. While Svyatoslav is an unforgettable silhouette, Vladimir Monomakh is a whole man.

His son held the fabric of the state together and kept the Kipchak at bay, but after this the central power of the grand princes began to disappear. Thereafter the provinces bordering on the steppe were forced to rely on their own weakened resources, which proved insufficient to stem the barbarians. Villages and towns were burned, crops destroyed and the people driven off into slavery until the fertile border provinces became once more a grassy wilderness. Even Kiev began to lose its supremacy, and though the shadow of a great name long drew rival princes into civil war for the throne of Kiev, few of them held it long and civil wars became continuous. As the twelfth century draws on, the Kipchak and other nomads no longer appear as the enemies or subjects of a united Russia but as participants in Russian civil wars.

The Church exhorted the princes to cease the shedding of Christian blood and to stand together against the infidel, but in the long run it was impossible to get combined action from a nation that had no organic unity. The barbarians had already made deep encroachments when the Tartar invasions of the thirteenth century struck not only the frontier provinces but the whole of the Russian land with a lasting devastation.

In the age of Kiev life was primitive, but there was as yet land for all and the black earth was fruitful. Trade brought most of its profits to those who were already well-to-do, but there were pickings for the poor too. War and slave-raiding were the most sinister sources of wealth, for the Russians both exported and kept slaves, though slave labor was never the main basis of their economy. When slave-raiding became less common toward the end of the Kiev period, the ruling class looked for compensation in a more intensive exploitation of the land and of those who worked on it. It was complained, rather surprisingly, that in the old days princes extracted their wealth from foreigners by war, but now they battened on their own people. Beneath the pressure of landlord and creditor, the free Russian peasant of early times soon began to lose his full liberty. It is hard to say what stage of enserfment had been reached at any given moment, but it is certain that throughout the Middle Ages a man had some freedom to migrate and to change masters. And in the palmy days of Kiev every material problem and every economic relation was eased by the teeming fertility of nature.

Memories of the golden age of Kiev have never quite died among the Russian peasants. Families of peasants driven from the Ukraine by the Kipchak and their Tartar successors trekked into the forests of central Russia. Centuries later some of their descendants continued their journey into the far north. In the Archangel province and round Lake Onega, ballads and songs preserved to this day tell of Vladimir and the great days of Kiev and of the heroes who were then upon earth.

3. Retreat to the North

In the days of Monomakh the region of the upper Volga still remained a poor and distant principality separated from the rich south by forests whose former impenetrability has left traces in the ballads of the Russian peasant. Travelers from the Ukraine to central Russia had to make a long journey up the Dnieper and across to the headwaters of the Volga basin and then down again to their destination.

But in the course of the twelfth century peasants driven from their land by the Kipchak began to make their way north into the forest. We must imagine each family migrating after harvest or perhaps in the early winter when the ground was hard. A little grain could be loaded onto the small carts which were the sole transport, but for the first year these pioneers must have lived mainly on what game and fish they could trap and on wild honey, eked out in the summer by mushrooms and berries.

Three generations of one family formed the typical settlement, if we may judge from later Russian custom. The grandfather ruled supreme and his choice of a site for the family hamlet was final, while the grandmother was free to rule her daughters-in-law with a rod of iron. The first task was to clear the trees and to burn any timber not needed for immediate use. The plows of those days scarcely scratched the ground, seed gave poor yields and as soon as the ground showed signs of exhaustion the family had to move to another site where more trees had to be felled and new shelter built. (Cf. p. 21.)

Each successive move brought settlers deeper into the forest, until in less than two generations the mesopotamia between the upper Volga and its great southern confluent, the Oka, had become one of the best populated regions in Russia. Population brought wealth and wealth brought power, so that already in the days of Vladimir Monomakh's grandchildren the north had become supreme over Kiev and the older cen-ters of power and civilization.

In the Ukraine the scarcity of water and the exigencies of defense forced men to build large villages near the streams, but in the north, where water was plentiful and the enemy distant, the settlements of man were tiny islands of one or two households amid a sea of forest and bog. To this day central Russia contains many broad wildernesses, and even within twenty miles of Moscow there are forests where, be-neath a gray sky, I have lost all sense of direction in a fea-tureless waste of pine and moss.

A different life has produced a different national character. The people of north and central Russia are called Great Rus-sians to distinguish them from the southern Ukrainians or Little Russians. In the north most of the soil was poor and the climate was as hard as the Canadian and as treacherous as the English. The Great Russian peasant must complete his field work in a few weeks of summer or he faces starvation. This has taught the Russian peasant to work in furious bursts while fate permits. No people in the world can work so hard while the mood lasts, but many of them have a correspond-ing incapacity for steady constant work. The uncertainty of nature has given the Russians a taste for risks, and there are moments when they stake all on a hazardous decision as if they were "opposing to the caprice of nature the caprice of their own courage. Indeed this inclination to tempt happiness, to bet on success is the Great Russian's 'Avos,' his 'perhaps it will be all right' " (Klyuchevski, Vol. I, p. 89, Russian ed.).

But when the short months of frantic toil are over, the Great Russian peasant has many months of autumn and win-ter to fill. He likes to drowse in the warmth of his log cabin, but poverty has driven him to eke out his living in various ways. While the women were occupied with spinning, some of the men kept bees in the hollow trunks of trees or caught fish and trapped game; others worked the iron which is found in the form of nodules in lakes and bogs, or boiled pitch or salt.

In later days changed circumstances have brought out new potentialities hidden in the Russian nature, but surroundings such as those just described have long provided the setting for Great Russian life. Their influence on human nature has been described by the greatest of Russian historians (Klyu-chevski, Vol. I, p. 89, Russian ed.):

"The impossibility of calculating in advance, of figuring out a plan of action and making for the chosen target in a straight line has left noticeable traces in the mental setup of the Great Russian and in the mode of his thinking. The uncertainty and irregularity of day-to-day life have taught him rather to weigh up the course already accomplished than to figure out what lies ahead; rather to glance round backwards than to look before. His struggle against unexpected blizzards and thaws, with unpredictable August frosts and January slush, has made him circumspect rather than foreseeing; he has learned rather to mark consequences than to fix targets; he has trained himself to draw up balance sheets at the cost of his ability to make estimates. This capacity is indeed what we (Great Russians) call 'after wit.' The saying 'Russians are strong in after wit' fits the Great Russians perfectly. But 'after wit' is not the same as 'arrière pensée.' In his habit of turning and tacking between the inequalities of the road and the accidents of life the Great Russian often gives an impression of crookedness and insincerity. He often thinks in two directions and that looks like double-facedness. The Great Russian always makes for a definite goal, even if this may often be insufficiently thought out; he walks on and keeps looking about him so that his gait seems evasive and uncertain. After all, the Great Russian proverbs tell us that it is no good banging your head against a brick wall and only crows fly straight. Nature and fate have so treated the Great Russian that he has learned to make his way onto the straight road by devious paths. He thinks and acts as he walks. After all, what could you find more crooked or winding than a Great Russian village footpath? You might think it was the track of a snake. But just try to do it straighter; you will only get bogged and come out in the end on the same winding path."

Like most generalizations this description leaves something out. It hardly allows for such tenacious planning as that by which eighteenth- and nineteenth-century Russian villagers would transfer whole communities to a chosen site in distant Siberia. But the circumspect Great Russian peasant is a character whom one still meets under a thin disguise in Soviet society and, one might add, at international political meetings.

The Russian peasant's attitude to his rulers has something in common with his attitude to nature. One, like the other, is the condition of his happiness, indeed of his existence, and both are unpredictable. He accepts good government and the oppression of tyrants as he accepts good and bad harvests. Petty oppression, incompetence and bureaucracy, like bad weather, are something that one seeks shelter from; bursts of sunshine are to be enjoyed. However, Russians do not forget grievances and injustices, although the fact that they will put up with so much has often led their rulers to the false conclusion that they will put up with anything.

4. Suzdal and Vladimir

North of the Oka the princes were in the land before most of their people and they set themselves to encourage colonization. One of Vladimir's younger sons, Yuri Dolgoruki or George Long Arm, received as his appanage the distant and unimportant principality of Rostov and Suzdal. But Suzdal lies in a northern salient of the black earth which at this point juts up far into the forest. Peasants escaping from the disordered south were drawn to this fertile land, protected from the steppe by forest and distance and from lawless neighbors by the strong arm of its princes. George and his son, Andrew of Bogolyubovo, welcomed all colonists and founded new towns with immigrant craftsmen, who brought skills that had been rare in the north, until the land of Suzdal became a little oasis of wealth and civilization amid the wastes of central Russia.

The shift of wealth, power and population from the Ukraine to the north hastened the breakup of the old empire of Kiev. In the south a man on horseback could ride anywhere and in the days of Kiev the road from the Varangians to the Greeks had bound the empire together, but in the north hundreds of settlements strung out on a spider's web of smaller rivers were separated from each other by forest and quagmire. These obstacles divided the country into endless little districts which could easily live in isolation from all neighbors, so long as trade and industry remained primitive.

The earlier princes may have been half barbarian, but they were accustomed to broad horizons. Soviet writers exaggerate the patriotism of early Russia, but it is true that the Russia of

Kiev had more sense of belonging together than any other area of comparable size in Europe at that time. In the north the spiritual descendants of the Vikings turned into a race of sluggish provincial landowners.

Russia has never been completely stagnant, but new ideas arrive later and circulate more slowly in a vast and remote country than in our well-knit Western world. In the days of Kiev trade stimulated Russia's sluggish circulation, but by the year 1200 trade was vanishing. Material development depended henceforth on the slow working of agricultural colonization. Landowning had become the only basis of wealth, but land without people was valueless, and it was the aim of every landowner to fix peasant families on his land from generation to generation. The simplest way to do this was to lend them money in bad times and not to let them leave until they had repaid the uttermost farthing. Some estate owners drove unconscionable bargains, but a landlord had to treat his tenants with at least some consideration if he did not wish to see his estate deserted by its cultivators.

The local aristocracy of the north had long ruled over a scattered population of Russians and Finns, but the new arrivals upset the existing social balance. The poorer classes were swollen by resourceful and determined pioneers from the Ukraine and by the skilled artisans who came to settle in the new towns. Andrew of Bogolyubovo boasted that he had made the land of Suzdal populous, and it is not surprising that he leaned on the new settlers for support. His father, George Long Arm, the most powerful prince of his day, was the first to base his power on the north. Andrew lived more than half his life without ever seeing the south. When at last George was firmly established at Kiev he gave his son charge over one of the neighboring towns, but Andrew hated the Ukraine and could not abide life in the south. Before the year was out he had left for the north against his father's will, taking with him the famous Madonna of Vladimir which is now in the Tretyakovsky Gallery at Moscow. Three years later, when George Long Arm died, the bitter antipathy between the Ukrainians and the Great Russians burst out: northerners were robbed and murdered and the palace of the grand prince was looted.

His father's death left Andrew the strongest and most ambitious prince in Russia, but he made no effort to seize the throne of Kiev, preferring to rule from his own city of Vladimir, twenty miles south of Suzdal. Andrew of Bogolyubovo had been cast in a different mold from previous rulers, and he did not affect either the standards of family solidarity or the manners expected from a Russian grand prince. Instead of governing through relatives, he expelled his brothers and nephews from their possessions and governed through his own creatures. Shunning the older aristocracy of Rostov and Suzdal, he ruled from a new palace at Bogolyubovo outside his faithful Vladimir. This city, perched high above the river Klyazma amid undulating fields famous for corn and fruit, still retains many of the buildings with which Andrew embellished his Kiev of the north. The most beautiful, if not the most splendid, is the Church of the Pokrov, or Veil of the Blessed Virgin, standing upon a little hill beside a stream. There is nothing here to match the mosaics and sumptuous materials of Kiev or the inexpressible aspirations of Muscovite architecture. The elegance and simplicity of line are nearer to the classicism of Petersburg or the West.

Andrew did not wish to rule in Kiev, but he had no intention of watching an effective rival for power establish himself in southern Russia and in 1171 he sent his army against Kiev. The mother of Russian cities was captured and sacked without mercy, and thereafter the grand prince of Kiev was little more than a puppet appointed and dismissed from Vladimir.

Andrew shocked his opponents as much by his manner as by what he did. For instance, in 1174 he placed Roman of Smolensk on the throne of Kiev, but a quarrel soon broke out and Andrew sent an emissary to Roman and his brothers with the following message: "Roman, thou and thy brothers do not walk according to my will, so begone from Kiev and thou, Mstislav, begone from Belgorod and thou David from Vyshgorod; go ye all to Smolensk and divide there your heritage as you can." Even in the north Andrew's imperious and capricious nature forbade him to share his diversions with the nobles whom custom assigned as his companions. He used to go hunting with a few chosen friends, telling the rest to find their own sport.

It may be that Andrew of Bogolyubovo was feeling his way towards a centralized autocracy resting on the support of the lesser gentry, artisans and pioneer settlers. If so, he was ahead of his time. But he was tactless to the old nobility and he did not know how to get faithful service from the new men in whom he trusted. The contemporary chronicler sums up by saying: "Wise as he was in all affairs and valiant as he was, Prince Andrew spoiled his intentions by incontinence."

In the end his excesses made even those who served him fear for their own safety and he was murdered by his body-guard. Assassination of rulers was rare in Russia until Peter the Great loosened all the ties of traditional sanctions. So Andrew's murder unloosed evil passions. For two days no one dared to bury the corpse, which lay naked in the courtyard of the palace of Bogolyubovo. While the mob sacked the dead prince's possessions, villagers came to share in the loot and everywhere the mob began to murder the officials appointed by Andrew. The chronicler makes the characteristic Russian comment that the people did not understand that "where there is law, needs must be many injuries."

On Andrew's death the aristocracy of Rostov and Suzdal expected to see the end of the upstart pretensions of Vladi-mir, for, said they, "Vladimir is subordinate to us and there do dwell our slaves, even stonemasons and carpenters and plowmen." But the people of Vladimir and other supporters of the new order successfully backed Andrew's younger brother Vsevolod through two years of civil war.

Vsevolod, who bore the name of "Big Nest" from his nu-merous offspring, was brought to power by the same forces that had supported Andrew. He achieved his brother's ambi-tion of dominating both northern and southern Russia from the banks of the Klyazma, but when he died in 1212, his in-heritance was divided among his progeny, in accordance with the disastrous custom which treated the domain of a Russian prince as an estate belonging to the royal family rather than as a kingdom whose unity must be preserved.

The settlement of the land between the upper Volga and the Oka continued for twenty-five years after the death of Vsevolod, and Russian colonization began to reach out north and east. In 1221 Nizhni Novgorod was founded in Finnish territory at the confluence of the Volga and the Oka as an outpost of war and trade against the Moslems of the middle Volga. But this quiet expansion was soon to be cut short.

The civilization of Vladimir before the Tartar invasion combined for a moment the width and refinement of Kiev with the strength of Moscow. But the plant had been cut at the root and the exigencies of medieval life in the northern forest would have had their effect even if Genghis Khan had never lived.

CHAPTER III

the resurgence
of the steppe

*That bitter and hasty nation, which shall march
through the breadth of the land . . . their horses
also are swifter than leopards and are more fierce
than the evening wolves.* Habakkuk i. 6-8

Drought and hunger have often driven the nomads
against their settled neighbors in both Asia and Africa. Some
historians have sought to connect these periodic irruptions of
Bedouin and Scyth, Hun and Tartar, with a climatic cycle.
But the Mongol irruptions of the thirteenth century surpassed
all previous invasions as a typhoon surpasses an ordinary
gale. No cyclical theory could account for the organized fury
and farsighted designs which distinguish the Mongols from
all their predecessors and from all those that came after
them.

In the destruction that they wrought, the Tartar invasions
of Asia and Europe were the greatest disaster in the history
of China, in the history of the Middle East and in the history
of Russia. But there is another side to the medal. Man has
never been so near to a world state as under the Mongol empire. Europe owes a debt to the Mongols for the wide horizons which inspired the age of Columbus. The great khans
ruled through an international civil service that had room for
statesmen and administrators of all nations. Among these
were Marco Polo and the great Chinese statesman Yeliu
Ch'u-Ts'ai. The organization of the Mongols was efficient;
their rule was ruthless to lawbreakers, but to the submissive
benevolent.

Nomadic tribes which live for any length of time on the
borders of the sown land have generally been converted to
the religion of their neighbors and have received some tincture of civilization. Thus the Seljuk Turks had become Mos-

51

lems and coreligionists of their future subjects before they conquered Hither Asia; so they did not destroy but invigorated the ancient civilization of the Middle East.

It was otherwise with Genghis Khan. He was born into one of the most remote and primitive of the wandering tribes of Asia. The son of an important chieftain, he was orphaned at the age of twelve and deserted by everyone except his strong-minded mother and his younger brothers. Genghis was an untaught savage whose school was the struggle from dire poverty to the lordship of upper Asia. Yet in the extent of his conquests he was the greatest of all conquerors; and he was greater still in his understanding of the springs of action and in his power to create those living organizations which make large action possible. In poverty and in greatness he chose his companions with unerring skill, and the friends of his youth became the faithful generals and governors of the Mongol empire.

Every man in his dominions was a warrior; and at a moment's notice every warrior must be ready with his horse and arms for a long campaign. Arms and equipment were standardized down to the smallest details in accordance with the lessons learned from many campaigns. In peacetime, men and horses were trained to disciplined maneuvers in the hunting field. In war, iron discipline and scientific tactics replaced the traditional hit and run of tribal warfare. "Arrow messengers" riding night and day kept the great khan informed of all important events and maintained contact between armies and divisions on campaign, while the careful collection of military and political intelligence discovered the weak points in neighboring states. Genghis had a hard struggle to establish the foundation of his power, but as soon as the new tactics were fully developed every difficulty seemed to vanish. Whenever he defeated a nomadic tribe, the great khan taught Mongol skill and discipline to his vanquished enemies, whose loyalty to their new master strengthened the Mongols after every victory with the increasing speed of a chain reaction. The Mongols at their best could probably have beaten any army that Europe put into the field before the invention of the breech-loading rifle.

The army was organized in units of 10, 100, 1,000 and 10,000. On pain of death, men of the same unit must never desert each other, whatever the odds, and Genghis Khan lived up to this standard himself. Enemies who were brave and loyal to their cause were often pardoned and rewarded

with high office, but treachery in friend or foe was never forgiven. Once, thinking to escape destruction, the tribe of the
great khan's worst enemy handed over their chief. Genghis
Khan exterminated the whole tribe, declaring that those who
betrayed their master could not be trusted.

When their organization was consolidated, the Mongols
soon became the lords of all the steppe lands from Manchuria to Turkestan, and Genghis Khan promulgated a new code
of laws based on the traditional morality of the steppe. Theft
and adultery were punished by death; caravans were protected and trade began to flourish as never before.

Had Genghis Khan died at the age of fifty he would be
remembered as a great and just ruler of nomads. We might
never have known of his youthful escapades, of his daring,
loyalty and prudence, and of his deep family affections, which
make him a man of flesh and blood among the phantoms of
nomadic history, but we should not have to record the account of blood which darkens the Mongolian conquest of
more civilized lands. For Genghis Khan lived to be an old
man and his armies tortured and killed men, women and children throughout most of Asia and half of Europe on a scale
never equaled till our own day. Judged by the standards of
right and wrong in which he grew up, Genghis Khan was a
good man, but to rule over city-dwelling Chinamen and Per-
sians set problems for which his bright but savage genius was
unprepared.

One day he asked his chief generals what was the greatest
joy in life. All were for hunting of one kind or another, but
the great khan shook his head at each answer. "The greatest
joy a man can know," he said, "is to conquer his enemies and
drive them before him. To ride their horses and plunder their
goods. To see the faces of those who were dear to them be-
dewed with tears and to clasp their wives and daughters in
his arms." Yet he could listen to unpalatable advice from the
upholders of ancient tradition. He solicited the wisdom of the
great Chinese sage Ch'ang Ch'un who addressed the khan in
celebrated words:

"A whirlwind does not last for a morning; a cloudburst is
over within the day; and by whose will is this? By that of
heaven and earth. If neither heaven nor earth can achieve
permanence, how much less can man do so? . . . To rule
over a great realm is like the roasting of little fish. One must
not rub off their scales; must not shake them too much, must

not scorch them and must be easy and tender in the way one handles them. Only he who is just to all his subjects is a good ruler. . . . We must work as the Tao, the way, the persistent, the true meaning works by inaction."

On hearing this Genghis Khan is said to have turned to his chief generals with the words: "What the sage speaks is wisdom that he has learned from heaven. I have preserved his words in the depth of my heart. Do ye the same but they must not pass beyond ourselves."

The Mongols had old scores to settle with China and a clash was certain in that quarter, but Genghis Khan aspired to peaceful trade relations with the West. When Mohammed Shah, who had succeeded to the inheritance of the Seljuks in west Asia, sent an embassy to the new great power that had arisen to the northeast, his envoys received the following answer:

"I already know the size and power of your shah's realm. He is the ruler of the West just as I am the ruler of the East and we should do well to live together on friendly terms. Our boundaries touch in the land of Kipchak and it would be to our advantage if merchants could move freely from one country to the other."

When the Caliph of Baghdad, who was an enemy of Mohammed Shah, tried to persuade the Mongols to attack him, Genghis Khan replied: "I am not at war with him," but Mohammed Shah, for his part, was less prudent and gave orders to execute some Mongols who had been found among a caravan that was seized by one of Mohammed's provincial governors. One hundred and fifty men were massacred, but one slave escaped to bring the tale to the nearest Mongolian post, whence he was immediately sent to the great khan. "With this command," writes the Moslem chronicler, "the shah signed his own death warrant. Each drop of the blood he then shed was paid for by floods of his subjects' lifeblood. Each hair of the victims' heads was paid for by a thousand heads and each dinar was heavily outweighed by tons of gold."

But Genghis Khan still did not want a quarrel and contented himself with sending an embassy to ask for the surrender of the official responsible for the massacre. Mohammed Shah in reply slew the ambassador and sent the rest of the embassy back without their beards. Genghis then prepared for total war.

Mohammed Shah believed himself secure behind the barriers of the Hungry Steppe and the Tien Shan Mountains with their 12,000 foot passes, but the Mongols and their hardy ponies overcame obstacles and hardships which had proved insurmountable to large armies since the beginning of recorded time. The Moslems were defeated and all central Asia and Persia fell into the hands of the Mongols.

Genghis Khan was a severe conqueror, but he did not at first go much beyond the limits of what was customary in that age and place, though he had very little use for soft city-dwellers who could not serve in the Mongol army of horse archers. But, when the inevitable revolts broke out, he made it a rule to massacre the inhabitants of offending cities. Not only were captives pressed into the conquerors' service, but lines of defenseless old men, women and children were often driven against their kith and kin to provide a screen for the Mongol hosts who followed. Sometimes after the inhabitants of a city had been massacred and the executioners had left, the survivors would creep out of their hiding-places in the smoldering ruins only to find that the Mongols had sent back a rearguard to complete the work of murder. None but artisans and men of skill or learning and beautiful young women were spared to adorn the court of their conquerors.

Terror was used with great effect as an instrument of policy. The Mongols, or Tartars as they were sometimes called, were believed invincible and Genghis Khan encouraged the belief that he and his hosts were instruments of the wrath of God. In Europe it was supposed indeed that they were called Tartars because they had issued from the gates of Tartarus or hell. At Yarmouth there was a glut of herrings one year because purchasers from the other side of the North Sea were afraid to sail at the mere rumor of the Mongols' approach. Where the Tartar army had passed, men with arms in their hands allowed themselves to be slaughtered in droves by one Mongol soldier. So great was the terror of the Mongol name.

Success beyond the dreams of Alexander the Great now encouraged the Mongols to believe that they were intended by heaven to rule all the world. Genghis Khan divided the earth in all directions between his sons. The west, "so far as the hoof of a Mongolian horse can travel," fell to Juji, the eldest, and in 1221 he was instructed by his father to undertake a three years' reconnaissance of the lands beyond the Caucasus.

The Georgians were defeated and most of the western Kipchak submitted in the first year's campaign. Juji went into winter quarters in the south Ukraine and proceeded to collect military and diplomatic information about Europe. This expedition was not more than a reconnaissance in force and Juji had no wish to become embroiled with the Russians, but a part of the Kipchak fled north to Russia asking for help from their traditional foes. The Russians decided to help the Kipchak against the unknown enemy and advanced with their allies into the steppe. Near the lower Dnieper ten Mongolian envoys appeared in the Russian camp, saying: "Why have the Russians taken the field? The Mongols have no quarrel with them. They have only come to chastise their disloyal vassals the Kipchak . . . who have frequently attacked and plundered Russian lands. The Russians would be better advised to make common cause with the Mongols and to take vengeance on the Kipchak." This overture was dismissed as a trap and the ten envoys were killed. The Russians crossed the Dnieper and dispersed the Mongolian advance guard.

Soon after this, two Mongol horsemen rode right into the Russian camp and cried aloud: "You have murdered our envoys, have attacked our outposts and want war. So be it. We had planned no evil against you. All the peoples have only one God and He will judge between us." The Russians were so surprised that they let the two riders depart unscathed.

Nine days later upon the banks of the river Kalka not more than thirty thousand Mongols faced a much larger army of Russians and Kipchaks, who were so certain of victory that they did not even attack in concert. But Mongol discipline, concentrating its blows where they were needed, drove the Kipchak back upon the already disordered Russians and then forced the confused mass into the river, whereupon a contingent of ten thousand men from Kiev, which had not taken part in the battle, was surrounded in its fortified camp. After three days scarcely one was left alive to take home the news of defeat. The victors celebrated the occasion by feasting upon a platform supported by the suffocating bodies of the Russian princes.

However, the Mongols were not yet ready for the conquest of Europe and after plundering some of the nearest towns they turned east to disappear from European eyes for fourteen years. The Russians hoped that the danger had passed and made no attempt to consolidate their scattered forces, for the northern princes felt safe behind their screen of forest, and trade no longer gave all Russians a common interest.

Genghis Khan died in 1227, but his empire, his military organization and his dream of world dominion lived on. A complete plan for the conquest of Europe had been drawn up from the knowledge obtained by Juji's expedition, and in 1237 Batu, the son of Juji, who had inherited the western fief of the Mongol empire, began to execute the plan. In the first six years Russia, Poland, Silesia, Hungary, Serbia and Bulgaria were conquered according to plan, and the rest of Europe was saved by the death of the great khan rather than by the prowess of her defenders.

Hitherto the deep Russian forests had been proof against invasion, but in the winter of 1237-38 Batu raged like a blizzard through central Russia, riding with ease over the frozen rivers and marshes, which had deterred all previous armies. Ice and snow had no terrors for the Mongolian warriors, who were inured to Siberian cold; and the supply of fodder to their horses gave no difficulty, for the hardy Mongolian ponies knew how to reach the winter grass by scraping through the snow with their hoofs. The Russian princes resisted at first with desperate courage, but they did not combine and the Tartars overcame them one by one. Every place was summoned to submit to its rightful lord, the great khan, appointed by the will of heaven. The least resistance was treated as treason and punished by massacre, which spared neither woman nor child. Vladimir was sacked and the churches were choked with the bodies of those who took refuge there. By the end of March 1238 Batu was little more than a hundred miles from Novgorod, but then he turned south, knowing that the thaw would soon make large-scale movement impossible. For two years Batu ravaged north and south, imposing Tartar rule on all Russia. In 1240 he destroyed Kiev, and five years later the Papal legate Fra Giovanni Piano Carpini records that barely two hundred houses stood in Kiev, while in the surrounding districts he saw "an enormous number of skulls and bones of the slaughtered men lying on the plain." Some of the towns destroyed by Batu were rebuilt later on new sites, but others disappeared forever. City life took centuries to recover, and the mason's art disappeared from Russia, for stone buildings were built no longer.

The rulers of the Golden Horde, as the western Mongols

were called, soon discovered that prosperous subjects paid more taxes than burned cities. Batu's massacres put back the settlement of northern Russia by several generations, but the Ukraine was already ceasing to count and the tragic loss of provinces on the southern border did not affect the main course of Russian development. The drain of tribute probably delayed the development of trade and industry, but the Mongols put down robbery with a firm hand and gave effective protection to such trade as had survived. So the wealth which the Tartars took away with one hand was sometimes given back with the other. If Russia was provincial and isolated in the thirteenth and fourteenth centuries, that was a consequence of her geographical position and of her stage of economic development. Tartar domination, insofar as it kept open the trade routes to the east and south, tended to draw Russia into contact with a wider world. For instance, the Genoese became firmly established in the Crimea under Tartar protection and Italian architects appeared in Moscow as soon as the country had recovered enough from its devastation for stone buildings to be built once more.

In the steppe lands the Mongol minority was soon absorbed by the Kipchak and the territory of the Golden Horde was still known as the land of Kipchak. The center of western Mongol power was the lower Volga, and here the house of Batu continued the traditional semi-nomadic life, deriving part of their wealth from flocks and herds, part from the tribute of neighboring lands and part from transit trade.

The khans encouraged the building of cities, and their capitals at New and Old Sarai on the lower Volga flourished exceedingly. At Old Sarai near Astrakhan "reservoirs of water at various levels unceasingly drove iron water wheels. Here there were countless workshops; smithies, tile works, potteries, smelting furnaces," and New Sarai near the site of the future Stalingrad "was traversed by canals, adorned with lovely ponds; the houses had water conduits, mosaic floors, walls covered with variously glazed tiles. In the ruins there have been discovered the vestiges of fine tailoring and shoe-making establishments and of jewelers' shops" (Pravdin, *The Mongol Empire*, p. 472).

The first generations of Mongols protected all religions, supposing that there was truth in each and that the prayers offered by priests of every creed would all contribute to the welfare of the great khan and his armies. Many influential Mongols became "Nestorian" Christians and at one moment it seemed that the myth of Prester John might come true in a Christian Mongol empire. But local traditions were too strong and in the end the Mongols of China became Buddhists, while the Ilkhans of Persia and their rivals of the Golden Horde embraced Islam. The difference of religion widened the gulf between the Tartars and their Christian subjects. There was no normal social intercourse between conquerors and conquered, no Mongol ruling class in Russia and little intermarriage between the races. Thus there was no fusion of culture between the Russians and their conquerors. For a short time Russian soldiers were forced into the Mongol service as far away as China, but the old order of state, church and society was left very much as before.

The Russian princes were responsible as vassals for law and order in their own dominions and for the punctual payment of tribute. Only in the first two generations was any attempt made to collect the taxes directly, though at least three times a searching census of the population was taken. The collection of tribute was first confided to Tartar residents in each important center, but after the first generation these were replaced by Jewish and Armenian tax farmers. This system again led to abuses, and the collection of tribute was finally delegated to the grand prince of Vladimir.

Every successor to the throne of Vladimir had to obtain on his accession a confirmation of his authority from the khan. For this purpose he undertook a journey to the Mongolian capital, where he was expected to pay richly in bribes and presents for any favor conferred on him and to outbid other competitors in his promises of tribute. Several princes did not come back from these expeditions. The suspicions of the Tartar court were easily roused and it was a short step from suspicion to summary execution, but those grand princes who returned armed with the khan's authority were in a strong position against their brother princes. The Russian grand princes used the great khan's commission to re-create, by degrees, a national unity which made it possible for them in course of time to throw off the Tartar yoke. The Russian Church, too, was fortified by the favor of the khan and by the grant of privileges which for the first time made the Church independent of the state. At a time of political division the existence of a united church independent of the local princes, but owning land everywhere, helped greatly to draw the country together. Thus one of the indirect results of the "Tartar yoke" was to hasten the reunification of Russia.

The Tartar example reinforced the lesson that strong government was needed and it appeared to show that strong government must be ruthless. A vast land with natural unity, but too scattered to be ruled by the milder methods which would have been suited to a smaller or more articulated community, was waiting for some strong power to deliver it from anarchy worse than misgovernment.

The Tartars bequeathed to Russia the knout and perhaps the germ of the secret police, but they also left behind them many words connected with trade, and the tsarist government's post system was the direct descendant of Genghis Khan's "arrow messengers." It seems fanciful, however, to suggest that the tsarist bureaucracy is a continuation of the Tartar civil service, for the period of direct Mongolian administration was too short and too distant from the first tsars to have produced such progeny.

The knout was no ordinary whip, but a three-tailed weapon of rawhide sharpened so that every blow inflicted a deep wound. In Russia torture long remained the ordinary method of obtaining evidence from those suspected of crimes, or of withholding evidence. Torture began with the knout and ended with a special engine designed to dislocate a man's limbs; torture by fire sometimes accompanied the use of this ghastly apparatus and in extreme cases boiling water was dripped slowly onto the shaven head of the victim. The Russians accepted these horrors with an equanimity that shocked visitors from Renaissance Europe. The post of executioner and torturer was considered respectable and even honorable. Well-to-do merchants would pay a substantial sum for the post, which brought sinister gains to its holder, who, retiring after a few years, would sell his office at a profit. The highest in the land were not exempt from physical punishment, and society does not seem to have considered that it was degrading to inflict or to suffer torture and the knout, until in the seventeenth century the influence of milder neighbors began to influence Russia. But even at the worst times the Russians were loth to take life by judicial process. In Russia a thief might be beaten with the knout while a government official stood by inscribing each stroke in a book for the purpose of official records, and he might even die under punishment. In western Europe he would have been hanged as a matter of course.

The Mongol empire retained its full vigor for a bare century, but the Mongol name did not easily lose its power over the loyalty of mankind. Even Tamburlaine sheltered behind the façade of a puppet emperor descended from Genghis Khan, and Tamburlaine's descendants when they became the emperors of India were proud to call themselves Mongols or Moguls. The last descendants of the great khan to rule a part of his domain were the emirs of Bokhara and of Khiva, who were driven out by the Bolsheviks in 1920.

The great days of the Mongol raiders passed with the invention of firearms which, for the first time, gave the settled cultivator a tactical advantage over the nomad. The Chinese and Russians then pressed their advantage and repaid many of the cruelties of former centuries, while the Mongols, having lost their ascendancy in war, became converted to Lamaistic Buddhism, the most peaceful of all religions. Altered circumstances and a new religion have changed the noble but merciless warriors of Genghis Khan and Batu into a race of mild-eyed herdsmen.

A Russian observer, G. N. Potanin, describes the Mongols as they were in the 1880s:

"Life among the Mongols proceeds quietly, their ways are gentle, brutal treatment of women and children is unheard of; crimes, especially murders, are of rare occurrence; Russian merchants living in Uliasutai assured me that during the seven years that they had inhabited the town they had never heard of a murder; there had been but one case of violent death and that was a suicide. To such a degree do the Mongols abhor death by violence that according to Mr. Shishmarev, our consul in Urga, when the Chinese authorities had condemned several men to death for political offenses, not a man was to be found amongst the Mongols to undertake the role of executioner. A heavy bribe induced one at last to carry out the sentence, but from that moment he was ostracized by all and becoming desperately poor was obliged to wander, a beggar, from place to place; all men strove to keep him at a distance, and when he stretched forth his hand for alms they gave, it is true, but at the same time called upon him to go away" (see John F. Baddeley, *Russia, Mongolia, China,* Macmillan, 1919, p. 52).

CHAPTER IV

roots of the
Polish problem

Кто устоит в неравном споре:
Кичливый Лях иль верный Росс?

(*Who will last out the unequal contest,*
froward Pole or trusty Russ?)

Pushkin, TO RUSSIA'S SLANDERERS

In south Russia the fall of Kiev left a political vacuum which began to be felt as the tide of the Tartar invasion receded. It became clear that the first strong rulers to raise themselves up would step easily into a rich inheritance, but the fate of centuries depended on the character and origin of the new rulers. By now the differences of ethos and of theological emphasis between the Eastern and Western branches of the Church had hardened into schism. Injuries given and received on both sides were renewed daily until the sense of a common Christianity was overlaid by an undying hatred. Could the marches of Poland and Russia provide a link between the two halves of Christendom or would they prove to be one more bone of contention?

If an Orthodox power could consolidate the Ukraine and the marches of eastern and western Europe, Russia would grow from a rich land placed within reach of the centers of Western and Southern civilization. If a Catholic power became established, it was probable that the Russians would, for a time at least, be forced back into the provincial poverty of the Great Russian woods and marshes, from which they would come out one day to challenge Western rule of the broad and rich debatable lands, which had once formed the kernel of the Russian empire.

In the thirteenth century a line of energetic Russian princes built up a powerful state in the provinces of Galicia and Volhynia. Wedged between Catholic Poland and the rich but exposed lands of the central Ukraine and protected by the Pripet marshes on the north and by the Carpathians on the. south, the two provinces were well placed for trade and large enough to form the basis of great power, as such things went in those days.

Forest gave some protection against the Tartars and, though Galicia and Volhynia were cruelly ravaged and compelled to pay tribute, they maintained a relative independence of the Mongol yoke even at the worst moments. Religion divided Galicia from Poland, but the organization of society formed a bond of sympathy and interest between Catholic and Orthodox neighbors. Great Russia, unlike the Ukraine and Poland, was the creation of organizing princes and enterprising colonists. The rank and file of the northern gentry had become established after the first wave of colonization was over and they had to accept the control of the great nobles who organized the new provinces. But in the south of Russia, as also in Poland, the old local gentry, who had grown with the land from the dawn of its history, remained and kept their customary privileges. Thus the great boyars of Galicia were never brought under the control which the northern grand princes imposed on those who entered their service, and the southern nobility used their freedom from restraint to impose fetters on their own tenants. In this way, long before the enserfment of the Great Russian peasants, the southern landowners were able to assert a complete domination over the men and women who worked their land. (Cf. p. 109.)

Western influence was strengthened by the wish of the Galician princes to enlist against the Tartars the support of their Catholic neighbors in Poland and Hungary. Political alliance had cultural and religious implications. The prince of Galicia was crowned king by the Papal legate, and abortive negotiations took place for the reception of Galicia and Volhynia into the Roman Church on a Uniate basis. In the end both people and rulers remained Orthodox, but the princes maintained a Latin secretariat and sealed their charters with a Latin seal, while German settlers in the cities of Galicia were encouraged to organize themselves under the German Magdeburg Law. A medieval synthesis of East and West would have solved problems which torment us all to this day.

It might have seemed that Galicia was on the way to just such a synthesis, but that was not to be.

By the fourteenth century the tide of civilization was flowing strongly from the West and, in 1340, upon a failure of the local dynasty, Galicia fell an easy victim to the rising power of Poland. Thereafter, Galicia remained an integral part of Poland till the first partition in 1772, when the province fell to Austria. Hapsburg rule proved enlightened in many ways. Lvov became a center of culture to which Polish patriotism feels a deep affection; but the peasants of Galicia remained Orthodox for the most part and continued to speak a Ukrainian dialect, though Galicia has never formed part of any Russian state from the fourteenth century till 1939, in which year the Polish Ukraine became part of the Soviet Union.

Volhynia did not go to Poland with Galicia but became part of the new Lithuanian state, and thereby hangs a tale. The Lithuanians, the Old Prussians and the Letts were kindred peoples inhabiting the shores of the Baltic and the lower valley of the Niemen, and speaking Indo-European dialects which closely resembled each other but bore only a distant relation to the Slavonic languages. History has next to nothing to say of the Lithuanians before the thirteenth century, but in the course of the next hundred years these pagans emerging from the forest produced a dynasty of great leaders who imposed their domination on the principalities of the Dnieper. The loosely knit empire of Lithuania soon became the dominant power between the Baltic and the Black seas, but its Russian subjects outnumbered the Lithuanians themselves and they were far more advanced in civilization. The official language of the empire was Slavonic. The existing social structure was maintained and the old ruling classes kept their position under Lithuanian rule.

At first the heathen Lithuanians tended to embrace the religion of their Orthodox subjects. If Orthodoxy had once struck roots among the Lithuanian leaders, Vilna might have taken the place of Moscow in Russian history. An Orthodox state placed along the length of the great divide between eastern and western Europe, and ruled from a capital lying within a short journey from the German trading cities of the Baltic, would have formed a link between two worlds, but the history of the Russian borderlands is unlucky. The swaying balance inclined decisively to the Catholic side and Lithuania, soon to be joined with Poland, became an alien power ruling lands that had once been Russian.

Poland, formerly poor, barbarous and divided, was in the fourteenth century united under strong kings and entered into the heritage of Western Christendom. The new three-field system of agriculture increased the national wealth, marshes were drained, forests were cleared and settlers from Germany and Flanders came in large numbers, both to work the land and to populate the cities which grew up along the trade routes. The burghers of these cities, who were often German, received the right to govern themselves under the Magdeburg Law, while Jews came in large numbers to enjoy the tolerance of the Polish state and they too were allowed to regulate their affairs according to their own law. Polish law was codified and enforced. Traders thrived and the poverty-stricken Polish landlords began to grow rich on the export of corn both east and west. In the fifteenth century Polish grain was regularly exported as far as Constantinople.

A university was founded at Crakow and the full splendor of the Renaissance came to Poland in the fifteenth and sixteenth centuries. Copernicus, the first modern scientist, was a Renaissance Pole. The nobility lived in Renaissance palaces and their tombs were adorned with Italianate sculpture. They were well versed in the ancient and modern literature of Europe. The events of contemporary history and court life were recorded and commented on in well-written Latin histories and elegant Latin epigrams. Poets wrote with equal ease in Latin and in their native Polish. In their dress the nobility combined national tradition with the sumptuousness of the new age, and shining heads shaved clean save for one lock, in the immemorial manner of the Ukraine, appeared above Renaissance doublets and ruffs. (Cf. p. 30. A similar custom seems to be referred to in Herodotus, Bk. IV, 23.)

Polish genius in the arts of peace was matched by courage and organization in war. Later ages have often seen Poland's martial skill and intrepidity tragically expended against hopeless odds, but in the conditions of the Renaissance the Poles were a first-class military power and able to meet all calls on their resources. Such a neighbor as Poland was bound to influence the infant Lithuanian state, but the extent and nature of that influence depended partly on accident. The old Polish dynasty became extinct in 1370, and in 1386, by a fateful act of statesmanship, Poland and Lithuania were united in a dynastic marriage. In the course of two centuries, the resulting union ripened into an association closer than the union of Scotland and England.

The landowning gentry, who held the power in the composite state, early learned to curb their kings by imposing conditions on every accession. In England the Great Charter imposed by the barons once for all on a monarchy that remained strong enough to rule effectively has become the foundation of liberty within the law for the whole people. But in Poland the "pacta conventa," imposed afresh and enlarged upon every accession in the interests of one class only, ended by making government nearly impossible. Moreover, by abstaining from trade themselves, while preventing any peasant from rising in the social scale, the gentry held back the economic development of the country and made it certain that trade and industry should be in the hands of foreigners, mostly Jews, Germans and Armenians. Jewish bailiffs were employed in the management of the big estates and the Hebrew community thus incurred all the odium which had been earned by their employers, as well as the unpopularity of being the only moneylenders and, in many places, the only traders.

There were few Jews in Russia proper and there was no discrimination against them until the end of the Middle Ages, but in later times, when the Russian empire gained large territories from Poland, she acquired therewith a large Jewish population and inherited the social problem that arose from the peculiar position which the Jews occupied in Poland. The Russian government tried to prevent Jews settling outside the old Polish boundary, which became known as the "Pale of Settlement." In spite of this, anti-Semitism invaded the Great Russian provinces and has left tragic traces throughout Russia.

Under tsarism the Jews were treated with stupid and brutal incomprehension, sometimes compelled to live where no living was to be had, often prevented from getting the education that their talents deserved, and occasionally subject to *pogroms*. Under Soviet rule they have fared somewhat better, being allowed to live where they like, and many of them have risen to the top in literature, science, and the arts. Yet they are still treated as a separate people. If one is a Jew it is entered on one's "passport" (or identity card), a document that must be produced frequently for a variety of official purposes. Since the 1930s Jews have been excluded from the Soviet diplomatic service, and custom—albeit unwritten and unavowed—has sometimes made it hard for them to get a higher education or to rise in their professions. At certain periods they have suffered the rigors of Soviet law far more than most other groups, and at times the Jewish community has been threatened by vicious attacks on "Zionism" in the Soviet Press.

In the long run the privileges of the gentry were sufficient to account for the subsequent calamities of Poland, but during the centuries of the Renaissance Poland could afford much unwisdom and the brilliance of her ruling class was a magnet for every eye. A delightful social equality reigned among the gentry, but who was entitled to enter this magic circle? Could the Orthodox nobility of the Dnieper expect to hold office and enjoy privileges in a Catholic state? Any Lithuanian subject who was a landowner and embraced Catholicism was admitted to the privileges of the Polish gentry, but every landowner who remained Orthodox was debarred from public office and from any education worthy of the name. His wife and daughters would be condemned to the tedium and seclusion of the home of a bucolic, Orthodox squire, while the splendor and amenity of a life modeled on Baldassare Castiglione's *Cortegiano*, as well as the fruits of public employment, awaited those families which accepted the Latin rite and the Papal jurisdiction (cf. p. 110).

At first the majority stood firm for the old ways of Orthodoxy, but in each generation there were converts until in the course of three centuries practically the whole of the landowning class of the Polish Lithuanian state had become Catholics; and for a Russian to become a Catholic meant to become a Pole; but whatever the landlords might do, the peasants of eastern Poland clung stubbornly to their own traditions, and a difference of language and religion gave a deeper meaning to the gap between lord and serf.

Throughout the ages the problems of Poland have been rooted in these fundamental conflicts.

CHAPTER V

the cities of the West

Once did she hold the gorgeous East in fee.

Wordsworth, ON THE EXTINCTION OF
THE VENETIAN REPUBLIC

1. Medieval Russian Republics

After the Tartar invasions city life throughout most of Russia fell into a long stagnation. But in the far west, beyond the reach of the Mongolian flood, the old Russia, "The Land of Cities," went on much as before.

Novgorod grew rich at the point where the river Volkhov debouches from Lake Ilmen. Vyatka, in what was then the far north, and Pleskov, or Pskov as it is now abbreviated, "the younger sister of Novgorod," were independent republics with their own proud traditions. But "Lord Novgorod the Great" with its teeming streets and warehouses full of German cloth and wines was far above all rivals. "Who can stand against God and Lord Novgorod the Great?" Thus ran the proverb.

Stone churches rose above the general level of crowded wooden houses and provided in their vaults safe storage for the merchant companies of Novgorod. Those who have seen Eisenstein's film *Alexander Nevski*, parts of which were shot at Novgorod and Pskov, will remember the simple and harmonious outlines of the eleventh-century Cathedral of St. Sophia at Novgorod.

The government of Novgorod was republican. The organization of defense and good order was entrusted to a prince drawn from Russian princely stock, but the republic, led by its merchant nobility, was capable of showing the door to any prince who did not give satisfaction. In 1221, so the contemporary *Chronicle of Novgorod* tells us, "The men of Novgorod showed Prince Vsevolod the road. 'We do not want thee. Go whither thou wilt.' He went into Russia to his father." In

68

those days "Russia" was a foreign country to the men of Novgorod, just as France is a foreign country to the French Swiss.

Again in 1270 the *Chronicle* records that

"There was a tumult in Novgorod; they set about driving Prince Yaroslav out of the town and they summoned an assembly in Yaroslav's court and killed Ivanko, and others escaped into the church of St. Nicholas; on the morrow Ratibor, the captain of the thousand, Gabriel Kiyaninov and others of his friends fled to the prince in the citadel near Novgorod; and they took their houses for plunder and divided up their dwellings and sent to the prince in the citadel a document setting forth all his faults: 'Why hast thou taken up the Volkhov with snarers of wild ducks and taken up the fields with catchers of horses? Why hast thou taken the homestead of Alex the son of Mortkin? Why hast thou taken silver from Mikifor the son of Manushkin, and from Roman the son of Boldyzh and from Bartholomew? And another thing, why dost thou send away from us the foreigners who dwell among us? and many faults of this kind. And now, prince, we cannot suffer thy violence. Depart from us and we shall think of a prince for ourselves.' And the prince sent Svyatoslav (his son) and Andrew the son of Wratislaw to the assembly with greeting: 'I renounce all that and I swear by the Cross on all your terms.' But the men of Novgorod answered: 'Prince, go away, we do not want thee: else we shall come, the whole of Novgorod, and drive thee out.' And the prince went out of the town against his will."

But the men of Novgorod could not manage without a prince and found it hard to get a substitute for Yaroslav. In the end, after various intrigues with the "tsar of the Tartars" and the grand prince of Vladimir, they agreed to take Yaroslav back on terms. But, as luck would have it, in the very same year Yaroslav succeeded to the throne of the grand prince. However, he remained titular prince of Novgorod and from this time it became usual for the grand princes to hold the title of prince of Novgorod but to carry out the functions of that office through a deputy.

The powers and revenues of the prince of Novgorod were strictly limited by custom and enshrined in a contract between townspeople and prince. The prince, or later the prince's representative, did not live in Novgorod but in the wooden citadel nearby. He could not own land in the territory of Novgorod or trade except through the intermediary of a native-born merchant. His executive power was limited by the popular assembly and by elected officers of whom the chief were the governor and the captain of the thousand. Without the governor the prince had no right to appoint local officials, to grant charters, to conduct trials or to punish without trial.

In essence Novgorod was an oligarchy of rich merchants, but the power of the ruling class was limited by the powers of the prince and tempered by the constitutional right of the city mob to make its power felt through the popular assembly. Summoned by the city bell the carpenters, potters, ferrymen, fishermen, smiths, tailors, silversmiths, moneyers, laborers and mountebanks of Novgorod would meet to debate affairs of state. Nobles and rich merchants were few but powerful in council; slaves were many but had no voice.

There were few, if any, rules of procedure and there was no appeal from the decisions of the assembly. According to ancient Slavonic tradition, a tradition which is still alive, the eventual decision had to be unanimous, as in a jury, but cudgels were often used to ensure unanimity. In a gust of passion the mob would condemn the houses and goods of unpopular rich merchants to be plundered. In such cases the citizens enjoyed an afternoon's looting. In extreme cases the victim might be executed by being hurled into the Volkhov from the famous bridge of Novgorod, but the crowd was not always deaf to appeals for mercy and victims were sometimes allowed to retire to a monastery—"they released his soul into repentance," in the phrase of the *Chronicle of Novgorod*.

The influence of city life tends to break up big families. Accordingly the patriarchal family of three generations living together was less firmly established in the territory of Novgorod than elsewhere in Russia. The historian Kostomarov, writing in 1860, records that in his own day family organization was markedly weaker in the villages of the ancient territory of Novgorod than in other parts of Russia. Organization by neighborhood and by voluntary association took the place of the older ties of blood. Merchants banded together into companies for protection against the many hazards of the age, and the inhabitants of each crowded street formed a loose corporation under an elected elder. Neighboring streets were confederated into wards or "ends" as they were called, and the whole city was divided by the river Volkhov into two "sides." The "Sophia side" with the fortified Kremlin and cathedral and the houses of the aristocracy lay west of the river; the "commercial side" on the east bank contained the trading center, with the buildings set apart for foreign merchants, and the assembly place and assembly bell, with its own bell tower. The rivalry of the two sides was intense and disputes were often fought out with cudgels upon the bridge. From time to time the bridge was carried away by storms and ice, and the pious chronicler opines that the Almighty did this in order to prevent the shedding of Christian blood.

As in Venice, a merchant aristocracy set the tone of society, exhibiting those qualities which come naturally to a nation of shopkeepers. The straightforward business methods of the merchant princes of the north contrasted with the tortuous ways of other Russian traders. The rich wore long red boots and loved to dress in crimson. The men had their beards carefully trimmed and put sticky perfumes on their hair; they cut their hair back from their foreheads and plaited it in a special way known as the *kika,* leaving a long lock hanging from the crown of their heads. The girls wore pigtails with ribbons and women wore headdresses tied under their chins with a kerchief. The poor were dressed in coarse russets and grays, with bare feet or shoes of bark much like their ancestors and descendants for many generations in all parts of Russia. Displays of singlestick and wrestling, mountebanks and every kind of show kept the streets continually animated. The rich were expected to maintain their social position by giving feasts at which foreign wines were served as well as native beer and mead. Minstrels were essential to the success of an "honorable feast" and the festivities sometimes ended in men and women dancing together to the great scandal of some of the clergy.

The Novgorod merchants exchanged the furs, wax and hemp of the north for the cloth and wine of Europe and the corn of Suzdal. Lake Ilmen and the Volkhov teemed with fish, but the poor forest soil could not provide enough bread for a large city. Novgorod's great weakness was her dependence on foreign supplies of wheat. After the destruction of Russian's southern regions, Suzdal was the only province that was still able to export wheat. So the citizens of Novgorod came to depend for their daily bread on the grand princes of Vladimir who controlled Suzdal. The merchants who brought corn from central Russia were in a delicate position toward society, for they trafficked in the very basis of life. When corn was scarce, the price soared and a fortune could be made in a few weeks, but it could also be lost in a night if the hungry mob plundered the house and store of some rich profiteer.

Famines are recorded time without number in the *Chronicle of Novgorod,* as in all medieval chronicles.

"In 1230 on the day of the Exaltation of the Honorable Cross (September 26) a frost killed the crops throughout our district and from that there arose great misery. We began to buy bread at eight kunos, a barrel of rye at twenty grivnas, or twenty-five in the courts, wheat at forty grivnas, millet at eight and oats at thirteen grivnas; our town and our country went asunder and other towns and countries became full of our own brothers and sisters; and the rest began to die. And who would not weep at this, seeing the dead lying in the streets and the little ones devoured by dogs? And God put into the heart of Archbishop Spiridon to do good. He put a common grave by the Church of the Holy Apostles in Prussian Street and engaged a good and gentle man by name Stanila to carry the dead on horses whenever he went about the town, and so continuously he dragged them every day; and he filled it up to the top; there were 3,030 in it."

After describing the political commotions of the winter of 1230-31, the chronicler returns—

"to the bitter and sad memory of that spring. For what is there to say or what to speak of the punishment that came to us from God? How that some of the common people killed the living and ate them; others cut up dead flesh and corpses and ate them; others ate horseflesh, dogs and cats; but to those they found in such acts they did thus—some they burned with fire, others they cut to pieces and others they hanged. Some fed on moss, snails, pine bark, lime bark, lime and elm tree leaves and whatever each could think of. And again other wicked men began to burn the good people's houses, where they suspected there was rye."

On top of all this a fire broke out and burned a great part of the city but "the same year God showed his mercy toward us sinners. He did his mercy quickly. The Germans came from beyond the sea with corn and with flour and they did much good, for the land was already near its end."

These and other smaller catastrophes kept the wheel of fortune turning. A fire or a riot would turn a rich man into a beggar overnight, someone else would rise to take his place, and others would watch in envy. The uncertainty of life at Novgorod bred a spirit of adventure; but it also kept the slave market well supplied, for those who lost all were often forced to sell themselves and their families to escape starvation.

Like Athens and Rome, Novgorod was a city-state which became an imperial power. All the north of European Russia from Murmansk to the Urals formed part of the domain of "Lord Novgorod the Great." This vast area could not be effectively administered by medieval Novgorod, but it was brought into the trading system of Europe by the tribute in kind which was exacted from the tribes of the forest and of the tundra. Ermine and sable bought or extorted from the Finns and Lapps went to deck the charming lords and ladies of our medieval manuscripts, and wax from northern bees was burned on the altars of Catholic churches.

In the more southerly parts of the empire of Novgorod there was a settled local administration under officials drawn from Russian princely stock and appointed by the republic, but it does not seem that this form of rule created any strong loyalty. The leading citizens of the subsidiary towns had little share in the politics of Novgorod and the common people had none. The peasants of the empire of Novgorod lived, like other Russian peasants of that age, in an uneasy freedom limited by the shackles of debt and poverty. For them the fall of Novgorod meant nothing but a change of masters.

In the fourteenth century Pskov became independent of Novgorod with a territory that was large enough to count for something in the world of those days, but small enough for the methods of rule natural to a city-state. Pskov maintained a not inglorious independence until its absorption by Moscow in 1510. Aristotle would have said that Novgorod was too large for a satisfactory polity, but that the land of Pskov was eusunoptos, the right size to look at. So, Pskov developed her own variant of the Russian culture, expressed above all in her architecture. You might think that all those whitewashed churches would be monotonous, but the Pskov architects knew how to combine the simple elements of dome, apse, porch and bell tower in strikingly original variations. Modern architects have something to learn from the way in which the simplest shapes are used in different combinations so that each church is beautiful in its own way. Pskov has kept more of its old traditions than Novgorod and it is here that one sees best how much local personality was lost when, in the sixteenth century, Russia became a state rigidly centralized on Moscow.

2. Novgorod between East and West

Till the end of the Middle Ages Novgorod was the main center for interchange between Russia and the West, but her relations with the neighboring Teutonic world were such that Lord Novgorod the Great became the last outpost of Byzantinism rather than a window on Europe.

In the Viking age and in the early Middle Ages the island of Gotland was the commercial center of northern Europe. The splendid stone churches, now serving shrunken villages, still testify to the enterprise of the merchant farmers who made Gotland great for more than a thousand years, and the tremendous cyclopean masonry of Thor's castle and the ancient carved stones of Gotland testify to a prehistoric civilization as impressive as any in Europe. Gotland is now an island of ghosts, but in Visby there is still a street called Novgorod Grän, as if to remind the world of the ancient links between Russia and Scandinavia.

In Novgorod the traders from Scandinavia were concentrated in a building known as the Court of the Gotlanders, but after the rise of German trade in the twelfth century this was eclipsed by the newer German Court and in the end even the Court of the Gotlanders fell into German hands.

The eastern shores of the Baltic, inhabited by Finnish and Lettish tribes, long formed a buffer between Russia and the West. The lower valley of the Dvina was at first under the loose suzerainty of Russian princes, but in 1202 the German Knights of the Sword, a crusading order modeled on the Templars, appeared at the mouth of the Dvina near Riga. Their ostensible aim was to convert the heathen tribes of the Baltic, but conquest was the only way to "convert" those who only knew Christianity through the sword.

The order took vows of celibacy rather than chastity and the adventurous youth of Europe's feudal nobility provided a never-failing stream of recruits. Two hundred years later

Henry IV as a young man fought side by side with the German knights and probably provided the model for Chaucer's "verv parfit gentle knight" who had crusaded in Lithuania and Russia:

In Lettow had he reysed and in Ruce.

The native tribes resisted as they could, but the well-fed, well-organized, armored cavalry of the West soon gained key positions on the lower Dvina and the Baltic coast. Soon they began to look with covetous eyes on the nearest Russian lands. In 1240, three years after Batu's devastation of Russia from the south, the Germans overran Pskov and began to prepare a great expedition against Novgorod. Attacks from east and west seemed to presage the utter disintegration of Russia.

The leading personality in north Russia at that time was Prince Alexander Nevski or Alexander of the Neva, so-called for his great victory on the banks of the Neva in 1240 over the famous Swedish King Birger Jarl, the founder of Stockholm. Birger and his Scandinavian army came with the blessing of the Roman Church, intending to seize Novgorod before the Germans got there and to spread the influence of Rome throughout northern Russia. The Russians, relying on native tribes to watch and report all unusual movement at the mouth of the Neva, learned of the expedition sooner than the Swedes expected. Alexander, at that time prince of Novgorod, mobilized Russian patriotism for the Orthodox faith and joined contingents from "Russia" to the army of Novgorod. The Russian forces caught the Swedes by surprise and won a decisive victory at the cost of only twenty men.

Alexander Nevski, who was the son of that Grand Prince Yaroslav whose quarrels and peacemaking with the men of Novgorod are described above, had passed most of his youth in the atmosphere of civil strife peculiar to the republic. Almost immediately after his victory over Birger Jarl, he quarreled with the men of Novgorod and left their territory. In the meantime the German knights, with new reinforcements from Europe, had overrun the Baltic lands and were busy dividing up their new conquests. German detachments were robbing, burning and slaughtering up to twenty miles from Novgorod before the imminent peril forced the republic to recall Alexander Nevski.

At once he began to win victories. In the winter of 1242

Pskov was liberated, but in the early spring a powerful German army with auxiliaries from the native tribes hastened to retrieve the situation. The Russians met them on the ice of Lake Peipus and the chronicler tells us that on seeing the Germans approach, Alexander raised his arms and cried out in a loud voice, "Judge Thou, O God, my quarrel with this froward people." The battle was fierce, but in the end the Russians won a decisive victory. In the pursuit the ice gave way beneath the weight of the invaders so that many knights were drowned with their horses. The plight of the armored men struggling with the treacherous ice has provided Eisenstein with a memorable episode.

After the "Battle on the Ice" there were countless wars and skirmishes between the Teutonic knights and the Russian cities, but the danger of conquest had passed and the frontier between German domination of one kind or another and Orthodox Russian civilization remained constant for many centuries along the frontiers of Esthonia and Latvia. But hard days still lay ahead for Alexander Nevski and "Lord Novgorod the Great." In 1247 Alexander as prince of Novgorod received a summons from Batu, khan of the Golden Horde, in the following terms:

"God has subdued many nations to me; dost thou alone refuse to submit to my power? But if thou wishest to keep thy lands, come to me; thou shalt see the honor and glory of my kingdom."

Such an invitation could not be refused, and Alexander with his brother Andrew hastened to attend the court of Batu, who forwarded the brothers to the court of the great khan at the other end of Asia. They endured hardship on the way and were able to observe all the terrors of the still recent Tartar conquests; but they were well received by the great khan and Alexander returned a firm supporter of the prudent policy of obedience to the Mongols.

For the first twenty years of Tartar rule Novgorod escaped both devastation and taxation, but in 1257 "evil news came from Russia that the Tartars desired a customs tax and a tithe on Novgorod; and the people were agitated a whole year." The nobility supported Alexander Nevski in submission to these demands, but the "lesser people" opposed him, fearing naturally enough that the burden of tribute would fall on them rather than on the rich. Alexander, whom the khan had appointed grand prince of Vladimir, had to put drastic pressure on the people of Novgorod before they would agree to pay the new taxes.

Frequent hostilities with the Teutonic knights did not prevent the development of a flourishing trade, but the "German Court" at Novgorod was kept under strict control by the Hanseatic League centered at Lübeck. The German merchants maintained a price ring, the Hansa regulated the types of goods which might be exported to Russia and, in order to make these controls effective, refused to sell except by wholesale. On the Russian side the trade was unorganized and buying was competitive, so that the Germans generally got the best of the bargain. No doubt the Russians resented this, though they do not seem to have thought of organizing to meet the German methods.

In the early Middle Ages Russian merchants used to visit the Baltic lands, but by the thirteenth century few, if any, Russians went much beyond the western boundaries of Novgorod. Likewise, if Hanseatic merchants lived permanently in London and Bergen, at Novgorod they were only seasonal guests. In order to maintain the monopoly of the Hansa, Germans were forbidden to teach Russians their technical skill and, though cloth from Flanders and from England was known in Russia, the German merchants gave preference to German wares. The Hansa even forbade grown-up Germans to learn the Russian language so that they should not become independent of the established organization. Chosen interpreters were, however, put to live with Russian families as children in order to learn Russian. Convoys of merchants arrived by specified routes every year at certain seasons, stayed a few weeks or months in the German or Gotland courts and departed when they had disposed of their wares. Western aloofness was answered by an equal coolness on the Russian side and Russians were not allowed to visit the German Court by night.

This strange symbiosis without contact reflected the emotional intensity of the quarrel between the Eastern and Western branches of Christendom. In 1229 the Pope had even forbidden all commerce with the Russians, as enemies of the Catholic faith. The Russian Church on its side began to regard everything as unclean that came from the hands of Roman Catholics. The Metropolitan Photius commanded that vegetables, wine and all food coming from abroad should be purified by consecration before it was consumed. If the difference of Church drew a kind of curtain across Europe, the toughness of the barrier was due to economic factors on both sides. On the German side a monopolistic organization of trade both facilitated and demanded a strict limitation of contact. On the Russian side the dislike of a foreign faith was enhanced by fear and jealousy of the greater material power and accomplishment of the aggressive foreigners who brought that faith.

Novgorod learned little from the West, but maintained her independence against every thrust from that quarter. On the other hand, she had little to learn from Great Russia on the east, but she was vulnerable from that direction. Whoever controlled the land between the Volga and the Oka controlled Novgorod's bread supply. After the rise of a strong power in central Russia the fall of Novgorod became a question of time.

Ivan the Great, who came to the throne of Vladimir and Moscow in 1462 (see p. 89), soon began to assert his rights as titular prince of Novgorod in ways incompatible with the traditional liberties of the republic. The men of Novgorod remonstrated and considered throwing themselves under the protection of Poland and Lithuania, but Ivan denounced this as heresy and treachery. He forced Novgorod to renounce all relations with Poland and to pay a heavy indemnity. Novgorod retained her autonomy under the suzerainty of Moscow for seven years more, but in 1471 a powerful Muscovite army crossed the frontier, the summer being unusually dry so that bogs, which formed an important part of Novgorod's defenses, were passed without difficulty. After one fierce battle the city capitulated and the empire of "Lord Novgorod the Great" was subjected to the Muscovite autocracy. Novgorod, like Venice, did not rouse the kind of patriotism which resists to the bitter end, but—

> Men are we, and must grieve when even the shade
> Of that which once was great is passed away.

After an attempted revolt, Ivan removed eight thousand of the leading families to his own domains and replaced them with merchants from Muscovy, who introduced the more devious methods of trade to which they were accustomed. In 1495 he expelled the German merchants, confiscated their goods and closed down the court of the Germans and the court of the Gotlanders. All those who might have kept the old traditions alive were thus removed and Novgorod soon became the sleepy provincial town which she still is. The old buildings suffered severely in the war against Hitler, but much remains. Those rounded domes like Saracen helmets, St. Sophia's and the red-brick Kremlin with the limpid, teeming waters of the Volkhov and the fairy-tale memories of Lake Ilmen testify to an older Russia. The Russian city-republics seem to have vanished without a trace in the ocean of Russian life, but there are a few people who look back to them with a touch of wistfulness; and the fact that they flourished for so long gives the lie to all theories that Russian human nature requires a personal autocracy.

COMPARATIVE DATES

B.C.

Second half of seventh century, Scythians invade western Asia. Middle of fifth century, Herodotus visits south Russia.

A.D.

862 Rurik.
973 Death of Svyatoslav.
988 Baptism of Vladimir, grand prince of Kiev, and reception of Christianity.
1113-25 Vladimir Monomakh rules in Kiev.
1147 First written mention of Moscow.
1157-74 Andrew of Bogolyubovo rules in Vladimir.
1169 Kiev sacked by Andrew of Bogolyubovo.
1176-1212 Vsevolod "Big Nest" rules in Vladimir.
1199-1205 Roman, King of Galicia and Volhynia.
1221 Foundation of Nizhni Novgorod.
1223 First appearance of Tartars, Battle of Kalka.
1237 Tartar invasion of Russia.
1242 Alexander Nevski defeats Germans.
1252-63 Alexander Nevski rules in Vladimir.
1235-66 David, king of Galicia and Volhynia

B.C.

480 Battle of Salamis.

44 Assassination of Julius Caesar.

A.D.

306-37 Constantine, Emperor of Rome. Converted to Christianity and founds Constantinople.
449 Hengist and Horsa.
622 Mohammed flees from Mecca to Medina.
768-814 Reign of Charlemagne.
786-809 Reign of Harun al Rashid.
845 Vikings sack Paris.
867-86 Basil Bulgaroktonos reigns in Constantinople.
871-99 Reign of King Alfred.
1066 Battle of Hastings.
1073-85 Pope Gregory VII (Hildebrand).
1096 First Crusade.
1204 Fourth Crusade, capture of Constantinople by crusaders.
1215 Magna Carta.
1265 Birth of Dante.
c. 1270 Thomas Aquinas completes *Summa Theologica*.
1348 Black Death.
1386 Union of Poland and Lithuania.
1369-1405 Tamburlaine reigns.
1374 Wycliffe becomes rector of Lutterworth.

the age of Moscow

Our money is spent; my lord also hath our herds of cattle; there is not ought left in the sight of my lord, but our bodies, and our lands: Wherefore shall we die before thine eyes, both we and our land? buy us and our land for bread, and we and our land will be servants unto Pharaoh: and give us seed that we may live, and not die, that the land be not desolate. Genesis xlvii. 18-19

CHAPTER VI

the rise of Moscow

Lo thus I make an end: none other news to thee,
But that the country is too cold, the people beastly
be.

George Turberville, English Ambassador to Moscow in the reign of Elizabeth I

After the invasion of the Tartars northern Russia settled down to five generations of poverty. The peasants worked poorer soil than in the spacious days of Kiev and the rulers had lost their old contact with the wider worlds of Byzantium and the Vikings. With each generation the princes sank deeper into an ignorant provincialism as their estates were divided among an increasing and boorish progeny till some of them were no more than petty chiefs ruling with absolute power over an impoverished hamlet. The vision of each ruler was limited by his neighbors' woods and fields, and the chroniclers of that age almost forgot the "Russian land" while they described local quarrels.

Her remoteness from the outer world ensured that Russia should start late on the path of European development. Scanty population and the barriers of distance, forest and marsh made it certain that her growth would be slow. New ideas and inventions, whether these were a better plow, improved military technique or commercial bookkeeping, took a long time to spread through the country, for it was impossible for advances to spread by the easy imitation of neighbors, when neighbors lived so far apart. Thus medieval strip agriculture and the three-field rotation of crops reached Russia late. Even when a new invention became known, it did not stimulate further development. The Russians had cannon by the end of the fourteenth century, but they did not develop a scientific art of war. When the first tsars met the armies of Renaissance Europe, the bulk of the Russian forces still consisted of feudal levies wearing the chain mail of the twelfth century.

Trade could not easily develop beyond a certain point in a land where distances were such that the cost of transport could easily exceed the value of the merchandise. Therefore until well into the nineteenth century many Russian landlords supplied the greater part of their needs from the produce of their own estates. Indeed, they bought and sold so little that the average Russian country gentleman kept no accounts until after the liberation of the serfs in 1861.

So Russia developed slowly. But on a long view Russia, like western Europe, shows a continuous growth, a steady material accumulation from century to century over the last 1,300 years. This dynamic peculiarity, together with her Christian tradition, distinguishes Russia from most of Asia and binds her to the West. But the broad similarities are masked by the fact that Russia often reaches a particular stage of development at a different time from the West. It is indeed true that concepts drawn from Western history can be misleading when they are applied to Russia, but it is still more misleading to try to interpret Russian history in terms of Asia. The Russian notion of autocracy, with much else that commonly passes as Asian, is Byzantine rather than Tartar, insofar as such things are not a native Russian product. The influences which formed China, India and the Moslem world affected Russia little or not at all. Yet Russia has diverged far from the usual European pattern and this divergence was completed before the year 1500.

In the Middle Ages western Europe laid the foundations of the modern world. The part played by medieval philosophy in preparing the ground for science has been described in a previous chapter. At the same time craftsmen in many trades were making the technical discoveries which led to the rise of capitalism and to the industrial revolution. A busy middle class was working out the principles of banking, bookkeeping and law which made it possible to exploit material advances. But during these centuries Russia had no articulate philosophy. Technique lagged behind and there was no real middle class, for the Russian merchants remained illiterate traders who made no attempt to improve their primitive methods of business.

Russia also missed that revolution in the relations of men and women brought about in western Europe by the cult of courtly love and the institutions of chivalry. No doubt there are approximate parallels to be found in other cultures, but on a broad view the modern West has been distinguished by the sustained and all-pervading influence of romantic love. There were no troubadours in Russia.

Other societies have adopted varying attitudes toward people who fall in love. Some societies are indulgent, others are wary or disapproving toward a passion which is so dangerous to society and seems so close to madness, but before the troubadours the madness of love had not been sought for its own sake. Still less had it been made the supreme object of life. But at the end of the eleventh century Provençal poets and aristocrats began to make it their chief aim to find means of supercharging their moments of rapture and prolonging this state throughout life. This had nothing to do with marriage. Indeed, the courts of love ruled that true love between a married pair was impossible. All physical fulfillment was despised by the purists. Courtly love fed upon the pure adoration, the distant glance and the secret sign peculiar to lovers who can never be united.

The historical antecedents of this unearthly passion are obscure. No doubt it had some connection with Christian love, but the connection is not direct. Indeed, in some respects the two things might be considered opposites. It has been well said that Christianity is the most material—one might add, the most earthy—of all the great religions. But courtly love is the offspring of an earth-despising spirituality such as is found in some Eastern religions, in the Gnostic and Manichean heresies and in Platonism, a philosophy which is never quite at home in Christianity. Yet courtly love soon came to terms with Western Christianity. The orthodox Dante languished for his Beatrice like any troubadour, but when she died he exalted her into a symbol of divine wisdom. Since Dante the romantic conception of love has changed in many respects, but it still bears traces of its distant origin. For good or evil Muscovy had no share in all this. When at last in the eighteenth century Russia became open to the West, the upper classes accepted a romantic conception of love and marriage. Romance ending in marriage is now the dream of every Soviet boy and girl, but in love the Russians remain more realistic than we.

In the Middle Ages Russia and western Europe were both "feudal" in the broad sense of the word. But the relations of the Russian social structure were very different from the feudal system of western Europe. In the West each man was

born into a position where he owed lifelong service to someone who was above him in the social scale and to whom he
could look in return for protection against enemies. These relations were hereditary and unescapable. In Russia, too, society was bound together by a chain of service. Each man
served a superior in return for protection, but everything was
a question of contract. While central Russia was still being
colonized, society remained more or less fluid. The peasant
agreed personally to serve his landlord and, unlike the Western villein, he was free to leave provided that he could pay
his debts, which indeed might not be easy. The landlord
served some greater lord who would be an independent
prince, unless he in his turn had found it expedient to take
service with the grand prince. In theory each landowner was
the absolute ruler of his own domains and of its inhabitants,
only owing service to his superior so long as his contract ran;
the "right of departure" was an essential part of the system.

In the West feudal rights and obligations were laid down
with a precision learned from Rome. In Russia each prince
or landlord administered customary law on such principles as
seemed good to him. There was no "common law" for the
Russian land and no judges appointed by central authority to
dispense even-handed justice. But the worst tyrannies were
abated by the acknowledged right of peasants to leave their
masters.

After the Tartar whirlwind Russia soon found a new level,
colonization resumed its course and the land between the
upper Volga and the Oka began to fill once more. The links
of trade began to bind the country together again, as in the
days of Kiev, and as the Tartars lost their first vigor it became possible to think of common defense. Vladimir, the first
capital of central Russia, was exposed to attack from the
steppe, and it was not a foregone conclusion which of the cities of the northern forest would in the end prevail over its
rivals. There were bitter wars for supremacy between Russian
and Russian, and still more bitter intrigues with the all-pow-
erful Tartar overlord whose suspicions against his resentful
vassals could easily be worked upon by their rivals. The natural aim of every pushing princeling was to be nominated
grand prince by the Tartar khan, for with the Tartars behind
him the grand prince had considerable authority over the
other princes. In return for this he had to carry out the will
of the great khan and to see that the tribute was paid punctually and in full.

The unimportant appanage of Moscow was ruled by a minor branch of the line of Vsevolod Big Nest, but Moscow was well placed, deep in the forest astride of the chief communications. Moreover she was ruled by a family who knew so well how to get on that within fifty years the princes of Moscow became the chief power in central Russia. Rambaud, the French historian of Russia, describes the early princes of Moscow as "wary and persevering princes, prudent and unpitying, of melancholy and terrible aspect, bearing upon their brow the seal of destiny." They acted, he adds, "by intrigue above all, by corruption, by buying consciences, by abasement before the khans, by treachery with their equals, by murder and delation." This judgment is scarcely too hard, but for all their faults the house of Moscow had the germ of statesmanship and, as their domains increased, Moscow became the natural focus of Russian patriotism.

At an early stage the metropolitan gave the support of the Church to Moscow by making it his seat. (In the Russian Church a metropolitan bishop ranks higher than an archbishop. Before the establishment of the Patriarchate of Moscow the metropolitan at Moscow was the head of the Russian Church.) The Russian Church was at that time the only expression of national unity. (See p. 59.) Moreover, it was to the interest of the Church to strengthen every focus of unity, for the Church, alone, owned land all over Russia and the Church was the biggest trader of the age.

The strength of religious influences is always open to doubt. Russia is large and evangelization was slow. Some of the clergy were corrupt and oppressive. Nearly all of them were profoundly ignorant. The old Slavonic gods were tenacious of life. They were not quite dead in the last century, perhaps even now they are still alive in some "bears' corners." But when every allowance is made, the Russian Church in the fourteenth century was a great power for good. Somehow or other something got through and many thousands were brought to Christ. It helped to civilize the great mass of half-believers, and those of the clergy who led truly Christian lives were deeply respected. The greatest of these was St. Sergius of Radonezh, a humble monk whose holiness was sufficient to compose the feuds of princes and to give courage to soldiers in their hour of need.

In those days, as again recently, many Russian monks worked the land to keep themselves alive, and their efforts to find ever more remote "wildernesses" in which to cultivate the land and lead a godly life produced a great movement of colonization. Some man of God, such as St. Sergius, would seek out an unknown corner of the forest where he could fend for himself with perhaps one or two chosen companions. Unremitting labor in that healthy climate would give tone to his body, and prayer would direct his thought and feeling. Before long other kindred spirits would discover the secret hiding place and join the little community, which would soon grow into a small monastery of simple-minded, laborious monks.

At this stage peasants and their families would begin to settle nearby in order to enjoy the protection of the monastery. Little by little the world obtruded upon the hermits' life and the monastery came to enjoy a worldly eminence. The peasants, who had settled nearby, almost inevitably became the tenants of the monks, who forgot their former industry when there were others to work for them.

At this point some pure, bold spirit among the monks would feel himself called on to seek out some new "wilderness" yet farther from the habitations of men, and the cycle would begin once more. This process, repeated hundreds of times in the later Middle Ages, brought the Russian faith and the families of hardy Russian peasants to the shores of the White Sea and to the approaches of the Ural Mountains.

Thus the purest efforts of the Russian Church to escape from the world involved her ever more closely in the affairs of the world, as each new monastery grew to be a center of wealth and power (see pp. 91–92). That is one of the reasons why the Russian Church and Russian society eventually became so closely intertwined that to many Russians they seemed to be one and the same.

CHAPTER VII

the first age of Muscovy

*What is sufficient for the salvation of souls may
be inadequate as a basis for a Christian culture.*

W. Weidlé, RUSSIA ABSENT AND PRESENT, p. 27

1. The Rise of the Tsars

After one hundred and fifty years of cowed subjection the reviving strength of Russia had become nearly equal to the declining force of the Tartars. The prince of Muscovy at that time was Dmitry of the Don, one of Russia's heroes. With boldness and judgment he built up his forces against the Tartars and in the year 1380 advanced with a combined Russian army deep into the steppe. Here, on the Field of Snipe by the upper waters of the Don, the Russian host, blessed by St. Sergius, met the onslaught of the Tartar horde and won a bloody victory. The memory of this battle vibrates in Russian hearts to this day, but the lumbering prose ballad in which a contemporary celebrated the victory has none of the joy of combat of Chevy Chase or Agincourt. The Russian bard laments with the wives and children of the fallen heroes and is struck to pity by the sight of the battlefield. "Brothers," he says, "then it was terrible and pitiful to see Christian corpses lying like stooks of hay by the great Don upon the bank. And the river Don flowed blood three days."

Russia had won a decisive victory but she had won by a hair's breadth and her losses had been such as to weaken her grievously. After the battle, Dmitry himself was found lying unconscious and all but mortally wounded, and a contemporary chronicler estimated that out of an army of 400,000 only 40,000 remained alive—although admittedly such figures are never reliable. Two years later the Tartars under a bold new ruler, Tokhtamysh, made a surprise attack, devastating central Russia, sacking Moscow, and reimposing the Tartar tribute. But this was a flash in the pan and thenceforth

Tartar suzerainty over Russia was but the shadow of its former self. A hundred years later the grand prince of Moscow had grown to be the tsar of all the Russias and the empire of the Golden Horde was in hopeless decay.

Ivan the Great, the first Russian prince to take the imperial title, was a cold, cruel, cowardly man, but his farsighted persistence and realism raised him above the ordinary level of rulers. He freed Russia from the Tartar yoke, but his manner of conducting this exploit was typical of the man. With no dramatic gesture, he withheld payment of the tribute, advanced with a large army to the banks of the Oka and waited developments. The khan moved with his forces to the opposite bank of the river. Here the armies exchanged arrows and taunted each other across the river, but neither dared attack. Weeks passed, while his counselors pressed Ivan to attack and he tried to screw up his courage. At one moment he withdrew to Moscow leaving the army in the field, but from Moscow the taunts of the populace and the scarcely veiled sneers of his advisers and of his own family drove him back to the army. There he still put off the day of action while the Tartar host watched, it would seem, in a like state of indecision.

When further delay seemed impossible, Ivan gave orders to retreat. But at that moment both armies were seized with an unaccountable panic and Tartars and Russians fled simultaneously from their terrified opponents. In this extraordinary way Ivan the Great gained his objective. No more tribute was paid to the khan and thenceforth Moscow had great influence at the courts of the succession states which grew up on the ruins of the Golden Horde.

Once freed from Tartar suzerainty, Ivan began to call himself "tsar" (which was the Russian form of caesar) and "autokrator"; this last word signified a fully independent ruler rather than an autocrat in our sense, but it was soon used to reinforce the autocratic pretensions of the tsars. Having assumed the imperial style, Ivan laid claim to the full inheritance of Kiev. In particular he claimed possession of the Lithuanian half of the Polish-Lithuanian kingdom and took this pretext for encouraging feudal nobles living on the border to transfer their allegiance from Catholic Poland to Orthodox Russia. At the same time the remnants of the independent principalities of central Russia were systematically suppressed, so that the tsar soon became in practice the only independent Russian prince under whom the feudal landowners could take service. Nobles still claimed that the traditional "right of departure" justified them in transferring their services from Muscovy to Lithuania, but the tsar treated this as treachery to himself and to the Orthodox faith.

The tsar's dominions were now the largest, though not the richest or most populous state in Europe. Muscovy seemed marked out by providence in the moment of her rise to greatness. In the past Russia had always looked to Constantinople as head of the Orthodox family and supreme representative of the true faith, but now the "second Rome" had fallen to the Moslems and it would seem that she had brought this calamity on herself by betraying her ancestral religion. As the Turkish claws closed round Byzantium, the Eastern empire made a desperate attempt to enlist Western help in a crusade against the sultan. A strong delegation from the Greek Church was sent to Italy and a union of the Eastern and Western Churches was agreed upon at the Council of Florence in 1439. But the differences had gone deep and a lasting union needed more statesmanship, more tolerance and more spiritual insight than that age possessed. In the atmosphere of Renaissance Italy neither side allowed enough for the strength of Orthodox feeling throughout the provinces of the East. The Union of Florence was rejected with indignation by both Greek and Slavonic Churches. In Russia the news that the Church of Constantinople had, as it seemed, fallen into heresy was greeted with horror and the fall of Constantinople fourteen years later appeared as a judgment of God.

In those years the star of Orthodox Muscovy was rising. Having thrown off the yoke of the Tartar unbelievers, and married Zoë, the niece of the last Byzantine emperor, Ivan the Great presented himself to the world as the inheritor of Orthodox tradition and the protector of true Christianity. The new Caesar adopted the double-headed eagle of Byzantium as his crest, and men of learning provided a theoretical foundation for his claims. The princes of Moscow were equipped with an imaginary genealogy tracing their descent from Caesar Augustus and with a prophecy of greatness to come. The first Rome had fallen before the barbarians and the second Rome, having embraced heresy, had become a prey to unbelievers, but Moscow was the third Rome. Moscow alone kept the true faith and her star would never set. These fond fancies probably had little direct hold outside court circles, but they helped to feed that Russian Messianism which has had so strong a hold on the imagination of many generations and was expressed in new forms after 1917.

The Muscovites had indeed certain unique qualities and it would have been good for the world to hear what they had to say, but they did not know how to express themselves in words. Such books as were written were the work of the clergy, but they produced no religious classics. Few of the Russian saints were in any way eminent as writers. But many excelled in the art of painting icons. It was in visual forms and above all in architecture that Muscovy's new greatness found its first expression. The Kremlin and the Red Square began to take on their present appearance and Italian architects called to Moscow by the tsar were absorbed into the Russian blood stream as only Russia can absorb. Muscovite fantasy and Italian skill were combined in those soaring pinnacles and colored domes that express some Russian quality which words cannot communicate. The Russian churches of the age between Ivan and Peter the Great combine exuberance and formalism, originality and tradition, in a way which gives the first hint of those incalculable depths which the "broad Russian nature" was to show in after ages.

It was the work of many generations to bring the gospel to every corner of the Russian land. Even in the last century there were still scattered settlements in the north which depended for marriage and baptism on the rare visits of traveling priests, but by the end of the Middle Ages every Russian villager called himself a Christian and knew the inside of a church.

The growing point of church life was the network of monasteries through the land and Muscovy's sudden greatness forced the monks to face an age-long dilemma of Christian life. They provided the best educated part of the ruling class and had become a necessary prop to a powerful state, but this involved them in much that was worldly and in much that was evil. Some of the best monks, seeing this, contended that religious houses should own no property. They were opposed by men of sincerity who maintained that monasteries must hold property in order to relieve poverty and misfortune and that they must be comfortable enough to attract men of good family so that the state, as well as the Church, might be served by a never-failing stream of well-born and educated monks. The issue seemed in doubt, but with support from the tsar the "possessors" prevailed and in so doing they bound the Church to the fortunes of tsarism. Four hundred years later the Russian church paid a bitter price for its political connections. Had the issue gone the other way we might have criticized the Russian Church, even more than we do already, for her lack of care for the good of society outside monastery walls.

The princes of Moscow were landowners whose estate had grown into an empire. When they had suppressed their rivals, neither law nor custom could limit their authority. The tradition of personal autocracy founded by Ivan the Great set the pattern for many generations of tsars. In the persons of Lenin and Stalin it survived the October Revolution. In Russia personal autocracy has deep roots, but it did not begin until the fifteenth century and it may not last beyond the twentieth. The great feudal nobles, who were princes in their own right, had long been accustomed to treat the prince of Moscow with deference as an "elder brother," but not to bow down before him as a supreme autocrat. Ivan's Greek wife brought the pomp of Byzantium to the court of Moscow and surrounded the person of the tsar with that wall of ceremonial which had always distinguished the Eastern Roman emperors from ordinary mortals. Earlier Russian princes had governed with the aid of a council of notables, but now the tsars would brook no infringement of their personal autocracy. A feudal noble who dared to press his opinion on Basil, the successor of Ivan the Great, was ordered from the tsar's presence with the words, "Begone, stinking villein, I do not need thee." It was complained that the tsar decided all matters of state with two or three cronies in his bed-chamber without consulting the council of *boyars,* as the nobility were now called.

2. Liturgy and Bureaucracy

The new formalism of the court ceremonial corresponded to a ritualism which pervaded life in all classes from the peasants to the tsar. In church services the smallest detail of word or gesture was formalized to express some living symbol. To this day in any Russian church you may still see the faithful approach the holy images with just such bows and prostrations as their ancestors used in the days of St. Sergius. But in the age of Muscovy, ritualism was not confined to church. In ordinary life, too, the pattern of conduct, style in dress, style in architecture and behavior at meals were regulated in accordance with rules which seemed to symbolize something deeper than words could express. It was, above all, this ritual way of life that marked off the Russians as a peculiar people who alone of all races had preserved the Christian life of the East in full purity. In its day this traditional way of life, in which everyone had his part to play, gave emotional security and sound direction to millions of lives, but in the end it stifled originality in thought and action. Since precedent ruled everything, even generals had to be chosen in accordance with strict rules based upon family and personal precedence. In consequence no one could ever serve under a leader from a family that ranked lower than his own without thereby creating a new precedent which impaired forever his own family's prescriptive right to office. This system led to endless disputes and blocked the promotion of able men, but it was not abolished till 1682.

The old Russian love of forms and formalities was weakened by Peter the Great, but it has found striking new forms of expression since Stalin's revolution. The Soviet feeling for protocol and external correctness has deep roots in the Russian past, and it has to be treated seriously by all who have dealings with Russians.

It was not easy for the tsars to hold together their vast and thinly peopled domains. Individual Russian administrators can be very good, but as a people the Russians lack "administrative sense." The first tsars had no trained officials, no means of remunerating their servants other than to allow them to batten on the countryside, and no effective means of keeping track of what happened more than a hundred miles from Moscow. For these reasons the administration was likely to be corrupt, incompetent and oppressive. It might also have been expected that the governors of distant provinces would become first irremovable and then independent, but this did not happen. The penalty for slackened control would have been anarchy and foreign domination such as Russia knew for a short time at the beginning of the seventeenth century, but the central government understood this well and therefore kept its local representatives on a tight rein. "Bureaucratic centralism" is slow and inefficient, but for centuries it seemed to be the only answer to a great and evident danger. In the growing days of Muscovy, heavy-handed administrative violence seemed a ready and effective means of maintaining law and order. Torture and savage floggings became the routine methods of an administration whose ca-

price and incompetence were subject to no effective legal control, but violence without system seldom achieves its object.
The autocratic willpower of the early tsars did not banish
disorder from Muscovy. Excessive centralization has now become a fixed habit of Russian administration, whatever regime is in power. The modern Soviet bureaucracy is a more
effective instrument of rule, but the aims of the Soviet government are harder to attain than those of the first tsars. So
today the Soviet bureaucracy still falls short, much as in an
earlier age the Muscovite bureaucracy fell short of an easier
aim.

   The problem of the early tsars was how to set up a bureaucracy without any trained bureaucrats. The taxes were
farmed, but the tsars exacted such exorbitant sums from the
tax farmers that these often made a loss. So it became necessary to compel rich citizens to take turns in shouldering the
burden of tax collection. The administration of justice was a
source of private revenue to the judge, who pocketed the
court fees and, no doubt, bribes into the bargain. Judgeship
was often considered as a reward for military service, and
judges were appointed openly and frankly "for the punishment of the people and for the ordering of the land in every
way, yea and for thy own quiet and sustenance." In other
cases the office of judge was sold to a private individual who
made what he could out of his office. Each department of
state made such laws as it saw fit, and as a rule nothing
effective was done to make new laws known throughout the
empire or even to inform other departments of the administration. Therefore a single fire might cause the loss of a
whole branch of Muscovite legislation.

   Western Europe was ahead of Russia in statecraft, in trade,
in technical skill and in the art of war, but Russia could not
learn from abroad without serious risk to the precarious balance of Orthodox Muscovy. Russians felt that their way of
life formed a closely integrated whole, whose every facet expressed some part of that Christian truth of which Russia was
the sole remaining guardian. To change a part was to change
the whole, so every new thing that came from infidel or he-
retical countries was itself tainted with heresy or infidelity.

   This gave Russian society from the end of the fifteenth century a rigidity which still leaves traces in Soviet society, but
the earlier Russia of "the Tartar yoke" was, for all its faults,
in some ways more open. In the absense of an extensive literature the Russian genius at this time found its most ample

expression in fresco painting, and before Ivan the Great this painting had a boldness and originality which were entirely lost by the end of the sixteenth century. Similarly, in the Russian Middle Ages a great variety of personality was expressed by a vast number of canonized saints. After 1500 saints became fewer, though the influence of religion was, if anything, more pervasive than before.

3. Muscovy and the West

During the reign of Ivan the Great, Russia emerged into the light of European history. Muscovy began to exchange embassies with the leading states of the day, and Western merchants, soldiers and craftsmen came to live in Moscow. From now on the reports of foreign ambassadors begin to be one of our chief sources of knowledge about Muscovy. The Russians could not fail to be conscious of their own backwardness in material accomplishments when they compared themselves with their Western neighbors, but they were not disposed to accept favors from peoples or potentates whose ways of living seemed to lack what was most important. So when the Holy Roman Emperor offered to confer the title of king on Ivan the Great, Moscow answered the emperor in a message whose haughty tone and loose syntax are typical of the age and country:

"And as for that which thou has said about the kingship . . . we too by the mercy of God are sovereigns in our own land from of old from our first ancestors, and we are instituted of God, as our ancestors were, so are we . . . and as formerly we desired no title from anyone, so now we do not want it."

Foreign embassies were received with overpowering pomp and magnificence but subjected to a tedious and pedantic protocol from the moment of their arrival on Muscovite territory. The Russians attached great importance to the repeated use of the full titles of the sovereign and never lost a chance of gaining face by making a foreign ambassador dismount first or uncover his head before the representative of the tsar, and they would employ strange subterfuges to gain some small point of procedure. Then, as now, small variations in formality were thought by the Kremlin to convey some insult to Muscovy. Even the intelligent and broad-minded Boris Godunov took offense because Queen Elizabeth did not always seal her communications to the Kremlin with the Great Seal. Regulating their own affairs by a minute regard for formalities, they seem to have assumed that the like symbolism and respect for hierarchical precedent would be equally effective in their relations with foreign states. Like their Soviet successors, the Muscovite officials insisted upon full translations and were meticulous in asking for written copies of proposals made orally. They combined deep ignorance and credulity about the affairs of the West with matchless skill in finding unexpected interpretations of agreements and in digging out precedents from previous negotiations. The delays of Muscovite procedure exasperated foreign envoys and the duplicity of Russian methods seems to have exceeded the crafts and wiles known to Western diplomacy. But there was no hypocrisy. When the Russian negotiators were caught lying, they laughed without constraint.

Foreign diplomats were kept in strict seclusion in a building specially erected for the purpose and were often held incommunicado under armed guard until their first audience with the tsar. After what seemed to the Kremlin a suitable interval, the ambassador and his suite were received by the sovereign with traditional ceremony and magnificence, for which purpose the court was augmented by those of the Moscow merchants whose venerable appearance would lend gravity to the scene. On these occasions no one would speak to the foreigners or acknowledge acquaintance with them by so much as a gesture or a glance. At the mention of the name of the ruler whom the ambassador represented, the tsar would rise and descend from the highest step of his throne, but throughout the proceedings he kept by him a ewer, in which to wash away all foreign contamination when the ambassador had gone.

From time to time an envoy would be invited to the tsar's daily banquet, when he would be amazed at the formality of the proceedings and the quantity of gold and silver, but might be put out by the absence of knives, forks and plates.

For a long time embassies were not allowed to buy anything for themselves, lest they should have contact with ordinary Muscovites. Their material needs were provided by officials who made all arrangements for foreigners and drew on their behalf rations on a scale which varied with the diplomatic rank of the foreign mission, much as the Soviet organization, long known as Burobin but now rechristened, arranges for foreign diplomatists. Drink was supplied on a generous scale, and it was a part of the task of those officials in whose care the ambassador was placed to make him drunk and worm out his secrets. Sometimes the only way to escape from these importunities was to feign sleep or hopeless drunkenness.

Theoretically, anyone was allowed to visit the embassy, but those who wished to do so were warned that it might be better to avoid diplomatic society and most of them took the hint. Above all, no women were allowed inside the ambassadorial quarters. On one occasion the Danish ambassador succeeded in marrying a Russian wife, but when the king of Denmark asked permission for the lady to come to Denmark he was met with a blank refusal, phrased as follows: "Inasmuch as in all our domains we are not accustomed to give free men into slavery, not only the people of our own domains, but people of other lands who are in our domains; but that wench belongs to our domains and it is not fitting that we should send that woman into slavery to your man Isidore" (i.e., to the Danish ambassador). This distressing anticipation of more recent cases seems to reflect something permanent. Russian governments often have their reasons for preventing their citizens from leaving the country and no doubt there are Russian men who resent foreigners having their women, but perhaps no Westerner fully understands Russian motives in these matters.

In the age of Muscovy, as in the Soviet age, resentment against foreigners was accompanied by intense curiosity and by the wish to impress. The passage of an ambassadorial procession was an occasion of the utmost magnificence and the people were bade to line the streets wearing their best clothes in order to create an impression of wealth. When Lord Carlisle arrived in Moscow as Charles II's ambassador, his procession was held up for a quarter of an hour on some imaginary pretext in order that the tsar and his family might observe the scene from a concealed viewpoint.

Their natural expansiveness and hospitality prompted the Russians to welcome foreigners and with one side of their nature they were anxious to learn everything that the West could teach, but at the same time they were held back by a dislike which was compounded equally of fear and contempt. The West on its side was distracted between admiration and fear of Russian strength and contempt for Russian barbarism. In the sixteenth century there were Western states, such as England, which were concerned to develop friendly relations with Russia and to bring her more fully into the Western society of nations, but the powers nearest to Muscovy tried to prevent the passage of skilled armorers bound for Moscow, lest the Russians might learn to emulate Western skill.

This fundamental pattern of attraction and repulsion on both sides has taken various forms in different ages, but it has not changed in essentials down to the present day.

4. Russian Villages

Great wealth and power were now concentrated at the court of Moscow, but the foundation of this glittering superstructure remained the labor of a scattered and poverty-stricken peasantry using primitive methods to wring a bare subsistence from wide expanses of soil.

Hitherto the Great Russian peasants had lived in scattered hamlets, but now the population was increasing and the three-field rotation of crops had come into use. This required large fields which, in turn, needed many hands to work them. So the peasants began to draw together into larger villages. In broad outline the system was that which prevailed in western Europe up to the agricultural revolution. Each village divided its arable land into three large fields, which lay fallow in turn for a year. Each field consisted of innumerable little strips, which were given out to the families of the village on a principle of rough equality, and the village as a whole, or rather a meeting of the heads of patriarchal families, decided how the strips should be divided, what crops should be sown, and generally regulated the work of the agricultural year. In accordance with Slavonic custom, every decision had to be unanimous, but heated argument often preceded agreement and the minority might keep their own opinion, even though they had voted with the majority for the sake of peace.

The origin of the Russian village commune or mir has been the theme of a long controversy in which various schools of politics appear in the guise of historical research. In the last century those who looked for the source of Russia's future greatness in her past were known as Slavophiles. They claimed that the *mir* was an original Slavonic institution of immemorial antiquity embodying the best principles of Socialism without the evils of an industrial society. The Slavophiles believed that the Russian peasant, with his life firmly based on Russian Orthodox Christianity and the village commune, was destined to rejuvenate the world. The numerous opponents of the Slavophiles looked to the West for salvation and were accordingly known as Westerners. They regarded the *mir* as a rigid framework which held back the growth of a free and flexible economic system based on private enterprise. All Westerners looked to the rise of capitalism, regardless of whether they were liberals or socialists. Liberals looked on a system of free enterprise as being in itself the economic embodiment of progress. Socialists, following the Marxist paradox, greeted with hope the rise of capitalism because it involved the creation of an industrial proletariat, and that was the first step toward socialism.*

The Westerners could point to the undoubted fact that the *mir* was useful to the administration and they claimed that it was a comparatively new institution which would never have developed as it did without the support of the state. The commune indeed rendered great services to the powers that be, for it was responsible through its headman for the collection of taxes and the punishment of minor crimes. Moreover, if any of the villagers fled to new land in order to escape debt or taxation, the rest had to pay for those who disappeared, so that every man had a strong inducement to prevent his neighbors leaving the village, even if he also had a secret wish to escape. For these reasons landlord, tax collector and police agent all found that the existence of the *mir* was highly convenient to themselves.

Whatever its origin, the Russian village commune has shown great vitality. Unshaken till the first Russian revolution in 1905, the *mir* suffered a partial eclipse in the last years of tsarism and the opening years of the Bolshevik Revolution. The establishment of collective farms at the time of the first Five-Year Plan, though it was a severe blow to many village traditions, was in theory also a means of reestablishing the traditional economic solidarity of the Russian village, but

* See also Chap. XV, p. 187.

the fact was otherwise. The village headsman in Tzarist days may have been as much a servant of the authorities as of those who elected him, but he was a genuine villager. The chairman of a collective farm is altogether an outsider. And he has to enforce a policy that is always unpopular and often unworkable. It remains uncertain how much village solidarity has survived the vagaries of Soviet policy, but the Kremlin has not spoken its last word about Russian villages.

CHAPTER VIII

Ivan the Terrible

Here's the smell of the blood still.

Macbeth, Act V, Scene 1

1. *Frontiers, Social Structure and Defense*

The economic and social structure of sixteenth-century Muscovy was too primitive to support an efficient Renaissance army. In particular, the ruling class was too ignorant and there were not enough artisans. But Russia could not escape from meeting her neighbors on the field of battle, for the domains of Muscovy followed no natural frontiers and the border regions would not be safe from incursions by turbulent neighbors unless the frontier were pushed forward. The only way for the Muscovite forces to hold their own against Western neighbors, let alone to advance their frontiers, was to put superior numbers into the field. A larger army meant heavier taxes at the best, but corrupt, cruel and inefficient tax gatherers trebled the burdens of the peasants who sustained the weight of Russian endeavor. The peasants' natural answer to taxation and debt was to move to fresh lands where, for a time at least, creditor and tax gatherers might find it hard to follow them. If this happened on a large scale, the state would be bankrupt and the army would melt away, for the Russian army was mainly drawn from landowners who could not leave their fields unless they had peasants to work the land (see below, p. 105). Moreover, in the general competition for labor, the larger and more powerful landlords were able to offer more attractive terms and more secure protection to their tenants and thus to entice away the pick of the peasants, leaving the smaller landowners dangerously short of labor.

Villages were self-sufficient and Russian landowners met most of their needs from the produce of their own estates, as has been observed above (see Chap. VI, p. 83). Towns were

101

few and small. There were indeed some rich merchants who lived sumptuously, but many shopkeepers lived and dressed like peasants, for fear that a display of wealth might invite spoliation by some powerful neighbor; and they thought like peasants, too. In these circumstances the artisan class had no one to teach it the skills of foreign lands and no great market for its wares. The nobility considered trade to be beneath their dignity and the fetters of serfdom made it ever harder for the peasants to rise. So between the poverty of the peasants and the self-sufficiency and rapacity of the landowners, little room was left for the growth of a middle class.

Muscovy had become a great power in Renaissance Europe, but, not for the last time, an increase in Russia's strength had rendered her difficulties more pressing than before. In Ivan the Terrible Muscovy found a gifted and strong ruler who saw some of his country's problems with that blinding Russian clarity which often inspires great undertakings only to bring them to a tragic conclusion. Russia's first revolutionary autocrat, Ivan succeeded to the throne as a small child. For the first few years of his reign Muscovy rested secure in the hands of the capable but unpopular queen mother but, when the infant tsar was eight years old, his mother died through poison, or so it was said, and the government was seized by a clique of grasping boyars who soon brought the country to the verge of anarchy. The boy was separated from those he loved and left cold, hungry, lonely and in fear of murder to learn what he could by observing the conduct of the boyars and by reading old books. In public he was treated with ceremonial servility, but any courtier who showed attention to the tsar outside the throne room roused the instant suspicion of the ruling nobles, who had good reason to fear the strong-willed boy.

It soon became apparent that Ivan had learned to conceal his thoughts and to trust his judgment. At the age of thirteen, with no warning, he summoned the chief boyars to appear before him and addressed them with bitter reproaches and threats. He announced that although many were to blame he would punish only the chief offender, Prince Andrew Shuiski. Then and there the small boy who sat on the throne had the guilty nobleman, who ruled all Russia, arrested and put to death.

Having shown his power, he confided the government of the empire to his mother's relatives until he was sufficiently experienced to take the cares of state upon himself. But from now on Ivan was master in his own house.

When Ivan grew to man's estate he sowed a plentiful crop of wild oats but he became a strong and successful ruler. His first great act was to attack the decaying power of the Tartars who were still entrenched on the middle Volga. In two well-conceived and well-organized campaigns, supported by excellent artillery, he captured Kazan and brought the whole Volga basin down to the Caspian Sea into the Russian empire, thereby opening the way for Russian expansion beyond the Urals as far as the Pacific Ocean. These exploits earned Ivan the name of Grozny, which may be translated "dread" or "formidable"; "Ivan the Terrible" is a title which is too familiar to be changed, but the epithet conveys an overtone which is not in the Russian.

As a boy he had seen the evils which follow when several tyrants exercise the power destined for one autocrat, and his early reading in scripture and history had implanted a firm belief that kingship was a thing divinely instituted for the purpose of abating the evils of society. The success of Ivan's early years confirmed his belief in himself and gave no hint of the tragedies which were to mar his work in the end.

The subjugation of the Volga did not free Russia from the fear of nomadic incursions. The southern frontier of the empire lay in the region of the Oka and beyond that the Tartar horsemen still ruled supreme in the Ukrainian steppe lands. Beyond the Ukraine stood the khans of the Crimea entrenched behind barriers set by nature and backed by the power of their overlords, the Ottoman Turks, now at the zenith of their power. The Turkish empire provided an insatiable market for slaves and the Crimea became the center for a vast slave trade whose raw material was provided by raids on the more exposed districts of Muscovy, Poland and Lithuania. The peasantry of the south Russian lands constituted an inexhaustible reservoir of humanity and year after year uncounted tens of thousands of men, women and children were carried away to swell the labor markets of the Levant and North Africa, to grace the harems of sultans and pashas or to give strength to the incomparable slave armies of Turkey. For three centuries a stream of vigorous Russian blood flowed into the Ottoman empire and dark-eyed babies were hushed to sleep by the lullabies of the Ukraine.

By degrees the settled peoples throughout the world were gaining the upper hand over their nomadic neighbors. In the sixteenth century the southern frontier of Muscovy began to be protected by strategically placed stockades and watchtowers manned by military settlers, who were given land, in return for which they were bound to defend the frontier. By degrees the stockades were moved farther south until at last the whole of the Ukraine was won for settled civilization and Potemkin's conquest of the Crimea in 1783 brought a long chapter to its close (cf. pp. 169 and 221).

In the flush of their eastern triumphs Ivan and his counselors debated the possibility of a southern campaign against the Crimea, but the tsar wisely decided that the risk of failure would be too great in so distant a campaign against a powerful enemy. He turned instead against a more accessible enemy to the west and decided, a hundred and fifty years before Peter the Great, to break through to the Baltic. His way was barred by the once-powerful Teutonic knights now undergoing the crisis of the Reformation. Startling victories of the Russian forces soon earned the intervention of Poland and Sweden, who began to be alarmed by the advance of their powerful neighbor. Poland offered terms which would have given Russia a useful outlet to the Baltic, but after deliberation the Russians rejected this offer and the one golden opportunity of obtaining a window upon Europe without undergoing crippling sacrifices was lost forever. The Poles, always brave and then at the height of their Renaissance might and glory, fought back vigorously and the war dragged on for twenty-four years during which time Russia was ruined by an effort beyond her powers. In the end Ivan was forced to renounce all his conquests and to surrender the westernmost parts of his inheritance.

But that outlet in the west, which was denied to Muscovy's sternest efforts, opened unexpectedly and of its own accord in the far north. English merchants seeking the northeast passage to China arrived unexpectedly in the White Sea and discovered new markets in Russia. After bureaucratic delays, which recall a more recent period, the English were forwarded to Moscow and received with honor by the tsar. Like most Russians, Ivan was repelled by the practical and commercial aims of the English diplomacy, but he saw in England a useful counterpoise to the power of his nearer Western neighbors and he was drawn to the adventurous honesty of the ambassadors who represented Elizabethan England at the Kremlin. He entered into long and curious negotiations for an English marriage, not shrinking from a union with

Queen Elizabeth herself if that were possible, and even put out feelers for a refuge in England if he should lose his throne.

2. A Revolution from Above

Since the time of Ivan the Terrible it has been a recurrent characteristic of Russian rulers never to think themselves secure unless every possibility of opposition has been destroyed. But Ivan the Terrible began his rule with no narrow conception of autocracy. It was understandable that he was suspicious of those tyrants of his childhood, the great nobles descended from former ruling princes, who formed the chief element in the traditional *duma* or council of state. So he took his important decisions in an inner council of well-chosen advisers drawn from outside the traditional ruling groups, while important reforms of civil and canon law were prepared in consultation with local opinion. From now on for about a century it became customary to call together from time to time consultative assemblies of representatives drawn from all Muscovy. These were not parliaments and it would be easy to exaggerate their value, but if they had been used with consistent wisdom in the formative decades, they could have helped to prepare the way for a more modern and efficient form of government.

Finding the feudal levies supplied by the great families both unreliable and inefficient, the early tsars began to draw their armies from a new class of their own creation. State land was given out for the sustenance of a professional soldier and of his family, so long as he remained in the service of the state. These grants were at first revocable, but since service to the state was lifelong and tended to descend from father to son, the grant of land, which made service possible, also tended to become hereditary. Such is the origin of most of that class of Russian landowners who live in the pages of Tolstoy and Turgenev. But land without labor to work it was useless, and the peasants living on the land which was granted out in this way were required to keep the master given them by the state. This duty imposed on the peasants was justified by the corresponding duty to serve the state which was imposed on the landowner by the original terms of his grant.

The development of a centralized bureaucracy depending directly upon the will of the tsar and the tendency to rely increasingly on the new class of landowners began before Ivan the Terrible and continued after his death. The older nobility disliked these trends and were often at loggerheads with the tsars. But in other reigns and at the beginning of Ivan's reign the relations between monarch and nobility remained tolerable.

In early manhood Ivan had a serious illness and as he lay between life and death he watched the courtiers intrigue for position after he was gone. In an attempt to secure the succession of his own line he tried to make the boyars swear fealty to his infant son, but the reluctance and evasions which he saw around him convinced the tsar that he was surrounded with enemies. On his recovery Ivan changed his counselors. There was nothing particularly vindictive or cruel about his conduct at this stage, but by degrees the feeling grew on him that he could trust no one. His wife died and he suspected poison, his punishments became continually severer as his mistrust grew, until Prince Kurbski, one of his chief generals, fled to Lithuania and gave his services to the king of Poland, in exercise of the outmoded "right of departure." Kurbski's defection moved the tsar to inflict increasingly cruel punishments, but this only multiplied disloyalty.

Meantime Ivan kept his own counsel and meditated a dark design. When the strain became unbearable, he withdrew to a stronghold near Moscow, declaring that he would rule no longer. The prospect of renewed anarchy brought immediate protestations of loyalty from the townspeople, and the tsar agreed to resume the crown on terms. He would divide Muscovy into two halves; one would be the tsar's private domain to rule as he saw fit. The rest would be ruled on traditional lines with the help of the council of boyars; and for this half of Muscovy Ivan appointed a new "tsar," one Simon, a baptized Tartar. It does not appear that Simon exercised much real power and he was soon set aside by Ivan, who had, in fact, no intention of allowing power to slip from his own hands.

Meanwhile Ivan the Terrible ruled his own half of the country with a new civil service recruited from men of low degree, who rode the country clad in black with a dog's head at their saddle bow. The activity of these dreaded agents who were armed with absolute power to suppress malcontents was by no means limited to the tsar's half of Muscovy. Indeed, the division of the land into two was, above all, a pretext for uniting strategically important districts in the tsar's hand and at the same time uprooting the old families from lands where historic associations had created local loyalties and settling them on new lands where they had no previous connections. The least resistance to the tsar's policy was treated as treason and whole families were exterminated with their retainers on suspicion against one member. It seems likely both that fear drove whole families into disloyalty and that private grudges were paid off in the name of justice. The old families were broken in a few years as completely as the English medieval nobility was broken in the Wars of the Roses a hundred years earlier.

Ivan the Terrible's reforms were in many ways well conceived, but to impose a revolution from above at the height of a desperate war showed a gross lack of judgment. Moreover, the tsar could not find trustworthy executants for his high designs. In general, those who rise suddenly to positions of power are more rapacious than those whose greed is sanctioned by long custom. Knowing how fast the wheel of fortune turns, they fear that they may have only a short season in which to enrich themselves and, being free from the subtle restraints of an hereditary position, they exact tribute with redoubled energy. The agents whom Ivan the Terrible recruited to carry out his reforms were men who enjoyed a precarious tenure of spectacular power. They robbed villagers and townsmen alike, sometimes exacting ten years' rent in one year, until at last the people began to flee from these extortions, villages were emptied and in some towns nine out of ten houses were deserted. Ivan the Terrible's rule drove many peasants and their families to flight, and at the same time the decline of nomad power made it possible for fugitives and adventurous settlers to push out into the rich lands of the "wild steppe" where they joined the mixed bands of adventurers from many nations who thrived lawlessly on the borders of settled civilization. The very success of the tsars in quelling "the accursed sons of Hagar" had made it possible for Muscovite peasants to quit the land of their allegiance, while the tyranny of tsars and landlords drove a great part of the population to seek new land outside the then boundaries of Russia. Stern efforts to bind peasant families more firmly to the villages where they ate the bread of affliction merely made escape the more desired. Central Russia was on the way to becoming a vacuum divided from the steppe by a belt of lawless and formidable runaways. At the same time like causes were producing a like result in Poland and Lithuania, which contained a large Russian population.

After a few years the division of the state into two was tacitly abandoned, but not before it had reduced the country to a state of misery and depopulation which brought many subsequent calamities in its train. To crown all, in a fit of rage, Ivan struck his eldest son a blow which proved mortal. Thereby he destroyed the hopes of his dynasty, while leaving his enemies to write the history of his reign. Ivan the Terrible was long held up to obloquy, but his severities struck down the great more often than the humble and he has lived in the memory of the Russian peasant * as a strong and good tsar. He was a contemporary of Queen Elizabeth, but his task was the task of William the Conqueror and it is fairer to compare him with the stark Norman who was more successful but scarcely less cruel than the Russian tsar. There is, indeed, much to be said for Ivan the Terrible, but the Stalinist school of Soviet historians put the whitewash on so thickly that one was bound to wonder whether the example of Ivan was not put forward in order to justify drastic methods of government in our own time.

To some contemporaries Ivan showed high gifts and a broad understanding. To others he seemed to veer neurotically between orgies which were often profane and a repentance which could scarcely be credited. But he is always a real human being and therefore he commands our sympathy even in the midst of his enormities. There is, indeed, something vividly personal about the utterances in which he addresses his enemies with bitter reproaches for the wrongs that they have done him. With him hatred was an "I—Thou" relation; he seems to have felt himself to be somehow involved in the fate of his enemies. At the monastery of St. Sergius near Moscow one is shown a strange list of all Ivan the Terrible's victims, left by Ivan himself with instructions to pray for their souls.

* Operagoers will be familiar with the old ballad about the capture of Kazan which supplies the words for Varlaam's song in the inn scene in *Boris Godunov.*

CHAPTER IX

the time of troubles

The plowers plowed upon my
back; and made long furrows.

Psalm cxxix. 3

1. The Ukraine

For two centuries Poland and Lithuania had been growing together in a dynastic union, but Lithuania still remained largely Orthodox while Poland was purely Catholic. In 1569 the two states entered into an organic union which, by placing the Lithuanian provinces under the direct rule of the Polish crown, increased the influence of the Catholic Polish landlords. These had already gained that complete domination over their peasants which Russian landlords would not achieve till two centuries later and, when it became known that after an interval of ten years all peasants in Lithuania were to be bound to the land as completely as their brothers in Poland were already bound, there began a wholesale migration of peasants to the east.

Peasants escaping to the unsettled parts of the Ukraine were soon followed by Polish landlords eager to exploit the virgin richness of the black steppe earth. A contemporary Polish writer, feeling himself unable to do justice to the wealth of corn and meadow and forest, of cattle and game and fish to be found in the Ukraine, exclaims, "Oh, why waste words when one phrase expresses all! This is the Promised Land. . . . Rivers of milk and honey flow here! He who has once been to the Ukraine can never leave her because she attracts men as the magnet attracts iron."

The gallant and generous Polish gentry found new scope in the Ukraine, but they brought with them the tragedies of Poland. The individualism of the ruling classes was pushed to a point where stable government became almost impossible, and the rights and liberties of the Polish gentry were such that little room was left for the rights of any other class or nation. In that age and place religion was the only living test of nationality, and Orthodox subjects of Poland were under continuous pressure to become Catholics. Toward the end of the sixteenth century the Polish Catholic authorities sponsored the establishment of a new "Uniate" branch of the Church which would retain the Eastern rite and Slavonic language while accepting Papal supremacy. By this means it was hoped to turn the flank of Orthodoxy. The idea was sensible in itself and capable of spiritual content, but there was too much cynicism in the move and the Catholic side showed little understanding of the deep hold which the Orthodox Church had on the Russian people. Some villages accepted the ministrations of the Uniate clergy and in the course of generations many of their flock acquired a deep affection for their new faith, but to the majority Catholic pressure was merely one more reason for escaping from Polish landlords.

The boldest fugitives from Russia and Poland alike went farthest into the steppe and joined the communities already known as Cossacks, which congregated round the rivers Don and Dnieper, beyond the effective control of either Poland or Muscovy. These intrepid brotherhoods owned no landlord as master, despised serfs and lived for fighting. Most of them were Orthodox, but adventurers of many faiths and nationalities were welcomed and the Cossacks were ready to fight in any cause. From their stronghold on an island hidden in the reeds and rapids the Cossacks of the Dnieper raided in light river vessels as far as the coast of Asia Minor, in turn providing the king of Poland with recruits or rebelling against his authority. If the Polish gentry had been willing to leave to the Cossack settlers their personal liberty, a little land and their religion, the Cossacks might have become contented subjects of the king of Poland and the Ukraine would probably have become permanently attached to Poland and not to Russia. In that event the Ukraine might have formed a link between eastern and western Europe. But the Polish gentry were not ready to admit the existence of a free yeomanry. According to the structure of feudal Poland, men living on the land must be gentlemen or serfs, but Cossacks were not gentlemen and refused to be serfs. The Polish government was forced to admit the right of a limited number of "registered Cossacks" to live in freedom, but tried assiduously and with varying success to reduce the rebellious remainder to serfdom. Strife never ceased until the failure of the Poles to achieve a settlement resulted in the transference to Russia of most of the Ukrainian land with its people and all their problems.

2. Boris Godunov

Ivan the Terrible was succeeded on the throne by his second son Theodore, an amiable, pious imbecile, who left affairs of state to his brother-in-law Boris Godunov, a cool-headed, intelligent man who had come to the front under Ivan. The Godunovs were gentry, but they did not belong to the higher nobility, and the great families were reluctant to accept Boris among those who had an hereditary right to great positions in the state.

For fourteen years Russia recovered peacefully from the disasters of the last reign, while Theodore prayed and Boris acted. Honest and competent men were appointed to public office, a few young men were sent to the West to learn what Europe could teach, trade and agriculture thrived and relations between landowners and peasants became more orderly if not more friendly. The holders of small grants of state land who provided the bulk of the army were in danger of losing all their tenants to richer and more powerful neighbors. Boris therefore took measures to prevent great landowners robbing labor from smallholders, but this inevitably made it harder for peasants to leave their masters. The government did not consciously intend to turn free men into serfs. The hard fact is that the Russian peasantry was on the way to serfdom and new fetters were continually forged, whatever government was in power.

Russian ecclesiastical diplomacy, supported by the prayers of Theodore and the wiles of Boris, secured the elevation of the head of the Russian Church to the rank of a patriarch, the highest position in the hierarchy of the Eastern Church. Muscovy was henceforth free from every vestige of tutelage to Constantinople, and the Russian Church and the Russian monarchy stood forth as the twin pillars of the third Rome, the greatest force in the Orthodox world.

While Theodore lived, Boris Godunov flourished, but his position depended on the fact that his sister was married to the tsar. The remnants of the great families were now ready to reassert themselves after the fearful buffetings of the last reign. For seven hundred years Russia had been ruled by descendants of Rurik, but the holy idiot Theodore had no children, and the only hope of the dynasty reposed in his infant brother, Dmitri, who died suddenly in mysterious circumstances in 1591. Soon it was rumored that Boris had murdered him. The case is uncertain, but the malice of his enemies and the emotion of the people have spun a tragic myth around the supposed guilt and certain doom of Boris Godunov.

Theodore died in 1598 and with him the royal house was extinguished. There was no law to regulate the succession, but Boris was in the saddle and with a show of reluctance, which may not have been wholly feigned, he secured his own coronation as tsar amid rejoicings which seemed to be universal. John Merick, the agent of the Muscovie Company, who had expected disturbances on the death of Theodore, was able to write: "But it hath been a very dead season. Yet (thanks be to God) through the wise government of Lord Boris Pheodorovich (Godunov) the Lord Protector unto the said late Emperor, since his death all things have been very quiet without any dissension; as the like in such a great kingdom I have not heard of." Yet within three years Boris Godunov's luck had turned and a succession of terrible famines drove many poor men to brigandage or to flight, while those who remained were often forced to sign a deed of bondage for themselves and their families in return for just enough food to keep them alive till harvest time. In a few places good people sold their substance to feed the starving, but up and down the land the rich "sold the needy for silver and the poor for a pair of shoes." The great nobles nursed their grudge against the upstart tsar and dreamed of heretic Poland where the rights of noblemen were respected. Supposed miracles were performed at the tomb of the dead infant Dmitri and then suddenly a rumor spread that Dmitri was alive and in Poland. With this began ten years of retribution for all the evil that had been done in Russia.

A short, thick-set, ill-favored Russian of common appearance had presented himself at the house of an ambitious Polish nobleman with the claim that he was the murdered Dmitri and the rightful tsar of Muscovy. For good or bad reasons the Poles accepted the claims of the false Dmitri, who was secretly converted to the Roman Catholic Church and married his host's beautiful daughter Marina. All historians agree that the pretender was not the youngest son of Ivan the Terrible, yet it seems that he believed his own claims and he showed resolution and intelligence worthy of a ruler.

Supported by a Polish army and accompanied by Catholic chaplains and his Catholic wife, the false Dmitri advanced against Boris. The fact that the pretender had abandoned Orthodoxy and the extent of his dependence on Polish support were not yet generally known in Russia and he soon gained many supporters. Moreover, he called in as allies the Cossacks of the wild borderland, who came cheerfully for a season to fight and stayed for ten years to plunder. As the pretender's army came within striking distance of Moscow, Boris died suddenly. It seemed that he had been struck down by the judgment of God.

3. Chaos and Revival

Thereupon Moscow passed into the hands of the false Dmitri and at once it became clear that the Poles and Catholics who had come with him meant to stay. This turned Orthodox Russia against the pretender, whose evident ability could not prevail against such odds. From the first moment his life was in danger and within a few months he was murdered, leaving the succession to the throne more doubtful than ever.

Thereon followed a time of darkened counsels and obscure intrigue, of civil wars in which it could scarcely be determined who was fighting whom or with what aim. Armies marched everywhere spreading misery and brigands took what the soldiers had left. Armies took to brigandage and brigands organized themselves as armies. The most powerful of the nobles proclaimed himself tsar without any shadow of legality, but could not make his rule effective. Other nobles bargained for a contractual monarchy on the Polish model, by which the monarch's instrument of accession should guarantee the rights of the nobility; but to most Russians the Polish form of oligarchy seemed likely to put many quarreling tyrants in the place of one rightful ruler. The king of Poland put forward his son as candidate for the throne of the tsars and then claimed the throne for himself. Through all vicissitudes a Polish garrison remained in the Kremlin and hordes of Cossacks dominated first one part of the country and then another.

A second false Dmitri arose and claimed to have escaped a second murder. This manifest impostor was known as "the thief," but he collected a sizable army and persuaded Marina, the beautiful young widow of the first pretender, to accept him as her husband. In the general decay of all authority, peasants revolted against their masters and the civil war became a class war. The peasants in revolt seemed to find natural allies in the Cossacks, but neither peasants nor Cossacks had any realistic or coherent political aims. They had grievous wrongs and they wanted to see a good tsar who would redress the wrongs of the poor and curb the power of the rich, but they did not understand the forces which impelled every tsar to strengthen the powers of landowners against their peasants.

The soundest forces in Russia are often hidden beneath the surface, and the miseries of civil strife and the scandal of a Polish garrison in Moscow touched hidden springs. The patriarchal customs of the grand princes of Moscow had provided no machinery for dealing with a constitutional emergency such as now confronted Russia, but the whole land was determined to have a strong and honorable government. The nerve center of Russian patriotism was the Monastery of the Holy Trinity founded by St. Sergius about fifty miles from Moscow. The monks manned their walls against the Polish army and stood a grim siege of many months. The heroic survivors of the siege set to with great energy to organize Russian patriotism, and letters were passed from town to town pledging all to work and fight for the common cause. Minin, a patriotic butcher of Nizhni Novgorod, set himself the task of organizing a national army and gave an example by selling his property to raise funds. Minin proved himself to be a first-class organizer, and soon a well-equipped army under Prince Pozharsky, a general of proved patriotism and ability, was advancing upon Moscow.

The victories of the national army soon made it possible to think of choosing a new tsar, and a "Council of All the Russias" was called to determine the succession. Eventually the choice fell upon Michael Romanov, a young man whose family had given Ivan the Terrible his first wife. But Michael was untried and the real ruler was the tsar's father, a nobleman who had been forced to take holy orders and gained great honor by his patriotic bearing in difficult days, first as metropolitan and then as patriarch of Moscow.

The Romanovs ascended the throne amid rejoicing, but they inherited a deserted land. Half the villages of central Russia were empty of people and the surveys of the next age abound in phrases such as "waste land, formerly village." The plowland in the possession of the Monastery of the Holy Trinity had been reduced in a few years to one twenty-fifth of its former extent, and this case was not exceptional. For a generation Muscovy was too weak to fight great wars. As the population began to return to the villages Russia was able to resume her slow ascent, but the peasants had learned that their revolt could be dangerous to the established power, and the rebellious had learned that pretenders could sit on the throne of the tsars. The rulers of Russia never again recovered their old security.

CHAPTER X

the last age of Muscovy

Ye shall cry out in that day because of your king
which ye shall have chosen you.

1 Samuel viii. 18

1. A Difficult Convalescence

The new dynasty of the Romanovs could not at first rely on a prescriptive right to rule as the house of Rurik had done. They owed their elevation to an assembly drawn from all Muscovy in accordance with the principle established by Ivan the Terrible and representing every estate from noble to peasant. For many decades they found it expedient to govern with the aid of similar assemblies. These councils, which were handicapped by the Slavonic tradition that no decision could be taken unless the voting was unanimous, did not aspire to rule. They did not have the legal rights or the carefully defined machinery of action which make a parliament, but they did keep the Kremlin in touch with local needs, and they enlisted local talent and experience in the business of government. The stages by which a council of estates and districts can become the nucleus of a representative government are often subtle and inconspicuous. In a happier setting the Russian assemblies might have developed by slow and indirect ways into the nucleus of a parliamentary system. But there can be no government by cooperation without many compromises and most Russians find compromise ignoble and distasteful. It was therefore fatally easy for the rulers and bureaucrats of Muscovy to suppose it better to impose their own or their sovereign's will rather than to seek for a patient accommodation.

Drastic government soon restored peace, but it could not create contentment. On crown lands the peasants were ruled by heavy-handed government officials, but the worst oppression was on monastic lands and private estates, where the

landlord held his serfs in the hollow of his hand. Nearly all
owed him more money than they could repay, and if the
landowner, who was also judge and policeman, chose to exact
his pound of flesh from his serfs, they had no defense except
flight or rebellion. Peasant revolts generated by the pressure
of landlords and officials broke out repeatedly in the wild
border lands of the south and east and sometimes spread to
central Russia. But the Kremlin was not strong enough to
curb the power of the landlords on whom it relied for the
defense of the country and the stability of the throne. Moreover, most of the landlords were not rich and the heavy demands of military service put upon them a burden which
they could hardly meet without squeezing their tenants. A
general lightening of burdens would have given the peasants
a chance to thrive; a prosperous peasantry could have been
ruled by milder methods and a contented countryside would
have released Russian energy for the accumulation of wealth
and ease.

It needed little for Russia to pass the dead point and join
the irresistible material upsurge of the West, but it was
scarcely possible to touch the tyranny of the landowners or to
make other fundamental reforms without sapping the foundations of national defense. Recent experience had shown once
more that Muscovy must be ready to defend herself against
dangerous neighbors. Yet, as things were, court, landlords
and administration bore down the whole country with their
weight. Heavy burdens unsettled the peasants, while the need
to raise revenue and to maintain a class of landholders for
the public service made it even more necessary to tie the
peasants to the land. Meanwhile, the state grants of land had
in practice become hereditary, the owners forgot that the
purpose of the grant was to enable them to serve the state,
and the peasants, who had longer memories, found themselves undergoing heavy burdens to support their masters in a
service which was often slackly performed.

2. *Hierarchy and Rigidity*

Societies which are subjected to too great pressure
sometimes become petrified. In the later Roman Empire the

need to maintain the fabric of the state forced the emperors at all cost to strengthen and make firm each separate part of the administrative system till the whole empire and the whole of society became one rigid structure which did not at once expose its brittleness. Likewise in seventeenth-century Muscovy, society became petrified and stratified until every function in society became hereditary. Landowners and their children served in the army and in the administration. Peasants and their families served by paying their taxes, if they lived on crown lands, or by maintaining their masters for the service of the tsar, if they lived on a private estate. The children of peasants or landowners could not become traders, and therefore the occupation of merchant must become hereditary too, in order that there might be someone to buy and sell. Even the artisans of the towns were bound to their station in life and to their birthplace. Where all classes were thus restricted, the calling of parish priest became hereditary too, for otherwise there might have been no priests.

Unlike the celibate clergy of Rome, the parish priest of the Orthodox Church is not set apart from the world. By tradition he is a peasant living among peasants. Distinguished only by his dress and by his function in conducting the liturgical worship of his church, he works the land like other peasants and he marries; indeed, he must be married before he is ordained. The Orthodox parish clergy have often shared the vices and limitations of their flock, but they are close to the people, whose aspirations they share, and in popular risings they were often found on the side of the peasants.

It needed training rather than education to conduct a set liturgical service; sermons were not called for. The fact that the Russian parish clergy have been for the most part simple, unlettered men has not prevented them throughout the ages from ministering to the deeper life of millions of Russian men, women and children. The Eastern service of the Eucharist may not have the variety of liturgical beauty or the ampler expression of the ministry of the Word, which are found in many Western forms of service, but it binds men together with links that cannot be expressed by words. The faithful believe that during the Eucharist the congregation become one with each other and with the glorious company of heaven in the communion of saints. This conception is touchingly expressed in the "cherubic hymn" which is sung by a part of the congregation who symbolize the presence of the angelic hosts. The worship and teaching of all the churches contain the same idea, but among the Orthodox it is put more in the forefront than is usual in the individualistic West. The feeling of union which is thus engendered might be described in scientific terms as a telepathic phenomenon. Christians believe that in the sacraments men are strengthened by forces beyond themselves, but even those who do not believe may wish to consider whether the concentrated practice of telepathy Sunday after Sunday for close on a thousand years may not have contributed to the Russian gift for spontaneous cooperation.

Since enterprise could seldom raise a man from the station of life in which he was born, wealth grew slowly in Muscovy, but the gradual development of a richer and more complex economy did not cease. Moscow was rather bigger than London in Queen Elizabeth's time, but other towns were small and many of them were less important for trade or manufacture than for the shelter which they gave in time of war. Such towns would have few houses and in peacetime they might lie almost empty, but their walls enclosed broad open spaces and during an invasion refugees and their cattle would fill every corner. The townspeople were often plowmen and landowners rather than shopkeepers and artisans. Such industry as there was made its home in the villages where peasant artisans were learning to turn the long winters to profit by indoor work with their hands. A whole village would often specialize in such trades as ironwork, leather, weaving or the manufacture of wooden tableware, and the products of specially skilled villages became known all over Russia. The skill of Russian craftsmen and the beauty of their work has not yet been fully appreciated by the West. The small beginnings of heavy industry, which were needed for the supply of cannon and other firearms to the army, were largely in the hands of foreigners, who found, however, that their Russian workmen were apt learners. Increasing trade with the outside world brought a small but important foreign colony to Moscow, where the foreigners were segregated in a special quarter known as the "German suburb." English merchants trading through the White Sea had long enjoyed the privileges which excited the envy of the Russian merchants, but these concessions were withdrawn after the execution of Charles I, an event which caused great indignation in the Kremlin.

3. Defense

The presence of foreigners in Moscow was bound in time to make holes in the curtain which divided Russians from the West. Foreign merchants could be segregated to some extent, and foreign doctors were too few to have much impact, but foreign soldiers would be useless unless they could rub shoulders with their Russian comrades in arms. In the course of the seventeenth century it became the policy of the Kremlin to attract foreign officers to the service of Muscovy. At one time there were as many as four foreign generals and a hundred foreign colonels in the Russian army as well as a great number of junior officers. High pay was offered and attracted many, but more were discouraged by the knowledge that foreign officers were often detained in Russia on various pretexts after the expiration of their contract.

Queen Elizabeth's ambassador, Giles Fletcher, reports that "the Russe trusteth rather to his number, than to the value of his soldiers, or good ordering of his forces." The artillery was good: it seemed that "no Prince of Christendom hath better store of munition, than the Russe Emperor. And it may partly appear by the Artillery House at Moscow, where are all sorts of great Ordnance, all brass pieces, very fair, to an exceeding great number." But "the footman hath nothing but his piece in his hand, his striking hatchet at his back and his sword by his side." The piece or arquebus had "a plain and straight stock" and the barrel was "rudely and unartificially made, very heavy yet shooteth but a very small bullet." Many of the foot soldiers had not even this equipment and few were full-time soldiers. Most of them were wont to eke out their pay by engaging in various trades, in which the tsars gave them invidious privileges instead of paying them properly.

However, the bulk of the army consisted of feudal cavalry supplied by the holders of service grants of land and equipped with bows and arrows. The serving class were compelled to attend throughout every campaign, but their equipment was not checked and the fact that neither age nor illness was accepted as an excuse for absence must have introduced an odd mixture into the ranks of the Muscovite army.

"Their marching or leading is without all order save that the four Polskey or legions (whereinto their army is divided) keep themselves several under their ensigns, and so thrust all on together in a hurry." These tactics, which had been evolved against the Tartars, were outmoded against a Western adversary such as Poland or Sweden, but may not have been quite so undisciplined as would appear at first sight. Maurice Baring observes that

". . . the Russians, who often lack individual initiative, have in a high degree that power of cooperative energy. They work altogether naturally without feeling the need for any special leader. I remember a striking instance of this kind in the Russo-Japanese war, in the retreat from Ta-Shi-Chao, when the retreat of a vast number of transport was effected without any supervising control; it seemed to go perfectly. Colonel Gaedke, the German war expert, who was a witness of this, told me at the time that he considered this automatic cooperation very remarkable, and he doubted whether German soldiers would be capable of similar behavior in similar circumstances."

Russian chaos is seldom quite so bad as it looks. To take a more recent example, during the war against Hitler a confused mass of "rude and unartificial" farm carts immediately behind the lines delivered supplies to the Red Army with an efficiency that surprised foreigners who had experienced the delays of Soviet civilian transport.

Muscovy prevailed against the Tartars both by better technical equipment and by more intelligent use of resources. The Muscovite prefabricated traveling fortress, composed of wooden wagons made so that they could be jointed together into a continuous rampart with loopholes, showed the Russian practical imagination at its strongest and was well suited to warfare in the steppe. But against Western neighbors the best efforts of the Russian feudal cavalry were unavailing; and the heroic devotion and stoical courage of the infantry, who were drawn from the poorer classes, were best seen in defense. "In a set field the Russe is noted to have ever the worse of the Polonian and Sweden."

The Muscovite soldier carried his meager provisions with him and accepted terrible hardships as a matter of course.

Giles Fletcher, expressing a general opinion, writes "if the Russe soldier were as hardy to execute an enterprise, as he is hard to bear out toil and travail, or were otherwise as apt and well trained for the wars, as he is indifferent for his lodging and diet, he would far exceed the soldiers of our parts." This assessment coincides with some modern appreciations of the Russian soldier, but it scarcely does justice to the enterprise which Russians will show when they are dealing with problems which are familiar to them. The "striking ax" which the Muscovite footman carried could be used to create a wooden bridge, a cart, a stockade or even a house at a speed which would have made Giles Fletcher open his eyes. During the Second World War I remember hearing a British general describe with professional admiration the manner in which the Red Army had accomplished an opposed crossing of a broad river with no bridging materials other than those obtained with the help of their "striking axes" from the surrounding forest.

The professional qualities of the Muscovite infantryman are sufficiently described by his adversaries and by foreign observers. But the sixteenth and seventeenth centuries have left us no Tolstoy to hymn the Russian footslogger and no Bernard Pares to describe his bearing in the relations of humanity or his almost sacramental acceptance of death when he is with his comrades in battle. Yet it is not hard to see the features of a man peeping out from the uncouth accouterments of a Muscovite foot soldier.

4. New Lands

The later Roman Empire and Muscovy were confronted with broadly similar difficulties, but there is a difference in the result. Rome fell where Russia rose.

There were many differences in the situation of Rome and of Muscovy, but the greatest difference probably lay in their supply of good agricultural land. Imperial Rome had no new land to develop, but Russia had some of the best land in the world waiting to be settled as soon as she could master the black earth steppe and Siberia.

The process of gradual enserfment deprived the state of

many colonists, who would have opened up new and fertile land if they had been allowed to do so, but on the other hand the very harshness of Muscovy drove many to flight into new lands on the southern and eastern borders, which they transformed into provinces of Russia.

Ivan the Terrible's conquest of the Volga had opened the way to Siberia, and the wealth of fur to be found in the northern forests drew the Russians on. Siberia, like Canada, is a land of great rivers and vast plains reaching from the Arctic tundra into rich cornland. Both countries have been found in the present age to possess fabulous mineral wealth and both were first explored for their furs. Both Canada and Siberia have a hot summer and an intensely cold winter, whose fantastic extremes are liked best by those who know them best. I have found half an hour's stroll at night in 70 degrees (Fahrenheit) of Siberian frost as invigorating as an afternoon's exercise in the milder climate of England. There are not many Siberians who will admit that the earth holds anywhere a better land than Siberia.

The native tribes of hunters and fishers were too weak and scattered to offer serious resistance, and the Russians advanced like wildfire down one river and up the next until within less than three generations from Ivan the Terrible's conquest of the middle Volga they stood on the shore of the Pacific Ocean. In Canada the Hudson's Bay Company organized the trapping of the northern fur and added vast unknown regions to the dominions of the British Crown, while in Russia the Stroganovs, a family of peasant origin who knew how to rise, were granted certain privileges in the northeastern part of European Russia which led on to the conquest of the fur-bearing forests. Sable was "the true, the golden fleece," the "lure,"

> That took the Russ on plunder bent
> Hot-foot across a continent.*

The Romanovs soon discovered that Siberia was a place from which exiles could not easily escape. For over three centuries a ceaseless stream of political exiles, common criminals and unfortunate people who have fallen foul of their commune, their landlord or their commissar, has gone to

* J. F. Baddeley, *Russia, Mongolia, China,* 1919.

reinforce the pioneer trappers and peasants who have made Siberia one of the most vigorous lands upon earth.

Meanwhile, in the south of Russia Cossacks were conquering for Orthodoxy a land that was richer even than Siberia but which was defended by the fierce successors of the ancient Scythians. The Ukraine is a Russian land; indeed, it is the cradle of all the Russian lands. But here the asperities of climate are softened by rich soil and a warmer sun, and in the course of time the southern Russian dialects have diverged to form a softer speech which is accounted a separate language. The Russian and Ukrainian speeches are not different enough to form an insuperable barrier to intercourse, but Ukrainian national sentiment has crystallized round the difference of language.

In their origin the Cossacks were equalitarian, but very soon some became richer than others and class differences arose. Yet all were united in their opposition to the Poles and in 1648 they rose against the Polish landlords. A well-to-do Cossack named Bogdan Khmelnitski had quarreled with one of the Polish nobility over a girl, and when he was unable to obtain justice from the Polish authorities he raised the standard of revolt. Cossack warriors streamed to the support of their injured comrade and were joined by thousands of Orthodox peasants who believed that the Cossacks would free them from their Catholic landlords. The Ukrainian host won a series of crushing victories and in a short space of time the Cossacks were the masters of nearly all the Polish Ukraine. Bogdan thus found himself suddenly and unexpectedly one of the most powerful rulers in Europe.

The Cossacks were superb soldiers, but they were illiterate and they had no civil administration. None of them had any clear idea what to do with their new power and independence. Bogdan was Orthodox, but he was also well-to-do and he had no interest in liberating the serfs. For this reason he soon lost his mass support. The Poles rallied and drove the Cossacks out of the western Ukraine, but Cossackdom remained entrenched and independent beyond the river Dnieper.

The Cossacks were always ready to ally themselves with the king of Poland, the sultan of Turkey or the tsar of Muscovy, as it might suit their interests for the moment, but this time a more serious decision was called for. They felt the need for a loose attachment to some king or emperor, but they intended to run their own affairs. After long negotiations the infant Cossack state decided to seek the protection of Moscow. The tsar hesitated before accepting his new subjects, for Muscovy needed a long convalescence before she could risk the enmity of Poland, but in 1654 there was signed a treaty of union, by which there passed to Muscovite sovereignty that part of the Ukraine which lay on the left bank of the Dnieper and which had maintained its independence since the revolt of Bogdan Khmelnitski.

Soon there was friction, for each party interpreted the union in a different sense. The tsar saw no great difference between his old subjects in Muscovy and his new subjects in the Ukraine. He meant to incorporate his new domain into the body of the Russian empire, but the Cossacks did not mean to give up that home rule which Poland had never completely denied to them and which they had recently enlarged in such a remarkable manner. The arrival of Muscovite governors to occupy and administer the chief towns was the cause of much grumbling and some disorder, but by degrees the fact of Moscow's increasingly effective rule was accepted. Within a generation the richer Cossacks had become landed gentry, and in two generations they were petitioning the tsar for an extension to their own land of the serfdom which brought profit and power to the Muscovite landlords. While the rich Cossacks were absorbed into the Russian gentry, the poorer Cossacks became increasingly conscious of their separateness from the peasants whom they despised, until by a sad but natural evolution the descendants of the "free Cossacks" became the tsar's most trusted agents for the repression of popular discontent.

The acquisition of the Ukraine brought to Muscovy much-needed intellectual resources. The Catholic offensive of the counter-reformation had induced the Orthodox of Poland and Lithuania to band together for mutual support, and the arguments of the Jesuits had forced the Orthodox to put forward a coherent defense of their position and to undertake the education of their own clergy. Guilds of Orthodox artisans rallied to the support of Orthodox institutions, and great Orthodox noblemen founded academies which were intended to rival the places of learning founded by the Jesuits. It would be easy to exaggerate the attainments of the Ukrainian schools, but they were the first step toward independent thought in Russia and they have become thereby the modest parents of an immense progeny. The need to state a case against the Jesuits did not at first bring the Russians to a rediscovery of their spiritual origins, but it did instill into the pupils of the Ukrainian schools the principles of logical argument; and the study of Latin opened the door to a wider world.

For a good century the Ukraine sent a stream of educated men to Moscow where they played an essential part in the great transformation of Russia which took place in the second half of the seventeenth century and the beginning of the eighteenth. In Moscow, schools were opened at which the sons of the gentry could for the first time obtain the rudiments of education. Printing had been introduced into Moscow in the reign of Ivan the Terrible, but even in the second half of the seventeenth century only a few books were printed and only a very few noblemen showed wide interest or studied foreign languages. Plays of a kind were performed before the tsar and insipid verses were composed in the Polish manner, but these first halting steps give little indication of the greatness which was to come.

There are scarcely more than two or three Russian books written before the year 1800 which it is possible to read with pleasure today. Before Peter the Great the Russians were a strangely inarticulate people, few personalities stand out, and if we did not know their descendants it would be hard to tell what manner of men the ancient Muscovites were. But it is impossible to doubt that many strong and varied characters lay hidden behind the mask of Muscovite uniformity, just as more recently the mask of Stalinist officialdom hid a varied humanity. The Muscovites lacked the power of expression in words and it seems that the ritual of the old Russian life absorbed intellectual originality, but their emotions remained unspoiled. Somewhere in hidden depths there was maturing a power of expression such as the world has seldom seen.

CHAPTER XI

the two nations

*... for the Jews have no dealings with
the Samaritans.* John iv. 9

Hitherto Muscovy had been a seamless fabric, whose unity was shown equally in church, in state and in society, but in the second generation of the Romanovs the pressure of knowledge from outside produced a rift. Since then the lines of cleavage have changed more than once, but Russia has continually held within her two nations—one might almost say two worlds.

The disorders of the times had called forth a group of conservative reformers in the Church of Russia, and prominent among these was a young archpriest named Avvakum (or Habakkuk) who received powerful patronage but drew on himself the vengeance of prominent neighbors by his fearless denunciations. Several times he was beaten savagely and there was more than one attempt upon his life. Avvakum and his friends, like most Russians, attached great importance to the minute observance of the traditions of the Orthodox Church, but increasing contact with other countries had begun to show that the Orthodox Church outside Russia did not always follow the forms and customs which Russians accepted as immemorial and therefore apostolic. A revision of the service books seemed to be needed, but no one had the scholarship and wisdom necessary to carry through a successful liturgical reform.

In 1652 Nikon, an able peasant who had turned monk, became patriarch of Moscow and set about the purification of church life and the revision of the Liturgy. The changes were small—e.g., should the ejaculation "alleluia" be sung twice or three times and should one cross oneself with two fingers or with three—but they raised a storm whose ground swell has not yet died away. Even the English have shown themselves capable of violent differences over wafers and wax candles, but to the Russians every word and every gesture of the Liturgy embodied some aspect of the deepest mysteries of the Christian religion. The smallest change in word or movement seemed to import a change of meaning; and every change of meaning was heresy. Nikon was a strong-minded, tactless man who pressed his reforms with the narrow-minded self-confidence of the enlightened soul and the brutal ruthlessness of the Kremlin bureaucrat. To the simple-minded faithful, who saw their sacred customs overturned, it seemed that the leaders of the Church had been got at by lax Ukrainians, who knew Latin and had come under Catholic influence, and by crafty Greeks, whose orthodoxy had always been suspect. Nikon believed that in following the Greek custom of his day he was returning to the apostolic tradition, but modern scholarship has upheld many of Avvakum's claims. The Russian usage preserved a more ancient tradition than the Greek.

Soon the resistance became amazingly bitter and drew in many of the best elements in the Russian Church, particularly among the poorer parish clergy, who had little sympathy for the rich monks and bishops who imposed the reforms. So when Avvakum denounced Nikon and his party as apostates, his words found an echo in the hearts of many hearers. The rift grew into formal schism and to this day large numbers of strictly Orthodox Russians remain outside the Russian Church constituting the sect of the "Old Believers."

Too dangerous to be tolerated in Moscow, Avvakum was exiled to Siberia. He was given a cure of souls at Tobolsk where, but for his impetuous nature, he might perhaps have led the quiet, unmolested life of many Siberian exiles. In his autobiography, Avvakum describes how when he was at Tobolsk

". . . a certain Ivan Struna, secretary of the archbishop's chancery, persecuted me. Without cause he tormented Deacon Anthony, and the latter ran away from him and came to my church. Ivan Struna called his attendants and also came to the church on another day. I was singing vespers, and he rushed into the choir and clutched Anthony by the beard, while I closed the church doors, and let no one in. Struna was alone in there carrying on like the devil. And I, interrupting the office, seated Struna in the middle of the church with the help of Anthony and thrashed him with a leather strap for disturbance in church. And the others, about twenty strong, fled, driven by the Holy Ghost. Having received Struna's repentance, I sent him home."

But Struna's kinsmen did not forgive the insult and for a month Avvakum did not dare to sleep at home.

Then, as now, ideological dissent was considered to be a form of treason and Avvakum relates how in eighteen months at Tobolsk he "was accused five times of treason against the tsar." After this he was sent to the farthest East to the banks of the Amur under Pashkov, a celebrated Cossack leader, who had a reputation for merciless cruelty. Avvakum tells us that Pashkov "had six hundred men under his command. He was a rough man, for my sins, and he burned, flogged and tortured people unceasingly. I had often tried to stay him, but finally I had fallen into his hands. From Moscow he had received Nikon's order to torment me." But Avvakum did not try to ingratiate himself with his formidable captor.

In a rough and long journey the wildest spot was the long rapids of the Tunguska river.

"Ah, poor me! the mountains were high, the forest dense; cliffs stood like a wall, one could break one's neck looking up at them. . . . Pashkov wanted to cast me out into these mountains, to live among the birds and beasts. So I wrote him a short letter, and it started thus: 'Man, fear God, Who sits on the Cherubim and Who watches over the abyss, before Whom tremble the heavenly powers and all creatures, including man. You alone despise Him and cause disturbance,' and so on. There was much I wrote in that letter, and I had it taken to him."

So Pashkov sent his executioners to fetch Avvakum.

"He roared like a wild beast and struck me on one cheek and then on the other, and beat me on the head and knocked me down and seizing his battle ax he struck me three times on the back, as I lay there. Then tearing off my garment he applied seventy-two strokes of the whip on that very same back of mine. And I cried 'Lord Jesus Christ, Son of God, help me!' And I repeated these words unceasingly and he was

sorely vexed because I did not say: 'Have mercy,'.* At each
stroke of the whip I recited the prayer; then, in the middle of
the thrashing, I cried out: 'Enough of this beating,' and he
ordered the thrashing to be stopped. I asked him, 'Do you
know why you beat me? Why?' And once more he ordered
that I should be struck in the ribs, and then they let me go. I
trembled and fell. And he had me placed in the ammunition
boat; they fettered me hand and foot and threw me onto a
beam. It was autumn and rain beat on me all night."

For years on end this man, who could at such a moment
pray in words that were chosen to annoy his tormentor,
suffered torture by flogging, by starvation and by freezing in
some of the coldest parts of Siberia.

In the spring they

". . . floated lumber for the builders of houses and forts.
There was nothing to eat; men died of hunger, and from
working in the water. Shallow was the river and the rafts
heavy, the taskmasters pitiless, the sticks hard, the cudgels
knotty, the whips cutting, our suffering cruel; fire and rack
and people starving! One more stroke and a man would fall
dead. Alas, what times were these! I know not how he
[Pashkov] could lose his mind in this way. My wife had only
one cloak left that had not rotted. It would have been worth
fifteen roubles in Russia, and more over here, but he gave
four sacks of rye for it, and they lasted one or two years
while we lived on the river Nercha, eating mostly grass. He
let all his men die of hunger; there remained a small troop,
roaming through the steppes, digging for roots and grass, and
we did as the others. In winter we fed on pine bark, and
sometimes by luck on horseflesh and the carcasses of beasts
killed by wolves. What the wolves did not devour we ate.
And some would feed on frozen wolves and foxes and every
other kind of filthy beast they could find."

In the belief that the last days had come, Avvakum and his
family accepted the inevitability of suffering for themselves
and for each other with a realistic resignation that was characteristically Russian. After recording that his wife and son,

* The point is that it was natural to expect Avvakum to use the
"Jesus prayer," which runs, "Lord Jesus Christ, Son of God, have
mercy on me."

like himself, were imprisoned in underground prisons, he adds:

"But what can be done about it? Let them all suffer bitterly for Christ's sake. So be it, with God's help. It is fitting to suffer for the Christian faith. This archpriest formerly enjoyed intercourse with the great, and now, poor wretch, let him delight in suffering to the end; for it has been written: Blessed is not he who begins, but he who perseveres to the end. But enough on that subject. Let us resume our previous topic."

Since persecution did not break the resistance of the archpriest, the authorities wooed him to compromise but, when it became clear that he was not to be won, Avvakum was burned at the stake after fifteen years spent in a subterranean prison in the north of Russia.

Violence and tenderness are never far apart in this extraordinary man. He combined a fierce narrowness of mind and an inability to distinguish the essential from the trivial with a greatness of heart and soul which almost justify his followers in revering him as a saint. He could hate, but for him hatred was a close relation which could come near to love. Describing his parting with Pashkov, he comments: "For ten years he tormented me—or I him, I know not which! God will decide in the day of judgment." When Avvakum's worst tormentor under Pashkov was about to be lynched by comrades whom he had "denounced and whose blood he had shed," the archpriest ransomed him, saying, "Let the poor wretch repent of his sins." And when he comes to tell the story the "poor wretch" is called "my friend Basil."

Avvakum typifies the Old Believers. Like him, they combine a narrow understanding with a tincture of Christian love and a staunchness of character which have sometimes proved explosive.

Thousands of Old Believers were hanged and tortured. Tongues were cut out and hands severed. Avvakum himself was only saved from mutilation by the interposition of the tsaritsa. But the resistance grew with persecution and communities of Old Believers fled to the hardships of the northern forest where they were safe for a time from the violence of man, or to the southern steppe where many became Cossacks. They believed that the end of the world was near. Avvakum had said: "Our misfortune is inevitable, we cannot escape it. If God allows scandals, it is that the elect may be revealed. Let them be burned, let them be purified." Many tens of thousands wandered in the forests north of the upper Volga enduring untold hunger and cold. When they could no longer escape from their pursuers, many thousands of them anticipated the day of judgment by burning themselves alive inside their stockades. But God's visible judgment was stayed while the first generation of Old Believers grew old and died.

At first they had many priests among them but they had no bishop; and in the absence of bishops no new priests could be ordained. What was to happen when the first generation of priests were all dead? All agreed that the rule of Antichrist had begun, and the extreme groups held that in the "last days" sacraments were done away with, so that priests had become needless. Some carried these premises to a madly logical conclusion, refusing all authority other than a supposed inner light, but after much searching of conscience a great part of the Old Believers arrived at a strange compromise.

The direct ministrations of the official Church were utterly rejected, but it was illogically conceded that official ordinations were valid. Thenceforth officially ordained priests were regularly enticed to the service of the schism by the offer of better pay and by the attraction which the old traditions have always had for many. But the Old Believers still cherished the belief that in some mysterious corner of the East there lived other Christians who preserved the traditions of the Fathers and would send Russia a bishop to restore the past as it had always been. The schismatics sent many expeditions to look for this Old Believing Prester John. They pursued many will-o'-the-wisps; and many impostors came near to deceiving their narrow but shrewd understanding, until the mid-nineteenth century when at last a genuine Orthodox bishop from Bosnia consented to ordain a new hierarchy among the Russian Old Believers.

In the course of time persecution was relaxed and the fervor of the schism found an expression in more than average diligence and honesty, which soon raised the community to comfort and even affluence. Serfdom was never established in the northern forest, whose poor soil did not attract serf-owning landlords. This made it possible for those who had fled to the north to live as free peasants. The very poverty of the land pushed men to supplement a poor living by crafts and by trade. The needs of religion led to the spread of education among the schismatics many generations before schools became established in other parts of rural Russia. Economically the Old Believers were the most progressive community in Russia, but their hearts and minds were set on a changeless Russia such as they conceived to have subsisted for countless ages in the time before Peter the Great and before Nikon. They preserved the old tradition and the old life down to yesterday, like a living fossil.

The Old Believers drink like other Russians, but they abhor tobacco, which was forbidden in Muscovy before the schism, and they account it a deadly sin to shave. In Moscow during the Second World War I was unable to visit an Old Believer church because my beardless chin would have revealed me as a heretic. To the straitest sect of the schismatics every invention introduced into Russia after the schism is suspect. Some would not even use the public highway because made roads were unknown in Muscovy. The Old Believers will often have strangers to stay in their households, but articles used by heretics are considered to be defiled; if, for instance, a guest eats off a plate which is used by the family, the plate is broken and the guest is expected to pay for a new one.

This peculiar people succeeded by degrees in restoring much of the old splendor. Humble monasteries concealed among the forests began first to attract gifts from the faithful and then to grow rich by trade and by the industrious practice of handicrafts, until there grew up inside the schism a hierarchy of honor among holy places and a powerful chain of ecclesiastical vested interests. Their monastic buildings were made according to strict rules, preserving each detail of the decoration which had been customary in the first half of the seventeenth century, but every resource of traditional art was employed to give them beauty. From time to time a monastery would be pulled down by official orders and its treasures confiscated, but the monks and nuns grew skilled at concealing the nature of their association and would often have themselves inscribed for official purposes as a company of merchants. The habits of adaptation gained under the tsars have proved useful under the Soviets and I have it from a generally reliable source that there was before the war at least one collective farm which fulfilled all its obligations to the state while at the same time operating as an Old Believers' monastery. As late as the nineteen-fifties two secret Old Believer monasteries and four convents were discovered hidden in the Siberian forest. This shows both the tenacity of the

Old Believers and their skill in camouflaging what they are doing. It also shows how little the Kremlin sometimes knows about what goes on in out-of-the-way country districts. (See *Religiya i Nauka* for Jan. 1963.)

Modern life is a solvent which is carrying away the few remaining relics of old Muscovy, and the Old Believers are losing numbers, but it would be a mistake to underestimate the hold of their peculiar traditions on a section of the Russian people. About the middle of the last century, the tsarist government conducted a secret inquiry into the schismatics. The high official charged with this inquiry reported that when he entered a peasant's hut he "was often received with the words, 'We are not Christians.' 'What, then are you infidels?' 'No,' they would answer, 'we believe in Christ, but we belong to the Church, for we are worldly frivolous people!' 'Why are you not Christians, since you believe in Christ?' 'Christians,' they reply, 'are those who stick to the old faith, and they do not pray in the same way as we do; but as for us, we have no time to imitate them.' "

Many of those who rejected the priesthood after the first generation maintained their moral discipline and social cohesion by a strict adherence to that part of the Church's ritual which it was lawful for laymen to perform. Thus they could baptize but could not marry, a disability which inspired some to the strangest views of sex. Others retained the fervor of their movement but not the discipline. They turned to ecstasy, rediscovering all those excesses which recur everywhere, from the later Roman Empire to the United States of America, when the powerful forces of religion are not subject to the discipline of community life. Russia has had her Shakers, her Holy Rollers and her perfectionists, who believed that their holiness would transmute the most disgusting actions into virtue. It is tempting to think that such ideas were handed down secretly from the wilder sects of late antiquity through the medieval Bogomils, until they met the boldest speculations of the priestless Old Believers. This is possible, but the case is uncertain.

Some brought sex unadorned and undirected into their religious practices, and the prolonged ecstatic dances of Christian dervishes ended in free embraces, while others denied the sexual emotions all place in the good life. There was even a brotherhood of those who had in the most literal sense become eunuchs for the sake of the kingdom of heaven. Up to the Revolution these parchment-faced men with their high-pitched voices were familiar to all, for they excelled so much in honesty and reliability that they were universally accepted as cashiers. Other sects, such as the Khlysty or Whips, maintained that, since repentance is pleasing to God, Christians should sin the more boldly so that they might have whereof to repent; and it would seem that they practiced what they preached both in the joys of sinning and in the ecstasies of repentance. Since the Revolution the wilder sects have been little heard of, but there is no doubt that some of them still exist.

It would be wrong to regard the sectarians as a whole as associations of religious maniacs. Even those who rejected marriage in theory often lived better family lives and treated their women with more respect than the Orthodox. Most of the sectarians showed themselves to be ardent seekers after God's truth and in time many of them came to a sober zeal that was close to Protestant nonconformity. When the British and Foreign Bible Society began to work in Russia under the august patronage of Alexander I, most of them became great Bible readers. Soon after this, Protestant sects emerged, revealing a dim memory of Protestant tradition reaching back in one case to some unknown English doctor in the time of Ivan the Terrible. It is hard to gauge Protestant influence in Muscovy, but the fierceness of some attacks on Protestant doctrine suggests that it may have been greater than would seem at first sight. However, by the end of the eighteenth century Muscovite intolerance was burning itself out and Russian Orthodox theology had been deeply penetrated by Protestant influences. At the same time German Protestants, who had been settled by Catherine the Great on the Volga and elsewhere, showed the sectarians that they had kindred spirits outside their own people.

Today nearly all of the Russian Protestants are members of the Baptist Church. They continue to show the characteristic virtues of Protestant nonconformity, and they have an added grace which is their own. The danger of every strict religion is that it will end in hypocrisy, but that danger is not so great among Russians as in the West. Many Russians tell lies, but they do not generally deceive themselves; and when a Russian is honest, his integrity goes deeper than the conventional morality which may pass for honesty in other countries. Many Russian Baptists combine this deep integrity with some of the delightful qualities of the Orthodox spirituality which surrounds them.

COMPARATIVE DATES

A.D.

A.D.

1325-41 Ivan Kalita (John Moneybag), prince of Moscow, and then grand prince.

1337 St. Sergius founds Monastery of Holy Trinity.

1362-89 Dmitri of the Don reigns.

1380 Tartars beaten at Field of Snipe.

1462-1505 Ivan III, the Great, reigns.

1471 Novgorod conquered.

1480 End of Tartar yoke.

1533-84 Ivan the Terrible reigns.

1552 Conquest of Kazan.

1553 English open White Sea route.

1558-83 Livonian War.

1564 First book printed in Moscow.

1581 Conquest of Siberia begins.

1589 Establishment of Moscow patriarchate.

1598-1605 Boris Godunov reigns.

1604-13 Time of Troubles.

1613-45 Michael Romanov reigns.

1645-76 Alexis reigns.

1652-8 Nikon patriarch.

1654 Union of Ukraine with Muscovy. Beginning of "Old Believer" schism.

1676-82 Theodore Tsar.

1400 Death of Chaucer.

1429 Joan of Arc raises siege of Orleans.

1439 Council of Florence.

1440 Gutenberg invents printing.

1453 Fall of Constantinople to Turks.

1492 Columbus discovers America.

1497 Vasco da Gama passes Cape of Good Hope.

1513 Macchiavelli writes *The Prince*.

1517 Luther's theses at Wittenberg.

1531 Negroes imported from Guinea to America.

1564 Birth of Galileo, Shakespeare.

1571 Battle of Lepanto.

1575 Akbar conquers Bengal.

1588 Spanish Armada.

1607 First settlement in Virginia.

1618-48 Thirty Years' War.

1642 Birth of Newton.

1658 Death of Oliver Cromwell.

1667 Milton's *Paradise Lost* and first important work of Racine and Leibnitz.

1678 Bunyan's *Pilgrim's Progress*.

1688 Accession of William III.

the age of
St. Petersburg

The carpenter-tsar was too busy knocking up his barrack to address himself to a trade that called for vastly more patience and leisure—that of a gardener.

W. Weidlé, RUSSIA: ABSENT AND PRESENT, p. 41

CHAPTER XII

Peter the Great and the foundations of modern Russia

*So much one man can do
That does both act and know.*

Andrew Marvell, AN HORATIAN ODE UPON
CROMWELL'S RETURN FROM IRELAND

1. The Last Days of Muscovy

Muscovy had purchased strong government at the price of rigidity; and rigid bodies are brittle. The servants of the tsar learned to expect brutal punishment if they exceeded their instructions, but they could always protect themselves by getting previous sanction for their actions from higher authority. In this way it became established that every important decision must emanate from the highest quarters, and local or subordinate officials were confined to the execution of policy laid down from above. The France of Napoleon or the Prussia of Hardenberg and Stein might have made such a system tolerable, but in Muscovy the crafty scribes and ignorant noblemen who guided the tsar's hands were barred from reality by a confused mass of precedents and *paperasserie,* while the intricacies of rule by paper delayed every decision and multiplied the opportunities for deceit and corruption.

Soviet administration is less corrupt and more intelligent than its Muscovite forerunner, but it bears the mark of its distant origins. Soviet officials find it hard to understand the extent to which the British government is accustomed to trust the man on the spot. For this reason a Soviet liaison officer attached to a British battleship during the last war could scarcely believe that the admiralty did not issue detailed instructions for day-to-day operations. When such instructions were not shown to him, he assumed that something was being hidden. My own experience was the same. Russians working for my department in the British embassy could hardly believe their ears when I made immediate decisions on matters of some consequence without first getting official cover.

In the seventeenth century the Kremlin was already accustomed to regulate the affairs of society with stifling paternalism. Trade and manufacture hung on the uncertainties of official action and towns were built and maintained by government order, yet the Kremlin felt little responsibility for the economic development of the country. No roads were made and even the rivers were only half used, for though merchandise could be floated swiftly and easily downstream, the return journey was cruelly laborious. In the youth of Gorki and Chaliapin, barges were hauled upstream by the unaided labor of men pulling on ropes from the bank, but two hundred and fifty years ago even these primitive means were unknown. When a boat needed to go upstream an anchor was thrown out ahead and all hands pulled on the rope till the boat was brought up to the anchor, whereupon another anchor was put out a little farther up and the whole process was repeated endlessly day after day for as many weeks as might be needed. Primitive conditions held trade back and red tape took the resilience out of the Russian economy, while heavy taxes bore down the peasants and the growing restrictions of serfdom made it ever harder for a poor man to better himself.

The first need of the age was lighter taxes and a careful husbanding of resources. A generation of good housekeeping would have given Muscovy some reserves to draw on and then Russia's inherent strength would have enabled her to assert herself in a competitive world, but the task of defense could not wait.

To the south Muscovite palisades and Russian settlements were extended slowly and steadily into the Ukraine, but they did not check the slave raids of the Crimean Tartars, while to the west Sweden at the height of her magnificent manhood barred Russia from the Baltic. The lands where St. Petersburg was to stand had been finally lost to Sweden during the Time of Troubles and they would not be easy to recover.

Western neighbors already feared Russia's potential strength as much as they despised Muscovy's present barbarity. European rivals tried to frustrate Russia's attempts to acquire Western skills and to prevent Russian merchants from developing their own trade connections. An enterprising Russian who shipped a cargo of furs to Holland was forced to take his wares back to Archangel before he could find a buyer. So Russia's progress would be slow, so long as she was cut off from the Baltic, but if she tried to break through at once the effort might be too great. Even success might be bought at a price which would stunt Russian growth.

Looking back on the past we can see that such was the cruel dilemma of Russia in the age of Peter the Great, but these issues were not clear to the men of that time and accordingly there was little deliberate choice of means and no calculation of resources or timing of moves. Peter was led gradually by a genius that seemed at first eccentric and almost playful to force himself and his country to exertions which flesh and blood could hardly stand. Dire necessity enforced endless improvisations touching every side of the national life in turn until the improvisations of genius grew into a system. When Peter died, modern Russia stood erect but buried to her knees in the rubble of Muscovy.

In Russia government depends upon the will of the autocrat. Yet for many centuries there was no fixed rule of succession to the throne. There was a general presumption that the eldest son of the tsar would succeed his father, but the will of the reigning tsar was supreme in this as in all else and even after his death the tsar could fix the succession by his will. This system lasted until the mad Tsar Paul, embittered by the thirty years' usurpation of his mother, fixed the succession by a law of primogeniture, which was respected until the fall of the monarchy in 1917.

Alexis, the second Romanov tsar, liked hawking and the quiet routine of church and family life more than the excitements of war. Known to history as "the most quiet tsar," he began to rule when Muscovy, still convalescing after the Time of Troubles, was not yet strong enough for any great effort.

Muscovy was managed as a family estate, and the reigning tsaritsa always brought fabulous wealth and influence to her family for a time, but only for a time. When the tsaritsa or her husband died, her family must expect to fall from favor, and it was a short step from fall to exile, for the sudden influence of the favored family was always resented and favorites make enemies. So a royal marriage was worth a desperate intrigue, and the frantic defenders of family interest

did not always stop short of poison. Alexis first chose a girl
named Eudoxia to be his bride, but when she appeared for
the first time in the royal robes the ladies in waiting had
plaited her hair so tightly that she fainted before the tsar,
whereupon the court doctors were induced to declare that
she was epileptic. Eudoxia and all her family were exiled to
Siberia and the tsar chose another bride, Marya Miloslavski.

Marya died in childbirth after bearing thirteen children, but
the boys were all sickly and only two, Theodore and Ivan, survived their father. The widowed tsar must needs marry again
to secure the dynasty. He spent much time at the house of his
chief minister, Matveyev, a man of wide views, who had married a wife from the Scottish family of Hamilton, who were settled in Moscow. In Matveyev's house the tsar noticed his
host's pretty ward, Natalya Naryshkin; she took his fancy and
he married her. Natalya, with a dash of Scotland in her upbringing, brought a breath of fresh air into the Kremlin. She
bore a son, the future Peter the Great. Four years later Alexis
died suddenly in early middle age.

Neither Theodore nor Ivan was likely to live long, but for
the moment Theodore succeeded to the throne, the Miloslavskis came back in power and insolence and the Naryshkins
fell. Peter was born to the pomp which hedged the caesars of
the third Rome, but now his mother and he were expelled
from the Kremlin to live in the country near Moscow. Here
the boy of four ran wild and began to learn more from the
companions of his play than earlier tsars had learned from a
stuffy upbringing at the court.

Theodore reigned for six years, moving cautiously toward
more up-to-date methods of government. The tables of family
precedence in public office, which blocked the promotion of
good men, were publicly burned, but Theodore's health was
not equal to the stress of kingship and he died, leaving the
succession more doubtful than before. Ivan was feeble-
minded and almost blind, but he was the eldest surviving
prince, while Peter was a well-grown and vigorous lad who
looked as if he was sixteen but was in fact only ten. It was
left to the Miloslavskis and the Naryshkins to fight out the
claims of the two boys.

The Naryshkins won the first round and Peter was proclaimed tsar, but the Miloslavskis soon found a weak spot in
their defense. The garrison of Moscow was drawn from a
corps known as the *streltsy* or musketeers. In time of peace
these men lived in the suburbs with their families, plying var-

ious trades and bringing up their sons to succeed them in the career of arms. They had grievous complaints against their officers; they had been cheated of their pay, flogged without mercy and compelled to work for the private interests of their officers under military discipline and without pay. They were a credulous, inefficient, patriotic body of men and it was easy to work upon their feelings by promises of redress for their grievances, skillfully combined with an appeal to their patriotism. The Miloslavskis insinuated that the Naryshkins planned to kill all the children of the Tsar Alexis and to seize the throne for themselves.

The musketeers became persuaded that it was their duty to rescue the royal children from massacre and to restore their power to the Miloslavskis, who would then give their just due to all honest soldiers. One morning the whole garrison of Moscow, with drums beating and flags waving, marched upon the Kremlin demanding with threats to see the royal children. The government slept unaware of what was brewing, and the musketeers were inside the Kremlin gates before anyone realized what was happening. The Tsaritsa Natalya, trembling with fright, brought Peter and Ivan out onto a balcony for the men to see. Peter was motionless, betraying no fear while soldiers climbed up to make sure that the listless boy beside him was in fact the Tsarevich Ivan.

The now aged Matveyev, who had once been a favorite commander of the musketeers, calmed them for a moment by a promise of redress and a reminder of their former services, but everything was spoiled by a hectoring speech from another senior officer. Maddened and uncertain of themselves, the mutineers threw the unfortunate officer upon their spears and, having tasted blood, they burst into the palace, cut Matveyev to pieces and rushed through the Kremlin in a mad manhunt for the Naryshkins and other "traitors." Some of Peter's closest relations and some of the chief ministers of the government were murdered in hot blood or tortured to death. Cruelty was multiplied by confusion, for the mutineers did not always know by sight the men whose lives they sought and were capable of killing one man in mistake for another.

At length the fury of the musketeers subsided, but they remained in control of Moscow, murdering and torturing but not looting. They were mutineers, but they did not quite forget that they were soldiers and that the motive of their mutiny had been at least half patriotic. It was deeply disturbing to them that there should be in effect two royal families. Ivan

was the eldest and had therefore the better claim, but Peter
had been lawfully crowned and the musketeers could not
bring themselves to ask for his dethronement. So they insisted
absurdly that the unwilling Ivan should be crowned too. For
a time the throne of Muscovy was shared by two boy tsars,
one of whom was feeble in mind and body, while the other
had enough vigor for two princes.

Peter did not forget his first acquaintance with bloodshed
and henceforth he looked on the musketeers as enemies. All
summer long the musketeers held sway and the Kremlin lived
in fear, while the ruling classes reflected upon the narrow
margin which divided cruel severity from more cruel chaos in
Muscovy. Amid the general panic the Princess Sophia, alone
among the royal family, kept her head and showed the courage and resolution of a man. She had indeed shared a man's
education with her brother Theodore and had then quietly
acquired much knowledge about affairs of state in the sick-
room of the dying Theodore, who ruled from his bed. A
French contemporary described her as "immensely fat, with a
head as large as a bushel, hairs on her face and tumors on
her legs, and at least forty years old. But in the same degree
that her stature is broad, short and coarse, her mind is
shrewd, unprejudiced and full of policy." During the crisis
Sophia became the head of the government because she alone
would take responsibility. For seven years she ruled with the
help of her lover, Prince Golitzin, an enlightened but inefficient man.

Peter was sent back to the countryside and for seven years
he grew to prodigious height and strength. To the end of his
days he wrote in a half-literate schoolboy scrawl, for he
would not learn his lessons unless they seemed to have practical use. But he had a passion to know how everything
worked; and at play he worked with an intensity that blotted
out all other interests. When he played at soldiers, he drilled
his playmates into regiments with the deadly seriousness of a
brilliant child. Real weapons were used for mock battles, until
at the cost of many wounds and a few deaths the toy regiments began to turn into real soldiers, becoming eventually
the nucleus of the modern Russian army.

Peter chose his companions from all classes. Promotion
in the toy army was strictly by merit and the tsar himself long
remained a bombardier, refusing promotion until he had
earned it. All his life he stuck to this principle, and all his
life he chose his friends and ministers from all classes.

On an ever-memorable day he found in a shed the remains of a boat of strange design. This turned out to be an English boat which could be made to sail against the wind, a thing unheard of in Muscovy, a new symbol of man's mastery over nature. The young tsar insisted on having the old boat mended up and rigged, and soon he was sailing on the river Yauza. Then with single-minded concentration he ordered bigger ships to be built on the nearest lake, and years later, when at last he turned his mind to serious war, his first act was to build Russia's first fleet.

All his life Peter the Great loved water, but he loved fire almost as much and no celebration was complete for him without extravagant fireworks which sometimes cost lives as well as money. The hectic joy of fireworks answered to his restless energy but the sea gave him tranquillity.

From childhood Peter loved to do things with his hands; he hated abstract theories, but he loved all knowledge that gave him mastery. He became a first-class carpenter and ship-wright, and was skilled in many trades, including the work of a cobbler, blacksmith, printer and drummer. He mended his own clothes, and an enormous pair of topboots which he made for himself is still shown in the Kremlin. He studied mathematics not for its own sake but so that he might learn navigation, fortification and shipbuilding. He learned dentistry in Holland, practicing with relish upon his courtiers, and studied anatomy with a lasting ardor, applying his knowledge to torture, in which art he became a passionate adept.

Peter's journeys from his country home into Moscow took him to the "German suburb," where he found that many skills unknown to the Muscovites were practiced, and he soon became a regular visitor to the foreign colony, learning assiduously what the foreigners had to teach. The foreigners in Moscow "were in the main a rough lot, adventurers or soldiers of fortune, but their style of living and their range of knowledge brought a gust of air from the busy, methodical inventive West" (Sumner, *Peter the Great,* p. 12).

When Peter was sixteen he was married off to a wellborn bride three years older than himself. He duly produced a son, Alexis, of whom more hereafter, but his marriage was little more than a short interruption of his passionate games. The boy took little interest in affairs of state, though he was precocious in physique and understanding, but as he grew up it became clear that he and all his family lived in a deadly peril that would increase with every year unless Sophia was de-

posed from the regency. One night a rumor that the musketeers were advancing on Peter's home brought things to a
head. In his nightshirt the young tsar rushed out into the
woods, where he dressed in a hurry and mounted a horse to
gallop all night to the Monastery of the Holy Trinity. He arrived in a state of collapse. Since the Time of Troubles this
monastery had combined its holiness and its strong fortifications with an unequaled reputation for Russian patriotism.
Here Peter and his party waited, secure in the knowledge that
no Russian army would attack a lawful Russian tsar who
took refuge in the Monastery of the Holy Trinity founded by
St. Sergius himself and hallowed by patriotic tradition. Soon
the army began to come over to Peter's side and Sophia, finding herself deserted in the Kremlin, submitted to her brother.

2. Apprenticeship

The Naryshkins took the place of the Miloslavskis in
the government, and Sophia was put in a convent, but for a
time everything else went on as before. Peter left the government to the elder members of his family and went back to his
games with renewed intensity; the mock battles became more
warlike and the fireworks became more costly and more dangerous.

After his night flight Peter was afflicted with a violent
twitching of the left side of his face which came on him in
moments of passion throughout his life. His limbs were
seized by convulsions, his face twitched, his eyes rolled so
that only the whites could be seen and he rained curses and
blows with fist, stick or sword on all around, collapsing exhausted when his rage had worked itself out. Whether he was
cobbling, raging, sailing, drinking or ruling, he was always
absorbed in what he was doing at the moment; and he was
always doing something, for his nature never let him rest.

Himself a giant, he loved dwarfs with a morbid love of
that kind which generally betokens a hatred of self. His restless energy, his endless, short-lived, loveless amours, his violent compulsive drinking, his hysterical fear of black beetles,
his terrible nightmares and fear of sleeping alone, his urge to
humiliate others, to make them drunk, to make each man eat

what he considered specially disgusting or to make those who were squeamish about anatomy bite through the muscles of a corpse, all this betokened a man at war with himself. But his high purpose of service to his people, his vigorous inquiring mind and his deep love for a few friends showed that he was no ordinary neurotic.

Peter loved to sing in church, he expressed belief in religion and he was unmistakably impressed by the Quakers and their meetings, but blasphemous orgies, parodies of religious rites and blasphemous processions were a part of his life from adolescence to death. There was no hypocrisy in this. All his moods were genuine and, if they were not consistent, that is because his character was not consistent. No man feels constrained to blaspheme unless he half believes, and Peter moved violently between the half-belief of blasphemy and the whole belief of worship; and the first article of his belief was that he was appointed by Providence to lead the Russian people out of darkness into light.

At first Peter's great qualities and his terrible contradictions were not unfolded. At an age when Augustus was already a finished master of statecraft, the young tsar was still playing at soldiers. At last, when he was twenty-two, Peter joined an expedition against the Turks, serving nominally as a bombardier under experienced generals. The aim was to capture Azov at the mouth of the Don and to gain access to the Black Sea, but the objective of the Russians lay at an enormous distance from their base and the expedition was badly planned. So the Russians endured terrible hunger and suffered fearful losses but achieved nothing.

Stung to exertion by this failure, Peter at last took over the government and just at that time Ivan died, leaving Peter sole tsar. Refusing to accept defeat, he planned a new expedition against Azov and this time he meant to have command of the water. Russia had never had a fleet, but Peter set to with fury to build ships on the upper waters of the Don. Ships' carpenters were brought from Archangel and shipbuilders came from abroad, a model galley was ordered from Holland and twenty-six thousand peasants were conscripted for unaccustomed work in the shipyards. Thousands deserted in the winter and those who remained had a foretaste of that compulsory labor under a hard-hearted bureaucracy which both Peter and Stalin used for their great enterprises. Eventually the fleet was built and the capture of Azov gave the Russians their first southern outlet to the sea. Peter began at once to

fortify and populate his conquest by sending unwilling settlers
to work on the fortifications of Azov, where they suffered
great hardships.

Peter ruled now, but he did not at first change his advisers
or the established course of policy. However, he was maturing a daring innovation. Hitherto no tsar had ever left Muscovy, but now Peter decided to go to the West with a "Great
Embassy." Officially the tsar was incognito, but Peter the
Great, who was nearly seven feet tall, could not be hidden,
and in practice he concealed or admitted his identity as it
suited his whims. His rough vigor and coarse habits, and the
spark of genius hidden within a nature that seemed as yet
more eccentric than great, astonished North Germany as the
tsar traveled to his destination at the shipyards in Holland.
Many other results flowed from this famous journey, but the
tsar's original purpose was to satisfy his passionate desire to
learn shipbuilding. In Holland he worked as a laborer in the
dockyards and found that good ships were built by rule of
thumb, but hearing that in England ships were built according to scientific principles embodied in mathematical rules, he
decided to come and work in the yards at Deptford. Here he
lived in John Evelyn's house for three months, working,
drinking and observing; when he left, £350 worth of damage had been done to his landlord's property.

He showed a boundless curiosity about technical matters
and he thoroughly absorbed the mechanical principles of European skill, but he did not penetrate to the philosophy, the
spirit or the traditions of ordered liberty which lay behind.
His observations were shrewd but they lacked ultimate wisdom. On visiting parliament he said: "It is pleasant to hear
how the sons of the fatherland tell the truth plainly to the
king; we must learn that from the English." Peter detested
the servile prostrations which were usual in Muscovy but, like
other Russian rulers, he did not understand that the price of
honest advice is that subjects should be protected from the
anger of their rulers.

Soon after Peter's return to the continent, news came that
the musketeers had revolted, and he hurried home. The rising was suppressed before he arrived, but Peter did not forgive the musketeers for their repeated turbulence, and, sus-
pecting that Sophia was involved, he set about a thorough
investigation. Torture was then the established method of
criminal investigation in most continental countries, and in
Russia torture was conducted according to a ritual of rack,

knout and fire already described. The tsar entered upon this task with his usual zest and attention to detail, and thirty torture fires burned day and night until 1,700 men had been examined. Very little came out of the examination, but over a thousand musketeers were executed publicly in the Red Square by hanging, beheading or breaking on the wheel, in the presence of their screaming wives and children; others were branded and sent into exile, and the corps of musketeers was disbanded. It is not certain whether Peter himself acted as an executioner, but he certainly compelled his courtiers to do so.

Even blood-hardened Muscovy felt deep horror and pity at such severity, but the tsar was not to be deflected. When the patriarch of Moscow went with a picture of the Blessed Virgin to ask for mercy on the musketeers, Peter answered him in a fury, "What wilt thou with thy image or what business of thine is it to come here? Hence forthwith and put that image in the place where it may be venerated. Know that I reverence God and His most holy Mother, more earnestly perhaps than thou dost. It is the duty of my sovereign office, and a duty that I owe to God, to save my people from harm."

To outward view Peter showed no pity or remorse, but debauches, which were wilder than usual, showed that he was fleeing from something within, and the rages and nightmares that grew on him were surely nourished from springs of blood welling up somewhere in the recesses of his memory.

The tsar had long lost interest in his wife and he now compelled her to become a nun, which was the equivalent of a divorce. Alexis, an affectionate child of eight years, was taken from his mother and engulfed in the whirlpool of Peter's life. He came to his father at a time when the house was filled with the shrieks of tortured men and the wailing of their wives and children at the palace gate.

Peter the Great would seem to illustrate Lord Acton's belief that great men are bad men, but behind that grim public figure there lay hidden another Peter, a man who sincerely loved five or six people in his life, a child frightened by nightmares who found the burden of life unbearable unless he could be soothed against the maternal breast of the woman he loved, a man whose simple love for his country was expressed in lifelong ardent service, an unaffected comrade who discovered friendship among all sorts and conditions of men and in many nations.

3. The Social Revolution and the Northern War

In an age when symbols were powerful, the shaven chin and the short coat of the western European were symbols of revolution and Peter decided to enforce their acceptance. Conservatives invoked scripture to justify national tradition, maintaining that since man was made in the image of God, with a beard, therefore to shave was to desecrate the divine image. But Peter shaved his courtiers with his own hands. Some, however, kept their shaved beards on their person so that they could produce them at the resurrection. Likewise, Peter ordered the upper classes to wear the knee-length coat of Queen Anne's day, and anyone who appeared at the gates of a city wearing a long Russian robe was made to kneel while amid good-natured hilarity his coat was cut to the knee.

With the musketeers gone, Peter began to construct a modern army on the foundation of his toy regiments, but the creation of the Russian fleet still held the first place in his strenuous endeavors. If the new fleet was to be a reality, Russians must learn new skills, so Peter sent chosen men from all classes to the West to learn shipbuilding and navigation. Few of them learned much about ships, but they did see foreign lands and that began to bring Russia out of her isolation. Yet a fleet without a seaboard made no sense, and Russia's contact with the technical civilization of the West would be precarious until she had free access to the Baltic.

Here the Swedes barred the way. At this time Sweden ruled the greater part of the Baltic shores, having stepped into the heritage of the Teutonic knights, as well as holding possessions in north Germany. The German language was used equally with Swedish in this mixed empire and it seemed that Swedish power was a permanent feature in the northern scene. The high valor and disciplined virtue of her people made Sweden formidable, her administration was among the best of the age and, so long as she kept control of the sea, the fact that her dominions were spread round three shores might be no disadvantage.

Sweden's neighbors were always ready to dismember her if they got the chance, and in the year 1700 they were tempted by the fact that a boy sat on the throne of the Lion of the North. But that boy was Charles XII, a berserker in the age of reason.

This baleful hero ruined his country, but he has never lost the first place in the affections of his countrymen. A delicate child, he steeled himself by Spartan endurance to become the hardiest soldier of the north. Cold toward women, he fell in love with glory. His wild love for danger joined to a passionate belief in his own destiny and divine authority had a mad intensity, and his vindictiveness to enemies had the blindness of neurosis, but his violent will bore all before it. When his mind was made up, he would brook no opposition and hear no suggestions. Charles's decision and energy in command of the best infantry in Europe gained great victories and won him a reputation for military genius. Yet his erratic judgment and narrow vision often threw away the fruits of victory.

Charles was a match for Peter in his eccentricity. He coursed a hare in the parliament house, he practiced for days on end cutting off sheeps' heads with his sword till the staircase of the palace ran with blood, he threw the bleeding heads out of the window to the great astonishment of passersby, he broke all the benches in the palace chapel so that the congregation had to stand. And in two years he spent the whole of the vast treasure laboriously collected by his father.

Such conduct suggested to envious neighbors that Sweden under her new ruler would be weak. So Poland attacked her, war broke out between Sweden and Denmark, and Peter joined the alliance against Sweden, not knowing that Charles had already brought Denmark to her knees.

Peter's great objective was to break through to the sea. Immediately he laid siege to Narva on the Gulf of Finland, but the first serious encounter showed that the Russian army could not stand against experienced Western troops. Their transport and provisioning were incompetent and the men did not trust their Western officers. So the Russians were completely thrown off their balance when Charles arrived suddenly with a small force of hungry, determined Swedes, at a time when his enemies expected him to be at the other end of the Baltic. The Swedes attacked in a snowstorm, which blew in the faces of the Russians and blinded them. The Russians fled in panic, losing all their artillery, and thousands of men were drowned in the icy Narva river. The play regiments had shown amateur courage, but they had not yet the disciplined skill of professional soldiers. The Russians "ran about like a herd of cattle, one regiment mixed up with the other, so that hardly twenty men could be got into line" (Schuyler, Vol. I, p. 486).

If Charles had followed up his victory Peter would have been lost, but Charles found "no pleasure in fighting the Russians because they do not resist like other people but run away." So, despising Russia, he turned against Poland, where an unbroken succession of victories compelled belief in his destiny.

Peter was never so great as in defeat. Using the respite given to him by Charles, he rebuilt his army with tempestuous energy, melting down church bells to replace the guns lost at Narva. Five months later, with superb confidence in the attainment of his distant goal, he founded a school of mathematics and navigation.

While the main force of the Swedes was elsewhere, Charles kept enough troops in the Baltic provinces to garrison the towns securely but not to protect the countryside. So the renewed Russian army burned villages and reduced the country to a desert, while the Russian generals drove herds of civilians into bitter captivity like any Tartar. Able-bodied men were made to work, and the women were made into camp followers. Among these was a buxom, good-natured peasant girl called Catherine, who acted as washerwoman to the troops, like Mademoiselle from Armentières two centuries later. Catherine took the fancy of Peter's friend Menshikov, who passed her on to the tsar. Peter had little tenderness for himself or for others, but he loved Catherine with a devotion that was not clouded until many years had passed. He married her and made her his empress and, when he died, she inherited his crown. She did not expect bodily faithfulness from her husband, but she was certain of his love and she gave in return a placid support and sympathy which helped Peter to bear the terrible burdens of his soul.

The Russian army soon began to win victories against the Swedish generals, though not against Charles himself. Peter reconquered Russia's ancient but short stretch of seaboard which lay in a barren region of swamp and fog, whose only inhabitants were scattered Finnish settlers. Here alone Muscovy could breathe sea air and here Peter planned to build a new capital amid the waste of waters. Every prudent calculation was against him. The site of St. Petersburg was waterlogged and could not be reclaimed without decades of piledriving, it was subject to floods, it could not be supplied from the surrounding countryside. The climate of the new capital combined northern cold with the damp and fog of London. The capital lay on the very edge of the empire, many days' journey from the centers of trade and population. Moreover, it was an expensive luxury and Russia could not afford luxuries in the midst of a desperate war.

The transfer of the capital was hated by all classes, but Peter meant to have his way. Public buildings were laid out and the nobility were compelled to build houses in St. Petersburg according to the government plan for the town. Myriads of peasants were forced to work on laying foundations of stone and wood. Many thousands added their bones to the slowly rising solid core and the survivors endured miseries like those of Magnitogorsk in construction, but by the end of the reign St. Petersburg already had shape, solidity and a certain elegance.

Four more generations created the "Palmyra of the North" as it is today. The main stream of the Neva flows majestically through the center of the city, while smaller branches make islands and canals whose banks are lined with the stucco houses of the vanished great, built in the simple and grand style of the classical eighteenth century. The exhalations of the marsh are no longer fatal to health, but the watery air still gleams with an ever-changing light in the slanting rays of the northern sun.

St. Petersburg was more than a window on Europe, she was a sort of Europe in Russia, where Western customs and Western ways of thought were grafted onto the Russian stock. To this day a European visitor to Russia is more easily at home in Leningrad than anywhere else in Russia. There is nothing to remind one of Muscovy; yet St. Petersburg is somehow Russian. The slender spire of the Admiralty, which dominates every prospect, is like no Western spire or pinnacle but seems to catch a faint echo from the wooden village churches of north Russia.

St. Petersburg could not rob Moscow of her ancestral importance, and henceforth Russia was oriented upon two poles. Moscow stands for the older traditions, but Petersburg stands for everything European in two centuries of Russian glory. More beautiful than Moscow, she is not so warm. Rus-

sian feelings about St. Petersburg have always been divided,
and opinions have ebbed and flowed. At first a monstrous in-
cubus, St. Petersburg soon became the embodiment of an
enchanting dream of the union of European and Russian civilization. Then, toward the middle of the nineteenth century,
the dream became a nightmare as Russian hopes turned to a
mockery. Then, again, at the beginning of the present century
it seemed to many that St. Petersburg expressed a new, reasonable, beautiful Russia struggling to be born. But great factories growing outside the magic circle of palaces and gar-
dens engulfed the city in a surge of revolution and the city of
Peter became the city of Lenin, a symbol of revolutionary
heroism.

   The spirit of St. Petersburg was expressed by poets and architects, in the Russian ballet and in Russian science, but to
most Russians the new capital was, above all, the home of
Peter the Great's new bureaucracy. Officials ruling from distant St. Petersburg were very far from the needs and feelings
of those whom they ruled. Russia has had her good public
servants, but many were too badly paid or too lazy to act unless they were bribed. At their worst they combined the faults
of the publican with the inhumanity of the Pharisee.

   To build St. Petersburg, to create an army and a fleet and
to fight Charles XII added greatly to the burdens which fell
on the poorest classes. As the war dragged on, the traditional
taxes were augmented with taxes on mills, bridges, ferries,
horse-fairs, beehives, private bath houses, wills, beards and
mustaches etc., etc. A new class of "profiteers" grew up, composed of men who suggested and collected new taxes. The
tsar was prepared to accept any suggestion which seemed
likely to bring in extra money, without much consideration of
how the burden would fall, until experience taught him that
ruined peasants pay no taxes. To all this there was added a
grievous taxation in men called away to the army or to public
works. Recruits for the army were conscripted for the duration of their working life. A quota of men was imposed on
each estate, but the landlord decided at his absolute discretion
whom to send and this great power was often used harshly,
corruptly or as a threat to keep independent men down. The
men left their wives behind and these unfortunate creatures,
lacking the protection of a man, lost all social or economic
status in the village, were universally despised and generally
became village prostitutes. This incredible system of recruit-

ment lasted until 1847 and is often referred to in Russian novels of the classical period.

Driven to desperation by these exactions, many peasants fled across the borders of Muscovy and villages became empty, as they had a hundred years before. In the unsettled border lands there were desperate peasant revolts which had simple but revolutionary aims. "And the bandits said among themselves that their business, said they, is with the landowners . . . and the profiteers and the officials, to hang them." The risings were put down with difficulty and they encouraged Charles to think that a Swedish army in the Ukraine would find local support. Mazeppa, the old and wily *hetman* or governor of the Ukraine, was persuaded to forget a lifetime of support for Muscovy and promised to join Charles if he invaded the Ukraine. Such a plan might have succeeded if it had been efficiently worked out, but Charles made no proper preparation. Moreover, it was already late in the autumn before he began his long march from Poland through unknown territory to the central Ukraine.

The Swedish forces were divided into two contingents, the second of which only got through after a battle in which it lost nearly half its men and all its stores, ammunition and medicine. This encounter was a turning point. Peter wrote: "This victory may be called our first, for we have never had such a one over regular troops. In very truth it was the cause of all the subsequent good fortune of Russia, for it was the first proof of our soldiers and it put heart into our men and was the mother of the battle of Poltava."

Thus Charles found himself in the Ukraine with a reduced army and without the stores and clothing needed for a Russian winter, the winter of 1708 and 1709, which has left a grim memory in the annals of climate. Even in Venice the canals were covered with ice, and in the Ukraine men were frozen by the cold winds and birds fell dead as they flew through the air. The Swedes jested grimly that they had no doctors but Dr. Garlick and Dr. Death.

Mazeppa joined Charles with a handful of Cossacks, but the rest of the Ukraine stayed loyal to Muscovy. The invaders might be the finest troops in the world, but all through the long winter they lost men while Peter collected his resources for a decision. When the armies met at Poltava in June 1709, the Russian force was four times larger than the Swedish force and it was well armed, well fed and trained in modern warfare, while the Swedes were hungry, ragged and short of ammunition. Yet the Russians still lacked confidence before so famous an enemy, while Charles felt for his enemies a boundless contempt that was nourished by the now-distant memories of Narva. At first Swedish courage and cool skill seemed almost to put the issue in doubt, but they could not stay the course and before noon the Russian victory was complete.

Charles with a small band escaped to internment in Turkey, where his outbursts of rage against his host-captors gave us the word "hullabaloo." Sweden was wonderfully loyal to Charles during the years of his internment, but the vigor had gone out of the war.

Peter was now the arbiter of unhappy Poland and the dominator of the North. But he came near to losing all in a war against Turkey in the Balkans, a region which was outside that strategic area in which Russia could now expect to win victories. The position of Peter and his army became almost as desperate as the Swedish position before Poltava, but either the Turks did not understand their chance or their general was bribed. Peter had to give up the hard-won fruits of the Azov campaign, but he and his army were allowed to retreat and soon a great naval victory over the Swedes more than made up for defeat in the south.

After five years in Turkey Charles XII escaped across Europe and showed that he had lost neither vigor nor intransigence, but he did not live long. In *The Vanity of Human Wishes* Dr. Johnson wrote of Charles's exile and death in famous lines:

> The vanquished Hero leaves his broken Bands,
> And shows his Miseries in distant Lands;
> Condemn'd a needy Supplicant to wait,
> While Ladies interpose, and Slaves debate.
> But did not Chance at length his Error mend?
> Did no subverted Empire mark his End?
> Did rival Monarchs give the Fatal Wound?
> Or hostile Millions press him to the Ground?
> His Fall was destined to a barren Strand,
> A petty Fortress and a dubious Hand;
> He left the Name at which the World grew pale,
> To point a Moral or adorn a Tale.

Charles's death cleared the way for peace, and at last, in 1721, after twenty-one years of war, poor, backward Russia had gained all her objectives and there was peace in the north.

The victorious conclusion of the Great Northern War gave Russia the Baltic provinces of Esthonia and Livonia. For the first time Russia ruled over Western peoples who were neither Orthodox nor Slav. The peasants belonged to tribes akin to the Finns or Lithuanians, but the ruling classes were Germans descended from the Teutonic knights and they despised the men and women of alien race who worked their fields. The Baltic Germans were a vigorous branch of the Teutonic family, with all the virtues and vices of their race. Their rule was arrogant and sometimes harsh, but it was not unprincipled. They readily accepted loyalty to the Russian empire, which in return respected their privileges and their Lutheran religion. For two hundred years the Baltic Germans gave public servants to the Russian state and bailiffs to the Russian landowners. The Germans were not loved, and perhaps they did not deserve to be loved, but they did much for Russia.

4. Reform

The creaking machinery of government inherited from Muscovy was not able to meet the endless demands for more men and more money to be squeezed out of suffering peasant families. The war showed that reform was urgent, but it also distracted Peter from internal problems. Nevertheless, in the intervals of campaigning the administration was reformed, at first piecemeal and then with more system. The empire was divided into eight enormous provinces, each under its own governor who was to take decisions on his own. But the central government soon found that under this system control was slipping from its hands, and eventually the eight great provinces were replaced by fifty smaller provinces whose governors had limited powers. Peter set up a sort of cabinet, called the "ruling senate," which was to act as the government of Russia when the tsar was away, to be the supreme court of appeal and, above all, "to collect money, as much as possible, for money is the artery of war." This scheme worked badly and two senators, convicted of gross peculation, were sentenced to be knouted and to have their tongues cut out; but the senate survived in a modified form until 1917. The fantastic tangle of government departments was abolished, new departments were set up, each with a task that was defined in businesslike terms, and at the head of each department was put a committee. The system of rule by "colleges" or committees was introduced in accordance with what was considered the best European model. There was a fashion for committee rule in northern Europe, and Leibnitz wrote to Peter: "There cannot be good administration except with colleges; their mechanism is like that of watches, whose wheels mutually keep each other in movement." Peter took this advice gladly, for the engineering mind is always tempted to think that men are like the parts of a machine, but, in fact, the colleges encouraged laziness and the evasion of responsibility without checking bribery. At the same time local self-government was thrust upon the middle classes of the Russian towns, but the interference of officials of the central government stultified this effort to encourage the growth of a self-reliant, public-spirited middle class.

Peter could not find the right men to work his new institutions. His servants tended to be shirkers of responsibility—lazy, slow and corrupt. He himself was too impetuous to have much administrative sense, and he had no advisers competent to help him with the complex and subtle problems of public administration. His administration was more efficient than what had gone before, but, when one of the main objects of government is to squeeze taxes out of the people, that is a doubtful advantage. Since Russian civil servants have often been corrupt and inefficient, it is fortunate that until the present century they have been few.

The heavy poll tax which was now imposed demanded a census of the population. Death was the penalty for concealment, and the census officers traveled round with a portable gallows which they used freely. The poll tax was paid by all peasants—serf, slave or free. Indeed, no more is heard of these distinctions, for all were now bound to the land by equal chains, and serfdom became more and more like slavery. Each village commune was assessed as a whole and was responsible for the collection of taxes from its members, so that the commune became more powerful over individuals. Soon landlords were made responsible for the tax paid by their tenants, which gave the landlords still more power than before. While Peter lived, this system was justified by the universal service imposed on all classes. Peasants served by paying their taxes, while landlords served in the army and the navy or in the administration. Moreover, seeing the need for trained men, Peter insisted that the gentry should be educated for service to the state. He decreed characteristically that no gentleman should be married until he produced a school-leaving certificate; but such laws cannot be enforced. The civil service was divided into fourteen ranks, and the higher ranks conferred nobility upon the holder. Promotion was to be by merit, and henceforth able men of humble birth could hope to join the upper classes. Peter broke the prestige of birth and substituted for it a snobbery of rank and public office which has survived the Bolshevik revolution.

In this way Peter the Great put before his people an ideal of service to the state, which took the place of the older personal service to a feudal lord, culminating in service to the tsar as supreme head of Muscovite feudalism. Henceforth every Russian was bound from his birth to serve the state in one way or another, but Peter asked nothing from his subjects that he would not do himself. He led three separate lives, each of which would have taken up the energies of an ordinary man. He rose at dawn or earlier to work at his lathe and then, the work of a craftsman finished, he did a busy day's work as ruler of an empire in troubled times. Toward evening he began a life of debauch, carousing with passion, forcing his companions to drink themselves under the table and encouraging their quarrels, so that in drunken rage they might betray their secrets to the listening tsar, who would on occasion moderate his own drinking so that he might be in a position to listen and remember.

Next morning he would be at his lathe again, for neither drink nor care affected his appetite for labor. Physical work soothed his troubled mind and he would show his calluses with pleasure. His mechanical bent led him to understand all that technical skill means to civilization several generations before it had become the fashion to see such things. Peter encouraged industry by word of command, but he did not create the conditions in which industry grows naturally. At the end of his life he wrote in a decree:

"That there are few people wishing to go into business is true, for our people are like children, who never want to learn the alphabet unless they are compelled by their teacher. It seems very hard to them at first but when they have learned they are thankful. So in manufacturing affairs we must not be satisfied with proposals only but we must act and even compel, and help by teaching, by machines, and other aids, and even by compulsion, to become good economists. For instance, where there is fine felt we should compel people to make hats, by not allowing the sale of felt unless a certain number of hats are made."

Merchants compelled to enter syndicates for the manufacture of cloth were glad to make money out of army contracts in accordance with the bad old ways, but they were not interested in the work of their factories. Since craftsmen were few, serfs from the fields were assigned to work in the new factories, but these unwilling hands bound to lifelong labor at work which they detested, under abominable conditions, worked as badly as they dared, remaining constantly on the verge of mutiny.

"The net result of twenty-five years of hectoring impulsion was that Peter bequeathed a large-scale new heavy industry and a greatly developed textile industry, introduced several new branches of manufactures, and wrenched foreign trade round from Archangel to St. Petersburg. Foreign seaborne trade by the end of his reign was quadrupled in value" (Sumner, *Peter the Great,* p. 163).

But those who are in a hurry to develop new industries commonly forget that a flourishing industry depends upon a flourishing agriculture and Peter's "efforts to improve agriculture were intermittent, sporadic and ineffectual" (*ibid.,* p. 161).

Peter's reforms hastened Russia along the road upon which she was already traveling. Before Peter, army reform was on the way, the first beginnings of industry were there and Western influence was already felt in education, in the arts and in ways of life. Paternal monarchy was already turning into bureaucratic despotism, and the loose ties of paternal feudalism were following their fatal evolution into a serfdom which came nearer to slavery with every generation. But Peter accelerated all these changes to the point where evolution becomes revolution or, to use the language of Marxism, the accumulation of quantitative changes turns into a change of quality. This forcing of the pace sharpened the contradictions of Muscovy's inherited policies. Everything else depended upon the creation of a sound economic basis, and at that stage in Russian evolution this demanded above all lighter taxes and freedom to create wealth, but the tsar's imperious demand for quick results entailed exactions which bore down the poor and could only be enforced by a strangling bureaucracy and the enserfment of the peasants.

If Peter forced Russia too much, he did in the main force her in the direction in which she was bound to go. He liberated the minds of educated Russians from the fetters of the Middle Ages. The square type of the modern Russian alphabet replaced the heavy pen strokes of the old Slavonic letters. In the whole of the seventeenth century only 374 books were published and of these only 19 were on secular subjects, but in the twenty-seven years that followed Peter's first journey to the West, 700 books were published on every subject that interests modern man.

Hitherto the language of Russian writing had been a form of Old Slavonic diluted with current speech, but now this dignified language, rich in emotion but limited in vocabulary, began to be replaced by a newly concocted jargon. This was not the pithy speech of the peasants, full of proverbs and untranslatable earthy wisdom, but the language of Peter's court, a Russian compounded with foreign words that were not yet naturalized, a crude jargon but the bringer of a new world. By degrees the habit of education began to take root among the gentry and even among the up-and-coming members of other classes, but the great mass of the people had no part in all this. Indeed, the nobility, by adopting a foreign education and foreign ways, seemed to have marked themselves off as aliens, not belonging to the same race as other Russians.

Very many men from all classes felt a stubborn antagonism to everything that Peter did, and this hostility was often expressed in a religious form. Many simple-minded Orthodox could not bring themselves to accept abrupt change in the Muscovite way of life, which was for them the incarnation in society of the Orthodox religion. These feelings could easily be allied to the bitter resentment of those who suffered from the tsar's policies. So it seemed that after Peter's death conservative churchmen might manage to undo a great part of his work and the danger was centered on the patriarch of Moscow. "Although the patriarchate had existed in Muscovy for not much more than a century, it occupied an exceptional and overtopping position and during that period it had been filled by two outstanding men who made the patriarch the equal or even the superior of the tsar" (*ibid.*, p. 145). When therefore the patriarchal see fell vacant, Peter appointed no successor and eventually he put the patriarchate into commission. The governance of the Russian Church was put into the hands of a newly established "Most Holy Governing Synod," and the effective voice in the synod was the tsar speaking through a lay procurator appointed by the civil power. Peter showed no wish to touch the doctrine or worship of the Church, but he established state control over ecclesiastical appointments, the discipline of the clergy, and all matters where church life touched upon politics.

The Church had supported the development of the absolute autocracy of the tsars in accordance with Byzantine ideas. She taught that the ruler was appointed by God and she expected, in return, rulership inspired by God's laws. Peter accepted the autocracy but his view of the state was purely secular and he valued the Church merely as a means of securing worldly ends. The supremacy of the tsar over the Russian Church, which lasted from 1721 to 1917, was used to make every priest an agent of the state. Original thought about religious questions was stifled in an age when the Church had to face many new problems. And religion was identified with reaction throughout two centuries when every thinking or feeling man must see the need for reform.

5. Father and Son

Peter's enemies waited long for the death of the great man, hoping then to put the engines in reverse, for his reforms would not be secure unless he left an heir of full age who was devoted to the new system. Catherine had given him only delicate boys who were scarcely likely to grow up, therefore the natural heir was Peter's son by his first marriage, who was grown up before his half-brothers were born. Alexis was delicate and easy-going. Inheriting from his paternal grandfather his love of peace and his winning smile, religious in a traditional way, intelligent and sensible when his mind was unfettered by fear, he grew up to be the unhappiest of men. Loyal, loving and lovable, he went from his mother to his father at the grimmest moment of Peter's reign. He had the look of his father, whom he admired but could not imitate. With the deep family feeling of an old-fashioned Russian he could not forget his mother either. Alexis suffered loyalties that could not be reconciled. His father stood for the new and his mother for the old.

As he grew older, the boy was dragged round on campaigns, but he could give his father no effective help. Peter had always neglected Alexis and now he was enraged by his incompetence. Soon neglect was changed to contempt, and contempt ripened into hate.

Half in rage and half in despair Peter wrote to Alexis:

"I am a man, I can die. To whom then shall I leave that which I have, by God's help, planted and increased? To him who is like the idle servant in the gospel, that buried his talent in the ground? I think, besides, what a bad and obstinate character you have. How much have I scolded you for it, and not merely scolded but beaten you for it! How many years have I not spoken with you! Nothing has been of help."

In these terms Peter appealed to his son to reform his ways or he would forfeit the throne and be "cut off like a blasted limb," but Alexis had not got it in him to do what his father wanted and the threats of such a father threw him into a paralysis of terror. His tutors and his father had already taught him to drink; now drink alone offered an escape.

In every monarchy the opposition looks to the heir, and in Russia there were many sources of opposition. The poor hoped for lighter taxes and the injured for the redress of grievances, the religious hoped for a restoration of the old ways, those who were out of favor hoped for renewed smiles, the ruling class hoped to shuffle off the burden of endless service and eternal learning; all hoped for fewer wars and for a less hectic pace, and all looked to Alexis.

"Peter knew well his own unpopularity from the reports of the secret police. It was said, 'If he lives long, he'll make an end of all of us [serfs]. I am astonished that he hasn't been put out of the way before now. He rides about early and late at night, with a few people and alone. He is the dark enemy of the peasants, and if he races about Moscow much longer, he'll lose his head one of these days'" (Sumner, *Peter the Great*, p. 65).

And Peter knew that his enemies put their hopes on Alexis.

It was true that Alexis could not keep pace with his father, but he was not a blind reactionary. His tutor wrote to Leibnitz:

"The prince lacks neither capacity nor quickness of mind. His ambition is moderated by reason, by sound judgment. . . . I notice in him a great inclination to piety, justice, uprightness and purity of morals. He loves mathematics and foreign languages, and shows a great desire to visit foreign countries."

Such a man would not have undone all Peter's work, but it seems that Alexis intended to abandon St. Petersburg, to abolish the fleet and to reduce the army to the minimum needed for defense. To Peter this was treachery, and as time went on the wrath and hatred of the father against his son became more terrible. Lazy and besotted, with no safe friends, Alexis longed for release, but there could be no release without the death of his father. Peter knew all this and the thought that his son might wish his death grew into the fear that he was plotting it. Alexis drank and waited, not knowing what to hope for, paralyzed by fear and by the guilt of wishing his father's death. He renounced his rights to the throne, but no renunciation could be final. So Peter pressed him to become a monk.

Forced at last to a decision, Alexis fled secretly to Austria with his mistress, a serf girl called Afrosinia who was disguised as a page. The embarrassed Austrian emperor tried to hide his puzzling guest in a remote castle, but Peter's spies tracked Alexis down twice and tricked him to return by a mixture of threats, promises and insinuations, and by bribery of his custodians. Alexis was promised an unconditional pardon, but he knew his father and he returned in abject terror, to find that his pardon was in fact conditional upon his revealing all his accomplices. Alexis was ready to confess almost anything if he could only live in peace with his beloved Afrosinia, but there was so little to confess. All his friends were examined under torture. Next to nothing came out, but the net of suspicion grew wider. No one was allowed to leave St. Petersburg, there was a sudden demand for poisons at the apothecaries and their sale was forbidden. "Peter himself, with great coolness, conducted the whole proceedings, was present at the inquisitions and sometimes at the tortures" (Schuyler, Vol. II, p. 426). Many great or humble men and women were punished with the usual cruelty. Nothing came of this beyond vague and general discontent. But the tsar-in-quisitor had one more card—Afrosinia, who escaped torture by turning king's evidence. She searched her memory for every rash word and every word of impatience or resentment that her lover had spoken. This showed once more that the tsarevich had wished for his father's death, as a man must wish for that which assures his own life. But there was no vestige of a plot. Yet Afrosinia's evidence was taken as proof of guilt. Alexis was tortured twice in the usual way and then examined for three hours under torture in the presence of his father and the chief members of the court.

"Alexis was taken back to his cell very weak. In the afternoon his feebleness increased; he sent for his father, asked forgiveness for everything and that the curse upon him might be removed. Amid the tears of all present his father pardoned him and bade him farewell. Subsequently he took the Communion and at six o'clock he expired." (Schuyler, Vol. II, pp. 432-33.)

The next day (July 18, 1718) was the anniversary of the battle of Poltava, and Peter attended the usual festivities as if nothing had happened. At the funeral of Alexis the sermon was on the text: "Oh Absalom, my son, my son!" No one except a few ladies wore mourning, but the tsar is said to have wept bitterly.

Peter the Great was now at the height of his fame. The northern war was drawing to a triumphant close, the reforms were beginning to show results, St. Petersburg was taking shape and, above all, there were at last some young men who understood what the tsar wanted and could serve his schemes with zeal and efficiency. But soon he discovered, what everyone else knew, that his beloved Catherine was working hand in glove with Willem Mons, the brother of Peter's first German mistress. The two were the center of vast corruption and they were probably lovers. Peter could rely on no one for honesty or fidelity. In killing his son he had come near to destroying himself. Now he attacked his body continually with debauch and hard work. He would not make old bones and no one knew how much of his work would outlive him.

He died in terrible pain from strangury on February 8, 1725, leaving no heir of full age and no arrangements for the succession. In his death agony he wrote "Give all to . . ." but his dying fingers could not form the last word.

Peter the Great had built more than it seemed possible for one man to build, but the weight of his building crushed the peasants who formed its foundations. So his inheritance was unsure. And his sins were visited upon his house to the seventh and eighth generation.

His love for his country, for his people and for his friends was sincere and strong, but his passion for mastery could turn his love into hate, whenever the object of his solicitude was not easily molded to his desires. But Russians love him for that courage in living which gave full rein to many diverse urges. They will always think that cold reason tells a half-lie when it judges a great man.

CHAPTER XIII

the eighteenth century

He doth ravish the poor when he getteth him into his net. Psalm x. 9

Peter the Great gave his country a jolt which set the direction for 200 years, but the different parts of society did not move at the same speed. The poorer classes remained embedded in Muscovite ways, while the gentry moved toward the life of western Europe.

At first the manners of the eighteenth-century salon were an affectation among the Russian upper classes, but soon a French veneer became their second nature and by the end of the century most of them spoke French in preference to Russian. Their clothes and houses were European; churches were built in a delightful mixture of the Muscovite and Italian styles.

Nor were these changes confined to externals. Modern Russian literature did not yet exist, and the natural sciences were at first the monopoly of imported foreigners, but science and the art of writing soon struck root among the Russians, though it was some time before they came to fruition. As the years went by, French and German books were increasingly read by the upper classes and more books were printed in Russian, but it is too soon to speak of Russian literature. Eighteenth-century spoken Russian differed little from the spoken Russian of today, but Russian writers had not yet learned how to use their language. The undigested mixture of old and new, native and foreign which was current at Peter's court was good enough for the translation of technical manuals, but not for literature. Upper-class writers soon began to make stilted experiments with European literary forms, but Russian literature before the turn of the eighteenth century was a dreary business.

The turning point was the work of Michael Lomonosov, "the Peter the Great of Russian Literature" (Belinsky, *Literary Reveries*), a man whose great and varied talents exactly

166

met his country's need. Born a free peasant in the province of Archangel, which was too far north for the serf-owning gentry to impose their dominion, he ran away from home to learn at the schools founded by Peter. He went on to Germany in order to learn more and returned home an accomplished chemist with a burning interest in all learning. Lomonosov died in 1765, having placed Russian science upon a secure foundation and having given its form to the modern Russian language. In Lomonosov's literary revolution, borrowings from Old Slavonic and the West were not expelled but digested and set in a vigorous modern syntax, through which all the resources of spoken Russian became immediately available. Lomonosov had created an instrument. At first there was no one to use it, but in less than a century Russian had taken its place with the great literatures of the world.

As the progress of culture made the upper class more European, it made them at the same time more remote from the common people. The gentry began to look upon the peasants as savages, and the peasants became sure that their masters understood nothing that was worth understanding. Even language was a barrier, for the Frenchified speech of the upper classes was hard for the peasants to understand, perhaps even harder than the old-fashioned, earthy Slavonic of the Church. Moreover, many landlords were absentees who might not even know their own peasants by sight and left the management of their lands to bailiffs whose chief concern was to feather their own nests. Since the bailiffs had no interest in the land, Muscovy's pitiful, medieval methods of cultivation remained unchanged. The bailiffs knew that no questions would be asked so long as roubles were sent on demand to their masters in St. Petersburg or Moscow; Russian absentee landlords did not know enough about country life to intervene effectively in village affairs.

In England at this time the great improving landlords were carrying out the agricultural revolution which made possible the industrial revolution. In England the natural selfishness of landlords was often mitigated by intimate knowledge of their tenants, while in Russia landlord and serf were becoming foreigners to each other. In England the enjoyment of country life has never involved the renunciation of civilized amenities. But in Russia a landowner of modest means who lived on his estate might have to travel many miles for educated society. In his own village his neighbors would all be peasants and new books would be hard to get. In these circumstances it was easy to fall back into a Muscovite idleness and squalor which would make Squire Western seem a model of enlightenment. The absentees were those landlords who could not face the rigors and boredom of Russian country life. Toward the end of the nineteenth century a balanced country society was beginning to grow, but the revolution swept all this away before it had time to become established.

After the defeat of Sweden, Russia's circumstances no longer provided any justification for serfdom—if, indeed, such a thing can ever be justified—but it was precisely at this time that the long enserfment of the Russian peasants reached its climax. At the end of the eighteenth century Russian serfs could be bought and sold apart from the land which they worked, their masters could marry them off as they wished, they could flog them savagely and have them sent to hard labor in Siberia. In the course of many generations free peasants in debt to richer neighbors had become serfs and serfs had become slaves. Hitherto it might have been argued that the state could not exist without the labor of serfs, which set their masters free to serve as soldiers or administrators. But Russia's neighbors—Sweden, Poland and Turkey—were all now past their zenith and Russia had become too formidable for any but a great power to attack. In these easier days the gentry soon found that in practice they could evade their service, and in 1762 Peter III freed the Russian gentry forever from their obligation to serve the state. After this it seemed just to the peasants that they in turn should be freed from the *corvée*. But this did not happen, the fetters of serfdom became still tighter than before, and Peter III was murdered. Many of the peasants concluded therefore that the tsar had, in fact, freed the serfs, but that the nobles had suppressed the decree of liberation and murdered the tsar to conceal the truth.

The tyrannical system of society was consistent from top to bottom. The sovereign ruled with powers that were only limited by his own insecurity, landowners ruled their estates with powers that were hardly less and in the villages "big families" of three generations living together were ruled by tyrannical grandfathers. Work, marriage, the upbringing of children and social relations were all subject to family discipline. Among the peasants, grown-up sons might have to submit without complaint even if the head of the household shared his bed with his daughters-in-law.

The life of the Russian peasants at this time may well seem intolerable. Indeed, it was not tolerated, and endless smaller riots and revolts culminated in the great peasant rebellion under Pugachev, which Pushkin has described with genius and fidelity in *The Captain's Daughter*. But there was one great mitigation: there was still enough land. After all, there was a limit to what the landlords and their hangers-on could eat, the only market for a surplus was the towns and they were small. So the residue stayed in the countryside and unless the crops failed there was enough food to go round.

Manufacture grew slowly, for there were very few free laborers from whom a class of artisans could be recruited. If, for instance, the state needed an arms factory, there seemed to be nothing for it but to assign serfs as workmen. If they had to leave their villages and land for a distant factory in the Urals, where they were little better than slaves, that could not be helped. This system seemed inevitable at the time, but it worked as badly as might have been expected. The owners of factories began to find that their workmen did better work if they were given or could buy their freedom. At the same time an example of thrifty independence was given by Germans from the Baltic Provinces, by Jews from the newly acquired Polish provinces and by foreign settlers in the new southern provinces which were opened up after the conquest of the Crimea by Catherine the Great (cf. p. 104).

Throughout the eighteenth century the succession to the throne was in doubt, and a sovereign whose right is questioned cannot act against powerful vested interests such as the serf-owning gentry. These found in Peter the Great's regiments of guards a perfect means to make their will prevail. All ranks were recruited from the gentry and the presence of guards' regiments in the capital made their views decisive. During the supremacy of the guards, serfdom was turned into slavery. But after the year 1800 the balance of power turned against the guards and at last the status of the serfs began to improve.

Catherine the Great fills the end of the eighteenth century as Peter fills the beginning. Lacking Peter's genius and strength, she yet approached Russia more thoughtfully than he.

Clever, coarse-grained and a good sort, Catherine was the daughter of one of those small north German princes whose best hope of worldly advancement lay in the marriage of their daughters. Entering with zest into the profession of a royal adventuress, she married the future tsar, Peter III, and embraced her new country with her whole heart. Her husband was unattractive and feeble-minded. His rule being considered intolerable, he was soon put out of the way and his German wife was declared empress. From 1762 to 1796 Catherine presided over the Russian empire, combining splendor and intellectual pretensions with horse sense. Being full-blooded and a widow, she took a succession of lovers and, being coarse-grained, she flaunted them in public, but many women whose lives have been equally profligate have passed through life with far less scandal.

She imported into Russia the ideas of the French Enlightenment, but she did not see—indeed, no one saw—how little the theories of France fitted the facts of Russia. Nor did she see, until the French Revolution opened her eyes, that the theories of Voltaire and Rousseau were dangerous to herself and that revolutionaries could be as intolerant as autocrats. In youth and in middle age she began to modernize the structure of the Russian state and encouraged bold speculations in philosophy and politics. But owing her position to a palace revolution she could not risk offending the serf-owning class. Indeed, she increased the number of serfs by giving state lands with their population to her friends and favorites.

Even so, she did more than Peter for the transformation of Russia in the next century. She abolished tax farming, export duties, and monopolies, decreeing that except in the two capitals, anyone could start a factory. She built and repaired roads and bridges. Henceforth, the Russian economy became dynamic. She laid sensible foundations for national education and public health, courageously overcoming her fears and setting a public example by having herself vaccinated by Dr. Thomas Dimsdale, an English Quaker brought to Russia for that purpose. But she remained untouched by the deeper currents of Russian life, not unlike some of those British servants of India who left home to give themselves to a strange land. They served with all their might, loved those they served, and, like Catherine, spoke their language almost perfectly, while yet remaining aliens.

In the eighteenth century the Russian educated classes learned much of a new way of life. What they learned made them conscious of their own backwardness, but it did not sap their self-reliance. The immense tasks which lay before Russia did not seem beyond her immense strength, but before the end of the century a forerunner of the next age, Radishchev,

had described the hard lot of the Russian peasant in words
that came home to his own generation. He wrote characteristically: "My soul is borne down by the weight of human
suffering." Here was a new type, the "conscience-stricken nobleman," a man who felt human solidarity too keenly to be
able to acquiesce in ease purchased by the suffering of others,
a writer who felt that his duty to society came before his
duty to his art.

Peter the Great had muzzled the Church but he could not
destroy the prophetic spirit. The ills of Russian society cried
to heaven and, in default of the Church, Russian writers
came to express the conscience of the nation. Therefore
"Russian nineteenth-century literature as a whole became to
the ordinary educated Russian a substitute for the Church"
(Victor S. Frank in the *Dublin Review,* Autumn 1960).
Hence the intense concern of nearly all Russian writers for
the state of society, and hence the Russian impatience with
art for art's sake. The social responsibilities of Russian writers were not without danger: "Throughout the last hundred
and fifty years or so there has not been one really great Russian writer who, at one time or another, for one reason or
another has not come into conflict with the authorities, first
Tsarist, then Communist" (*ibid.*). Tolstoy was excommuni-
cated by the Church. Dostoyevsky was sentenced to death,
reprieved when he was already before the firing squad and
then sent to hard labor in Siberia. "And after the Revolution
—Blok, dying of a broken heart; Gumilev, shot as a monarchist conspirator; his widow Akhmatova howled down by
Zhdanov; Mayakovsky and Tsvetayeva" and Esenin "commit-
ting suicide. The list, which could easily be extended, now
ends with Pasternak" (*ibid.*). The tradition by which writers
are unavoidably involved in social and political responsibility
helps to explain why the Soviet Government insists that all
writers must actively support the regime, and why writers
who resist this are crushed with a thorough violence that
shows by contrast how amateur the tsarist repression was. In
spite of this, Boris Pasternak, Alexander Solzhenitsyn and a
few others have shown that even under Stalin a Russian
writer's conscience remained his own.

foundations of the nineteenth century

The world's great age begins anew,
The golden years return.

Shelley, HELLAS

Russia was now a great European power with a part to play in the wars and upheavals which flowed from the French Revolution. So the personal character of her rulers was an important matter in European politics.

In 1796 Catherine the Great was succeeded by her son Paul, the "mad tsar," a coarse and cruel man embittered by the long usurpation of his mother and deprived of all practical experience of affairs by her jealousy and suspicion. As soon as he came to the throne, Paul put the army into clothes of unbearable discomfort, and exacted cruel punishments for the slightest breach of his odiously minute regulations. He treated society as he treated the army. In 1801 he was murdered, his son Alexander I was declared tsar, and Russia began to breathe easily once more. But all Paul's sons were martinets like their father, and two of them were to be tsars.

There have been two or three moments in Russian history when it seemed that a new age was beginning in which every wrong would be righted and Russia would go forward to a future of incredible happiness. Such a moment was the accession of Alexander I. The new tsar was known to be full of generous intentions, and it was supposed that the pains which Catherine had taken with his education had fitted him to be a great progressive monarch. But alas! Alexander turned out to be one of the first victims of a "progressive" education. His grandmother confided the young Alexander's political education to a high-minded Swiss republican who filled his mind with abstract ideas of liberty and equality, and fed his imagination on the lives of the heroes of freedom as told by Plu-

172

tarch and Livy. Russian history and Russian reality were brushed to one side. He was not taught to concentrate or to think anything through to the end, and he learned too little of the means by which his heroes translated their ideals into achievement. So Alexander learned to talk but not to think and still less to act. Finally, when he was sixteen, he was married off to a German princess and with that all study ceased.

Succeeding to the throne at the age of twenty-four, he called together an idealistic group of friends with whom he began to plan a new age. All right-minded people at this moment assumed that Russia would now move toward a constitutional government, and the tsar himself seemed to agree with this, but in his heart, if one may judge from his later actions, he was only ready to do good to his people on condition that they took their good from him. For the moment, however, all was concord.

The only question was where to begin. Serfdom made Russia backward, and that very backwardness made it difficult to bring in liberal reforms. A land where most of the people were illiterate serfs and where there was no educated middle class would not have been able to work a constitution. The only way out was more education, and the new government set to work with a will to organize higher education. Grandiose plans for village schools were drawn up, but they took second priority and little came of them. How, indeed, could the poorer classes learn until there was someone to teach them? The first thing was to educate the middle and upper classes, and by now many of them were hungry for higher education. So for a few years university life flourished in Russia as never before, and the spirit of free inquiry pushed deep roots.

Western Europe was now entering on the industrial revolution. By comparison, Russian commerce and manufacture grew slowly but, even so, Russia was visibly outgrowing her serf economy. Every year there were more free workmen in the factories, and many poor men worked their way to ease and even to affluence. A serfowner would put one of his serfs to ply a trade in the town on condition that he paid so much in place of seignorial dues. These men remained liable for their share of the village taxes and the uncertain exaction of their lords lay like a shifting yoke upon their necks. But their status became more like that of free craftsmen, and if they earned enough they could generally buy their freedom from their masters. Or, again, a serfowner needing a new house or family portraits would train one of his serfs to be an architect or a painter. Or he might run a private theater and make some of his serfs into actors and actresses. Some of these educated peasants made good in their professions and earned their freedom. Thus in many ways a new middle class and a new class of artisans were recruited. They were not many in relation to Russia's needs, but they were enough to start the dissolution of the old society.

Alexander looked with nebulous benevolence upon projects for freeing the serfs, but practical measures designed to make radical changes in society always touched the position of the tsar, and at that point he drew back. He did not like to see his vague liberal principles worked out in practical measures entailing the consequences of harsh reality, and soon war provided a reason for putting off reforms.

The twists and turns of Alexander's policy toward Napoleon gave Russia some relief from continual war, but led in the end to the French invasion of Russia in 1812. In that memorable year the Russian people showed their greatness, and Alexander, putting aside every vacillation, behaved as a worthy leader. Several months before the French attack the Austrian ambassador wrote to Metternich:

"The emperor has little confidence in the talents of his generals . . . he puts his trust in the courage of his troops, their discipline and their passive obedience, but even more so in the obstacles which in his dominions are offered by the terrain, wooded, swampy, unimproved and sparsely populated. His majesty greatly relies on the difficulty of supplies and the rigor of the climate. The emperor also depends on public spirit, the sacrifices which are promised to him in the name of the nation, and the justice of his cause which he considers sacred."

In all this the emperor saw more clearly than many who have cut a better figure in history.

Moscow was burned, countless humble families were ruined and the vast tracts of country laid waste in the track of the contending armies did not recover for many years, but the Russians won a complete victory and two years later Alexander and his soldiers were in Paris.

This was the first time that large numbers of Russians had been in any of the great centers of Western civilization. They brought home new customs and manners which made them seem more different than ever from the merchants and serfs who still thought the thoughts of Muscovy. Moreover, many of them were infected by a ferment of new ideas and new impressions which made Russian intellectual life after 1812 far more lively than it had been before.

About the same time a momentous change took place in the tsar himself. As a young man brought up in the skeptical traditions of the eighteenth century, Alexander showed no religious inclinations until about 1812 when he came under strong mystical influences. Having no grounding either in the Bible or in the classics of Christian thought, he was not always able to distinguish wheat from chaff and was sometimes taken in by religious charlatans. But there can be no doubt of the zeal with which he began to read the Bible. In December 1812, while the ashes of Moscow were scarcely cold, a Russian Bible Society was formed and the emperor soon enrolled himself among its members. The new society, which worked in close cooperation with the British and Foreign Bible Society, spread copies of the scriptures energetically throughout the empire, and the habit of Bible reading was established in thousands of homes. Bible reading nourished the growth of free-church tendencies among many who were dissatisfied with the established Church and in this way contributed to the growth of the Protestant sects (cf. Chap. XI *ad fin.*). But even more important than this, it brought very many loyal members of the Orthodox Church to look for the foundations of their faith and their way of life in the Bible. The work of the Russian Bible Society ceased with the Bolshevik Revolution, but its results will long be seen.

At the end of his reign Alexander seemed to go back upon the generous aspirations of his youth. Liberty of thought was drastically curtailed and the tsar turned to heavy-handed methods of enforcing his will. For this purpose the only instrument ready to his hand was the Russian bureaucracy, which now took on its classical nineteenth-century form. Less ignorant than before, it was more than ever paperbound and curtained off from reality by its complicated departmental procedure. Elaborate precautions did not prevent corruption, but they made decisions slow. The Russian civil service was composed of human people, but their remoteness from the scene of action and their fear of their superiors often made them do inhuman things; and there was little chance of redress from the consequences of red tape or bureaucratic caprice, for to criticize the tsar's servants was considered tantamount to attacking the tsar himself.

Russian bureaucracy could be very cruel. This was not generally the result of deliberate purpose, but rather of incompetence and corruption. Every summer, droves of convicts were marched to Siberia in chains and very large numbers died on the way through gross failure of logistics. Overcrowding at reception points and in the barges on which part of the journey was made resulted in insanitary conditions and killing diseases became endemic. On arrival some prisoners were allowed to live in comparative freedom and comfort, others were confined to a living death in the mines and prisons of the far north and far east. Local officials grew fat on the meager stores intended for the prisoners. From time to time local officials suggested improvements, but nothing could be done without permission from St. Petersburg where the simplest proposal could get lost for twenty years or more in the files of the Circumlocution Office. The Soviet systems of prison and exile inherited all the vices and much of the slang of their tsarist predecessors. Stalin's work camps were equally inefficient in caring for the welfare of their denizens but more effective in bending people to the will of the authorities.

There was a hidden touch of Tsar Paul in Alexander I, and toward the end of his life this came out in his establishment of "military colonies" of peasants. It was hoped by this means to provide for the recruitment and support of the army, but the experiment worked badly, being spoiled by the pedantry and cruelty with which it was carried out by Arakcheev, the tsar's friend and minister. In 1825 Alexander I died, having disappointed both himself and all who had believed in him.

The reign of Alexander I is full of deluded hopes and chances missed, but for all that it is great in achievement. Russia was now one of the great powers. In intellectual studies the country was forging ahead. Already Lobachevski, whose name, if not his achievement, has been made familiar by a song of Tom Lehrer's, had formulated non-Euclidean mathematics, which made possible the discoveries of Einstein a century later. And Russian literature had suddenly risen to its full stature.

Pushkin, the first great Russian writer and the greatest of them all, was at the height of his powers. He was the first to use to the full all the riches of the Russian language, yet his earliest poetical works seem to have absorbed all the inheritance of Europe. He was a poet of the Romantic age, but he is always very close to reality. Without comparison Russia's greatest poet, he wrote the best of all Russian prose, concise, clear and somehow inspired. In one mood or another he seems to understand almost everything, but his genius was still unfolding when he was killed in a duel at the age of thirty-seven. In his last years he turned more and more to the history of his own country, and bade fair to become the greatest of Russia's historians if he had lived a little longer. It is often said that Pushkin holds in embryo everything that was to be unfolded in later Russian literature, but if Pushkin stands for what was to come, most of his compatriots still looked to the past. Some of their aspirations are better expressed in the medieval figure of St. Seraphim.

Seraphim was forty-seven years a monk before he began at the age of sixty-six the work of spiritual counsel that made him famous. For more than thirty years he had led the life of a hermit, and for the last fifteen years he had not spoken a single word. During this time he learned how to live in the unseen world of good and evil spirits and held intercourse with its inhabitants. He emerged from this long training gifted with the power to read men's minds and hearts. Sometimes he knew in advance who would come to see him and what their problems were. For himself he practiced an extreme asceticism, but he was cautious in advising rigor for others. His biographer relates that

". . . he always commanded, not only that one should eat one's fill, but even that one should take some bread along when going to work. 'Put a piece into your pocket; when you are tired and faint, do not be depressed. Eat some bread, and on to work again.' Even for the night he ordered that some bread should be put under one's pillow. 'If despondency and perturbing thoughts beset you, get your bread out and eat; your depression will leave you, bread will drive it away and will give you, Mother, a good sleep."

He held that the greatest spiritual danger was accidia, that deadly despondency and dull despair which besets monks and hermits, and he advised a cheerful sociability as a remedy.

Once he had healed a serfowner of a terrible illness and bade him sell his land, liberate his serfs and buy a small plot to live on. The man did as he was told and became a devoted follower of the saint. Another man came with pious tears, but before the man reached his cell, St. Seraphim said to the novice who was bringing the visitor, "This man is an impostor," and so he confessed himself to be. Once a barefoot pilgrim wearing chains came to see him; St. Seraphim told him to give up his way of life and return to his wife and family who were missing him. "The man was moreover to go into the grain business. 'This business is very good,' Father Seraphim added. 'I know a grain merchant in Yelets. Go to him and tell him that poor Seraphim sent you. He will hire you as a clerk.' " On the way out the pilgrim said that he had always been in the grain trade, but without due reflection and advice he had left his family to become a perpetual pilgrim.

St. Seraphim had a gift of direct access to divine things and he brought some of his friends to share his visions of heaven, visions which were accompanied by a brightness and fragrance that were beyond anything on earth. Dressing as a peasant rather than as a monk, he taught that the hermit's communion with another world was not peculiar to the solitary life but ought to be shared by all Christians. He came out of solitude in the year of Alexander I's death and died in 1833, having shed his influence abroad throughout Russia for eight years.

St. Seraphim seems to have stepped out of an earlier age, but in one respect his life pointed to the future. He was the first of those *startsy* or "elders," men like Father Zosima in *The Brothers Karamazov*, who came to have such a great influence in Russian life. These elders were simple monks. They held no office of authority in the Church, but their known holiness and wisdom attracted many who felt the need for spiritual counsel or support. It was by no means unusual for a peasant to walk from the other end of Siberia in order to seek help from a renowned *starets*. But their influence extended to all classes, and carriages of varying degree of comfort or discomfort were found outside their cells.

CHAPTER XV

shades of the prison house

The abuse of greatness is when it disjoins Remorse from power.

JULIUS CAESAR, Act II, Scene 1

1. The Decembrists and Nicholas I

Thinking Russians were beginning to see that something was seriously wrong with their country, but they could not see clearly what should be done, and insofar as they had specific reforms to propose, they did not always agree with each other. Moreover, the lower and middle ranks of society seemed to form an inert mass, though events were already ripening which would eventually bring them into active political life. For the present, leadership must come from the gentry, and the leadership of the gentry still lay with the officers of the guards.

The Emperor Alexander I had no children. By the law of primogeniture he should have been succeeded by his brother Constantine, but Constantine had renounced the throne. This renunciation had been embodied in a secret rescript naming the next brother Nicholas as heir, but the vacillating Alexander had not published this when he died suddenly in November 1825. Nicholas was now the legal heir, but no one knew it, and he had made himself unpopular with the guards' officers by his despotic spirit and by the narrow-minded pedantry shown when he had held a military command. The cast of his mind was German rather than Russian, and he touched no chord of sympathy in the hearts of his people. Nicholas I was called "Nikolai Palkin" or "Ramrod Nick" on account of his unbending severity and his ready recourse to birch and rod. But he was not a bad man in the ordinary sense of the word. Indeed, his lifelong severity was based on strict obedience to the promptings of a narrow conscience.

Nicholas could not take the throne safely without either

179

the active support of the guards' officers or the public renunciation of his brother Constantine. The latter confirmed privately that he had already renounced his right to the throne,
but refused to make a public statement or to come to St. Petersburg. In this strange crisis there was a fortnight's interreg-
num which seemed to the more liberal elements among the
guards' officers to give a chance to extort a constitution, a
chance which might not come again. Having brought over to
their side a regiment of the guards and some smaller units,
they embarked on a badly staged demonstration in front of
the Winter Palace. Most of the men had only a hazy idea what
they were about. Some of them, so it was said, thought that
"Constitutsiya" was the wife of the Grand Duke Constantine.
The demonstration was quelled without much difficulty, but
the governor of St. Petersburg was killed and the youngest
brother of the tsar was shot at. Such was the celebrated "Decembrist" revolt, the work of bungling amateurs, but an event
whose echoes have not yet died away.

Nicholas was now tsar, but it had been a narrow shave and
he determined to get to the bottom of the conspiracy. Several
hundred people were arrested, and the tsar himself directed
their examination, not with torture as in the days of Peter,
but with the milder methods of the nineteenth century. The
prisoners included many of the leaders of the intellectual
world, and they answered questions about their aims openly
and sincerely. Nicholas was horrified to discover the extent to
which radical views had spread. But for all that, he ordered a
summary to be made of the constructive proposals of the De-
cembrists. Some of the conspirators seemed to him the offspring of hell, but for the others he felt marked sympathy. He
treated all with even handed severity, but he helped the families of those for whom he felt sympathy. In the end, five ring-
leaders were executed and large numbers were exiled.

The arrival of so many intelligent and public-spirited men
stimulated the development of Siberia but, on the other hand,
the removal of so many brilliant men at one swoop lowered
the whole tone of St. Petersburg society. After this time the
Russian upper classes began to feel themselves prisoners of a
system which they could not alter but for which they remained responsible. Thereafter conscience-stricken despair
and futility gained a hold on the Russian gentry which was
never lost, until the Russian gentry were blotted out by the
Bolshevik Revolution.

Nicholas believed sincerely that Russia needed autocracy

for her preservation, but he had been taught that the tsar's advisers should be outspoken. He said to the French ambassador: "I distinguished and shall always distinguish those who want just reforms and wish these to come from the lawful power from those who want to undertake them themselves and God knows by what means." Russian revolutions generally come from above, and such words might have meant much in the mouth of a worthy successor of Peter the Great. But Nicholas I was one of those resolute, narrow-minded men from whom Russia suffers so much. Moreover, his advisers were such as a man of his type might be expected to gather round him, and his only tool for government was the Russian bureaucracy.

The educated classes were no longer content to remain passive spectators of public affairs, but their views were severely repressed by the censor and the political police. In practice the emperor did not welcome advice from his subjects any more than the man at the wheel likes advice from the passengers. "The tsar is a father, his subjects are his children, and children ought never to reason about their parents, or we shall have a France, a rotten pagan France," said the assistant chief of police. Under Nicholas, education was designed to inculcate obedience and religion; in his mind the two were closely connected and in consequence many of his subjects began to think that religion consisted in obedience to a bad order of society. Textbooks of philosophy could be printed, but the censorship regulations laid down that other books on philosophy "being full of fruitless and pernicious theorizing of the present age ought not to be printed at all." But, of course, this did not prevent philosophy from being read. This was near to the golden age of German philosophy, and thinking Russians turned from the French teachers of the Enlightenment to the bold speculations of the Hegelians, which they found to their taste. Neither French logic nor the empirical common-sense wisdom of the English have ever had a deep hold on Russians. The passionate metaphysics of the Germans speaks a language nearer to their hearts. But if they could appreciate the greatness of German thought, they were also easy victims to its faults, to the turgid emotions and to the ambiguities, both casual and studied, which sometimes spoil it.

Under Nicholas the press was allowed to explain the government policy, but that was all. The press regulations even forbade the publication of any proposal for the improvement of the public service. It was feared, not without reason, that such proposals would become the vehicle for concealed criticism. These restrictions were enforced by a cumbrous machine of censorship which would have prevented any political comment of interest being published if some of the censors had not been as stupid as they were strict.

The frustration caused by red tape was doubled by the caprice of officials. Uncertainty was and is one of the great evils of Russian government, but there are times when even uncertainty has advantages. In Russia more than anywhere the rigorous intentions of governments are turned aside by the unpredictable behavior of those who carry them out. The censorship inside Russia might be all-pervading, but Hertzen's famous journal, *The Bell*, published in London and forbidden in Russia, was known everywhere. A copy of each issue arrived punctually, by an unknown means, on the tsar's desk and was read carefully and with respect. Once when some courtiers were implicated in guilt by an article in *The Bell*, they had a false copy printed for the tsar. Hertzen discovered it and had a true copy placed before the tsar. Even administrative caprice was useful insofar as it made it possible for liberal or humane officials to give an elastic interpretation to their instructions.

Nicholas was a typical child of the age of reaction. He was drastic in his treatment of symptoms, but he could not see the causes of the break-up of the old society which he deplored. A century later it is easy to see that the Western world was now in the full surge of the industrial revolution, and that Russia could not stay untouched. Manufacture grew slowly because serf labor was slack and because it was still hard for serfs to rise to independence and found their own small businesses. But as the years went by, more factory owners were finding that it paid them better to employ free labor, and more landlords were finding that many peasants could pay their dues better if they were encouraged to ply a trade and migrate to the town.

In the villages, for the most part things went on in the bad old ways. The tyranny of some landlords was slightly limited by the gradual extension of more regular government, but most Russian landlords were not tyrants. Laziness and caprice were their worst faults, and the nineteenth century brought no cure for these vices.

By now, the population had grown to a point where there was a shortage of land in some provinces. In such regions the peasant plots were divided and redivided, so that with every generation it became harder for the peasants to gain a decent living. There was rich land and to spare in other parts of Russia, and many landlords would have been glad to let some of their surplus labor go. It would have suited them to exchange their hordes of unwilling serfs for a compact force of paid laborers whom they could take on or sack at will. But that would have involved the end of serfdom and the end of the village commune, the two chief bulwarks of society as it was. The tsar would not contemplate that.

The scene was set for change, and society was indeed changing, but not so fast as ways of thought and manner of life were changing among educated people. Therefore it seemed to impatient minds that Russia was going backward.

2. Intelligentsia and Slavophiles

The old rigid stratification of classes was breaking up and there began to appear men who belonged to no estate known to Muscovite tradition. Sons of priests learned the language of unbelief and were lost to the Church; serfs who had learned to be actors, architects, portrait painters or composers in the service of their masters were lost to the peasantry; sons of landless gentry lost their position in prosperous society but kept their aspirations for education. These groups did not join the society of the traditional trading class, the merchants, for these still for the most part lived upon Muscovite traditions, neglecting education beyond the rudiments and eschewing the world of ideas. Since no existing class was ready to receive them, the new elements coalesced into a new social group which was soon called the intelligentsia. Having no fixed place in the order of things, these men and women tended to reject Russian traditional values, but the manner of their rejection was very Russian.

The hero of *The Brothers Karamazov* embodies the all or nothing of the Russian intelligentsia:

"When he began to think seriously, scarcely had he been struck with the conviction that God and immortality exist when immediately and naturally he said to himself: 'I want to live for immortality and I accept no compromise.' Just the same, if he had decided that there was no God or immortality, he would have joined the atheists and socialists at once (for socialism is not only the workers' question . . . but chiefly the question of atheism, the question of the contemporary incarnation of atheism, the question of a Tower of Babel, which is built without God, precisely because it is not to reach heaven from earth but to bring the heavens down to earth)."

Generally poor and always insecure, with no abiding place in the Muscovite framework of Russian society, the intelligentsia rejected the autocracy and the old way of life which went with it. Rejecting the autocracy they rejected the Church which tyranny had made into an ally, but they could not leave behind their Orthodox longing for an all-embracing faith, nor the deep feeling for fellowship which the Russian Church had roused but not satisfied. That which they put in the place of Muscovite tradition and religion they embraced with the dogmatic fervor of their Muscovite upbringing. Emptying their hearts and minds of all Muscovite content, they filled them again with the ideas of Western emancipation, but they turned the hypotheses of Western intellectuals into the dogmas of the Russian intelligentsia. This was not because the Russians are a dogmatic people by nature—they are not—but the Russian context of thought subtly transformed every new theory that came from the West. In Germany and France, educated people were accustomed to new ideas. The latest theory was analyzed and compared with many other competing ideas, and it might not be taken very seriously. But in Russia there was little competition among ideas. Each new theory was like a ray of light in the kingdom of darkness. It must be embraced with fervor or rejected decisively. Above all, it must be taken with deadly seriousness.

Every type of mind was to be found among the new intelligentsia. But it is broadly true that

"The intellectuals from the nobility had a certain urbanity, a certain belief in good manners that the *raznochintsy* * lacked. The former were aware with their minds of the poverty and

* The *raznochintsy* were those who belonged to none of the traditional estates. In this context the word means the radical intelligentsia.

suffering of the Russian masses; the latter had lived in the midst of it, were not only aware of it but felt it. There is a venom and fanaticism in the language of the *raznochintsy* which are not found in their gentlemen predecessors, and which became and have remained an essential part of the Russian revolutionary tradition. This intolerant and savage attitude to the world is to some extent responsible for the growing indifference of the new intellectual generation to merely political reforms, for its insistence that it is more important to increase the material welfare of the people than to give Russia constitutional liberties. It was Belinski, the first of the radical *raznochintsy,* who said, 'The people have a need for potatoes but not the least for a constitution' " (Seton-Watson, pp. 58-59).

But this savagery of expression was closely related to a passionate feeling for human solidarity. Belinski expressed the feeling of many warm-hearted radicals in words that have become famous.

"What care I for the existence of the universal when individuality is suffering? What care I if genius on earth lives in heaven when the crowd is wallowing in the dirt? What care I . . . if the world of ideas is open to me in art, religion, and history when I cannot share it with all those who should be my brothers in mankind, my neighbors in Christ, but who are strangers and enemies to me in their ignorance? . . . Away then delight, if it is given to me alone out of a thousand . . . Grief, poignant grief, overcomes me at the sight of the barefooted little boys playing in the street, of the tattered beggars, of the drunken cab-driver, of the soldier returning from sentinel duty, of the official hurrying along with a portfolio under his arm, of the complacent officer, and of the haughty grandee. I all but cry when I give the soldier a farthing, I run from the beggar to whom I have given a farthing as though I have committed an evil deed." (Letter to V. P. Botkin written on Sept. 8, 1841. Earlier in the same letter Belinski expressed the same attitude in a more philosophical form: "Reality springs from a soil, and the soil of all reality is society.")

Extremity of reaction had encouraged the extremes of revolutionary thought, and it seemed that there was no place for moderation. Trotsky saw this with his usual penetration and his views are ably summarized by his biographer:

"The Russian intelligentsia were compelled to defend their most elementary rights by the most extreme and wasteful means. 'It became their historical calling . . . to use watches for knocking nails into walls.' A Russian had to become a Darwinist in order to justify his decision to marry according to his choice; he had to invoke revolutionary ideas to excuse his craving for education; and he had to have recourse to socialism when all he wanted was a constitution" (Isaac Deutscher, *The Prophet Armed,* p. 189).

Ardor to read, to understand, now became widespread and was nourished by thick periodicals whose editors developed great skill in outwitting the censors, and whose articles helped to rouse and to form public opinion. In all this the intelligentsia took the lead, but since they were shut out from all effective share in public affairs, their thoughts were often unreal and sometimes fantastic. De Tocqueville, speaking of the educated classes in France before the revolution, uses words which apply equally to the nineteenth-century Russian intelligentsia and, indeed, to the thinking part of the gentry:

"Dans l'éloignement presque infini où ils vivaient de la pratique, aucune expérience ne venait tempérer les ardeurs de leur naturel; rien ne les avertissait des obstacles que les faits existants pouvaient apporter aux réformes même les plus désirables; ils n'avaient nulle idée des périls qui accompagnent toujours les révolutions les plus nécessaires. Ils ne les pressentaient même point; car l'absence complète de toute liberté politique faisait que le monde des affaires ne leur était pas seulement mal connu mais invisible."

("They lived at an almost infinite distance from practical life, so they had no practical experience to temper the ardor of their natural disposition; nothing warned them of the obstacles which the facts of existence could put in the way of even the most desirable reforms; they had no idea of the perils which always accompany the most necessary revolutions. They did not even have any foreboding of them; for the complete absence of all political liberty made the world of affairs not only badly known but invisible to them." [*L'Ancien Régime,* p. 195. Ed. J. P. Mayer.])

The Russians are the most loyal and patriotic people in Europe, even more patriotic than the British, but under Nicholas even the conservative classes began to feel themselves increasingly alienated both from official Russia and from the great mass of the Russian people. With every decade their life became more European and less founded on Russian custom. But if the landowners were far from the peasants, the intelligentsia were still farther. Breaking with every Russian tradition, they moved in a world of ideas that were completely inaccessible to most of their countrymen.

Shocked by this rift in the Russian community, a tiny handful of thoughtful, religious, country gentlemen began to think more deeply about the Russian and Orthodox tradition which their hearts opposed both to the soulless bureaucracy and to the rootless intelligentsia. They believed that Russia had taken a wrong turning under Peter the Great and that her salvation lay in a return to what they took to be the Muscovite traditions. The Slavophiles, as they were called, were no ordinary reactionaries, and their views on the freeing of the serfs were sufficiently liberal to be frowned on by authority. The Slavophiles wrote much nonsense and their idolization of Russia sometimes went to extreme lengths. One of them, Danilevski, wrote that "even an ordinary rebellion going beyond the limits of a regrettable misunderstanding has become impossible in Russia, so long as the moral character of the Russian people does not change." Even the best of them were unable to give a realistic answer to the social, economic or political problems of their beloved Russia. Yet they stirred men's minds and hearts almost as much as the Westerners did. (For Slavophiles and Westerners, see also Chap. VII, pp. 98–99.)

Confronted with the challenge of Western ideas, they began to give expression to the philosophy of the Orthodox Church in terms which the contemporary world could understand, a task which was several centuries overdue. The West owes a debt to those Russian laymen who have opened for us the door to Eastern Christianity. In politics they are forgotten, but in religious life they became the source of a stream whose fertilizing influence is only now beginning to be felt.

Both Slavophiles and Westerners simplified too much. To most of the Westerners, Russia was a country without a past, a blank sheet of paper on which to write the word Europe. Bring European progress to backward Russia and all would be well. To the Slavophiles, Russia was a Messianic country and the West was decadent. The future belonged to Russia and her present troubles were chiefly due to Western contamination. The Westerners were sometimes too easily impressed by Europe, whereas the Slavophiles were sometimes moved by a senseless animosity against the West; but the best of them saw how much Russia had to learn. One of the wisest Slavophiles, Alexis Khomyakov, said, "learn but at the same time do not forget." He believed that the greatest treasure possessed by the Russian people was the wisdom bequeathed by their ancestors. Russia was a living community, the result of a continuous organic growth, whereas most of the Western countries were artificial creations, or so he believed. England alone among Western nations had an organic life of her own. England was Russia's natural rival, but a rival from whom much was to be learned. He was repelled by what seemed to him the formalism of the British constitution, but he warmed to men such as Wilberforce, the Duke of Wellington and Charles Metcalfe, the Anglo-Indian statesman. He believed that in such men religion and statesmanship went hand in hand and patriotism was married to a practical love of all humanity. For Khomyakov the British jury with its rule of unanimity represented the creative, organic side of British life, but parliament with its rule by majorities stood for deadening formalism. He quoted with approval Disraeli's "English manners save England from English laws." He thought that Russian moral principles were higher but that the English with their organic view of life as a whole lived up to their principles better.

The reign of Nicholas I is remembered for floggings, exiles, red tape and censorship, but it is equally memorable for the awakening of the Russian conscience to the perils and evils of serfdom, for the first wonders of the Russian novel, the rise of the intelligentsia, the beginnings of Russian music, the beginnings of Russian political thinking and of modern Russian theology. It seemed to some of the finest natures that Nicholas I had turned Russia into a prison. But what a prison!

CHAPTER XVI

the beginning
of modern Russia

С трудом великим здание я строю,
Тот светлый храм, ту мощную державу,
Ту новую, разумную ту Русь.

(*With great labor I build that shining temple, that
mighty power, that new, reasonable Russia.*)

A. K. Tolstoy, TSAR THEODORE, Act V
(Boris Godunov is speaking)

1. Liberation of the Serfs

The Crimean War brought the Russia of Nicholas I
up against reality with a bump. The policy of Nicholas had
sought justification from the needs of strength, but the test of
war showed that Russia could not defend her own territory.
Her soldiers were as stoical as ever, but tsarist transport and
commissariat could not supply them with the arms and ammunition needed against a modern enemy, and the Russian
economy could not stand the strain of war. Russian soldiers
armed with the flintlocks of the Napoleonic wars stood
against French and British soldiers with rifles. Officers who
had served their time under the narrow discipline of Ramrod
Nick could maneuver their troops smartly on the parade
ground, but that was all. On the field of battle the Russians
would move in dense columns with disciplined 'courage, pre-
senting an easy target to their enemies, but neither officers
nor men could master the open-order tactics needed against
modern firepower. At sea well-trained Russian crews in sailing ships met the steam battleships of England and France.
Russian industry turned out bad gunpowder and too few
arms. There were only three railways in the whole country.
None of these led to the Crimea, and all supplies had to be

brought over cart tracks which had scarcely changed since the Varangians.

Failure broke the heart of Nicholas I and he died. Failure broke his policy too, and his son Alexander II succeeded to the throne amid universal hope that the new reign would bring a new deal. Alexander II would have preferred to maintain his father's system unchanged, but he saw the needs of the new situation and he made it clear that he would make changes. For a short time all his subjects wished him well. Steady, old-fashioned, loyal Russians, liberals who lived for their "idea" and passionate revolutionaries all agreed that first of all the problem of serfdom must be tackled. By now everyone but a few archconservatives was against serfdom—humane people on humane grounds, progressive people on progressive grounds, economists on grounds of political economy, administrators for practical reasons. Even the serfowners wanted a change, since the families of the peasants had now increased on the better land to a point where landowners were burdened with a host of unwilling, inefficient workers whom they could neither usefully employ nor get rid of.

They reasoned that if the peasants were to be freed from all feudal obligations by a stroke of the pen and, if that was all, the land would still belong by law to the landowners. In that case, the peasants could only live by working their land on such terms as the landowners might give them. The landowners would take the pick of the labor market, competition for employment would keep wages down, and the landlords would be freed from all liability to keep alive those for whom they had no work.

But the tsar and his best advisers shrank from a step which under the disguise of liberation would have reduced millions to a poverty and dependence worse than serfdom; and a large section of the landowners was farsighted enough to understand that nothing would be secure unless the peasants were firmly established on their own land. It was decided therefore that the serfs should be freed with some land. But how much land were they to have? By law all the land cultivated by serfs belonged to their seigneur, but by custom and by peasant notions of right and wrong that part of the estate which the serfs cultivated for their own use belonged to them. "We are yours but the land is ours," they would say to their lords.

For four years the great debate fluctuated between timidity and realism, avarice and idealism, between self-interest enlightened by a grasp of the dangers of doing too little, and self-interest darkened by fear of change. In the end it was decided that the serfs were to be freed from their masters and that they were to have most but not all of the land which they were already working for themselves.

When the great day of liberation came, most of the peasants were glad to be freed from formal bondage to their masters, but they remained bound to the *mir* or village commune. (See Chap. VII *ad fin.*). They could not leave the village without a passport from the village elders, they remained liable for their share of the village taxes, and they must cultivate their land as the village meeting decided. The tsars carefully preserved the *mir* because it was felt that the social and administrative solidarity of the village made for political stability. They feared above all things the creation of a rootless proletariat.

The Russian village commune might have been as stable as the tsar and the gentry wished it to be, if it had been self-sufficing. But it was not. The law now recognized what custom had always sanctioned, that the peasants owned some land of their own, but in return for this they were compelled to pay compensation for what they had always considered to be their own. All pasture and woodland belonged to the landlords and even parts of the arable land hitherto cultivated by peasants were "cut off" for the benefit of the landlords. Balanced or efficient farming was not possible on the land left to the peasants. Impartial judges have held that the compensation payments imposed on the peasants were often more than the value of the land. It is certain that the burden proved to be crushing and that a large proportion of the payments could never be collected. Without enough land of their own to live on, the peasants had to work for a part of the year on the land of their former master for what wages he would pay, or to rent land from him at the price he chose to exact. Thus, the peasants remained dependent on the landowners in spite of the liberation. Were they better or worse off in the generation after the liberation than they had been before? It was hotly disputed. Socialists said worse, others said better, but the very fact of the dispute shows that improvement was not so marked as to be incontestable. In any case, it is not for Anglo-Saxons to throw stones. Russia made better provision for the needs of freed serfs than Britain or America made for liberated slaves.

The peasants thought that they had been cheated by the landlords. When shown the texts of the liberation decrees they would listen politely to the explanation, but at the end they would say, "We are ignorant people; we know nothing. What we say is that what the tsar orders, that is what must be done. You show us a book and tell us that it is the will of the tsar. But how should we know? We are ignorant and as for what is written in this book we know nothing." So they obeyed the decree, as they needs must, but in their hearts and minds they rebelled.

Material reasons for discontent were fed by reasons of pride. The memory of servile status was kept alive by laws dividing the peasants from the rest of society. Not only must they have passports to leave their village, but they were subject to their own village courts with power to flog them cruelly, not for breaches of the general law of the land, but in accordance with a customary law whose provisions were uncertain. The late Sir Paul Vinogradoff said that these village courts administered "a kind of shifting equity tempered by corruption." In all their dealings with authority, the peasants were liable to hectoring and caprice which it was wiser to accept without grumbling. The gallingly superior attitude which the rest of society adopted toward the peasants has survived the Bolshevik Revolution. Soviet snobbery pronounces the word *kolkhoznik,* or collective farmer, with that tone of contempt which earlier generations gave to the word *moujik.*

During the sixties and seventies silent resentment was slowly piled up, but the rebellious spirit of the peasants still looked to the tsar for redress. Had he not shown how in one day he could alter all the relations of property and society, and could he not again change all for the benefit of his faithful peasants? They looked back to a time before the landlords were in the land when woods and pasture had been free to all and plowland had belonged to him who worked it. The revolutionaries, who now began to abound, did everything to stimulate these memories.

The hope or belief that sooner or later the tsar would supplement the liberation of the serfs with "real freedom" often went with an intention of the peasants to help themselves, as soon as they had the chance, to what they conceived to be their rights, in a "black division" of the landlord's lands. This phantom hope hovered continually in the mind's eye of millions of Russians for nearly sixty years.

In the days of serfdom there had been rich villages and poor villages, according to the quality of the soil, the pressure of population, the conduct of the landlord, the industry of the peasants and the nearness of markets. But all who lived in the same village had lived roughly on the same level. Now with greater freedom to acquire property, some began to rise and others to fall. At one end of the scale a race of independent farmers began to rise out of the ruck, and at the other end a class of laborers without land fell into unrelieved poverty. It is tempting to think of the independent farmers as English yeomen or smallholders and the landless peasants as English agricultural laborers. But the comparison would be misleading. In the continually developing economy of Britain or America men without work in the countryside have generally been able to move elsewhere, but in Russia with her poor economy and vast distances, a man without land might have nothing to live on but seasonal work at certain times of year and charity at other times. At his best the Russian independent farmer was a true yeoman, but he had fought his way to the front in a hard school, and such a man soon became known as a *kulak,* which is the Russian word for "fist," or as an "eater of the *mir.*" A man and his family had to work hard to rise, and an illness, a fire or some other calamity could destroy the results of years of sober work. But once a man had taken the first hard steps to independence, his easiest way to wealth was to exploit the need of his least fortunate neighbors by lending money at usury, by hiring out his horses or implements at cruel rates to those who had none, or by getting others to work for him at the wages just above starvation level which the conditions of the market enabled him to impose.

2. Reform and Revolution

Before the reign of Alexander II, Russian law was administered by ignorant and dishonest clerks. Everything was done by writing, a case might drag on for years, the parties might never see the judge or each other, the decision would be communicated in writing. Moreover, involved and inaccessible laws made justice uncertain and often gave a bribed judge plausible grounds for any decision that he was paid to give. Alexander II set up for the first time courts with properly qualified judges, where cases were argued in public. At first the dearth of lawyers gave many opportunities to sharks, but soon qualified lawyers began to appear, well skilled in their profession. At the same time trial by jury was introduced and thereby law was brought nearer to the ordinary man's sense of justice. But it often happens that countries which introduce the English jury system fail to see that juries bring their great benefits to justice only so long as they are confined to the assessment of facts. In the Russian courts the juries found themselves involved in all those many intangible matters which concern judges giving sentence, rulers exercising their prerogative of mercy and prison officers watching over the execution of sentences, but do not help to establish the facts of innocence or guilt. The decisions of Russian juries were often capricious and in political cases every trial became a public debate on the political motives of the accused and on social justice in general. So it is hardly surprising that political trials were soon withdrawn from the ordinary courts. Moreover, the judges were often under severe pressure from the bureaucracy. Nonetheless, Russian law had henceforth some able and devoted servants, and its administration became much better.

After the reforms a subordinate official who committed a gross injustice, such as flogging peasants to enforce payment of taxes, was sometimes punished. Respect for law was slowly growing in the last decades of tsarism, but in Russia the sense of law has never been strong enough either to prevent the government breaking its own laws when it suited it, or to secure a respect for the letter of the law by the public. At no time has Russian law been altogether worthy of respect; only a few Russians have seen that the remedy is not to break bad laws but to make better laws. The French chronicler of nineteenth-century Russia writes:

"We have often had to observe the fact that there is a greater gap in Russia than elsewhere between law and custom, between what is officially permitted and everyday practice" (Leroy-Beaulieu, Vol. II, p. 419).

De Tocqueville describes the way in which the French an-

cien régime educated the makers of the French Revolution to lawlessness.

"Le pauvre était déjà beaucoup mieux garanti qu'on ne l'imagine contre les atteintes d'un citoyen plus riche ou plus puissant que lui; mais avait-il affaire à l'Etat, il ne trouvait plus . . . que des tribunaux exceptionnels, des juges prévenus, une procédure rapide ou illusoire, un arrêt exécutoire par provision et sans appel. . . . C'est ainsi qu'un gouvernement doux et bien assis enseignait chaque jour au peuple le code d'instruction criminelle le mieux approprié aux temps de révolution et le plus commode à la tyrannie. Il en tenait école toujours ouverte. L'ancien régime donna jusqu'au bout aux basses classes cette éducation dangereuse."

("The poor man was already much better protected than one supposes against the attacks of a citizen richer or more powerful than he; but if he had to do with the state . . . he found nothing but special courts, judges with preconceptions of the case, a rapid or illusory procedure and decisions that were expressly mandatory and without appeal. . . . It was thus that a mild and well-established government taught the people every day a code of criminal procedure that was the most appropriate to revolutionary times and the most convenient for tyranny. The government kept its school always open. Right to the end the *ancien régime* gave this dangerous education to the lower classes." [*L'Ancien Régime,* pp. 234-35, Ed. J. P. Mayer.])

In Russia the same bad lesson was taught by the same means, but the effect was sharper, for nineteenth-century Russia was less mild and more arbitrary than eighteenth-century France.

3. Disappointment

For a few years at the beginning of Alexander II's reign, the spirit of reform affected every part of public life. The censorship was relaxed, and elected local government authorities were set up. The constitution of these last was conservative, but peasant interests had some representation and for the first time local men could work effectively for the public good of their locality. Leroy-Beaulieu observes that the Russians, being opposite to the Victorian English in this respect, are disposed to expect everything from the initiative of public bodies. For instance, private enterprise had failed to provide insurance against the terrible fires which continually prevented millions of peasants from keeping their heads above water; the local councils stepped in with compulsory fire insurance. Writing in 1882 of the vast extension of this principle which was already discussed, Leroy-Beaulieu observes:

"Though such proposals have as yet small chance of success, Russia is by her custom and traditions, by her communal and social organization, one of the countries which are most exposed to the dangerous experiments of state socialism."

From the 1860s on, much public spirit of various kinds was enlisted in the service of local government. Much was done for education, public health and the well-being of the countryside, and more would have been done if the tsar's bureaucracy had not been suspicious of every initiative. Under the tsars local self-government never had a chance to come to full growth, but enough was done to show that Russians can run their own affairs with sense and enterprise if they are allowed to do so.

As modern life began to bring new ways of getting rich, a new kind of trader arose. The old type of merchant was a survival from Muscovy—ignorant, inefficient and easy-going. But now the medieval homes of these men began to be invaded by education, Paris fashions and the arts, and their ranks were swollen by restless energetic peasants who had made good after the liberation. Individualists and often very rich, these practical self-made men break in on the most futile scenes of Chekhov with their breezy common sense.

The modern Russian middle class did not have time to set their seal upon the pattern of Russian society and it is customary to write them off as a futile by-product of history. But this is too hasty. A middle class of the kind that the West has known since the end of the Middle Ages did not exist in Russia before about 1860, when such things as banks and limited companies began to be known. But the growth of middle-class society between the liberation of the serfs and the Bolshevik Revolution was fast and vigorous. The Russian middle class had all the active spirit of the West. Were they not Russia's response to the impact of "Western" conditions? The futility of the "conscience-stricken noblemen" was alien to them, for they had done no wrong to society—their class was too young for that—and they did not immediately conceive a frustrated ambition to rule Russia. But they produced men who knew how to make money, lawyers, doctors and intellectuals, a few first-rate scientists, some farsighted patrons of the arts and a few great artists and writers such as Chekhov and Blok. It is from them more than from the gentry that Soviet Russia inherited the capital of intellectuals and technicians which helped to carry her over the first generation of revolution.

Russia entered upon the 1860s with high hopes, hopes that were not unreasonable. If the supreme ruler had used his power unswervingly to press reforms for twenty years without haste or rest, the lasting foundations of a modern state could have been laid.

The difficulties, though great, were not insuperable. But the tsar was torn between incompatible aims. He wanted to do his duty as the ruler of a modern state, but yet the sacred autocracy received from his fathers must not be impaired. So new things could only be done if they did not seem to damage the traditional structure of Holy Russia, the repository of the Orthodox Christian faith. The government was at heart doubtful of its own position, and therefore it could not be consistent even in heavy-handedness. For instance, the censorship of newspapers was arbitrary and severe, but the papers were permitted to print full reports of a prosecution in which the censor appeared in a most ludicrous light, being woken up in the middle of the night by an irate editor (see Leroy-Beaulieu, Vol. II, p. 473).

The official censorship nourished the solidarity of the radical intelligentsia who read eagerly anything to their liking which escaped the censor's net, and cold-shouldered all that they did not like so effectively that they have been described as an unofficial censorship. Authors who pleased neither radicals nor die-hards found it hard to get a hearing. Political writings were eagerly read. Those that had no political content often fell flat.

So in a few years the reign that had started with such promise had settled down to sullen discontent. Both peasants and intelligentsia were discontented with the reforms, but their opposition had flowed in separate channels. The peasants had solid grounds for their discontent, but they were inarticulate. The revolutionary intelligentsia were filled with a generous indignation at the wrongs of the peasants and they were articulate, but they were as far removed from the peasants as was the bureaucracy. Since Peter the Great, the gap in comprehension between classes has always been greater in Russia than in England. The English landlord living on his country estate for most of the year, if not for all of it, has generally known how to talk the language of his tenants and laborers even when his relations with them have been bad. Victorian social reformers settling in the East End of London found barriers of misunderstanding between themselves and those whom they wished to benefit, but these barriers are not to be compared with the gulf of blank incomprehension and deep suspicion between the peasants and their well-meaning landlord which is described by Tolstoy in *Anna Karenina*. In the seventies many ardent young men and women decided to "go to the people"—that is, to go among the peasants, to live with them, to rouse them to a sense of their wrongs and to show them the way to better things through revolution. But the ground was not prepared, the peasants did not understand what these eccentric creatures were driving at, they were suspicious of them and sometimes even handed them over to the police as disturbers of the peace.

The failure of these first halting steps of the Russian revolutionaries made the intelligentsia see that they must think again, and it helped to turn their thoughts toward Marxism. But the "going to the people" had alarmed the government, which accordingly strengthened its police measures. Some of the revolutionaries felt that terror was the only answer to reaction, so they began to assassinate high officials who had incurred their special displeasure. The government answered with still more severe repression and began to think that against such an enemy as the revolutionaries every method of struggle was legitimate. Police spies multiplied and penetrated the terrorist organizations. The revolutionaries on their side felt that every method of struggle against tsarism was legitimate. Noble ends were distorted by Machiavellian means, and the whole level of political life in Russia was lowered. It has not yet recovered.

In 1881 the terrorists brought off their greatest coup. The "liberator tsar" was murdered by a bomb. Those who organized the assassination thought that the removal of the man whom they considered their archenemy would smooth the path for revolution, but they had made no plans to profit by the murder. So all that happened was that the comparatively liberal Alexander II was succeeded by the reactionary Alexander III.

It has been said that in tsarist Russia tyranny was tempered by assassination, but this macabre paradox contains more falsehood than truth, for assassination commonly strengthens just those fears which make rulers into tyrants. The tyranny of the Russian tsars was indeed tempered, not by assassination but by the laziness and the incompetence of its agents, by the humanity of many officials, by the infiltration into government posts of those who sympathized with reformers and even with revolutionaries, and by the lack of self-assurance which often prevented the tsars and their servants from pushing their policies through to the end.

CHAPTER XVII

the first age
of industrialism

*То над степью пустой загорелась
Мне Америки новой звезда.*

(*The star of a new America has caught fire over
the empty steppe.*) Alexander Blok, THE NEW
AMERICA

Behind the new tsar, strong, narrow, honest, "the last effective symbol of the Russian autocracy," there stood his former tutor, Constantine Pobedonostsev, soon to be procurator of the Holy Synod, and for twenty-five years the most powerful man in Russia. Gaunt, tight-lipped, high-principled and not inhuman, Pobedonostsev despaired of humanity. He saw clearly the forces of chaos growing among the younger generation, and he believed that nothing could restrain the evil propensities of man except the strongest government. He had studied English law and he wanted to see a rule that should be honest, intelligent and efficient as well as firm, but he knew that many of the agents of the government were not honest, not intelligent, not efficient. Then let them at least be firm. That was the only hope.

Absolute autocracy must not be impaired by legal guarantees of the rights of the tsar's subjects, by the calling of a consultative assembly which might insist on its right to give unpalatable advice, or even by the office of a prime minister who might stand between the tsar and his other servants. The unlimited power of the tsar conferred upon his servants powers which were limited only by the superior powers of the tsar. As in earlier days, so now; the despotic principle went right through the official conception of society. The old village commune was maintained as a source of discipline for the peasants, and the heads of patriarchal households continued to rule both the communes and their own families with rods of iron. In private life Pobedonostsev was a kindly man, but to the public he seemed the grand inquisitor of the Russian empire, the incarnation of all that was narrow and heartless and oppressive in the last decades of tsarism.

Whatever tsar and procurator might determine, the ferment of the nineteenth century was breaking up the old structure of Russian life, and inexorably the changes made in 1862 brought forth their delayed fruit. The government and the Slavophiles might wish to keep the village commune unchanged, but increasingly often workers were given passports by their village to enable them to work in the town. In the eye of the tax gatherer they remained members of the commune, but in fact their links with their village were weakened with time. In the villages the heads of patriarchal families began to lose ground. Education was spreading, and grownup married sons conceived the ambition to set up on their own.

The grievous burdens of rent and taxation kept most villages poor, but within this general poverty differences of degree became more marked. There were more *kulaks,* and more ways for *kulaks* to increase their often modest wealth. The misfortunes of primitive life, illness of man or beast, fire and drought put more unfortunates at the mercy of the *kulaks,* who would lend the means to rescue a man from his immediate plight but extort unconscionable terms in return. These "eaters of the *mir*" had "the hard unflinching cruelty of a thoroughly uneducated man who has made his way from poverty to wealth and has come to consider money-making, by whatever means, as the only pursuit to which a rational being should devote himself" (Stepniak, *The Russian Peasantry,* p. 55).

The financial structure of Russia increased the burden of the poorer peasants automatically, for

"the payment of foreign loans and the maintenance of the currency depended on a favorable balance of trade, and this was secured above all by great grain exports. The grain available for export was the property of the big landowners, and to a much lesser extent of the richer peasants (*kulaks*). It was produced by the labor of the landless peasants and dwarf holders, who received low wages in cash or in kind or in both. If the land had belonged not to the big landlords but to these peasant laborers, they would have eaten more, and less would have been available for exports" (Seton-Watson, *The Decline of Imperial Russia*, pp. 122-23).

There was no social insurance to take the edge off individual misfortunes, but village solidarity took its place to some extent. If anyone lacked bread, others would give him help until his harvest came in, and the receiver could give in his turn to others. "As long as a moujik has one loaf of bread left in the house his wife will give morsels" of bread to others. If

". . . you were to ask the peasants whether they assist the poor, they would certainly answer, 'Oh, dear me, no!' . . . But if you observe more closely, you . . . discover . . . a vast system of cooperative assistance given to the aged, the orphaned and the sick; . . . only the peasants do not look upon this as charity. . . . The old man whose corn the whole *mir* turns out to carry on a Sunday afternoon, receives only what is his due as a *mir's* laborer and taxpayer of several score of years' standing. The orphan receives but a benefit on account of labors to come" (Stepniak, *The Russian Peasantry*, pp. 290-91).

A man who is in need

". . . enters the house as if by accident and on no particular business beyond warming himself a little; and the mistress of the house, so as not to offend his modesty, will give him 'the morsel' incidentally and 'unawares.' . . . The moujik is very delicate in the management of such matters, because he knows that some day he, too, may perhaps have to seek morsels" (*ibid.*).

That was the best side of Russian village life, a side that is often forgotten. No reader of Russian novels is likely to forget that there was another side. If many orphans were brought up by loving foster parents, many others were left to starve or beg.

The people were increasing and already in many places the land carried more mouths than it could feed. In such districts misery and the hunger for land increased with every decade. There was good land lying untilled in Siberia and in "New Russia"—that is to say, in the region between the Ukraine and the Crimea—but peasants could not leave their commune to open up new land without the permission of the *mir*.

At first the government, anxious to keep things as they were, discouraged emigration inside Russia, but when repeated flights of peasants from their villages made it clear that movement could not be prevented, the government decided to encourage it. From the 1890s large numbers of peasants left to open up the black soil districts of southern Siberia, magnificent land where there had never been serf or master. Here a man worked for himself, and a free society with many American virtues began to grow up within the walls of tsarism. The Siberian peasants were vigorous, hardy and alert beyond the average, and their houses were cleaner and more spacious. A new life was created from the elements provided by nature with the help of the simplest instruments. James Mavor, the Canadian historian of Russia, describes how he

". . . lived for a short time with a group of Russian peasants who had just migrated to a new neighborhood. They took with them practically nothing but some flour, some leather, some iron bars and their tools for carpentry and blacksmithing. Immediately upon their arrival on the site they had chosen, they searched for clay, found it, made bricks, sun-dried them and built two sets of ovens. In one set the women made the bread for the group, in the other the men burned wood for charcoal. Within two days after their arrival they had six blacksmiths' forges going by means of the charcoal, and bellows which they made out of the leather. Within another two days they had made several dozen spades and a wagon, whose wheels were rimmed with iron forged by them on the spot. During the same time they had made shoes for their horses. During the four days some of them had been engaged in building houses, and within a few more days these were completed. Yet not one of these peasants could either read or write."

Overpopulation in the villages needed more than one outlet. So large numbers of Ukrainian peasants went to the USA and Canada to settle on the land, where they found a climate and soil not very different from what they had known. The Ukrainians of North America have prospered and form coherent groups which are loyal to their new home while remembering many Russian traditions and keeping the Orthodox religion.

Others, as has been said above, went to the towns to earn their tax money and, if possible, a little extra for themselves. Some of these left their villages for good, whereas others went to the town while work on the land was slack, returning every year for the harvest. While they were working in the town such men and women lived and slept where they could, often lying down at night beside the loom where they worked all day.

The labor of this new proletariat nourished the quick growth of capitalist industry, and in the later years of the nineteenth century Russia entered on an industrial revolution. At first industry was heavily concentrated in certain regions such as the Donbas in the Ukraine and in certain large factories, of which the Putilov works at St. Petersburg is the most famous. Large areas remained unaffected, but the fact remains that the transformation of Russia into an industrial country was on the way long before 1917, and the factory workers of the eighties and nineties provided fresh soil for the revolutionary movement. Trade unions were forbidden. That did not prevent them from existing, but it did prevent the development of an efficient trade union organization. So it fell to the revolutionary intellectuals to give the working class such leadership as they could. At first strikes were sporadic and not particularly effective, but the revolutionaries learned as much from their failures as from their successes.

The revolutionaries were coming of age. In the eighties there began to be Russian Marxists, and in the nineties there were organized Marxist groups, but it was not until the opening years of the present century that Marxist political parties were organized. Marxism appealed only to a section of the intelligentsia but where the appeal was felt it was powerful. Marxism proposed systematic action in place of endless talk and sporadic action. Moreover, there is in Marxism a kind of structural correspondence with Christianity which made people brought up in the Church feel oddly at home. In Marxism the Saviour becomes the Proletariat, the Church becomes the Party and the universal triumph of Communism takes the place of the Second Coming. In Soviet times the press has sometimes written "in almost overtly religious language of the first fruits of the classless society ('the age to come') already enjoyed in the USSR." (*The Ecumenical Review*, Oct. 1952, p. 90.) The Russian form of Christianity creates an intense longing for fellowship. The Russian form of Marxism, which has now been re-exported to other countries, tried to satisfy this longing. Where Communism is alive, it draws its life from the revolutionary fellowship. It is the tragedy of Russian Communism that this fellowship has gone dead. In saying this I make no judgment, one way or the other, about what is happening to the Communist Party in China or in any country other than Russia.

The Marxists looked to the new proletariat of the towns as the mainspring of revolution, but Marxism did not altogether displace the older stream of revolutionary thought which in a peasant land looked to the peasantry. Those who thought on these lines were known as Socialist Revolutionaries or S.R.s. The greater part of the poor and the oppressed were countrymen, and their aspirations were voiced by the S.R.s rather than by the Marxist parties, until the victorious Bolsheviks suppressed all rivals. The first Marxists had a hard task to establish the idea that revolutionaries should turn their backs on the peasants at least for a time.

For a long time Russian history has seemed to be dominated by the majestic figure of Lenin. To many, even of those who abhor his teaching, it seems that Lenin alone foresaw the inevitable end. To them it seems that Lenin is at the center of everything that gives meaning to his generation, sometimes guiding, sometimes just placing himself with perfect understanding in the center of the main stream. This view has a somber magnificence and it is not wholly untrue, but neither is it the whole truth.

Lenin's aims were universal, but his philosophy was limited and the use which he made of that philosophy was even more limited. Within the limits which he had set himself Lenin had a marvelous mastery of his material, but it has been shrewdly observed by Berdyaev, himself once a Marxist, that Lenin was not so much a theoretician of Marxism in the accepted sense of the phrase as—

"a theoretician of revolution; everything he wrote was but a treatment of the theory and practice of revolution. . . . Hence his narrowness of outlook, his concentration upon one thing, the poverty and asceticism of his thought, the elementary nature of the slogans addressed to the will. Lenin . . . read a great deal and studied much, but for a definite purpose, for conflict and action and for controversial purposes, in order to settle accounts with heresies and deviations. . . . He fought for wholeness and consistency in the conflict, which was impossible without an integrated dogmatic out-

look, without a dogmatic confession of faith, without orthodoxy. He permitted any method in the fight to achieve revolution. Lenin's revolutionary principles had a moral source;
he could not endure injustice, oppression and exploitation,
but he became so obsessed with the maximalist revolutionary
idea, that in the end he lost the immediate sense of the difference between good and evil; he lost the direct relationship to
living people; he permitted fraud, deceit, violence, cruelty.
He was not a vicious man, he was not even particularly ambitious or a great lover of power, but the sole obsession of a
single idea led to a dreadful narrowing of thought and to a
moral transformation which permitted entirely immoral
methods in carrying on the conflict" (*The Origin of Russian
Communism,* pp. 138-40. Slightly condensed).

The problem of the early Russian Marxists was to find the
right starting point for their revolutionary task. At first a
large part of the Marxists wanted to start with immediately
practical objectives. If the workers combined for economic
ends they could improve their material conditions, and "a
workman who began by demanding shorter working hours
would, in Russian conditions, very soon be shouting 'down
with the government.'" (Schapiro, *The Communist Party of
the Soviet Union,* p. 32.) But Lenin saw in this a danger that
Russian socialism might become bogged down in the redress
of petty grievances which could bring no lasting benefit. He
was convinced that the whole system of society must be
ended before it could be mended. For the same reason the
Bolsheviks did not practice sporadic assassination as some of
the S.R.s did. To kill the reigning tsar and a few of his chief
agents would not alter the system. Lenin bade his followers
raise their eyes to the distant hills beyond the revolution,
where alone were "solid joys and lasting treasure."

"To assist in the economic struggle of the proletariat is the
job of the bourgeois politician. The task of the socialist is to
make the economic struggle of the workers assist the socialist
movement and contribute to the success of the revolutionary
socialist party" (Lenin, *Sochinenya,* 4th ed., Vol. IV, p.
270).

To establish this was only the first battle. Lenin believed
that ultimate victory depended upon the organization of a devoted and disciplined body of revolutionary shock troops who

would prepare the revolution with obedient intelligence and ruthless determination. His party must be a brotherhood sworn to obedience and united in Marxist orthodoxy. He believed that a party whose membership was open to all would be spineless. But most socialists, at the beginning at least, wanted to have a party that all sympathizers could join. There was a deep question of principle behind this tactical question. Must the socialist revolution wait until the time was ripe, until the proletariat knew how to use power, or could a group of determined men force history and do for the working class what they were not ready to do for themselves? If the first view was right, the masses must be drawn into the Socialist Party and trained by it for a great corporate undertaking. If the other view was right, socialism needed a party formed on Lenin's model. Probably no one, not even Lenin, saw all this clearly at the time. Still less did anyone foresee the ultimate consequences, but such thoughts were never far from Lenin's mind and in 1917 he seized time by the forelock.

Such were the issues which split the Marxists into Mensheviks and Bolsheviks at the famous party congress in 1903, a congress which took place abroad, partly because the meeting would not have been permitted in Russia but also because most of the leaders of Russian socialism were exiles. This famous quarrel dominated the Russian revolutionary world for the next twenty years, but the issue was so tangled at the party congress in 1903 that it is scarcely possible to see what was at stake unless one uses hindsight gained from looking at the original quarrel in the light of the way in which the Bolsheviks and Mensheviks grew apart in the years that followed. A shadowy unity between the two factions of the Marxists flickered on for several years with much recrimination. The real differences between the revolutionary groups were much aggravated by the frustration and demoralization of a political *émigré* life. "There were days and weeks with nothing to do but quarrel and intrigue. To anyone so naturally quarrelsome and predisposed to intrigue as Lenin the atmosphere of exile was especially harmful" (Seton-Watson, *The Decline of Imperial Russia*, p. 292), (cf. also Deutscher, *The Prophet Armed*, p. 80).

"Lenin's twisted maneuvers and intrigues in the following years can only be understood if it is realized that he considered all the principles of party membership of which he talked as applicable only within his own faction. . . . The Mensheviks were not comrades. The nominal 'Russian Social Democratic Workers' Party' was not 'the party' at all. The Mensheviks felt loyalty to the whole party, and felt obligations to Lenin as a comrade; Lenin recognized no loyalty either to the wider party or to the Mensheviks. Any promise made to them was a tactical concession, to be withdrawn as soon as convenient." (Seton-Watson, p. 293).

While the revolutionary sects in exile quarreled with a true *odium theologicum*, the revolutionaries in Russia prepared the ground. Abroad and at home the atmosphere of revolutionary work was quite different. In exile a leader needed intellectual brilliance, Marxist scholarship and the power to convince. Inside Russia he needed courage, discretion and the power to organize. Lenin stood head and shoulders above the rest of the *émigrés*.

Stalin, ten years younger, was slowly working his way up among the organizers of revolution on the spot. The school of conspiracy steels the character but provides no training in democracy. Even if an illegal party wants to have genuine elections to party offices, it is impossible to conduct proper elections when all meetings have to be secret. Moreover, Lenin mistrusted the capacity of the masses to recognize their own interests unless the party leaders told them what to do; and Lenin's successors have inherited his mistrust. To this day elections to office in the Communist party of the Soviet Union take place under the supervision of a senior party official. He is instructed to "direct" the election without, however, going so far as to "impose" a list of candidates, whatever that means. (See, e.g., pp. 575 and 589 of *The Communist Party of the Soviet Union*, by Leonard Schapiro.)

The faithfulness of the socialist revolutionaries to each other and their readiness to suffer for their cause showed that they were as high-minded as their predecessors in the seventies and eighties. But in their view ends and means were not on the same moral plane, and in the opening years of the present century unscrupulous methods reached a new height. The revolutionaries had their spies in the government, and the government had its spies among the revolutionaries. Who was to know which was which? The same man might take money from the government for denouncing his revolutionary brothers to the police and at the same time organize effective revolutionary work. Those who relished intrigue sometimes hardly knew themselves which side they were working for. Azev, the head of the battle organization of the social revolutionaries, took money from the police for betraying his comrades, while at the same time he organized the murders of the tsar's uncle and the minister of the interior.

At moments the opposing groups became intertwined in the strangest ways. In 1902 an enterprising chief of police saw that trade unions were popular, but did not see why the revolutionaries should reap all the benefit of this. He proceeded therefore to instigate the formation of trade unions which would receive protection instead of persecution from the police. These unions gained a few benefits from the employers, but a leadership which looked both ways achieved nothing solid. The employers objected violently and the experiment of "police socialism" was soon brought to an end, but the idea that the working class could combine effectively for its own purposes had taken root.

the foundations crack

Unstable as water, thou shalt not excel.

Genesis xlix. 4

In 1894 Alexander III died and was succeeded by his son Nicholas II, the last of the tsars, a good man fated to bring evil upon his country. Lovable, weak and fairly intelligent, Nicholas conceived it to be his duty and his fate to carry on his own shoulders the whole burden of the Russian autocracy. His duty to his family, to his country, and to God were indistinguishable to him. He felt bound unconditionally by his office and by his coronation oath to preserve Russia holy and Orthodox under his own absolute rule while he lived, and to hand on undiminished powers to his son when he died. To limit his own powers by the acceptance of basic laws that even the tsar must not break, to accept the merest shadow of a constitution or even to appoint a prime minister would be an offense against God and against his own son even more than a political imprudence.

The center of Nicholas' life was a radiant home circle dominated by the empress, a granddaughter of Queen Victoria, who loved her family with a deep possessive love. She did not like to go outside her narrow family circle and she had little contact with outside events, but she loved Russia, or rather her idea of Russia, with a passion that was an extension of her love for her own family. The Russian empire was the family estate and the government thereof was the household business of the Romanov family. Left to himself, the tsar's weak nature might have been open to good advice, but he could not stand up to his wife. If the tsaritsa had been a bad woman her influence might have been held in check, but she was good by her own lights and her narrow integrity became Russia's greatest danger.

Daughters were born, but for some years there was no male heir, and when at last in 1904 a boy was born he was a "bleeder"—that is to say, he suffered from hemophilia. The slightest bruise became a serious illness and his life was in continual danger.

Nicholas came to the throne at a time when the old order was breaking up. In the old days everyone had an inherited position, but now a rootless proletariat was growing fast, and found a natural ally in the rootless intelligentsia. The land was passing into the hands of *kulaks* and merchants, and the *mir* was slowly but visibly losing strength and cohesion, while the new middle class was growing rapidly. There were healthy tendencies in what was new, and a government that was both firm and imaginative could have built on solid foundations, but the tsar and his government were more than ever out of touch with all that was dynamic in Russian society. Alexander III had known how to make himself respected, but weak, vacillating Nicholas soon lost the trust, though not the affection, of his ministers. The government no longer had an effective head.

Discontent was now more dangerous, not because the people were more miserable than before, but because they had begun to think that things might be otherwise. Tsarism as understood in the ruling circles was an all-embracing way of life, with all its parts depending on each other. So a strike against the authority of the employers carried by implication a threat to the whole principle of authority. The government could not regard a strike as a private quarrel between workers and their employers. The Bolsheviks were at one with the tsar in regarding the political side of a strike as more important than its economic side. After the turn of the century strikes began to be better organized and more effective.

Discontent can be met with reform, repression, or distraction. Having no stomach for reform, the government of Nicholas II continued repression on traditional lines and embarked on new policies of distraction. To turn away the people's attention from their own grievances the government worked up the latent hatred against the Jews, diverting the general malaise into pogroms. When discontent still remained, they hoped that the distraction of a victorious foreign war would rally the loyalty of the Russian people, but they misjudged both their adversary and themselves.

The Chinese empire of the Manchus was at the point of death, and Russia and Japan were rivals for the control of

Manchuria and Korea. The issue was important for both sides, but if there had been a will to peace there was no reason why it should not have been settled peacefully. Russia picked a quarrel, but made no effective preparations to fight. The Japanese saw they would have to fight and made a surprise attack in February 1904, before the Russians had brought the necessary reinforcements and supplies from Europe.

In the Russo-Japanese War the Japanese showed for the first time that an Oriental people using Western technique and Western organization can sometimes beat Europeans at their own game, while the Russians failed once more as they had failed in the Crimean War through bad organization, bad communications and corruption. The Trans-Siberian Railway, which was scarcely finished, could not supply the distant front. Japan won battles, but she exhausted herself. So the Russians were able to negotiate a tolerable peace, but not before the Russian state had been shaken to the foundations. The turning point was "Bloody Sunday," January 22, 1905. Loyal strikers marching through St. Petersburg to present a petition to the tsar were shot down and several hundred people were killed or wounded. By this one action the tsar lost forever the confidence of thousands of loyal subjects. Immediately a true revolutionary fervor was unloosed in a wave of strikes. Soon the government seemed not far from collapse.

In October 1905 the tsar, forgetting his scruples for the moment, issued a manifesto proclaiming guarantees of personal liberty in the form of fundamental laws, and the establishment of an elected assembly or *duma*. The fundamental laws were not always observed and the *duma* did not have all the powers of a parliament, but when all is said Russia had taken a big step toward freedom. After this the government had to reckon with public opinion.

But the country was not satisfied with this. In the Black Sea the crew of the battleship *Potemkin* mutinied, the peasants in many districts rose and began to seize the land, and an armed rising in Moscow held parts of the city for several days. In October 1905, at the height of the revolutionary fervor, the workers of St. Petersburg set up a soviet and this example was soon imitated in Moscow and other centers. The word "soviet" is nothing but the Russian for council, but henceforth the word had a political overtone. At first councils of strike committees, the soviets soon became the organs through which the various sections of the working-class movement met to control their affairs and to put forward their political demands. Until the October manifesto in which the tsar promised to establish the *duma*, all the elements in the opposition were pushing in the same direction, but the October manifesto split the opposition. Liberals felt that something important had been gained and their opposition to the government became half-hearted. The real revolutionaries saw a chance to press for more drastic reforms, which frightened the liberals. If the opposition had been united and if strikes, mutinies and peasant revolts had been coordinated, the tsar might have been driven from his throne, but he was able to deal with his enemies one by one. Within a year Russia was reduced to order; but things could never be the same again. The liberty of expression exercised during the "year of freedom" could not be wholly taken away and the *duma* remained in existence, albeit with greatly limited powers and based upon a restricted franchise.

The Social Revolutionaries in the countryside and the Mensheviks in the towns had generally a larger following than the Bolsheviks, but the Bolsheviks had taken the lead in the Moscow rising and Lenin had noted every lesson of "the first Russian Revolution." In particular he saw in the soviets a spontaneous expression of the active spirit of the Russian masses which might lend itself to his designs at the critical moment. Trotsky, not then a Bolshevik, had played a leading part in the Petersburg soviet, but Lenin alone saw the revolutionary possibilities of this form of organization.

As soon as things quieted down, the tsar repented of his promise to set up a *duma*. He narrowed its sphere of work as much as he could and was grudging in all his dealings with it. It is true that there were substantial groups of radicals and revolutionaries in the *duma* at every stage, but most of the members were loyal Russians who wanted moderate reforms. Some of the tsar's ministers were ready to work with the *duma*, but that made them suspect with their master and with the power that stood behind the throne.

In the last years of tsarism the tragedy of the imperial family and the fate of their country are closely intertwined. The tsaritsa was stronger than the tsar and everything that she did was done for the sake of her son. It did not seem that he could live without a miracle, but why should there not be miracles? Just at this time an uncommonly shrewd Siberian peasant began to make a stir in St. Petersburg. Rasputin passed for a wonder-working holy man and he evidently possessed unusual powers which to some observers seemed hypnotic and to others demonic. He had been under the influence of the strange sect of the Khlysty (see p. 135), and he oscillated between emotional religion and a violent debauchery which seemed itself to be part of his religious being. In spite of the dark side of his life he was taken up by a section of St. Petersburg high society, who showered upon him rich presents which he gave away to the poor or squandered on riotous living. Introduced to the imperial family he exercised his healing gifts on the tsarevich, and it appears that by hypnotic or other means he was able to stop the bleeding and, so it would seem, saved the boy's life more than once.

This extraordinary circumstance gave Rasputin an ascendancy over the tsaritsa, who was convinced that he had been sent from God and began to take his advice in everything. Rasputin soon began to get his own disreputable nominees into high positions in Church and state. His scandals were public and notorious, but every attempt to unmask him brought the undying hatred of the empress, who attributed every slur on "our friend" to the envy and malice of enemies. He was the only real contact which the imperial family had with anyone outside the court circle, and in their eyes he typified the Russian people whom they idealized by contrast with the rotten aristocracy and the godless intelligentsia.

After the "first revolution" it became customary to appoint a "prime minister," though this did not prevent other ministers going straight to the tsar. Not infrequently the tsar would fail to tell his ministers what he had done, what he intended to do and what he had said to their colleagues. Often the prime minister would find his policy overruled through the intrigues of rivals and the vacillations of the tsar.

In the summer of 1906 the tsar appointed as premier Stolypin, a provincial governor who had shown firmness and tact in the late upheavals. Stolypin was brave, farsighted, firm and a devoted servant of the Russian monarchy. He dissolved the *duma* and by the use of questionable means got a more conservative body elected in its place, but once he had done this he tried to work with the new *duma* in spite of the tsar and his wife. He saw that Russia could not be ruled effectively unless the tsar took at least a part of the nation into partnership. Stolypin wanted to gain wider support for the monarchy, so he was ready to work with liberals, but he was ruthless in suppressing revolution. In the three years 1907-09, four thousand people were condemned to death and at least two thousand were executed. Such numbers horrified an age which was not accustomed to mass murder; the hangman's noose was grimly called a "Stolypin necktie." And his name has been preserved in the railway wagons still used in the Soviet Union for transporting prisoners.

Economically, Stolypin began to transform the countryside.

"In the past conservative landlords had idealized the commune as the repository of the fine old Russian traditions of the peasantry. Now when they saw the peasants rising together again themselves . . . they began to believe the Narodnik * Theory that the commune was a potential basis of socialism. They therefore . . . began to agitate for the strengthening of peasant private property and the dissolution of the commune" (Seton-Watson, p. 231).

This suited Stolypin, who relied on the "strong and sober," the energetic and progressive peasants who were held back by the *mir*. He allowed and encouraged the peasants to leave the village communes and to set up as individual smallholders owning a compact share of the village land. In less than ten years the number of peasant families owning their own land was more than doubled, and by 1915 there were already more than seven million households of peasant proprietors. Moreover, the cooperative movement began to spread fast among the farmers and brought to the countryside many of the advantages of large-scale organization. But if some went up, others went down, and those who went up were tempted to become "eaters of the *mir*," tyrannizing over their poorer neighbors, while there were more and more landless peasants every year. Some of the landless went to the towns to get jobs, but many remained in the villages in precarious misery.

Stolypin's policy was not a cure-all, but it released creative energies. It had a chance of bringing Russia through her impending crisis, but Stolypin had enemies and rivals. He said in private that he expected to be assassinated by a police agent, and on September 14, 1911, he was shot dead at a gala performance in the theatre at Kiev. His assassin had been both a Social Revolutionary and an agent of the police. He had a police pass to enter the theater. Was he acting for the police or the revolutionaries or for both? It is not certain.

* The Narodniks were the predecessors of the S.R.s in stimulating revolutionary feeling among the peasants (cf. pp. 198, 205).

The tsar never had another servant to compare with Stolypin; but whatever the government did, Russia was growing. Russian scientists and men of learning now stood in the front rank and educated life was becoming broader. This was not the greatest age of Russian literature, but it was the most brilliant. Virtuoso poets expressed new emotions and Russia was in the vanguard of esthetic experiment. The Russian Edwardian poets are untranslatable and therefore little known abroad, but the greatest of them, Alexander Blok, sometimes overcomes even the barrier of translation. This was the age of Diaghilev, an age when Russian artists had a cosmopolitan accomplishment which they have never had before or since. Diaghilev and his circle drew on all the inheritance of world civilization to make ballet into a new form of art which expressed the whole range of human emotions. Painters such as Kandinski and Malevich rivaled the boldest experiments of Braque and Picasso. All in all the art of the twentieth century owes more to the Russia of this time than to any other country, excepting only France.

The fresh thinking about religion which had begun among the intellectual laity in the last century began to bear fruit at this time and to affect a section of the radical intelligentsia. Some who had been Marxists came into the Church and gave it intellectual leaders such as Bulgakov and Berdyaev, who afterwards came to the West and had a deep influence on Western Christendom.

This brand of intellectual religion should not be idealized; it was immature and some of it was phony. But it was a portent. Fifty years later its influence was still visible, both for good and for bad, in Pasternak's novel *Dr. Zhivago*. With time these and other new ways of thinking would have transformed the Church, but time was not given. Up to the Bolshevik Revolution a great part of the Church still lived in the age of Muscovy and the established system of church government ensured that conservative forces would predominate. The hierarchy were rigidly controlled by the state. The sons of priests often went to church seminaries whether they had a vocation or not. Many of the pupils, and Stalin among them, turned against the Church. Poverty and administrative pressure forced many others to become priests against their inclination. There was much to reform in the Church. Reform was on the way but it needed time.

Russia was backward, but she was not stagnant. Industry was developing and the working class were learning to organize in trade unions. The peasants were still very ignorant, but they were beginning to learn to read and write and to organize cooperatives. In 1912 the *duma* passed a law to provide universal compulsory education. The war came too soon for this to come into full effect, but great changes were on the way.

Looking back on this time after thirty years, the exiled Fedotov wrote:

"Fifty more years and the Europeanization of Russia, down to her lowest layers, would be accomplished. How could it be otherwise? The Russian people were made from the same ethnographic and cultural dough as the gentry which successfully went through the same school in the eighteenth century. Yet these fifty years were not given to Russia."

CHAPTER XIX

the time of the
breaking of nations

Quem Jupiter vult perdere dementat prius.

(*Him, whom Jove would destroy, he first makes mad.*)

Latin Proverb

The outbreak of war in 1914 seemed to unite the tsar once more to his people. Even Social Revolutionaries and Mensheviks were carried away by the general enthusiasm for the national cause which they identified with the cause of democracy. A war against German despotism fought with democratic Britain and France as allies seemed certain to bring freedom to Russia. Only the Bolsheviks and some of the Mensheviks and S.R.s opposed the war, which they treated as a struggle of rival capitalisms in which all the governments were the enemies of all the peoples. However, for the first year or more the Bolsheviks had little influence over the workers, to say nothing of the peasants. Rasputin was no friend of the Bolsheviks, but he was with them in opposing the declaration of war, and he sent a characteristic telegram of warning to "Papa," as he called the tsar: "Let Papa not plan war; for with war will come the end of Russia and yourselves, and you will lose to the last man." In this his peasant shrewdness was more penetrating than the calculations of statesmen and intellectuals.

The *duma* threw itself wholeheartedly into the war, but it opposed the incompetence and corruption of some government departments. Since the war with Japan, the fleet and army had been reorganized to good purpose, but the army ran out of ammunition after a few months. Sometimes three soldiers had only one rifle, so that men had to wait for arms till their comrades were killed. But fearful losses did not shake their morale. Fresh drafts of peasants and workers fought as bravely as those who had gone before, and succeeding cadres of officers accepted without flinching losses even greater than those of the rank and file. A new war minister did wonders with supplies, working as closely with the *duma* as his master would let him, but by the autumn of 1915 the country was bled white. In the first year of war Russia had lost about four million men in killed, wounded and prisoners.

Every reasonable calculation pointed to a separate peace with Germany, but the Russians do not always know when they are beaten. So the tsar and most of public opinion were at one in their determination to fight on. Two sensible courses lay before the tsar: he could make peace with Germany in spite of public opinion, or he could give his people a share in the government and rely on their active support in the conduct of the war. He did neither. He continued the war and at the same time did his best to exclude every part of his people from any share in the government. To crown all, the tsar himself went to army headquarters and took over the supreme command of the army. He had the good sense to leave the conduct of the fighting to his generals, but the tsar's long absence from the capital left the administration of the Russian empire to the tsaritsa, and that meant to Rasputin.

Naturally the empress was incapable of coping with the problems of a great empire at war, but she believed that all would be well if she only maintained the autocracy and followed faithfully the divine guidance of "our friend." She worked devotedly in a war hospital, but otherwise hardly ever went outside her own tiny family circle, for she considered Petersburg society to be immoral and her dislike was cordially returned.

Rascals and puppets were appointed to the highest offices in the state, while honest men refused office in order to avoid dealing with Rasputin. Soon the cities began to grow hungry, not so much because there was not enough food in the country as because in the prevailing confusion not enough food reached the towns. At last revolutionary propaganda began to take root. The dangers were plain. Many of those who had access to the tsar warned him where his folly would lead, but he rejected every warning—or, if he weakened for a moment, his wife strengthened his obstinacy.

Russian government is a stiff, brittle structure which does not bend until it breaks. The end came abruptly. In the late winter of 1916-17 riots broke out in the capital; the tsar dissolved the *duma,* the *duma* refused to be dissolved, mutinous troops refused to fire on the people; and suddenly no one obeyed the government. For a moment Russia, conscious of her latent strength and rejoicing in her new freedom, looked forward to a happy future, but soon chaos came between the Russians and their hopes. The tsar was forced to abdicate, but he made no effective arrangement for handing over the government. A provisional government was set up with the support of most of the *duma,* but it had no authority received either from the tsar or from the people, nor did it have the material means to establish a power emanating from itself. The police had been used too often against the people to be trusted by the Revolution, so they were soon disbanded and no effective new force took their place. Hitherto the army had remained loyal and heroic, but now revolutionary propaganda was allowed at the front and began to spread like wildfire. The discipline of the army collapsed. After this the provisional government was left with no reliable organized force for the maintenance of law and order. It was continually defied with impunity. Yet most of its members did not see their own weakness and continued to behave as if they were a properly constituted government with means of imposing their will.

Soviets were formed on the 1905 model, but with the addition of deputies from the soldiers and peasants. There was no time to establish set rules for the constitution of the soviets and no body of experience to draw on. The soviets were therefore extremely informal. The Petrograd * Soviet sprang up almost of its own accord on the first day of the Revolution. The example was imitated in every center. Factories, workshops and army units were the normal bodies to send deputies but there was no control of numbers. It was in effect the keen socialist and working-class groups who appointed deputies and it was the keen deputies who turned up to meetings of the soviet. If anyone was dissatisfied with his representative on the soviet, he could start an agitation to get him recalled and to have someone else appointed in his place. The

* St. Petersburg has been rechristened twice, once as Petrograd early in the war and again as Leningrad after the Revolution.

Bolsheviks did this systematically in order to get their own people into the soviet.

In a body with so little formal constitution as a Russian revolutionary soviet, the inner group of officeholders was bound to hold decisive power. The inner group of the Petrograd Soviet expended hectic energy, often going without sleep for days on end if the cause of the Revolution so demanded. They made the Petrograd Soviet into a power whose influence was felt throughout the Russian empire. The soviets were originally the expression of the Russian working class's instinct for spontaneous and informal cooperation, at a time when all organized power was collapsing into rubble. They evolved into the institutional expression of the domination of a revolutionary elite.

The soviets had an enormous moral influence with the working class. From the very beginning they had as much effective authority as the provisional government and as much right to govern, if, indeed, either had any right at all. By a strange arrangement the staid *duma* and the turbulent Soviet of Petrograd occupied different wings of the same building, the famous Tauris Palace given to Potemkin by Catherine the Great after the conquest of the Crimea. For a short time it was almost as if two hostile governments were sharing the same building.

Lenin was an exile in Switzerland, but now the Germans, hoping to foster Russian defeatism, sent him home to Russia in a sealed train. The Bolsheviks were not at first so influential as the more moderate revolutionary parties, but Lenin's arrival transformed the scene. Seeing at once possibilities that went far beyond the accepted Marxist analysis, he began to work for an immediate proletarian revolution without an intervening stage of bourgeois democracy. Trotsky stood head and shoulders above the other revolutionaries and Lenin stood head and shoulders above Trotsky. The two needed each other. Trotsky lacked the massive brain power and solidity of Lenin but there was fire in his thought. With his brilliance and energy, his courage and *panache*, and his powers as an orator, a writer and an organizer he supplied something essential to the Revolution. Ten years younger than Lenin and the same age as Stalin, Trotsky had long been a prominent revolutionary, skirmishing on the border between Mensheviks and Bolsheviks, outraging the Mensheviks by his truculence and the boldness of his ideas but not joining the Bolsheviks. In the spring and summer of 1917 Trotsky moved rapidly nearer to the Bolsheviks and soon became Lenin's chief ally.

After some hesitation the astonished Bolsheviks accepted with all their heart the new theory that they should not wait for Russia to pass through the normal stage of a "bourgeois" revolution but should work for an immediate proletarian revolution. Lenin saw that the key to control of Russia was to gain control of the soviets, where the Bolsheviks were at first in a minority. For this purpose the soviets had two advantages over the *duma*. In general the soviets drew their strength from the working class, whereas most members of the *duma* came from the upper classes. From the tactical point of view—

". . . the essential feature of the soviets was that they represented the primitive, politically inexperienced masses. . . . The mass of members . . . were persons of no fixed program, easily swayed by the events of the moment and by the most attractive of the slogans put before them. In any parliament, the parties would be represented by experienced politicians, already possessing deeply defined political convictions. If the Bolsheviks took part in parliamentary politics, they would have to bargain and make concessions to other parties. But if they could capture the soviets, they would make themselves the leaders of the masses" (Seton-Watson, p. 365).

Lenin believed in his cause and he believed in the proletarian masses. Indeed, to him the two were almost the same thing, for the supreme virtue of the Communist cause was that it alone could raise up the proletariat, and the supreme virtue of the proletariat was that it could accept Marxism in the form that Lenin had given it. The position of the proletariat, ground down and with no attachments to the existing order, was the guarantee of that. The Russian masses at the moment wanted two concrete things, peace and land. The provisional government, which included Mensheviks and Social Revolutionaries, believed that if Germany won, the Russian Revolution would soon be finished. This, and a feeling of solidarity with their Western allies, made them reluctant to conclude a separate peace. Though most of them favored giving a great part of the land to the peasants, they held that this should be done by due process of law. That meant delay. The Bolsheviks had no use for legal forms and they decided to risk a German victory. Thus they were able to outbid the other parties by offering to the peasants both peace and an immediate division of land.

The Bolsheviks were determined to destroy the discipline of the army, believing that the old army must pass into dissolution before a new army devoted to the Revolution could be formed. The provisional government were caught between their wish to defend Russia from the Kaiser's Germany and their wish to defend the Revolution from Russian reactionaries. Their natural allies in the first task were the patriotic reactionaries who were enemies of the Revolution. Thus, it was well nigh inevitable that the efforts of the provisional government to defend Russia, ineffective as they were, should be taken by left-wing socialists to be a betrayal of the Revolution. So it seemed to the left that the provisional government was lining up with dark reactionaries and it seemed to conservatives and moderates that the Bolsheviks must be in German pay.

With supreme lack of realism Kerensky tried to find a way out of his difficulties by ordering a general offensive. The Germans had taken advantage of the Russian Revolution to move some of their forces to the western front. It seemed plausible, if only one could ignore the condition of the Russian army, to think that an offensive might succeed and that a successful offensive might restore morale and make it possible to consolidate the Revolution on a constitutional basis. With understandable shortsightedness the Western Allies, locked in a desperate struggle with Germany, put strong pressure on the Russians to make the eastern front active once more. This may be compared with the agitation for a second front twenty-five years later, at a time when the roles of East and West had been reversed. In both cases sentiment and a feeling of desperation played a greater part than military calculation.

In the second case it was mainly a matter of time before an effective invasion of Europe could be launched from the West, whereas in the first case it would have been more realistic for the Allies to have faced the fact that Russia was no longer capable of putting up an effective fight and to have accepted the inevitability of a separate peace. In 1917 there were, however, some warning voices even from the West. " 'The Russian army is nothing but a façade,' said General Pétain, 'it will fall to pieces if it makes a move.' The American mission, for another example, expressed the same view." (*The History of the Russian Revolution*, by Trotsky.) Nonetheless orders were given for a general advance, but when the arrangements for the offensive were supposed to be ready, many of the troops would not go forward. If some regiments turned out in full force, others appeared with reduced strength, and yet others refused to come out at all. In such cases the officers were powerless to restore discipline. After many delays a sprawling attempt to advance without much coordination was begun on the 16th of June on the southwestern front and at the beginning of the second week in July on the other fronts. Some gains were made where the opposing forces were weakest but the advance soon petered out and the army began to get out of hand even more menacingly than before.

The leading generals were thoroughly disgusted with the provisional government and made preparations to replace it with something more congenial to themselves. The head of this movement was General Kornilov, the commander in chief, but he relied on influential civilian support. It was never clear what exactly Kornilov and his supporters intended to put in the place of the provisional government or what degree of force they were prepared to use. At the end of August troops began to move on the capital, but the movement was badly organized, its leadership was lifeless and there were not enough troops to overcome any stiff opposition. The generals were right in thinking the government a thing of straw to which no one felt a real loyalty, but they did not see the weakness of their own position in ordering an already mutinous army to fire not on the enemy but on its own people; and they failed grievously to discern the rising strength of the left.

It was intended that on the approach of Kornilov's forces his supporters in the capital should seize control of Petrograd. They failed even to make an attempt, but the left-wing workers of Petrograd threw up barricades and formed armed detachments while workers of the famous Putilov factory worked all out to produce arms for the defenders of the Revolution. Trotsky describes the political warfare which stopped Kornilov's advance even more effectively than firearms:

"The railroad workers in those days did their duty. In a mysterious way echelons would find themselves moving on the wrong roads. Regiments would arrive in the wrong division, artillery would be sent up a blind alley, staffs would get out of communication with their units. All the big stations had their own soviets, their railroad workers' and their military committees'. The telegraphers kept them informed of all events, all movements, all changes. The telegraphers also held up the orders of Kornilov. Information unfavorable to the Kornilovists was immediately multiplied, distributed, pasted up, passed from mouth to mouth. The machinists, the switchmen, the oilers, became agitators. It was in this atmosphere that the Kornilov echelons advanced—or what was worse, stood still. The commanding staff, soon sensing the hopelessness of the situation, obviously did not hasten to move forward, and with their passivity promoted the work of the counter-conspirators of the transport system. If you follow on the map the fate of the Kornilov echelons, you get the impression that the conspirators were playing at blind man's buff on the railroad lines.

" 'Almost everywhere,' says General Krasnov, writing his observations made on the night of August 30, 'we saw one and the same picture. On the tracks or in the cars, or in the saddles of their black or bay horses, who would turn from time to time to gaze at them, dragoons would be sitting or standing, and in the midst of them some lively personality in a soldier's long coat.' The name of this 'lively personality' soon became legion. From the direction of Petrograd innumerable delegations continued to arrive from regiments sent out to oppose the Kornilovists. Before fighting they wanted to talk things over. The revolutionary troops were confidently hopeful that the thing could be settled without fighting. This hope was confirmed: the Cossacks readily came to meet them. The communication squad of the corps would seize locomotives, and send the delegates along all railroad lines. The situation would be explained to every echelon. Meetings were continuous and at them all the cry was being raised: 'They have deceived us!' " (Trotsky, *The History of the Russian Revolution.*)

In this way, the revolutionary workers of Petrograd overcame Kornilov's revolt without even having to fight. Kerensky, the head of the provisional government, had behaved ambiguously toward Kornilov and this ambiguity reflected his government's position. They were against reaction and they were against the extreme left but they had no powerful organized support from the center. If Kornilov had succeeded they would no doubt have greeted him as a defender against Bolshevism. As he failed, they hailed the workers as defenders against Kornilov; but they did nothing effective to bring the conspirators to book. Kerensky's government tottered on for a few more weeks but its credit was now utterly exhausted. Most of the able men who had belonged to the provisional government in its first weeks were now out of office, but at this stage even the greatest resolution and intelligence could scarcely have saved the day.

The socialist members of the provisional government may have been honest men, but they did not show either resolution or competence in their advocacy of the cause of the downtrodden. It might well seem that the determined, bustling, unscrupulous Bolsheviks were more likely to get things done. Moreover, the people who came to the Bolshevik meetings looked like real working-class men and women, whereas the meetings of the other socialist parties often took their tone from middle-class intellectuals. It was obvious which would have the greatest appeal to the factory workers with whom in fact lay the immediate future, though it was not obvious that a working-class party would be able to dominate a country of peasants. Thenceforth the history of Russia, in one of its aspects, has been a long inarticulate struggle between peasants and town workers. In 1917 the peasants had the advantage of numbers but in the nature of things the proletariat was gathered in the key centers. Moreover Russia's growing but still undeveloped heavy industry was dominated by a few large factories, among which the Putilov works at Petrograd was pre-eminent. So it was comparatively easy to organize the factory workers, and once they were organized they would exercise an influence out of all proportion to their numbers. On the other hand it was extremely difficult to organize the peasants, spread out in many tens of thousands of villages and hamlets, with very few roads worthy of the name. The only party that had roots in the countryside were the Social Revolutionaries, who had inherited the Narodnik tradition going back to the time before Marxism came to Russia. The Marxist Mensheviks and Bolsheviks did not talk the language of peasants and had no hold on the countryside but it was the Marxists who had the great leaders. The peasants may have been scattered and backward but their numbers and their control of the food supply gave them an inherent weight which an able leader could have used to overcome the tactical advantages of the town workers. The Russian peasants wanted a revolution but they wanted a different revolution from that which the Bolsheviks gave them. If the Social Revolutionaries had thrown up a leader with half the ability of Lenin or Trotsky, the Russian Revolution might have taken a very different form.

As things were, the firm discipline and devotion of the Communists won rapidly growing support both in the soviets and in the country at large. The troops at the front were now heartily sick of the war and ready to listen to the Communists. Continually heartened by their successes, the Bolsheviks, acting mainly through the soviets, made a brilliantly conducted series of encroachments upon the discipline of the army, the power of the government, the authority of the factory owners and the property of the landlords. The power of the provisional government began to sink away both at the front and throughout the land, till by the autumn of 1917 it was little more than a façade. The rank and file of the garrison of Petrograd could not be relied on to obey orders, unless these were endorsed by the Petrograd Soviet, and the senior officers had little use for the incompetent provisional government.

The Bolshevik preparations for a *coup d'état* were scarcely concealed. At that stage it would have taken very little force to crush the military organization of the Communists. At that stage there were progressive elements which were ready to oppose the Communist rising if they had been properly organized, but the clever fools, nonentities and half-baked idealists who made up the provisional government showed little understanding of their peril and made no determined effort to organize resistance. In October 1917 the greater part of the proletariat was exhausted by the months of hardship and confusion which it had already gone through; the workers were not willing to lift a finger to help the provisional government, but it did not follow that most of them were ready to fight for the Communists. It was only a tiny minority who took an active part in the Communist rising. There were hundreds and thousands of men and women with high courage, sincerity and intelligence among the active members of the Communist Party. Such men and women were heroes, but only a few of those who supported the Bolsheviks throughout Russia were like them. An acute observer from the non-Communist extreme left wrote in description of the delegates to the second all-Russian congress of soviets which met in Petrograd during the crucial days: "Out of the trenches and obscure holes and corners had crept utterly crude and ignorant people whose devotion to the revolution was spite and despair, while their socialism was hunger and an unendurable longing for rest. Not bad material for experiments, but—those experiments would be risky" (Sukhanov, p. 635).* The same writer, who was editor of Gorki's left-wing paper, *New Life*, records that at this time his editorial office was "swamped with letters from the trenches," letters which showed an unbearable longing for peace, "if only it would end; nothing else mattered—parties, politics or revolution. Anyone would be supported who produced even a ghost of peace."

It was not clear what the Bolsheviks would do if they could get into power, nor was it clear what their passive supporters expected them to do. But the provisional government was doing next to nothing, while it seemed clear that the Bolsheviks would do something and do it vigorously, and in particular that they would try to make peace and that they would give the land to the peasants. With such a program they gained the acquiescence of the great majority and the enthusiastic support of a few. The army was no longer ready to fight with determination in any cause at all, but almost the whole of the army was ready to acquiesce in a Bolshevik rising, and some army units were prepared to march, if not to fight, on Bolshevik orders. The morale of the fleet was higher and a considerable number of the sailors were ready to fight for the Bolshevik cause. Some of the armed factory workers were brave and determined, but they had no military training or discipline. Such forces hardly seemed sufficient for a rising, but against such an enemy as the provisional government it was enough. There was very little resistance to the final blow which was struck on October 25, Old Style (November

* As late as 1927 less than 10 per cent of the Russian Communist Party had completed higher education, less than 8 per cent had received even secondary education, and over 2 per cent were illiterate. The low level of education among the Communist rank and file was one of the things that made the party so singularly malleable in the days when first Lenin and then Stalin were establishing their hegemony. In 1956, 14.7 per cent of all members of the party and candidate members had received complete or incomplete higher education and 22.2 per cent had completed secondary education. It is a reasonable assumption that nowadays the great majority of officeholders in the party are well educated. An instructive picture of changes in the character of the party's membership can be gleaned from Leonard Schapiro's *The Communist Party of the Soviet Union*. See especially pp. 232, 311, 317, 322, 328, 435, 439, 454-6, 512, 515-6, 523-4, and 565.

7, New Style), and in a few days the Bolsheviks were supreme throughout the greater part of Russia.

There were no mourners at the funeral of the provisional
government. It seemed to have died quietly in its sleep. Its
head, Kerensky, was a young left-wing lawyer of striking personality who rose to a sudden eminence in the February Revolution. Having a gift for words he mistook rush for action
and deceived himself into thinking that Russia could be ruled
by oratory. During eight months no leader had arisen from
the bourgeoisie capable of coping with the mounting crisis.
This is a criticism of Nicholas II more than of the Russian
bourgeoisie. While he was on the throne the tsar had given
his people no chance to learn the art of ruling, and after his
abdication things soon became past mending. Even a few
months of transition from autocracy to constitutional rule
would have given a chance for new men to prove their practical worth.

For all its futility, the provisional government made one
lasting change in the structure of Russian society. It ended
the system by which, since Peter the Great, the Church had
been subjected to the State through the "Holy Synod." One
of the new government's first acts was to install a new and
liberal procurator of the Holy Synod who replaced the reactionaries in the synod with more liberal bishops. Thereupon
the whole body of the Church took on the air of revival and
reform, and on April 28 the Holy Synod issued a proclama-
tion which stated that "with the change of regime the Established Church could not preserve the old order, which had
outlived its time." (*People, Church & State in Modern Russia,* Paul R. Anderson, SCM Press, 1944.)

In August a council of the whole Russian Church assembled for the first time since 1696 and received from the government authority to "elaborate and present for the approval
of the provisional government, legislation covering the new
order of free self-administration of the Russian Church." At
that stage it was expected that the new Russia would be a
constitutional monarchy and the council expected the Orthodox Church to enjoy a position of moderate privilege in the
new order. In the general uncertainty it was impossible to
work out a detailed constitution for the Church but a momentous decision was taken by a majority vote to restore the
Patriarchate of Moscow and to establish a synod of bishops
to replace Peter the Great's "Most Holy Governing Synod."
The voting was 141 to 112. "Many delegates, laymen, clergy

and bishops would have preferred a less monarchical form"
of Church government (*ibid.*, p. 61). A substantial minority
held radical views on politics which they applied also to
Church government. Nearly half the members of the council
were laymen. They included people like S. N. Bulgakoff who
had come from Marxism to Christianity, and among the
clergy many of the parish priests still felt a bitter traditional
jealousy against the prelates of the Church and against the
rich monasteries from which the bishops were recruited. On
November 5, as the Bolshevik Revolution was already breaking, Tikhon, the Metropolitan of Moscow, was elected to be
the new Patriarch. No one foresaw the fiery trials that were
to be his lot. At this stage there was a fair amount of anti-
clericalism, or rather antimonasticism. The vast estates of the
richer monasteries were resented by the peasants and by
many of the parish clergy. The militant atheism of the Bolsheviks was not yet fully apparent but men like Bulgakoff must
have known what was in store if the Bolsheviks prevailed.

Ostensibly the Bolsheviks with some support from other
left-wing revolutionary elements had seized power in the
name of the soviets. But it soon became clear that the Communist Party would rule the soviets and that Lenin would
rule the party with the help of a small group of trusted leaders. At this time it seemed as if anything might have come
out of the welter. The Bolsheviks were deeply divided about
the rising and it is doubtful whether they would have attempted to seize power if Trotsky had not been driving them
on. Without Trotsky's courage, inspiration and practical ability it is doubtful whether the revolt would have succeeded.
Even after the October Revolution, neither the Bolsheviks
nor their enemies found it easy to believe that they would remain in power. Looking back on the Revolution, one is
tempted to rationalize and to tidy history up. From this van-
tage point it looks as if the Bolshevik Revolution was the
predestined end to which events had long been moving. But
this account leaves out too much. Contemporaries saw things
which we may easily forget, and they were right to think that
chance played a part in these fatal happenings.

There is no doubt that Russia was headed for revolution,
but it was not inevitable that the revolution should take that
particular form. If the characters of the tsar, of his wife or of
Rasputin had been different, things might have taken a different turn before the fall of the monarchy. Foolish as Nicholas was, it could hardly be foreseen that he would aban-

don the ship of state without placing the tiller squarely in the hands of a successor. And in the events between February and November the activity of Lenin was decisive. Such at least was the opinion of Trotsky, who wrote many years afterward: "Without Lenin the October Revolution would not have been won." One might add that without Trotsky Lenin would scarcely have succeeded either in seizing power or in winning the ensuing civil war.

COMPARATIVE DATES

A.D.

1682-89 Sophia, regent; Ivan and Peter, tsars.

1694 Peter the Great begins to rule.

1700-21 Great Northern War.

1703 Foundation of St. Petersburg.

1718 Death of Charles XII. Execution of Alexis.

1721 Establishment of Most Holy Synod.

1725 Death of Peter the Great.

1741-62 Elizabeth, empress.

1755 Foundation of Moscow University.

1762 Edict freeing gentry from service to state.

1762-96 Catherine the Great, empress.

1772 First Partition of Poland.

1783 Conquest of Crimea.

1793 Second Partition of Poland.

1795 Third Partition of Poland.

1796-1801 Paul, tsar.

1799 Suvorov's campaign in Italy.

1801-25 Alexander I, tsar.

1807 Peace of Tilsit.

1808-09 Conquest of Finland.

1812 The *"War for the Fatherland."*

1825-55 Nicholas I, tsar.

1825 Decembrist revolt.

1830-31 First Polish revolt.

1853-56 Crimean War.

1855-81 Alexander II, tsar.

A.D.

1694 Birth of Voltaire.

1715 Treaty of Utrecht.

1729 The Wesleys begin meetings at Oxford.

1755 Johnson, *Dictionary.*

1756-63 Seven Years' War.

1762 Rousseau, *Social Contract.*

1772 Warren Hastings appointed governor of Bengal.

1776 American Declaration of Independence.
Adam Smith, *Wealth of Nations.*

1789 French Revolution.

1805 Austerlitz, Trafalgar.

1809 Birth of Gladstone, Lincoln and Darwin.

1815 Waterloo.

1818 First steamer crosses Atlantic.

1823 The Monroe Doctrine.

1825 First railway from Stockton to Darlington.

1827 Dr. Arnold becomes Headmaster of Rugby.

1840 Introduction of penny postage in Great Britain.

1848 Revolutions on continent.
Communist Manifesto.

1853 Commodore Perry opens Japan to American trade.

1856 Bessemer's process for steel.

1861 Emancipation of serfs.
1863 Second Polish revolt.
1864 Local government re-
forms.
1864-85 Conquest of Central
Asia.
1866 Dostoyevsky, *Crime and
Punishment.*
1881 Assassination of Alexander II.
1881-94 Alexander III, tsar.
1885 First important strike.
1891 Beginning of Trans-Siberian Railway. Famine.
1894-1917 Nicholas II, tsar.
1896 Wave of strikes.
1903 Split of Bolsheviks and
Mensheviks.
1904-05 Russo-Japanese War.
1905 First Russian Revolution.
1906-11 Stolypin, prime minister.
1910 Death of Tolstoy.

1859 Darwin, *Origin of Spe-
cies.*
De Lesseps begins Suez
Canal.
1861 Outbreak of American
Civil War.
1865 Founding of Salvation
Army.
1867 Karl Marx, *Das Kapital.*
1870 Franco-Prussian War.
1871 Paris commune.
1883 Maxim invents gun.
1889 London dock strike.
Shaw, *Fabian Essays.*
1890 Fall of Bismarck.
1901 Death of Queen Vic-
toria.
1903 First flight by Wright
brothers.
1913 Einstein's general theory
of relativity.
1914 Opening of Panama Canal.
First World War.

PART IV

the Soviet age

And they said, Go to, let us build us a city and a tower, whose top may reach unto heaven; and let us make us a name. Genesis xi. 4

CHAPTER XX

a new time of troubles

I am the master of my fate:
I am the captain of my soul.

W. E. Henley

1. First Steps of New Rulers

The early victory of the Bolsheviks reflected the weakness of their opponents rather than their own strength. The Communists had no clear idea of how they were going to govern or how the new society would work. Marxist thought had concentrated on the dissection and overthrow of capitalist society. Not even Lenin had made a blueprint for socialism. Indeed, as Mr. E. H. Carr has pointed out, "on the eve of the revolution his contribution to the economics of socialism was 'Imperialism as the Highest Stage of Capitalism,' a searching analysis of the economics of the latest phase of capitalist society." So when the Bolsheviks came to power they had to improvise a new organization of society as they went along, and their first ideas of administration were vague. Trotsky "required nothing of the officials of the former Ministry of Foreign Affairs but the surrender of the 'secret treaties. . . .' The People's Commissioner of Finance demanded the surrender of the funds of the state bank, but was otherwise indifferent to the procedures of financial administration." (Carr, Vol. V, p. 113.)

Russia was exhausted by war and revolution, the police had been disbanded and the Bolsheviks themselves had destroyed the discipline of the army. The task of re-creating an ordered society would have been formidable even to experienced rulers, but the Communists had no experience of ruling or of large-scale organization, and there was no one to teach them. They learned by costly experience.

Moreover, Russia was not altogether in a serious mood. The working classes celebrated the Revolution by a gigantic

236

spree which went on for several weeks. A large part of the army got drunk for weeks on end and dissolved into the countryside. Large consignments of liquor on the railways were seized by units which had got out of hand, cellars were broken into and wine shops were rifled. In the capital, mass orgies threatened to paralyze the Revolution. In particular, the tsar's cellars were an irresistible temptation. The most famous regiments of the Russian army got drunk in succession while doing guard duty at the Winter Palace. They were replaced by mixed guards selected from different detachments; these got drunk and were replaced by leaders of the revolutionary movement in the army, but they also got drunk. The fire brigade was sent to flood the cellars, but they too got drunk. In the end, sailors from Helsinki put an end to this "alcoholic lunacy," binding themselves not to drink by an oath under pain of death.

The Bolshevik leaders had had a foretaste of difficulties to come and had seen how slight was the basis of their power. They could rely on prolonged and almost superhuman efforts from the hard core of their supporters, but for the rest it would be a question of spasmodic effort and there would be much indiscipline and evasion wherever the chance was given. Yet they trusted to their own indomitable spirit and they were sure that the Revolution would spread to western Europe. "The majority of Russian workers in 1917 . . . standing at a level of subsistence not far removed from starvation and maddened by the meaningless sacrifice of the war, had neither hope nor belief in any existing institutions and were desperate enough to accept with alacrity the revolutionary leadership of a small group of determined men bent on overthrowing them." (Carr, Vol. III, p. 221.) The Bolshevik leaders could not believe that "the majority of the workers of western Europe—and not merely a privileged minority . . . had a standard of living which, poor as it may often have been, was still worth defending. At any rate they were unwilling to sacrifice it lightly in pursuit of the prospective benefits of revolution." (Ibid.) The Bolsheviks long miscalculated the force of conservatism among the working classes in the West. For some years after 1917 they lived in continual expectation of a European revolution.

Bukharin said that the Revolution was "a simultaneous wager on international revolution and on the peasant." (Syedmoi S'ezd Rossiiskoi Kommunisticheskoi Partii, Moscow, 1923. Speech of Bubnov [p. 63]. Cf. also speech of Ryazanov [p. 87].) The first bet was lost, but there was still hope that the Revolution might fulfill the aspirations which it had inspired, if it could gain the general acquiescence of the peasants or, better still, their active support. The Bolshevik leaders were determined that the rights of the proletariat as they conceived them should prevail over the interests of property owners and the prejudices of the peasantry. For that purpose they envisaged a "dictatorship of the proletariat," but this was a paradox in the Russia of sixty years ago. The dictatorship of the proletariat "did not rest on the strength of the proletariat, which was for the present extremely slight. Its declared political program was to make the proletariat strong, and to create the conditions in which a dictatorship of the proletariat in the Marxist sense might become a reality. But these conditions included a remolding, psychological as well as material, of the proletariat". (Carr, Vol. V, p. 134). The Communist leaders may not have had a conscious intention to set up a personal dictatorship, but they were acting in the name of the proletariat to be, not of the Russian working class as it was.

The Marxist analysis of society seemed to ensure that the working class would support the leaders of the socialist revolution, and no one had thought what was to be done if this expectation proved false. All the revolutionary parties— Bolsheviks, Mensheviks, and S.R.s—expected the Revolution to bring freedom. If Lenin had doubts, he did not express them before 1917, but when he was in power, he never hesitated to use his unique authority to persuade the Communist Party to accept the use of dictatorial methods whenever these seemed to be the best means of maintaining Bolshevik power or of establishing the predominance of the ruling group within the party. The rank and file of the party might not have followed their leaders if they had known where Lenin was leading them.

The establishment of socialism entailed a new organization of industry and farming, but for the moment there was no question of setting up elaborate institutions. The peasants were already helping themselves to the land, and the Communist authorities encouraged and helped this process. After a few months almost all the land was held by peasants, not on any socialist principle but as individual cultivators. This had been the policy of the Social Revolutionaries, not of the Bolsheviks, but the Bolsheviks now saw to it that the peasants got the land while the Social Revolutionaries talked about legal forms. The Bolsheviks stole the clothes of the S.R.s while they were bathing and they found that they fitted. A few state farms and collective farms were scarcely noticed in an ocean of smallholdings, worked by the labor of a man and his family, commonly owning one horse. In the same spirit the workers began to seize factories, but since they were not able to run the factories themselves, it was generally necessary to ask the old owners and technicians to carry on for the new authorities. Many fled, others were unable or unwilling to adapt themselves to the new requirements, but those who remained managed somehow or other to run such industry as still kept going. The resulting situation was described as "workers' control." This does not mean that the workers were in executive control and took responsibility for running the factory; the word "control" was used in the Continental sense of supervision. The management could not in practice resist the workers' demands, but it remained responsible for the consequences. Such a system could not work for long, if indeed it was meant to work at all. "Workers' control" was useful as a slogan for destroying the old economic order and for gaining the support of the workers in 1917, but as soon as that was done "workers' control" had served its purpose. The Soviet government went forward from "workers' control" to the full nationalization of all major industry and from that to the formal but ineffective abolition of private trade.

The Communists had promised peace, but imperial Germany saw no reason to grant easy terms to the Russian Revolution. The old army was no longer capable of resisting a determined attack, and the Communists had not yet created an effective army of their own. At first they could not bring themselves to accept the German peace terms and Lenin had to use all his weight to make his colleagues agree to the Treaty of Brest-Litovsk by which the whole of the Ukraine was lost to Russia.

2. Civil Strife

Bolshevik rule had been established with surprising ease over most of the empire, but nowhere had it been consolidated and as the months drew on chaos became worse.

The railways scarcely moved, industry was grinding to a standstill, the towns were very hungry. Everything was in a turmoil. The enemies of the regime were everywhere. In the summer of 1918 their opposition flared up in open revolt. In September a Social Revolutionary, Dora (Fanny) Kaplan, nearly succeeded in assassinating Lenin. The Bolsheviks used drastic methods from the start, but what passed for tyranny in 1917 seems mild by the standards of a generation later. When the events of 1918 showed Lenin that he could not maintain his power without making free use of the firing squad, he did not scruple to do so. The Red Terror dates from this time, but it took long to reach its full development.

In 1918 the Allies were still engaged in a desperate struggle with an unbeaten Germany and they could not be indifferent to the Russian civil war, for the Bolsheviks had taken Russia out of the war, while their opponents denounced the Treaty of Brest-Litovsk and dreamed of revenge against the Kaiser's Germany. While the war continued, it was inevitable that the Allies should support those who were trying to overthrow the Bolsheviks, but to continue this support after the defeat of Germany was another matter. The support given to the White forces was not, as it turned out, large enough to influence the result, but it was enough to prolong the fighting and the suffering which flowed from it. So the Allies became involved in atrocious civil confusion and were blamed for every tragedy where they were present. Moreover, the Allied intervention convinced the Bolsheviks that the capitalist countries would always try to destroy the work of the Revolution. This notion fitted in with Marxist preconceptions and long remained an *idée fixe* with Communist statesmen.

For the best part of four years the civil war raged with varying fortunes. At one time Communist rule was confined to an area that corresponded roughly with the territory of the grand princes of Muscovy in the fifteenth century, but in the end the Bolsheviks were left in command of nearly all the former Russian empire with the exception of Poland, Bessarabia, Finland, and the Baltic States. If the enemies of the Soviets could have worked together and coordinated their attacks, they could doubtless have beaten the Red forces, but their victory could hardly have lasted without more unity of aim and more statesmanship than they possessed.

Landlords and their sons joined the White armies organized by tsarist officers, and fought for the restoration of their estates and the reestablishment of traditional values. School-boys from the "better" schools joined them and fought with pathetic heroism for ill-defined notions of honor and patriotism. The Allies intervened in the hope that they could bring Russia back into the war against Germany or at least secure a decent and respectable government. The Ukrainians and other nationalities fought for independence from Moscow. Anarchistic bands fought for an end to all government. Bandits fought for themselves and joined all armies indifferently. Armies, partisans and marauding bands followed each other in such quick succession that the same place might change hands several times in a few days. Each new army that entered a town shot those whom it supposed to be its enemies. It is hard to say which side was the most cruel.

Generals had an imperfect control of their armies in the hideous confusion, and few tried to restrain the fury of their subordinates. If the commander of a detachment ordered a massacre, it was not likely that he would be brought to book. Nearly all had something to avenge. If a man's property had been robbed, his wife raped or his parents murdered, he might not be able to find those who had wronged him, but he could always find other workers and peasants or other landlords and officers to shoot in vicarious vengeance. Each act of revenge raised up new avengers, until the combatants regarded every man on the other side as a mortal enemy.

The tsar and his family, held as prisoners in the Urals, prepared themselves for death with a spiritual courage which wipes out the folly of their lives. They were shot on the orders of the local Communist leaders for fear that they might be rescued and restored to power. Millions of humbler victims were killed or died of hardship, hunger and epidemics. They left behind them countless orphans to live by begging or stealing. These unfortunate children joined together into bands of outlaws who paid back to society the injuries which they and their parents had received.

In the midst of all this, there were still some heroic men who were ready to die for their principles, but most were puzzled, not knowing what to think or what to strive for, though it was clear that the conflict concerned all. The Social Revolutionaries and Mensheviks had more supporters in the country than the Bolsheviks, but they were reluctant to take up arms against the Soviet government for fear that to do so would result in a victory of the reactionary and barbarous White armies and a restoration of the old order. The White armies had no such scruples, but they "lacked the moral authority which could have won them popular support" (Schapiro, p. 348). The Red Army, improvised with great determination and skill as the fighting went on, had a hard core of determined Communist fighters, but its ranks were filled with conscripts. At first it was officered by former officers of the tsarist army, many of whom had been pressed into the Red Army on pain of prison or death. It is not surprising that many of them deserted to the enemy. The morale of the rank and file was not much better. In two years the number of deserters recaptured or surrendering voluntarily was over half of the whole army. Such discipline and coherence as the Red Army possessed depended on the amateur military commissars appointed by the Communist Party.

Many of the working class were ardent Communists and many landless agricultural laborers were for the Soviets, but most of the peasants were of two minds. Lenin put their attitude in a sentence: "We are Bolsheviks, but not Communists. We are for the Bolsheviks because they drove out the landowners, but we are not for the Communists because they are against individual holdings" * (Lenin, *Sochinenya*, 2nd ed., Vol. XXVI). The biographer of Stalin and Trotsky brings out yet other elements in their attitude:

"Rural Russia, vast, illiterate, boiling over with revolt and revenge, had little grasp of the involved disputes between the urban parties. It would be futile to try to put the attitude of that Russia into a clear-cut formula: it was confused, changeable, self-contradictory. Nothing characterizes that attitude better than the following scene described by historians. In one rural area a large body of peasants concluded a meeting with a religious vow that they would no longer wait for any land reform; that they would at once seize the land and smoke out the landlords; and that they would consider as their mortal enemy anybody trying to dissuade them. They would not rest, the peasants proceeded to swear, until the government concluded an immediate peace and released their sons from the army, and until 'that criminal and German spy' Lenin had received exemplary punishment. In the election to the constituent assembly (see below) peasants like these un-

* Lenin claimed indeed that this attitude was confined to Siberia and the Ukraine but there is no reason to doubt that it was fairly general throughout the country.

doubtedly cast their votes for a Social Revolutionary. But
they did so because they attributed to the Social Revolutionaries, the party which had had its roots in the country, the
firm intention of carrying out the program to which the
Bolsheviks alone were determined to give effect. That is why
each of these two parties, the only broad movements left,
. . . could claim, each with some reason, to enjoy the peasantry's support. 'Do not the peasants abhor Lenin, the German spy?' the Social Revolutionary said with self-confidence.
'But do they not declare those who, like you, delay the dis-
possession of the landlords and prolong the war as their mortal
enemies?' the Bolshevik retorted triumphantly" (Isaac
Deutscher, *The Prophet Armed*, p. 320).

That was at the beginning of the Revolution. Later the decisive factor in the minds of the peasants was their fear that
the Whites would take away their land and punish them for
their part in the Revolution. If the White armies had tried to
reach an understanding with the S.R.s and had treated the
peasants decently, they would have had a good chance of
overthrowing Soviet rule. But the White cause attracted to its
ranks narrow-minded reactionaries who hated the Revolution
with a hate that prevented them from distinguishing between
the Bolsheviks and Mensheviks or Social Revolutionaries.

All those who had property to lose and most of the educated classes were against the Revolution, not only because
they stood to lose material advantages, but also because the
Revolution had brought the great unwashed to positions of
command and ignorant hands were ruining "the great work
of time." The Church was against the Revolution partly because the Revolution was against the Church and partly because the organization of the Church had been closely identified with the tsarist order of society. Parents were against the
Revolution because they did not want their children to be
drawn into the turmoil. And for this reason the Bolsheviks
became savage in denouncing traditional family life. They
maintained that the authority of parents in a bourgeois society depended on control of the purse strings. Under socialism
the young would be free, free to love as they liked and free
to make the Revolution here and now. Without the enthusiasm of the very young the Revolution would hardly have
prevailed, but those who were young in 1917 were middle-
aged in 1937 and already looked on family ties from a different point of view (cf. Chap. XXII, Section 5). However,

in the revolutionary years Communists were borne along by unbounded faith in the future and in themselves as the architects of the future. They were building the new heaven upon earth and they had the inexpressible thrill of feeling that every event in the whole world concerned them personally. Those who found brothers and sisters in every proletarian could give up the familiar ties of blood if the Revolution so demanded.

There was at this time a real union between the mass membership of the Communist Party and their leaders. Lenin did not always do what the mass of the party wanted —let alone what the rest of the Russian people wanted—but at this period of his life, if not at all times, he did identify himself emotionally with the masses of the Russian workers and he took a pleasure that was almost perverse in embracing the aspirations of the poorest workers, however crudely and violently they might be expressed.

A constituent assembly elected just after the Bolshevik Revolution gave a large majority to the other revolutionary parties, but the Communists dismissed this assembly at once. It may be doubted whether the constituent assembly would have thrown up leaders capable of ruling Russia in those turbulent times, but the Communists gave it no chance to try.

They believed that in taking power into their own hands they were acting for the people as a whole, or at any rate for the working class upon whose leadership the good of society depended. In his controversies with Lenin many years before, Trotsky had prophesied that if the party "substituted itself in this way for the working classes, the party organization would then substitute itself for the party as a whole; then the central committee would substitute itself for the organization; and finally a single dictator would substitute himself for the central committee" (Deutscher, *The Prophet Armed;* Trotsky, *Nashi Politicheskiye Zadachi*). But no one remembered this, perhaps not even Trotsky himself.

If part of the Russian people could not see their own good and there was no time to persuade them, they must be forced into line. Since there was not enough food in the towns to feed the factory workers and the Red Army, squads of Communists went out into the countryside to take food from the peasants. It was a vicious circle. With industry nearly at a standstill, there was nothing for the peasants to buy in exchange for their produce. So they cultivated less land and did not bother to go to market. That meant that there was still less for the factory workers to eat, and they began to leave the towns and go back to their villages. This in turn meant still fewer goods in the shops, and so it went on. If the Communists tried to right this by taking food from the peasants, then the peasants were still less inclined to sell what they had left. Looking back on this, Lenin said:

"We really took from the peasants all their surpluses, and sometimes even what was not surplus but part of what was necessary to feed the peasants, took it to cover the costs of the army and to feed the workers. We took it for the most part on credit, for paper money. Otherwise we could not beat the landowners and capitalists in a ravaged small-peasant country" (Lenin, *Sochinenya*, 2nd ed., Vol. XXVI, p. 332).

Money loses its value when there is nothing to buy, so wages had to be paid chiefly in kind. This did not seem an evil in itself to those who considered money and markets unnecessary in a socialist society, but it did produce practical complications.

"If the government was to go on requisitioning food and enforcing the ban on trade, it had to increase the pressure on the peasantry first in making it produce more food and then in requisitioning the food. It might also offer special rewards to food growers; clothing, footwear, agricultural implements. It could not do so, however, before the famished workers had repaired and set in motion the destroyed and dilapidated industrial plant and begun to turn out the goods for which the peasantry craved. The government was therefore compelled to press for more industrial production. Unable to offer incentives to the workers, it had to apply more force to them as well as to the peasants" (Deutscher, *The Prophet Armed*, pp. 490-1).

"The requisitioning of food and the prohibition of private trade for the time being helped the government to tide over the direst emergencies. But in the longer run these policies aggravated and accelerated the shrinkage and disintegration of the economy. The peasant began to till only as much of his land as was necessary to keep his family alive. He refused to produce the surplus for which the requisitioning squads were on the lookout. When the countryside refuses to produce food for the town, even the rudiments of urban civilization go to pieces. The cities of Russia became depopulated. Workers went to the countryside to escape famine. Those who stayed behind fainted at the factory benches, produced very little, and often stole what they produced to barter it for food. The old, normal market had indeed been abolished. But its bastard, the black market, despoiled the country, revengefully perverting and degrading human relations" (*ibid.*).

It should be added that townspeople who fled to the countryside might find that they had jumped from the frying pan into the fire. Countless villages were pillaged and burned and the people decimated or massacred in the name of "law and order," of "socialism" or of "anarchism." The inhabitants sometimes deserted their villages to escape marauders of every kind. Men, women and children lived (or died) as best they could in the forest, leaving behind them the unreaped crops to be eaten by vast swarms of mice that multiplied without let or hindrance.

3. Discipline, Centralization and Tyranny

In spite of all, the Bolsheviks won the war, and as fighting ceased at the fronts units under military discipline were transferred to other urgent tasks.

"The stage was set for what came to be known as 'the militarization of labor.' This was the new issue which the ninth party congress had to face when it met toward the end of March 1920. Labor armies were appearing everywhere in the form of detachments of the Red Army employed, now that fighting was at an end, on heavy work of all kinds, including forestry and mining. Nor was there any doubt what this implied. Trotsky, who believed that the problems of industry could be solved only by the methods and by the enthusiasm which had won the civil war, spoke of the need to 'militarize the great masses of peasants who had been recruited for work on the principles of labor service,' and went on: 'Militarization is unthinkable without the militarization of the trade unions as such, without the establishment of a regime in which every worker feels himself a soldier of labor, who cannot dispose of himself freely; if the order is given to transfer him, he must carry it out; if he does not carry it out, he will be a deserter who is punished. Who looks after this? The trade union. It creates the new regime. This is the militarization of the working class' " (9 S'ezd RKP (b), *stenographicheskii Otchot*, 1920; Carr, Vol. II, pp. 212-3).

When everything was turned to the winning of the civil war, all work became a sort of service to society; to require some men to fight and others to work was another form of Peter the Great's principle of universal service.

"The existence of an overwhelming national purpose made it easy and imperative to press forward with policies for the direction and disciplining of labor. The question of the relation between the trade unions and the state was fallaciously simplified now that both the state and the unions depended for their survival on mobilizing every man and every machine in the interests of military victory over the 'white' armies. Under war-communism labor policy became a matter of recruiting workers for the war effort and of sending them where they were most urgently required; the trade unions were the instrument through which this policy could be effectively carried out. So long as the civil war lasted, every issue of principle seemed clear-cut, straightforward, uncontroversial" (Carr, Vol. II, p. 198).

But as soon as the end of the civil war was in sight it became urgent to decide whether the proletarian democracy so drastically abridged in war could be restored in peace. At the tenth congress of the party held in March 1921, Lenin refused to proclaim an open divorce between the dictatorship and proletarian democracy, whatever his private opinions may have been, but he made it clear that he did not intend to rely on full democratic methods. His roundabout way of saying this is summarized by Deutscher.

"The party had to override trade unions, to dismiss their recalcitrant leaders, to break or obviate popular resistance and to prevent the free formation of opinion inside the soviets. Only thus, Lenin held, could the revolution be saved. But he hoped that these practices would give his government a breathing space—his whole policy had become a single struggle for breathing spaces—during which it might modify its policies, make headway with the rehabilitation of the coun-

try, ease the plight of the working people, and win them back
for Bolshevism. The dictatorship could then gradually revert
to proletarian democracy. If this was the aim . . . then the
party must reassert the idea of that democracy at once and
initiate no sweeping measures suggesting its abandonment.
Even though the regime had so often had recourse to coercion, Lenin pleaded, coercion must be its last and persuasion
its first resort. The trade unions ought therefore not to be
turned into appendages of the state. They must retain a measure of autonomy; they must speak for the workers, if need be
against the government; and they ought to become the
schools, not the drill halls, of communism. The administrator
. . . might be annoyed and inconvenienced by the demands
of the unions; he might be right against them in specific in-
stances; but on balance it was sound that he should be so inconvenienced and exposed to genuine social pressure and influence. It was no use telling the workers that they must not
oppose the workers' state. That state was an abstraction. In
reality, Lenin pointed out, his own administration had to consider the interests of the peasants as well as of the workers;
and its work was marred by muddle, by grave 'bureaucratic
distortions' and by arbitrary exercise of power. The working
class ought therefore to defend itself, albeit with self-re-
straint, and to press its claims on the administration. The
state, as Lenin saw it, had to give scope to a plurality of interests and influences. The tenth congress voted by an overwhelming majority for Lenin's resolution" (Deutscher, *The
Prophet Armed,* p. 510).

Those who voted for these rather confusing resolutions did
not foresee either that they would be ruled by Stalin or what
the monolithic structure of state and party would become in
his hands, but, however the facts were wrapped up, they were
in fact voting dictatorial powers to whoever controlled the
party. As they voted, the sailors of Kronstadt, the pride and
glory of the revolution, rose in revolt against the dictatorship
of the Communist Party. They demanded, among other
things, the immediate re-election of the Soviets by secret bal-
lot, freedom for the peasants "to do as they please with the
land" and freedom of speech and of the press for workers,
for peasants, for left-wing socialist parties and for anarchists.
The Kronstadt revolt was the last effective demand for
"proletarian democracy." It was soon suppressed.

Whether they were prepared to face it or not, the aims

which the Bolsheviks had set themselves, together with their miscalculations of popular reactions, indeed the whole logic of their situation, compelled them to rely on force not merely as a temporary expedient but permanently. From the beginning, the political parties of the opposition had rough treatment from the Bolsheviks, but among rank-and-file Communists the idea "that those parties should be suppressed on principle had not taken root before the end of the civil war" (Deutscher, *The Prophet Armed*, p. 517). In theory, "the government still looked forward to the end of hostilities when it would be able to respect the rules of Soviet constitutionalism and to readmit regular opposition," but when the time came it got cold feet. It had too many enemies to be able to rule democratically. Lenin had admitted to the tenth party congress, "We have failed to convince the broad masses."* The Communists "had half suppressed their opponents in order to win the civil war: having won the civil war they went on to suppress them for good" (*ibid.*, p. 518).

Liberties denied to other revolutionaries could not in practice be given to Communist opponents, for if opposition had been allowed inside the party it would unavoidably have become a focus for the bitter discontent of those who were not Communists. This was the reason for the famous rule against "fractionalism" which was now adopted. The theory was, and is, that free discussion inside the party was permitted until the party had given its decision on the point at issue. After that, there must be no more argument and, to quote Lenin, all party members must "act as one man." It was now decided that even before the party had officially made up its mind, there must be no "fractionalism"—that is to say, no one was to organize a group inside the party "on this or that platform"; and by a secret rider added to the resolutions of the tenth party congress the central committee of the party congress was given "full powers in case(s) of any breach of discipline or revival or toleration of fractionalism to apply all measures of party sanction, including expulsion from the party." This ensured that whoever controlled the central committee controlled the party; and the technique of control was now nearing perfection. A card index of all party members was being prepared, and by this means it was becoming possible to keep track of every nucleus of opposition, to break it

* *Desyaty S'ezd Rossiiskoi Kommunisticheskoi Partii*, Moscow, 1921, p. 208. Cf. also Bukharin on pp. 124 and 176.

up by transferring its members to other parts of the country and to place the most reliable supporters of the party line where they were most needed. This operation was in the capable but unscrupulous hands of Joseph Stalin who had now become the Secretary of the Communist Party, a position which gave him a decisive say in the control of the party membership (pp. 266, ff.) He used his influence to get his supporters into the key positions everywhere.

None of the liberties taken away during the civil war were returned afterward. In order to win the civil war, the trade unions were turned into an instrument of coercive government and, for all Lenin's brave words, they never recovered their original function of protecting the workers. The political police, the Cheka, were set up at an early stage when the new rulers might well feel insecure. The first head of the Cheka was Felix Dzerzhinsky, an intellectual inquisitor. He was ruled by a sense of duty, but one cannot touch tar without getting one's hands dirty. The Cheka under various names, OGPU, NKVD, MVD, KGB, soon came to have a powerful and corrupt vested interest in oppression.*

Compulsion went hand in hand with centralization. Unable to trust the loyalty and competence of their subordinates, the leaders of the Revolution felt obliged to hold all the threads in their own hands. When for a time during the civil war the territory which they held shrank to the dimensions of fifteenth-century Muscovy, this extreme centralization was not obviously absurd. Indeed, during the civil war there was no alternative, but habits of overcentralization acquired at the height of the civil war remained as a lasting feature of Soviet rule. Both tsarist tradition and Lenin's conception of party organization favored centralization. Every mass movement tends to an extreme either of anarchy or of discipline, and Lenin had chosen discipline. Under Stalin, the tendency to overcentralization was reinforced by a morbid suspicion of all subordinates.

The Bolsheviks gained power because, as Berdyaev pointed out, they turned everything Russian to their own ends.

"Bolshevism . . . made use of the Russian traditions of government by imposition, and instead of an unfamiliar democ-

---

* For convenience, the Soviet political police are generally referred to as the "OGPU" in this book. A "Chekist" is a member of the Cheka.

racy of which they had had no experience proclaimed a dictatorship which was more like the old rule of the tsar. It made use of the characteristics of the Russian mind in all its incompatibility with the secularized bourgeois society. It made use of its religious instinct, its dogmatism and maximalism, its search after social justice and the Kingdom of God upon earth, its capacity for sacrifice and the patient bearing of suffering, and also of its manifestations of coarseness and cruelty. It made use of Russian Messianism and faith in Russia's own path of development. It made use of the historic cleavage between the masses and the cultured classes, of the popular mistrust of the latter. . . . It absorbed also the sectarian spirit of the Russian intelligentsia" (*The Origin of Russian Communism*, pp. 168–9. Slightly condensed).

The Bolsheviks had gained an unshakable hold on the government, but the recalcitrance of the material on which they worked continually frustrated their attempts to realize Lenin's dreams. The Bolshevik view of man and society contained much truth, but it was incomplete. Marx and Engels made many new and valuable observations about economic influences in human affairs. Their mistake was to conclude that they had found the key to all the problems of society. Their Russian followers embraced their views with a narrow but ardent orthodoxy. They believed that theft and other crimes against property were the direct result of a vicious economic system. In a socialist society there would be no need to steal and therefore no theft. Likewise, prostitution and most of the unhappiness of family life resulted from the economic structure of bourgeois society. Substitute socialism for capitalism and these evils would soon disappear. If this were true, it followed that the socialist revolution was the supreme good by which all actions were to be judged. A lie told in the interest of the Revolution was a noble lie, and every cruelty might be excused if only it served the Revolution. It might be a duty to kill or to deceive. There was no limit.

This view of evil leaves out of account those weaknesses of human nature which flow from man's own being, not from any social system. The Bolsheviks had no means of distinguishing between true and false elements in their theory. They held the whole Leninist faith with the unshakable ardor of fundamentalists, and they were sure that their faith was incarnate in the policy of their party, for theory and practice were one. So it was treachery even to ask those questions

which had to be asked before the Bolsheviks could discover
where they had gone wrong. .

The Russian Revolution is a gigantic classical tragedy. A
fatal flaw in the Communist view of the nature of things has
perverted noble aspirations. It is in this that "the unity of
theory and practice" has been shown. Before Lenin was removed from control by his first stroke in May 1922, the fatal
acts had been performed, but their tragic consequences were
not yet unfolded.

CHAPTER XXI

a breathing space

The NEP, the most false and ambiguous of all Soviet periods.

Pasternak

1. The NEP

The civil war was accompanied and followed by typhus and famine. In those regions which normally produced a surplus, the peasants were fairly well fed until the bad harvest of 1920, though even here the townspeople went hungry, but in those districts which depended on imported grain "the consumption of food was slightly lower than that enjoyed by the state-assisted starving peasantry during periods of famine before the war"; that was in the countryside; in the towns it was estimated that people ate only two-fifths of what they had eaten before the war. No one could count the victims, but it is thought that over 7,000,000 died from hunger and epidemics in the first two and one-half years of Soviet rule (Schapiro, pp. 215-6).

At last, with the new harvest of 1923, the country could make a new start. The old society had been swept away, but the new foundations had not yet been laid. There was no question of the expansion of industry for the present. It would be much if such industry as existed before the Revolution could be brought back into full production and if farming could be revived sufficiently to feed the towns. Hitherto the Bolsheviks had tended to assume that it was only necessary to extract from the countryside food which was already there. They did not readily take in that production could fall so low that there was no longer enough food to go round even in a land as rich as Russia. Eventually famine brought this rather elementary lesson home.

The main purpose of NEP, the New Economic Policy first introduced at the tenth party congress in 1921, was to **give** the peasants an incentive to produce more. Under NEP forcible requisitions of food ceased, and the peasants were encouraged to sell their produce on the open market, while in the towns small private businesses were allowed to spring up and even to thrive for a short time.

As Russia recovered from her wounds, visitors from the West began to arrive once more, and they found much that pleased them as well as much to cause somber thoughts. "Old wooden Russia" was still alive in all her indescribable charm. The peasants had the land and worked it with their families as independent small holders. Many children were going to school for the first time in their lives. It was true that there were not enough schoolteachers, not enough doctors, not enough people trained in any of the skills which the country needed, but the poor had a fair chance of getting whatever was available. All shortages and hardships could be blamed on war and civil disturbance. It was still possible to believe that plenty was just around the corner. The Communist Party controlled everything, but their leaders did not at that stage take much more than their share of conveniences which were not available for all. The continuance of vigorous and open disputes among Communists seemed to show that there was still a sort of democracy within the party even if no one outside it could express his opinions. The Cheka was an unpleasant part of Soviet reality, but it had not yet become an all-pervading tyranny and it was not altogether foolish to hope that severe measures taken at a time of extreme crisis would be gradually relaxed. Socialism would soon be built, criminals and enemies of the Revolution were the result of a vicious social system. This would be changed, society would cease to breed criminals and there would then be no need for repression.

The outlines of a new economic morality were becoming generally understood, if not always accepted. Offenses against public property were treated as a form of treason against socialism while theft of private property was officially regarded with comparative indulgence as a consequence of the former capitalist order of society. "Speculation" and "exploitation" were treated as heinous crimes. The essence of "speculation" is to buy cheap in order to sell at a profit. The worst kind of "speculation" is of course to buy food in a cheap market in order to sell it at an extortionate price to starving people. But in Soviet law the man who buys and sells again after adding a retail margin is equally guilty of speculation. However, in Soviet Russia you may generally sell anything that you have produced yourself at whatever price you can get. But you must not charge a commission for taking your neighbor's goods to market. If all this made distribution expensive and inefficient, that was one more reason for hastening the development of socialism to the point when private production would become a negligible factor. In the meantime the peasants continue to sell food in the town markets. Much of this trade is on the edge of the law or downright illegal. The authorities watch it with suspicion and make occasional swoops but sixty years after the October Revolution it shows no signs of disappearing.

"Exploitation" is the crime of making money out of someone else's labor. You may employ labor for personal services. Until recently it has been fairly easy to get domestic servants in Moscow. Well-to-do people, such as the late Alexis Tolstoy, might employ a gardener and a chauffeur. It was quite legal to do this but if he had tried to make money by selling garden products or getting his chauffeur to ply for hire as a taxi driver, he would have become liable to severe penalties. Under the NEP the party had to allow exceptions to these rules, but it went against the grain.

During the NEP Russia's economy was sluggish. There was much unemployment, and a very high turnover of labor. Those workers who were not firmly established in the towns often went back to their villages. The skilled workers, who formed the aristocracy of labor, could generally hold on to their jobs. They suffered much poverty, hardship and overcrowding but they were better off than most of their neighbors and their hours of work were not excessive. The Soviet trade unions did not and do not take an effective part in collective bargaining over wage rates, as this is understood in the West, but they could sometimes get their members holidays by the sea, rests in sanatoria, and other advantages.

The shape of a new society was beginning to appear. At the top were the higher officials and army officers, leading scientists, writers and the like. Near to these came the skilled workers and after them the unskilled who were often unemployed or continually changing their jobs in search of something better. Outside the main stream of Soviet life there was another class, the *"byvshye"* or "those who had been" in positions of importance before the Revolution; the gentry, army officers, the tsarist police force, the clergy, the bourgeoisie and the families of all these. All were suspect but some were useful to the regime and held down good jobs; some lived by the sale of jewelry and others scraped a living in various ways. The peasants, as before, stood apart from the life of the towns with their own peculiar class structure. It was usual to divide them into three classes: the *"kulaks"* or "rich peasants," who hired labor as well as working their own land; the "middle peasants" who had enough land to keep themselves but not enough to need hired labor; and the "poor peasants" who did not have enough land to live on and had therefore to work for the *kulaks*. These divisions were not hard and fast; a family of middle peasants might suddenly find themselves called *kulaks*. The Bolsheviks and the *kulaks* recognized each other as natural enemies. If the new regime was to have any mass support in the countryside, this must come from the "middle" and "poor" peasants.

During these years Russia was intensely alive intellectually and spiritually. Stimulated by the brilliant leaders of the Revolution, great numbers of young men and women were discussing Marxism and found the experience exhilarating. The application of Marxist theory to the circumstances of the day was a fascinating subject for eager and open debate. The Revolution had stirred Russia to the depths and during the civil war the government had been too busy to set up a thorough-going control of intellectual life. During the NEP "thought control" was tightened steadily but it was still possible to believe that the restraints imposed by a Marxist control of intellectual life were necessary for the full flowering of the human spirit.

Many of the best writers and artists left Russia during the civil war or the early years of NEP, but others found that the new circumstances of their native land moved them to creative work. Others again felt that for them, at least, to leave Russia would be spiritual death and they were prepared to remain, come what might.

A large section of the avant-garde artists hailed the Revolution as the fulfillment of their dreams. Where previous generations of artists had drawn their raw material from nature, experiments with abstract art were now suggesting the possibility that man might construct a brand new world for himself. (See Camilla Gray, *The Great Experiment*, Chaps. 7 and 8.) Malevich claimed that "Cubism and Futurism were the revolutionary forms of art foreshadowing the revolution in political and economic life in 1917" and the aim which he proposed was to "seize the world from the hands of nature and build a new world belonging to man himself." Some of the best artists used their skill to give visual expression in posters, books, stage decor and films to the Revolution as they understood it; some worked for a fusion of industry and art. Russia was too poor, too disorganized, to execute most of the plans conceived by these artists of the twenties, but some of their designs have a touch of genius. They have left to posterity one great monument, the mausoleum of Lenin in the Red Square. In the early nineteen-twenties, ideas were still welcome provided that they fitted into the Soviet pattern.

The overt expression of disloyalty was severely repressed, but loyal satirists such as Mayakovsky and Zoshchenko were encouraged to castigate the failures of Soviet human nature in general and the follies of Soviet bureaucracy in particular. "The intelligentsia was . . . able to maintain some sort of autonomous existence, under increasingly difficult circumstances, during the first decade of the Soviet régime. Censorship and general control . . . were not in principle different from what they were before 1905, being designed mainly to prevent obvious propaganda against the régime. Until the end of NEP even non-Bolshevik and anti-Bolshevik writers were enabled to reach a wide public through private or cooperative publishing firms which were not under direct party control and, indeed, a considerable amount of scarcely veiled criticism of the regime and party ideology was published in this manner" (Max Hayward in *Soviet Survey* for Nov.-Dec. 1957).

This was the age of Soviet experimentalism when bold new forms in poetry and the theater, in education and in life rivaled and outbid the *avant-garde* of Paris and Berlin. In London "the bright young things" scandalized society by setting the Thames on fire or dressing up in baby clothes. In Moscow they practiced free love and nudism, they advocated the emancipation of schoolchildren and campaigned against religion and family life. For all the differences, Russia did not escape the *Zeitgeist* of the twenties.

The young seemed to be in perpetual effervescence. It was exciting to live amidst such bold experiments and to share in making a brave new world. The hardships of Soviet life appealed to youthful idealism. Was it not worthwhile going hungry for a few years in such a noble cause? Dirt and shabbiness were as alluring to the Soviet youth of that day as to their spiritual forebears of the sixties and seventies.

It is tempting to take a romantic view of Russia in the

NEP period. Indeed, it is impossible to understand the driving force of the Bolshevik ideals without entering into their romantic side, but the romantic view leaves out something vital. The stern men and women who led the Bolshevik Revolution were literal-minded and pitiless theorists. Whatever the cost, they meant to see Marxism applied line by line, until everything fitted into the pattern. Such men were not likely to acquiesce in a compromise, but Russia of the NEP was essentially a compromise, only half socialist. All industry of any size had been nationalized, but many smaller businesses and the greater part of the land were still in private hands. And the worst of it was that the socialist half of the Soviet economy depended on the other half.

The middle and poor peasants should have been the mainstay of the regime in the countryside, but "the individual peasant, left to himself with the small holding which any approximately equal distribution of the land must inevitably produce, had relapsed into subsistence farming to feed himself and his family, and met his other needs by barter with his neighbors and by seeking employment for himself or members of his family in casual labor or in rural handicrafts. It was beyond his capacity, and did not enter into his view of life, to produce food for sale to the cities, much less for export." (Carr, Vol. V, p. 239.) If the towns had relied on the poor peasants for their food they would have starved. On the other hand the *kulaks* produced a surplus for sale but drove a hard bargain. If they had been encouraged to prosper they could have fed Russia and, no doubt, produced for export too, but was this tolerable in a socialist country? The *kulaks* were capitalists and if they had been given their head they would have undone much of the Revolution. They were afterwards treated so cruelly, and so many innocent men, women and children were confounded with the guilty, that one is tempted to idealize them, but the typical *kulak* was no prosperous yeoman farmer living on friendly terms with his neighbors. The *kulaks* were hated for the way in which they ground work and money out of men and women who could find no other employer. Wages were seldom paid in cash and many subterfuges were used to conceal the extent to which one man was battening on another. Often a rich peasant would "cultivate the poor peasants' land in return for a major share of the harvest, so that the rich peasant, in virtue of his ownership of animals and implements, became the principal beneficiary from land which he neither owned nor rented" (*ibid.*, p. 235). The Trade Union of Agricultural and Forestry Workers, which should have protected the workers, was ineffective and was viewed with general contempt, while the *kulaks* got the cooperative movement into their own hands so that it was not possible to use it either as an instrument to curb *kulak* power.

Kulaks were hated but it was not clear who was to be considered a *kulak*. Those, such as Bukharin, who wanted to let the peasants get rich if that was the only way to feed the socialist towns, said that not all "rich peasants" were regarded as *kulaks* by their neighbors. In an expanding economy it might have been possible to encourage the peasants as a whole to become rich without allowing the *kulaks* to rise on the shoulders of the weak and inefficient, but in the stagnant economy of Russia in the mid-nineteen-twenties a "wager on the *kulak*" meant restoring a rural tyranny worse than the old landowners'. However, it was not easy to see another way out. For a time concessions were made to the *kulaks*, but it was found that even so food did not come into market unless industry produced the things which the *kulaks* wanted to buy. Yet industry could not increase its output without more capital which could only come from a farming surplus. The problem remained unresolved until the advent of the Five-Year Plans.

In the towns, the counterpart of the *kulaks* were the *nepmen*, men who had grown rich suddenly under the New Economic Policy and often showed the disagreeable qualities of the *nouveau riche*. There was a real danger that socialism would be strangled by the *kulaks* and the *nepmen* at home; and the Communists were convinced that before long they would be attacked by their enemies from without, an expectation which came true on June 22, 1941.

Urged on by such fears, the Communist leaders hurried Russia toward the goal which they had set. Industry was reestablished and the nation was taught the new learning which was to be the key to the future. All who stood in the way were crushed without mercy. The old ruling classes, the Mensheviks and the Social Revolutionaries, had all been destroyed as organized groups, and anyone who had been connected with them was in perpetual danger of Siberia or execution.

2. Religion Under Communism

The Church was doubly suspect. It alone maintained its organization, it alone continued to put forward a view of life which undermined Marxism, and without Marxism there could be no socialism; or so it was supposed. Therefore relations between Church and State could not be easy. Already in February 1918 the attacks on Church property had induced the Patriarch and Synod to issue "instructions to the Orthodox Church against Government acts"; it was laid down that "in cases of attack by despoilers or graspers of Church property, the Church people should be called to the defense of the Church, sound the tocsin and send out runners, etc." In 1918 the Soviet government was not expected to last and the Church authorities thought that if they could postpone any calamity for a few months, the danger would have passed. Matters came to a head in the terrible famine of 1921-22. In Russia's desperate straits voluntary charity was allowed to make its last appearance.

The Patriarch Tikhon offered to collect valuables belonging to the Church and to offer them as collateral security for a foreign loan to buy food for the starving. Objects consecrated for sacramental use were excluded from this offer. At first the State accepted this but on second thought the Bolsheviks saw grave objections to letting the Church take part in social work which according to their view ought to be a Communist monopoly. Moreover all Church property had been nationalized; it was true that most of the Church plate or other valuables still remained in the churches or undestroyed monasteries, but according to the letter of the Soviet law the Church had no property to offer. The Kremlin therefore demanded the surrender of Church valuables. Tikhon maintained that the surrender of consecrated articles would be contrary to the canons of the Church, but enjoined the faithful to give up whatever was not consecrated and to pay the value of the rest.

The government took no account of this and sent out its own agents to seize those valuables that were not of religious significance. As might have been foreseen, the agents of the atheist government did not distinguish accurately between one kind of religious article and another. Many of them simply took what they found, whether it was consecrated or not.

Thereupon Tikhon issued a famous appeal to the faithful to resist the despoilers of consecrated Church property. As a direct consequence of this, 1,414 "bloody conflicts" took place in various parts of the country and were officially recorded, while no doubt many other similar conflicts went unrecorded. Many Church people were arrested and sent to Siberia or shot, and the Orthodox Church lost many of its leaders. The first effect of persecution was to draw Church people together into a closer fellowship. The Church was reduced from power and riches to poverty and oppression, but the subtler forms of Stalinist pressure were not yet invented. It was possible for one who lived through those years to write, "That was a happy time. The Church was strong. (*Plenennaya Tserkov*, by Rar [Vetrov], published by Posev, Frankfurt am Main, 1954, p. 9).

The Roman Catholic minority adopted the same attitude as the Orthodox at this point and suffered the same fate. But those sects which could be regarded as having broken away from Orthodoxy were treated with relative favor by the Kremlin, on the principle of "divide and rule," until it became clear that their vigor would be as dangerous to Communism as was the Orthodox Church itself.

At the climax of this campaign against the Church the Patriarch Tikhon was arrested. Thereupon some of the leaders of the radical movement inside the Church made strong representations to the Patriarch that the Church was suffering from his absence and asked leave "to open the chancery of your beatitude and start it functioning." Tikhon gave them permission to open the patriarchal chancery but with instructions to hand it over to certain senior members of the hierarchy to whom he entrusted responsibility to act for him during his arrest. The radical Church leaders did open the chancery but instead of handing it over to the persons designated by Tikhon, they proceeded to operate it on their own account and called a new council of the Church. This council voted to abolish the Patriarchate and substitute a more democratic form of Church order and called on "every faithful churchman . . . to fight with all his might together with the Soviet authority for the realization of the Kingdom of God upon earth . . . and to use all means to realize in life the grand principle of the October Revolution."

This new movement, known as the "Living Church," succeeded for a time in getting control of most of the parish churches and had support of a kind from a very large number of bishops and clergy. But it was suspect to the rank and file of the faithful.

The leaders of the "Living Church" were in part time-servers, but many of them were also moved by a genuine desire for radical reforms of the Church or for the development of Christian-socialist ideas which they believed to be in harmony with the ultimate aims of the Communists. They failed to understand that a passionate atheism forms an essential part of all real Communism and they did not realize that the Bolshevik leaders were using the "Living Church" as a tool to be thrown away as soon as it had served its purpose. On the other hand Tikhon's policy of resistance seemed to have brought the Church into a blind alley, and it was natural to hope that a fresh start would bring better results. The clergy in particular were put under cruel pressure from the Communist Party to support the new movement. Moreover many of the parish clergy were moved by hatred and jealousy of the "monastic autocrats, who had prevented able married priests from rising to positions deserving of their talents" (Anderson, p. 65). This predisposed them to think well of the schism, which was strongly antimonastic.

If the motives of the supporters of the "Living Church" were various and complex, the views of its opponents were simple and downright. The vast majority of the faithful remained true to the Patriarch and regarded the formation of the "Living Church" as treachery to Christ. They kept away from those churches which joined the schism, and before long repentant clergy began to make their peace with the patriarchal Church. The "Living Church" soon crumbled away and its last pitiful relics were received back into communion by the Patriarch of Moscow after the Second World War.

Some of the uncertainties which led to the schism were also reflected in the patriarchal Church. In June 1923 Tikhon was suddenly released by the Soviet Government and issued a famous "confession." The Patriarch declared: "Having been nurtured in a monarchist society, and until my arrest having been under the influence of anti-Soviet individuals, I was filled with hostility against the Soviet authorities. I repent of all my actions directed against the government. . . . I hereby declare that I am no more an enemy to the Soviet government."

This dramatic declaration proved a turning point. The

Church had broken decisively with its past political affili-
ations and now sought to find its position in the new society,
whatever trials might lie ahead. But at the time there was intense confusion and it is still not clear how far Tikhon may
have been influenced during his imprisonment by pressure
from the OGPU and by misrepresentations of the Church's
situation during his enforced absence. A great assembly of
the faithful greeted the Patriarch with joy at his 'appearance
in church after his release. Others shook their heads. Was the
"confession" a forgery or extorted by force or could it be
that the Patriarch had gone over to the enemy?

Some purists rejected the ministrations of a Church which
had made a pact with the anti-Christ, as it seemed to them.
Henceforth a section of the Church existed in secret. The
succession of bishops and priests was maintained but they
worked secretly, concealing their identity from all but trusted
brethren. Secret churches were fitted out in inner rooms, attics
or cellars, and served by priests who never went out by daylight. Other priests traveled, making themselves known to
each other on journeys by an elaborate system of pass signs
which were changed at frequent intervals. In the nature of
things it is impossible to know how many adherents Russia's
"underground church" has at any time. The inner circle of
those who know the pass signs must always have been small.
But there were many more who would welcome the services
of a traveling priest when he appeared suddenly in a village.
At the times of greatest confusion and greatest persecution it
seems likely that the "underground church" had the tacit
approval and even support of very many, rather in the way
that many Russian peasants in the eighteenth and nineteenth
centuries held to the belief that the Old Believers were the
true Church even if they themselves had not the courage to
join them openly. In the quieter days that followed 1945 the
underground church has been quietly growing back into the
legal church, as its leaders gave permission for their followers
to use the ministrations of trusted priests of the legal church.
Yet it is always possible that renewed persecution might lead
to a revival of the "underground church."

Tikhon died in 1925. The Church was not allowed to elect
a new Patriarch and the deputies who should have taken Tikhon's place were not allowed to assume office. For about two
years the Russian Church was left without any legally recognized central administration. The only organs of the Church
whose existence was recognized by the Soviet law were

groups of twenty people in each parish who took formal responsibility for the Church. In the Soviet view larger organizations such as dioceses "existed only in the imagination of
the faithful." A bishop had no legal right to give even the
most necessary instructions to the priests under him. If he did
so, he was infringing the freedom of a Soviet citizen—a serious crime. Similarly the parish priests were in theory completely in the hands of the "twenties elected by their parishioners." In fact the wishes of ecclesiastical superiors were ascer-
tained and carried out, but those who did so were at the mercy
of any informer. The loyalty of the believers to each other and
the Russian power of informal cooperation were enough to
prevent an immediate collapse of the ordered structure of
Church life but it was clearly desirable to bring this system
to an end as soon as possible. In 1927, in return for renewed declaration of loyalty to the Soviet state, the Metropolitan Sergius was allowed to assume the office of Locum
Tenens of the Patriarch. The organization of the Church
remained very rudimentary for another 15 years, but the
Russian Church at that time needed no more elaborate organization for its survival.

The restoration of an embryonic administration in 1927
did not lead to any greater favor being shown to the Church.
Those who worked in the Patriarchate knew that they were
marked men but they knew too that it now suited the government to have a central Church administration to deal with.
One of them has written "we compared our position with that
of chickens in a shed, from whom the cook seizes victims in
turn—one today and one tomorrow, but not all the chickens
at once" (Rar, p. 105).

There was more than one reason why the Bolsheviks regarded religion as dangerous to themselves. The Orthodox
Church had been closely identified with the tsarist regime—
too closely for the health of its spiritual life. So it was natural
that the Communists should look on religious people as coun-
terrevolutionaries. Moreover, a religious man will not hate at
the word of command, whereas the Communists enjoin
hatred of the class enemy as an imperative duty. A religious
man keeps a final independence, however obedient to the
state he may be, and that prevents him from being a good
Communist. The Bolsheviks regard religion as something that
confuses and weakens a man and may make him a bad Soviet
citizen. Man's happiness is to be found here or nowhere. The
key to the future is in man's own hands and to pretend other-

wise could only be a weakening distraction. Holding these beliefs, the Bolsheviks did what they could to squeeze their religion out of the Russians.

They denounced the Christians as enemies of the Revolution, they unmasked every pious fraud and invented numerous imaginary charges. They prevented the printing of religious books and newspapers. They kept up a barrage of rationalist propaganda showing the iniquities of the Church and maintaining that religion was disproved by science. Crippling taxes were placed on churches and priests, and the weight of the burden was doubled by the manner of its collection. A sudden demand would be made for taxes (or for insurance of the church building) and if the money was not forthcoming at once and in full the church would be closed. For many years all who took a leading part in the congregation were liable to be arrested and severely punished, not ostensibly for their religion but on a trumped-up charge. It is still forbidden to teach religion to children under eighteen except in private houses and in groups of not more than three. For many years the children of priests were excluded from higher education. Only the staunchest believers were likely to seek ordination under these conditions, but in the fervor of their faith they made up for the fewness of their numbers and the inadequacy of their training.

Under this pressure those who are "most zealous when religion goes in his silver slippers" soon left the Church; and some simple souls were bowled over by statements such as "Darwin has proved that there is no God," but even those who did not know how to answer such arguments were not always convinced. The Russian peasants are suspicious of clever townees, particularly if these are people in authority. So though the atheist propaganda had a considerable effect, the Church still had a hold on a great number of people, particularly in the countryside.

Even those who had themselves thrown off religion would often allow some older relative to teach their children how to pray. If the poison of religion was not to be stopped in the 1920s and spreads among the new generation even now, that is largely the work of the Russian grandmothers. From the Marxist point of view, however, it was reasonable to suppose that religion was a dying superstition. The life of the nation was being restored after the time of troubles, the party was strengthening its hold on the nation and Stalin was strengthening his hold on the party.

CHAPTER XXII

Stalin's revolution

*My father . . . hath chastised you
with whips, but I will chastise you
with scorpions.* I Kings xii. II

1. Stalin's Rise to Power

The death of Lenin in 1924 left a vacuum, but there were many able men waiting to fill it. Trotsky seemed to stand head and shoulders above the rest, but if Trotsky should prove, for all his brilliance and resolution, to be too erratic for supreme rule, there were other old comrades of Lenin who might aspire to succeed him.

The brilliant internationalists of the first Bolshevik generation overlooked Stalin in their plans for the future, so they have left no vivid picture of their supplanter in his ascent to power. To many of them he seemed nothing but "a gray blur looming up now and then dimly" (Sukhanov, p. 230). Very short, pockmarked, with a slight malformation of one arm, his speeches were flat and his writing pedestrian. Moreover, he spoke Russian with a strong Georgian accent, which was comically out of keeping with his place in history. Stalin typified everything that was provincial in the Russian Revolution, yet in his way he was closer to Russian realities than the brilliant men who despised him but were nonetheless ready to seek his help in their quarrels with each other. Lenin had his reserves about Stalin's character and judgment, but he saw that Stalin was supremely competent and he gave him important tasks. Indeed, as secretary of the Communist Party Stalin had already gained control of the keys to supreme power when Lenin died, but no one realized this. Stalin was still a backroom boy, not to be compared with the magnetic figures of the leading revolutionaries, but enormously useful as an organizer who was ready to give his full energies to tasks which others found boring. Stalin resembled the first grand princes of Muscovy in his lack of color, in his lack of scruples and in his effectiveness. He was recognized as an important member of the government but no one thought of him as a potential successor to Lenin, except perhaps Lenin himself.

On December 25, 1922, with the shadow of death already upon him, Lenin dictated but did not show to the other Communist leaders a document which has become known as his "testament." He saw the danger of the party being "split in the near future" and gave a warning that the personal relation between Stalin and Trotsky constituted "a big half of the danger of that split." "Comrade Stalin having become general secretary has concentrated an enormous power in his hands; and I am not sure that he always knows how to use that power with sufficient caution. On the other hand comrade Trotsky . . . is distinguished not only by his exceptional abilities—personally he is, to be sure, the most able man in the present central committee—but also by his far-reaching self-confidence." A few days later Lenin wrote a famous postscript to his "testament" in which he said:

"Stalin is too rude, and this fault, entirely supportable in relations among us communists, becomes insupportable in the office of general secretary. Therefore, I propose to the comrades to find a way to remove Stalin from that position and appoint to it another man who in all respects differs from Stalin only in superiority—namely, more patient, more loyal, more polite and more attentive to comrades, less capricious, etc. This circumstance may seem an insignificant trifle, but I think that, from the point of view of preventing a split and from the point of view of the relation between Stalin and Trotsky which I discussed above, it is not a trifle, or it is such a trifle as may acquire a decisive significance."

This postscript, like the "testament" itself, remained secret but the conclusion that Stalin should be removed from the post of general secretary marked Lenin's increasing disillusionment with his successor. As late as October 1922 his trust in Stalin seemed unshaken. "Then, in November, or at the beginning of December, something happened that shook that trust irretrievably" (Deutscher, *Stalin*). News of Stalin's part in the brutal repression of discontent in Georgia began to reach Lenin's ears. But there seem to have been other factors at work besides this. When Lenin had recovered sufficiently from his illness to be "back in office, he sensed a vague and yet unmistakable change in the atmosphere around him. The creaking of the administrative machine had got worse during his absence. It had become more difficult to get straight and quick answers to queries. People grumbled about rudeness in some offices, red tape in others, and abuses of power in yet others. His own instructions and orders often got stuck in unidentified places without reaching their destination. He had the feeling of obscure happenings behind his back. Even before his illness he had confided to the party his uncanny sensation that the whole government machinery had been moving in a direction different from the one he, the man at the wheel, had believed" (*ibid.*, p. 247).

Three days before Lenin dictated his testament, his wife, Krupskaya, had a violent quarrel with Stalin. In the following weeks relations between Lenin and Stalin grew steadily worse until by the beginning of March Lenin seems to have been ready to take open action against Stalin, but on March 9 Lenin had his third stroke. He was not to recover, though he lingered on until January 1924. When Lenin had this stroke his "testament" was not known to any of the leaders of the party. The twelfth party congress was to meet in a few weeks. If Lenin had retained his faculties until then, the congress might have removed Stalin from his post as party secretary. But with Lenin absent from the scene, Trotsky hesitated to act against Stalin, who showed Machiavellian skill in managing the congress. Thus Trotsky lost his only real chance of securing the succession.

Stalin's methods of political warfare were simple and effective. First as secretary of the Communist Party, while Lenin was still alive, he put his own supporters in the key positions in every district throughout the country. Then, when Lenin died, Stalin banded together with Zinoviev and Kamenev to oppose Trotsky. When Trotsky was safely excluded from power, Stalin joined with Bukharin and others to attack Zinoviev and Kamenev. Finally, when this maneuver was in its turn successfully completed, Stalin turned against his last associates with the help of assistants who owed their own careers to Stalin himself. After this there was no one left to share Stalin's power but those who were completely dependent on him.

But why did Stalin's opponents let him get away with it? The short answer is that they underrated him. Even in 1927, when it is now possible to see that his dictatorship was already consolidated, his clever rivals tended to despise him.

Under Lenin he had gradually collected enormous power in his own hands. The culmination came on April 3, 1922, when he was made secretary to the central committee of the party, or, as it was sometimes expressed, general secretary to the party. Lenin was still in full vigor and no doubt he felt sure that he could control Stalin, but within two months Lenin had his first stroke. This gave Stalin a clear field.

He controlled the membership of the party in every way. Through patronage he could get his supporters into the key positions everywhere and he could see. that his opponents were posted where they could exercise no decisive influence. He could see to it that troublesome people lost their jobs and in those days of unemployment to be out of work was a very serious matter. As secretary of the Politbureau he prepared its agenda, supplied documentation for every decision to be taken and could influence the execution of the decisions after they were taken.

If the other Bolshevik leaders had been trained in the school of administrative experience, they would have seen that such power was dangerous, but they had neither the experience nor the common sense needed to gauge their rival. Trained on the story of the French Revolution, they were looking for a Danton or a Bonaparte. Trotsky might be a Bonaparte, but not Stalin. The general secretary's lack of personality seemed to make him the ideal vehicle for the anonymous forces of class and party (*ibid.*, p. 273). He never seemed to push himself forward. At meetings of the Politbureau he would listen quietly and then vote with the majority, often a majority that he himself had engineered. In his original controversies with Trotsky he left it to Zinoviev and Kamenev to make the most withering attacks. Stalin used more moderate language. "He was more accessible to the average official or party man than the other leaders. He studiously cultivated his contacts with the people who in one way or another made and unmade reputations, provincial secretaries, popular satirical writers and foreign visitors. . . . Sometimes he would be seen in a corner of a staircase pulling at his pipe and listening immovably, for an hour or two, to an agitated interlocutor and breaking his silence only to ask a few questions. . . . The interviewer . . . rarely reflected on the fact that Stalin had not revealed his mind" (Deutscher, *Stalin*, pp. 273-4).

The leaders of the opposition to Stalin always found themselves outvoted at meetings of the Politbureau or of lesser party organs, but party solidarity bound them not to ventilate their disagreement publicly. Stalin kept Trotsky in the Politbureau, sharing the unpopularity of its decisions, until his position had been so completely undermined that his open opposition could be risked. Trotsky could not organize a group of supporters without being guilty of "fractionalism." Still less could he appeal to public opinion outside the party. That would have been treachery to Communism, and Stalin's opponents still felt themselves bound by the rules of party loyalty. If they had been as unscrupulous in that respect as they were in other matters, their opposition might have been more effective.

To build and to overthrow do not call for the same qualities. If there had been no Stalin, there is little doubt that some other organizer would have come to the front and elbowed aside the more spectacular men who had made the Revolution. It was likely that the man who did this would have learned his trade in the dangerous but plodding work of undermining the old order bit by bit in distant parts of the Russian empire. Sometimes he would be in prison, sometimes exiled to Siberia, learning the art of double-crossing in a world of spies and counterspies, seldom outside Russia, his mind formed by contact with the Russian intelligentsia and the half-intelligentsia. Such men were cut off from the broader views of revolutionary exiles in London or Paris or Zurich, but they were learning all the time how to handle men and how to get things done. Such a man was likely to be narrow, determined, unscrupulous; and so Stalin turned out to be; but such a man would also be brave, efficient and ready for great sacrifices in what the Bolsheviks believed to be the universal cause of mankind; and Stalin was that too.

When he was young he identified himself with his cause and showed that he could suffer for it. When he was old, he identified the cause with himself. Whoever had played Stalin's part in history was likely to do that.

In the first years of his rule, displaced leaders were not executed. Trotsky was sent to a distant part of the Soviet Union and then exiled to Turkey. It was not until the thirties that Stalin undertook the final liquidation of his chief enemies. In the meantime the party rule against "fractionalism" covered his needs. At first he tolerated opposition in the sense that dissident Communist leaders could express their views if they could find someone to listen; but Stalin controlled all the

most effective means of publicity and was able to drown the
voices of those who opposed him. The rule against fractionalism gave him an ever-ready pretext for suppressing the nucleus of an organized group. Even this was not strong enough
for Stalin at the height of his power. To his strong but rigid
mind the slightest murmur of criticism seemed dangerous and
was suppressed with ruthless and thorough violence.

When he was at the beginning of his ascent, did he foresee
the end? As time went by, the tyrant's appetite grew with eating, but when Kamenev and Zinoviev wanted to take drastic
action against Trotsky, Stalin replied, "We have not agreed
with Zinoviev and Kamenev, because we know that a policy
of chopping off [heads] is dangerous and infectious. You
chop off one head today, another one tomorrow, still another
one the day after—what in the end will be left of the party?"
This enabled him to pose as a moderate, leaving colleagues to
bear the odium of having advocated extreme measures, but
also leaving the future open for drastic measures if at any
time he judged this necessary. He felt his way forward from
step to step, with a strong sense of direction but not, it would
seem, with any clear vision of the goal toward which he was
steering the Soviet Union or of the part that he would play in
the last twenty years of his life.

Sometimes principles as well as personalities were involved
in the struggle for power, but it is not always easy to disentangle the issues, for the contestants sometimes said what
they hoped would favor their chances of success rather than
what they really thought. All of them were ruthless and all
were certain that they alone were right; if one of them at any
moment advocated greater freedom of discussion, it does not
follow that he would have given his own opponents a fair
hearing if he had been able to silence them. What, then, was
the issue of principle between Trotsky and Stalin? Trotsky, it
may be said, believed that world revolution must come before
socialism could be built in one country, while Stalin held the
opposite opinion. "Socialism in one country" involved the
creation of a new socialist industry; so it follows, on this
view, that Stalin was bound to push forward with the rapid
industrialization of Russia through the Five-Year Plans or
something very like them, and that Trotsky was bound to oppose this. That is what happened, but if their roles had been
reversed, perhaps, Trotsky would have advocated Five-Year
Plans and collective farms, and Stalin would have been
against them. Indeed, Trotsky advocated planning and a more

rapid development of industry at a time when Stalin was opposing him for being a "super industrializer" who wanted to go too fast. It may well be that subjectively the leaders of the rival factions were fighting for a particular interpretation of Marxism, and for the policies which they believed to flow therefrom as a corollary, but that objectively they were fighting for power or for their skins.

This, however, does not account for the stronghold which the phrase "socialism in one country" gained over a whole generation. Stalin seems first to have used the phrase almost casually but he was quick to see that his words had a resonance. The words "socialism in one country" embodied "a synthesis between socialist and national loyalties. It was the point at which Russian destiny and Marxism joined hands. By the same token it was a landmark in Russian history. Hitherto the economic development of Russia and the Westernization of Russia had been integral parts of the same process. After 1925 they were separated. Industrialization would be pursued independently of the West and, if necessary, against the West." (Carr, Vol. VI, p. 50.) Henceforth the Soviet regime drew its vital force at least as much from Russian patriotism as from international Communism. In the 1970s both these forces are still operative. I make no judgment concerning China or any other country, but in Russia patriotism has shown more staying power than Marxist ideology.

To simple-minded Russians, whether they were party members or not, "socialism in one country" meant the end of the agonizing feeling that Russia's future depended on a coming international revolution which never happened. Henceforth poor, backward Russia would stand on her own feet. Indeed she was no longer backward, for the land of *moujiks* had made a Revolution such as none of the advanced countries had achieved. This Revolution depended for its survival and development on no foreigners but on the Russians themselves. To Bolshevik determination nothing was impossible.

Zinoviev and Kamenev admitted cynically after their quarrel with Trotsky that to them "socialism in one country" was just a stick to beat Trotsky with. It was the reward of Stalin's patient listening and self-effacement that he came to have a unique understanding of what counted with party members. It was he who gave power and content to the phrase "socialism in one country."

2. The Five-Year Plans

By about 1928 Russia had reached a crossroads. Her economy was half socialist and half not, the balance was unstable and the time seemed ripe for a decision. Moreover, Stalin had now consolidated his power and had at his command a disciplined and all-penetrating body of servants who were capable of carrying out the boldest decisions. All sizable industry had long been nationalized, but the greater part of the land was still farmed by smallholders. There were far more peasants than workers in Russia, and the peasants still made their livelihood by selling produce for private gain. So the more they prospered, the more they became attached to the processes of buying and selling. Thus the peasantry formed a rural petty bourgeoisie, and like all bourgeois they were creating capitalism every day in the ordinary course of their activity. If farming had remained as it was, the new Russia would eventually have taken her character from her smallholders. That might have been a very good thing, but it was not what the Communists intended. Moreover, there were practical as well as theoretical objections against leaving things to take their course. If Russia was to go forward there must be a big expansion of industry; that meant larger towns and more people to feed. But Russian farming was inefficient and barely succeeded in feeding the existing towns; moreover, it was very labor-consuming and could not spare the large number of men who would be needed by an expanding industry. For these reasons industry could only be developed as fast as agriculture could provide more food and more labor for the towns. How fast could Russia go? The question was urgent.

The Communists had little doubt that sooner or later they would be attacked by one or another of their enemies, and they knew that they would not be able to defend themselves unless in the few years that remained they could create and arm a powerful modern army. That could not be done without industrial resources which did not yet exist. Stalin put the problem in a nutshell:

"Old Russia . . . was beaten by the Mongol khans. She was beaten by the Turkish beys. She was beaten by the Swedish feudal lords. She was beaten by the Polish and Lithuanian gentry. She was beaten by British and French capitalists. She was beaten by the Japanese barons. All beat her—for her backwardness: for military backwardness, for cultural backwardness, for political backwardness. . . . We are fifty or a hundred years behind the advanced countries. We must make good this distance in ten years. Either we do it or they crush us."

Once Stalin was launched on the first Five-Year Plan and the collectivization of the peasants he saw his problem with pitiless clarity and pushed his solutions through with pitiless severity. But he had blundered into the situation with a lack of forethought that would be incredible if he had not recorded his original views beforehand. As late as June 1928 he maintained that "under present conditions the expropriation of *kulaks* would be folly" and even in the spring of 1929 that "individual poor and middle peasant farming plays and will continue to play a predominant part in supplying the country with food." (*Problems of Leninism,* Moscow, 1945, pp. 221 and 267.) In his report to the fifteenth party congress in 1927 he expressed contentment with the state of Soviet industry and gave no hint of any preparations for the first Five-Year Plan, though it was to be launched within a year. When Trotsky, Zinoviev and Kamenev had suggested a much slower rate of industrial development than that of the Five-Year Plans, Stalin had dismissed his opponents as "super-industrializers." At this stage he turned down a project for the great Dnieper dam, which afterward became the chief glory of Soviet planning, and is said to have remarked that for Russia to build this dam was like a *moujik* buying a gramophone instead of a cow. (*The Case of Leon Trotsky,* N. Y., 1937, p. 243.)

In January 1928 there was a serious crisis in the supply of food to the towns. The grain bought from the peasants was two million tons short of the minimum needed. No doubt the *kulaks* were exploiting a seller's market. The Politbureau ordered "emergency measures" to get more grain out of the peasants. This in Stalin's own words led to "administrative arbitrariness, violation of revolutionary law, raids on peasant houses, illegal searches." The peasants resisted by all the tricks known to a farming community. To give in to them might have meant leaving the factory workers to go hungry and that was one thing which Stalin did not want to risk. So he decided to apply drastic remedies.

He was still comparatively new to the experience of unbridled power and though he had a vast experience of one kind of administration he had not so far been specially concerned with economic affairs. He was therefore inclined to suppose that economic problems both in farming and in industry could be resolved by the methods of administration to which he was accustomed. His new responsibility for industry led him to conclude, rather hastily, that Soviet industry could now be developed much faster than even the "super-industrializers" had dreamed.

If the decision to embark on the first Five-Year Plan was taken without sufficient consideration there were nonetheless real reasons for it. The rulers of Russia faced the cruel dilemma which had faced the first Romanovs. Russia could not defend herself without undergoing a burden which would cripple her. But there is one notable difference. The means by which Muscovy defended herself prevented the growth of Russia's productive resources, whereas Stalin proposed to make Russia defensible by bringing about an enormous increase in industrial production. In both cases one is bound to ask whether in the long run lighter burdens and a steadier pace would not have given both a better defense and a higher production, but Stalin would have answered that he did not expect to have time for such methods, and that if he had not pressed on with his plans Hitler would have crushed him in 1941.

Such were the reasons for Stalin's iron determination to push through the first Five-Year Plan at any cost. This "plan" was at first conceived as a rapid but balanced development of complementary resources, but under the pressure of circumstances it soon became more like a race than a plan in the ordinary sense. The experts who made the plans for each industry were pressed to fix their targets high. If their estimates of what was possible were too cautious, they courted the accusation of sabotage, while if they were too optimistic someone else would get the blame for nonfulfillment of the plans. So the plan gave every basic industry a target so high that it bore little relation to previous performance. Everything was calculated on the most optimistic estimates of "yes men." There was no allowance for contingencies, for the mistakes that would be made by unskilled men learning skilled jobs in a hurry, or for any other human weakness. Yet the responsibility for carrying out each part of the plan was pinned down to the managers of individual factories who often paid with their life or liberty for failure to produce what was demanded. If they failed they could not blame the planners for demanding the impossible of them. That would be to criticize the party line which was deemed infallible, unless and until the party itself admitted that it had made a mistake. Each factory, indeed each unit of each factory, was individually committed to fulfill its part by a process of consultation that ran from top to bottom of Soviet industry. Higher authority proposed a plan for each industry and for every enterprise in that industry. The draft plan was then discussed industry by industry, factory by factory and workshop by workshop. Suggestions were welcomed so long as they were suggestions for raising the target, but it was dangerous to suggest that the target should be lowered or to resist proposals for raising it still higher. So everyone who held a responsible post in Soviet industry was publicly committed to carrying out his bit of the plan whatever his private feelings might be.

To exceed the plan was the road to favor, to fall short was to invite severe punishment. In practice it was often impossible to fulfill the plan without serious breaches of the laws for the protection of labor. Safety was neglected, men were made to work illegally long hours, machinery and human beings were cruelly overworked. Factories might be unheated in the Siberian winter, men and women fresh from the field might be set to work in an unfinished factory with no proper training in their new work. If there were no houses, they slept in sheds. Nothing mattered so long as the plan was fulfilled, but if it was not fulfilled there would be an inquiry. The management would be blamed not only for its failure to deliver the goods but also for its breaches of the law and for its callousness to the workers. Those who were held to be chiefly responsible would be sent to Siberia or shot.

Yet to fulfill the plan did not guarantee that the country got what it needed most. Plans are expressed in figures, and figures can be manipulated or falsified. So the most successful factory manager might be he who was best at covering his tracks. It is impossible for any plan to specify in every detail what is to be produced. For instance, a plan for some factory would say that so many articles were to be produced, but if there was any imprecision in defining the articles to be made, the factory might well make whatever was easiest, even if the country had enough of that thing already but needed desperately something else that the same factory could also make. Provided the right number of things were made, there would probably be no questions asked, even if they broke the first time they were used. Efficient and fearless auditors could have prevented many of these things, but Russia has no profession to compare with our accountants. Moreover, it was not safe to bring to light faults in which powerful people might be implicated.

A planned development of industry in the ordinary sense of the phrase means, above all, that the supply of one factory is linked with the production of another factory which makes the raw material for the first factory, but in the chaos of the first Five-Year Plan no factory could rely on its supplies. The fact that no raw material had arrived might be grounds for punishing those who had failed to deliver it, but lack of supplies was no excuse for not fulfilling the plan. Enterprising managers overcame these difficulties by scrounging, by bribing, by falsifying accounts, by every kind of subterfuge and even by theft of supplies intended for others. So long as you succeeded no questions were asked, but if you failed to fulfill the plan no excuse was accepted. In these ways Communist planning bred a new kind of rugged individualism.

In spite of all, the foundations of a modern industrial society were laid by the first Five-Year Plan. All the effort went into heavy industry. The shops were empty and the industries which produced consumer goods were not given enough of the nation's scarce resources to produce the pots and pans, the boots and shoes, the clothes and all the other everyday things which ordinary men and women ardently desired. Russia must go short now, so that there might be plenty later on. This boldness captured the imagination of many, and youthful idealism was fed by a vision of plenty which seemed to be just round the corner. The present sufferings were severe, but that appealed to the ascetic spirit of Russian idealism and made success even more desirable.

3. The Revolution in the Countryside

The first Five-Year Plan went hand in hand with a
revolution in the countryside which surpassed all previous revolutions. The party reasoned that if smallholdings divided
into medieval strips did not produce enough food and took
too much labor, these holdings must be abolished. All the
land of a village would then be merged in one "collective
farm." This would belong to the village as a whole and could
be cultivated by modern methods which would produce more
food and take less labor. Then men and women whose labor
would no longer be needed on the land would go to the
towns where the Five-Year Plan needed them and would eat
the extra food to be produced by these up-to-date arrangements. This plan might have worked if it had been introduced at the wish of the majority of the peasants, or at least
of the natural leaders among them, and if there had been
enough men trained in modern farming and enough tractors
to make a reality of the talk about improved methods. But
there were not enough tractors or other machinery and there
were very few skilled instructors who had the confidence of
the peasants.

The Communist Party did not have deep roots in the countryside. As late as 1939 not one in twenty villages had its
own Communist cell. To set up collective farms seemed an
ideal way to spread rural communism and to strengthen the
party's control over the undisciplined Russian peasant, but
the townsmen who came to explain to the peasants what the
party now intended did not know how to gain the confidence
of their hearers any more than did the young men and
women who "went to the people" in the 1870s. It was clear
that the peasants were being asked to give up that which was
dearest to them—their land—but it was not clear what they
would get in exchange. The party had not thought out in concrete terms what exactly was involved in collectivization.
Would everyone be paid alike, and if not, how were wages to
be calculated? Would everything be put into the pool, or
could a family still own their house, a garden plot, tools,
fowls, pigs, a cow or a horse? Policy fluctuated about such

matters, and when the peasants thought that their animals would be taken from them, they were tempted to kill and eat them. Indeed, the government had promised tractors, so draft animals might not be needed. Between 1929 and 1933 the number of horses in the Soviet Union went down by more than half, the cattle were reduced by nearly a half and the sheep and goats by nearly two-thirds. A good half of the livestock on which Russia depended had been slaughtered as a direct consequence of collectivization.

Those who had the least to lose were the most likely to welcome the new arrangements, while those who owned the largest plots of land were sure to be the bitterest opponents of the collective farms; and the *kulaks* already had their special reason for hating the Communist system. So the government based its drive for collectivization on the landless peasants who were promised that in the new society they would have a share in the land that would be taken from the *kulaks*. Not unnaturally many of the better-off farmers resisted; they were transported with their families to Siberia. Soon it was assumed, not without reason, that all *kulaks* would resist; so all were transported. But who was a *kulak*? Any family who was slightly better off than its neighbors were liable to be called *kulaks* and treated as such. And anyone, rich or poor, could be accused of *kulak* mentality. Once a man was accused, it became dangerous to defend him. An accusation was an easy way to pay off a grudge and there were many malicious accusations. Millions were deported. Most of them were not really *kulaks,* but ordinary peasants who did not want to give up their land. Sometimes a whole village was recalcitrant. All resistance was crushed without mercy, but the members of the Communist Party who had to enforce the government's decrees did not always like their task. Mr. Isaac Deutscher, in his life of Stalin (p. 325), describes a chance meeting with a colonel of the OGPU in a railway carriage:

"The colonel was completely broken in spirit by his recent experiences in the countryside. 'I am an old Bolshevik,' he said, almost sobbing, 'I worked in the underground against the tsar and then I fought in the civil war. Did I do all that in order that I should now surround villages with machine guns and order my men to fire indiscriminately into crowds of peasants? Oh, no, no!' "

There were indeed many Communists who were revolted by the pace and consequent inhumanity of the collectivization. Until all open opposition was liquidated, such men and women had a mouthpiece in Bukharin and his group of "right opportunists," who believed in a slower evolution and considered that for the present Russia could not get on without some smallholders. Bukharin thought there was something to be learned from the example of the United States, where farmers, freed from the burden of excessive rents, had grown prosperous, and where the development of industry and agriculture went hand in hand. (See article by Bukharin in *Pravda* for September 30, 1928.)

Somehow or other, the peasants were hustled into collective farms, but they did not put their backs into making the new system succeed. Men and women worked slackly and tried to evade work for the collective, reserving their energy for any little plot that they had managed to keep for themselves.* During the NEP the *kulaks* had helped greatly in feeding the towns, but now they were out of business. Moreover, great numbers of cows, pigs, sheep and fowl had been killed. For all these reasons less food than ever came into the towns, which were swollen by the Five-Year Plan. The towns were not far from starvation, and even in the countryside there were large areas where people died of hunger. Something was wrong, and Stalin admitted publicly in a famous article entitled "Dizzy from Success" that the party had gone too fast. The pace was slackened and a little more common sense was henceforth applied to agriculture. The system began to settle down and people knew where they were. Agricultural production increased, though not fast enough to feed the towns without difficulty. And the peasants still had bitter grievances. There is much to be said for the Russian collective farms in the abstract, but being imposed by force and without adequate preparation the new system defeated its chief purpose. It was intended to give the towns more food at once, but in fact its first result was to produce a sharp fall in food production.

* In 1938 the private plots of the peasants formed only 3.3% of the total cultivated area but the peasants owned privately on these plots over half of all the cows in the country and 40% of the sheep. In 1937 the production of the peasants' private plots was 21.5% of the total agricultural production.

It might have been expected that the collectivization would at least have released large numbers of peasants for work in industry. In the long run it has had this effect but not at first. Many of the industrial workers still felt themselves to be peasants who had taken a job in the town, which they regarded as more or less provisional so long as they still owned land in the villages. Thus any upheaval in the villages affected the town workers too. Collectivization sent them hurrying back to their farms for fear that the collective farm might take over their land in their absence. (See *Labor in the Soviet Union* by Solomon Schwarz.)

4. The Great Terror

In all these ways the first Five-Year Plan led to hardship, injustice and resentment. Thus the plan fostered resistance to itself, and this resistance prompted Stalin to repression. By cruel efforts the first Five-Year Plan was completed in four years, but even this brought no respite, for the completion of the first plan did little more than show how much still remained to be done; and the second Five-Year Plan, which began in 1933, coincided with the rise of Hitler. Time pressed more than ever. But if Stalin pressed his people harder, this made the muddle worse, so that there was more hardship and therefore more discontent. The fear that discontent would flare up into resistance made Stalin become even more oppressive. The fear that war was imminent made him press on all the faster to his goal of industrialization. But a faster tempo set the vicious circle turning faster still. Nonetheless, real progress was made and by 1934 it was possible to hope that the worst was over, though the Soviet Union was still under great strain. Then suddenly, Kirov, the popular Leningrad party secretary, was murdered. The circumstances were suspicious and it is almost certain that he was killed on Stalin's orders. In any case, Kirov's murder was the occasion for a thorough attempt to extinguish every vestige of criticism or independent thought, let alone of opposition.

Suspects were arrested, their examination led to more arrests, the examination of the newly arrested suggested wider ramifications of discontent, which in turn led to more arrests in an ever-widening circle. Denunciations were called for in public meetings and anonymously. Denunciation was taken as proof of guilt, and the omission to denounce an acquaintance who came under suspicion was itself treated as a crime.

Those who were arrested had no peace until they confessed. "Who recruited you?" "Who did you recruit?" Many had nothing to confess, had not been recruited by anyone and had recruited no one. But ceaseless examination, lack of sleep, fearful threats and insidious cajolery, occasional torture and many other devices broke all but the strongest wills. Many were able to avoid implicating the living by confessing to have plotted with someone who had died. Very few held out to the end without confessing.

So the waves of denunciation and arrest spread even more hectically in ever-widening circles. A tap on the door at night and a man or woman would disappear. His arrest endangered all his family and all his friends, through the principle of guilt by association. It seemed that there would be no end until those who remained at liberty were too few to guard those who had been arrested.

For three years the terror grew continually. Many hundreds of thousands were shot, some for real but more for imaginary offenses, millions were sent to Siberia or the far north, and countless numbers of men and women rotted in prison without trial, sometimes for many months or even years. Several millions died of hardship, but many have survived to tell of these days and their accounts tally. Physical torture was not always eschewed, but the NKVD had a wider range of pressure at their command than Peter the Great had, and they were more patient than he, being ready to spend many months if necessary on breaking down the resistance of a single witness.

The Great Terror of the thirties differed from previous waves of terror, not only in its extent and duration but still more in those whom it struck down. The leaders of the opposition, the enemies of the Soviet system and those whose social origins were likely to make them critical of the new regime had long been accustomed to persecution, but loyal rank-and-file Communists had felt fairly secure. Now no one was safe. The natural enemies of the regime were arrested and punished in anticipation of the crimes that they were likely to commit, while Communists were arrested on the suspicion that their very enthusiasm might lead them into forbidden paths. To hold a responsible post was to risk arrest, for any failure might be put down to sabotage. Theory and practice are one in the Bolshevik view. The theory of the party is beyond criticism: so every failure in practice must be due to treason or to sabotage. Those members of the Communist Party who held responsible posts were the most suspect of all, particularly if their party membership dated from revolutionary days. Old revolutionaries were too independent-minded for Stalin. Those who had made one revolution might always be tempted to make another. People who had important jobs generally kept two suitcases packed, one at work and one at home, so that they might always have their things ready whether they were arrested by day or night.

Every connection with potential enemies of the Soviets was a cause for mortal suspicion. The Jews suffered out of all proportion to their numbers, not because they were Jews but because most Jews had relations abroad. All personal links with the West were broken. The leaders among the older revolutionaries had been men with wide contacts and rooted in European traditions. Now they were replaced for the most part by raw recruits of the new school who knew nothing but what they had learned in the years of turmoil, men and women whose spiritual ancestry went no further than the revolutionary intelligentsia of the 1860s.

The Church suffered with all Russia in the Five-Year Plans and the collectivization, but religious people were hit harder than the rest. To be a priest was to be suspect, and to be suspect was to be deemed guilty. Very many religious people were sent to Siberian concentration camps, where their fortitude and meekness sometimes created an impression as powerful as that of the heroic revolutionaries in tsarist prisons. The Russian Church had not the intellectual equipment to stand up to the Marxists, but the heroism of a martyr is sometimes more convincing than a logical argument.

Very many of the responsible jobs in the Soviet Union changed hands not once but several times during the Terror. Junior engineers or clerks found that the removal of their superiors suddenly brought them to the top of the tree. If they in turn proved unequal to their new tasks, they followed their predecessors to Siberia or the firing squad. Not surprisingly production fell, great projects remained uncompleted or even reached such a state of confusion that they could never be completed.

The OGPU itself suffered the same purge as every other department, and officers of the secret police who had extorted confessions found themselves sharing cells with those whom they had examined. Twice the head of the OGPU fell a victim to his own terror.

Then Stalin called a halt. Beria, the new chief of the OGPU, was no milder than those who had gone before him, but he recognized with greater realism the practical limits of terror as a means of ensuring loyalty and achieving greater production. He began by quietly releasing many thousands of prisoners. Under Beria the OGPU remained cruel, inhuman and unscrupulous almost beyond belief, but it was not mad. Denunciation was less often taken as proof of guilt, and people began to sleep quietly in their beds. Beria reigned for fifteen years over the secret police, and in that time Russia began to settle down in spite of war and turmoil. The Great Terror of 1936-38 has burned into our imagination till we often assume that terror is the norm of Soviet life. It is true that the Great Terror can scarcely be exaggerated. It is also true that terror has never been far from the surface since the Revolution. Those who lived through the terrible years will never forget, but even a few years later some of the younger generation who had grown up under Beria seemed to be strangely unaware of what had happened when they were youths or children. One consequence of this was that they were less guarded in their contacts with foreigners.

What caused the convulsion? "Why?" "What for?" "Why are we here?" These questions scratched upon prison walls and the coaches of prison trains were discussed endlessly among prisoners awaiting trial. Many explanations have been given and most of them contain a grain of truth. Undoubtedly some prisoners were guilty of sabotage or even treason. Stalinism had many enemies for many reasons, and every opposition had to work by conspiracy, for there was no possibility of legal opposition. It is also true that scapegoats were needed for the insufficiencies of the first two Five-Year Plans. But the demand for scapegoats is measured in hundreds or thousands, not in hundreds of thousands or in millions.

It is said that the OGPU became an enormous agency for the recruitment of slave labor for public works, particularly in the far north and Siberia. This is true, but this method of public works contracting is costly and inefficient. Moreover, a high proportion of the prisoners were skilled men and women whose skill was badly needed elsewhere but could not always be used by the OGPU.

Why did so many confess to crimes that they had not committed? Why were the examiners so bent upon getting confessions which they must often have known to be false? It is true that those who would not confess were punished without publicity, while the full glare of a public trial was turned onto those who made the most dramatic confessions. It is also true that subtle and brutal pressure maintained over a long enough time makes most people ready to confess to almost anything. Yet after every proper discount has been made, the output of confessions remains staggering.

It is no longer plausible to ascribe this willingness to confess imaginary crimes to the vagaries of the Russian soul, since Chinese and other non-Russians are found to behave much the same before Communist tribunals. It is more relevant that those among the accused who were loyal Communists needed at all costs to preserve their faith in the Communist Party. Otherwise the world would be empty for them. Some of these men admitted afterward that they indulged in extraordinary prevarication to convince themselves that the regime represented by the OGPU was right, and that they themselves were wrong. After all, what are "right" and "wrong"? The party might be "right" in the only way that mattered. Come what might, in the eyes of some of the accused the party remained the savior of the world. In the ultimate analysis its policy must be right. The enemies of the Revolution must be destroyed and must be shown to be destroyed. If innocent people suffered, too, that could not be helped. "Fell a forest and chips will fly," runs the Russian proverb. If a false confession served the party, that sacrifice must be loyally accepted. Those who reasoned thus confessed willingly to imaginary crimes if that was the last service they could do for their beloved party in whose bosom they had found the only true fellowship of their lives.

But most of the accused were not party members. Why did so many of them confess? In a sense, all were guilty, or at least felt guilty, for everyone had at one moment or another doubted the wisdom and justice of what the party did. Many had expressed their doubts. All had broken the law, for it is not possible to keep the law when ordinary buying and selling or even barter may become the crime of "speculation," but yet the conditions of life are such that no one can survive without such exchanges. In Soviet Russia the commonest amenities and even the barest necessities might be impossible to get without a wangle that would not bear close inspection by any tribunal. In particular, everyone who held a position of responsibility felt guilty toward society, for everyone "had at some time cooperated with the system to a greater or lesser extent, minimized in his own mind its mistakes and defects, shut his eyes to accessible facts, tried to justify them against his own better conscience" (Beck and Godin, *Russian Purge*, p. 182).

Moreover, the OGPU had become a vast vested interest. Conspiracies must be continually unmasked or there would not be enough jobs for the boys. Why then did not the OGPU stick together to defend their professional interests? There is no certain answer, but it looks as if after 1937 the old Chekists who had a sense of professional solidarity were replaced by a new set of Stalinists from the central organization of the party. It may even be that these new men were deliberately given the task of rooting out the old hands on the ground that they knew too many secrets to be trusted.

The worst of all was that the OGPU had been caught up in the methods of the Five-Year Plans. If the Kremlin ordered the discovery of conspiracies, conspiracies must be discovered. If any investigator failed in this task or discovered fewer conspiracies than his colleagues, that must be because he was in the conspiracy himself. The investigators knew that they were often investigating imaginary plots, but they knew too that if they did not secure enough confessions they would join their victims in the cells. It was almost as if each official of the OGPU had been given the unmasking of so many conspirators as his part in the Five-Year Plan, a task that he must fulfill on peril of his life. If he took the short cut of killing his victims too soon, in order to spare himself and them agony, he risked trouble with his superiors for destroying valuable witnesses before they had given all their evidence. The plan demanded conspirators, not victims.

5. Return to Tradition

In a few years Stalin swept away many landmarks which had survived the Bolshevik Revolution, but for all that Stalin's Revolution went with a return to many traditional values and a renewal of Great Russian nationalism. In the first flush of their victory the Communists had wanted to throw aside everything old. There was to be a new heaven and a new earth, and all things were to be made new. The literature of the past was only valuable insofar as it pointed to the socialist future. Family life as it had been known hitherto was an expression of the ties of bourgeois economic life and would now be replaced by a free and glorious morality founded on the relations of a socialist society. Youth owed no respect to age. Children must defy their parents and their teachers where these stood in the way of Marxist progress. Such ideas expressed the logic of revolution. To make a revolution you must recruit young people, and the younger the better. Those who are over forty seldom want drastic changes, nor do they wish their children to be involved in dangerous adventures. So in 1917 the Bolsheviks encouraged the young to break away from their parents; but when the boys and girls who made the Revolution began to have their own families, they wanted their children to treat them with respect. Moreover, the relaxation of traditional discipline in the 1920s produced evils which the 1930s could not ignore —promiscuity, broken homes, venereal disease, the instability of labor, and children who took to the lives of hoodlums and bandits because they had no one to look after them—all these formed a complex of intractable problems. So a demand for the restoration of traditional disciplines arose of its own accord. Children were no longer encouraged to defy their teachers, and experiments in school democracy ceased. Indeed, the methods of teaching became exceedingly conventional, not to say conservative. Divorce became less easy and the state threw its weight increasingly on the side of family stability.

At the same time the classics were rediscovered, the Russian literature of the great age was put back on its pedestal and the glories of the Russian past were accepted as precursors of the glory of the Russian Revolution. But it was a return to Peter the Great, not to Dostoyevsky, who was considered a weakening influence. The new age insisted upon greater discipline than in Peter's time. Men and women must work where and how the state required. Natural science was fostered in order that it might minister to the needs of society, and the value of scientific work was judged by its economic consequences. Literature and the arts, too, had to serve the state by showing men their duty to help in building a socialist society. Paper and print would not be allocated to a publication which did not do this. And an author who did not come into line was considered guilty of a frivolity which was criminal at such a moment.

In all this Stalin was simply pushing to a madly logical conclusion principles laid down by Lenin. In an article on "The Party Organization and Party Literature," published in 1905, Lenin had written: "The principle of Party literature consists in the fact that, for the socialist proletariat, not only may literature not be an instrument of gain for individuals or groups but also in that it may not be an individual matter at all, independently of the general proletarian cause. Down with non-party writers! Down with literary supermen! Literature must become a *part* of proletarian activities in general; it must become 'a wheel and a screw' of the single great social-democratic machine which is driven by the whole conscious vanguard of the whole working class." One of the chief aims of Stalin's policy was to substitute a collective loyalty to the Soviet regime for "group and even family loyalties and spontaneous mutual ties of any sort." (Max Hayward in *Soviet Survey* for Nov.-Dec. 1957.) But the most usual consequence, particularly among intellectuals, was that "the vaunted *Kollektiv* . . . became a conglomeration of isolated, lonely, mutually suspicious individuals whose only alternative to futile martyrdom was humiliating dissimulation" (*ibid*). To this day one of the chief aims of Kremlin policy with regard to writers is to prevent *gruppovshchina,* the emergence of "pernicious cliques" or groups of friends who support each other's literary undertakings. In literature "pernicious *gruppovshchina*" corresponds to the crime of "fractionalism" in politics. The case against *gruppovshchina* was put in a well-known resolution of the central committee of the party in August 1946 as follows: "Obviously unsuitable works are permitted to appear in print for fear of hurting friends. Such liberalism, which sacrificed the interests of the people and state . . . to friendly relations and which muffled criticism, led to writers losing their sense of responsibility to the people, the party, the state. . . ." One of the methods used to combat the natural tendency to solidarity among colleagues was the continual reshuffling of editorial boards.

The arts languished under the deadly conformity imposed by Stalin. Month after month the newspapers reiterated the same things in almost the same words at interminable length. Indeed, the very rigor of the control encouraged long-winded banality. It was safe to use the tired Stalinist phrases, how-

ever trite they had become, but original turns of expression
might always be suspected of some concealed meaning. Every
newspaper article on every subject had to present the official
view in proper balance and no one could risk that a last-min-
ute cut by the editor would remove some vital qualification.
So journalists repeated themselves again and again, so that however their articles were cut they might still contain every essential ingredient of the party line.

These repetitions of Soviet slogans in speeches and books,
newspapers and magazines, in broadcasts and films, became
like an endless liturgy, and it was not altogether fanciful to
describe Stalin's Revolution as a gigantic experiment in the
power of liturgy to change man and to establish complete
control over all material resources. An ex-Communist describing the very typical articles addressed to Stalin in a provincial
newspaper has said:

"It sounded solemn almost like a great litany from my childhood. It was written . . . 'thou art the Greatest Leader and
Teacher, the Wisest Man of our Time, our Beloved Father and
the Light of our Lives. . . . We were able to fulfill our tasks
only because we obediently followed thy orders. For thine is
the Party which constantly directed us as well as through thyself
who never left us without thy attention'" (Borodin, *One Man
in His Time*, Constable, London, 1955).

Indeed, communism had many of the attributes of a religion,
but it did not give men all that they had found in their traditional religions.

Under the Five-Year Plans many millions of people learned
to read and write, millions received a higher education, good
doctoring became available for all, or at least for most, the
army became strong, and the Soviet Union became a great industrial country. All this was achieved at great cost and with
many setbacks. The plans failed in the production of food and
the provision of housing. The natural sciences were greatly
developed but the social sciences were held back by bureaucratic ideology. The enjoyment of the theater and of other arts
was brought to many millions and most of the classics were
performed with brilliance, but new works were stereotyped.

Stalin was hardly more cruel than Peter the Great or Ivan
the Terrible, but he was singular in the thoroughness of his
cruelty and in the way that he degraded the moral standards of
his subjects. His methods encouraged unscrupulousness and in-

humanity to subordinates among the upper ranks of society and in all classes hypocrisy and talebearing. Yet idealism was never quite quenched. There was always a streak of principle and more than a streak of unselfishness among those who worked the system. And ordinary people were strangely untouched by the corruption of their rulers. Even at the worst moments the ordinariness of people's lives was more striking than the extraordinary circumstances in which they lived. There was plenty of fraud, cruelty and cant, but there was still more of simple natural goodness to be found among the Russians.

6. The New Society

By 1940 the outlines of a new society could be seen. The old aristocracy and bourgeoisie as distinct classes had disappeared, but a fair sprinkling of their children had entered the new dominant groups. A Stalinist breed of factory managers, army officers, technicians, intellectuals and highly skilled workers were already secure in the enjoyment of a modest material prosperity, and had begun to assume the right to more than their share of the good things of the world. Under the pressure of the plans, piecework had become nearly universal. Between the highest and lowest incomes earned by free workers there was a large gap, even if it was not so large as the gap between a millionaire and an English unemployed miner in the 1930s. Below the bosses and the skilled workers came the army of the less skilled, who had a hard life but were not at the bottom of the social scale. Social services which had been established since the Revolution gave valuable help in need to those classes of people who seemed likely to help actively in the building of socialism, but there were not enough resources to go round. The provision made for those who were too old or too ill to work was often pathetically insufficient. Very many of the old and the ill had relations to look after them. Indeed, a grandmother with time to stand in endless queues might be an asset. But the full weight of human misery lay upon the old and the ill if they had no family. There were many orphans and there were many children whose parents had been sent to forced labor. If anyone showed kindness to these children he was likely to share the fate of their parents. Some orphans were looked after with loving care in model "children's homes," but not all Soviet orphanages were models of their kind. In the worst orphanages the authorities had lost all control and the toughest of the children reigned supreme amid dirt and violence. Rather than live in such establishments, most of the children preferred to run wild in the streets, banding together in gangs and living as they could.

In the countryside, villages which were near their markets or had good communications might become prosperous, but most of the peasants remained very poor. The new rural aristocracy was the directing staff of collective farms, together with the staff of the machine tractor stations which supplied machinery for the harvest and acted as general agents for the Communist Party.* These country bosses lived better than their neighbors, but they did not belong to the village and they were not numerous enough to form their own society. Country life had become intolerably boring for educated people, and it was difficult to get able men to take posts in the villages.

By this time the millions of men and women doing forced labor in concentration camps had become a well-established feature of the Soviet social structure. Some were ordinary criminals, some had broken the economic laws of the Soviet Union by "speculating" and some, no doubt, were active opponents of the Soviet regime, but many had done nothing to deserve punishment. Life in the labor camps was fearfully hard, yet in most camps many of the inmates survived. In Soviet society one often meets people who have done time in Siberia or Kazakhstan. The work of the prisoners was not efficient, but for many years it was an important element in the Soviet economy and in particular made it possible to develop valuable resources in inclement regions where free labor could hardly have been induced to live.

The scheme of Soviet life was such that it might have been expected that everyone would find a place, even if only in a concentration camp, but anyone who observes the Soviet Union attentively catches glimpses of a whole world of people who do not belong to Soviet society. In the 1940s there were still people who had never done any work and still lived on the

* In 1958 most of the machine tractor stations were disbanded and their assets sold to the collective farms.

sale of their jewelry. There were religious sectarians who lived monastic lives under the outer form of a collective farm. There was the "underground church," previously mentioned. There were gypsies who slipped through every net, and there were men and women who had become bandits, living in secret hideouts in the forest, sometimes caught and sent to concentration camps but returning to their former life as soon as they were released. The Soviet underworld was recruited from many sources, but not least from the gangs of child bandits.

Stalinist society did not attempt to produce uniformity of condition, but it will be asked whether there was not equality of opportunity. The answer depends on what is meant by the question. It will always be the case that the child of clever and well-connected parents living in the capital is more likely to get on than a child brought up in some "bears' corner" where there is nothing in his surroundings to stimulate imagination about a wider world or to add to his store of knowledge. In theory, primary education has been universal for many years, but even now there are probably some exceptions. In 1955 the Soviet teachers' newspaper complained that the children of poor parents are sometimes "kept out of school so that they can work," and that "year after year the national economic plan in regard to universal education is not fulfilled. Many schoolchildren still receive no instruction and the numbers of children who leave school is still extremely large" (*Uchitelskaya Gazeta* for November 30, 1955). It is broadly true that until about 1940 a boy or girl from a working-class peasant family who worked hard at his books had a good chance of getting his foot on the ladder, and promotion was quick for those who had special qualifications. In the 1940s Soviet officials holding responsible jobs were often ten, twenty or even thirty years younger than their British opposite numbers. But in the year 1941 a new system was established by which every year some hundreds of thousands of boys in their middle teens were conscripted into technical training schools. By this measure, which remained in force until 1959, a substantial part of the boys in the Soviet Union lost their chance of a higher education. It is true that in Russia, as in the West, it is possible for those who leave school young to go to the university, but it is not easy. Up to 1936 the children of bourgeois parents, tsarist police officers or priests were subject to discrimination. When these disadvantages were removed, Soviet society had already begun to form its own hierarchy of privilege. So at no time was there equality of opportunity for all, but at all times there were good opportunities for many, and perhaps for most.

Soviet society was beginning to take shape, but it had not solidified and the Soviet rulers had strong reasons for trying to postpone the armed clash with the West which they believed to be unavoidable in the end. For nearly two years the Russians kept out of the Second World War with the help of some cynical diplomacy.

CHAPTER XXIII

war and cold war

*Say not the struggle nought availeth
The labor and the wounds are vain.*

Clough

1. War

Under the second and third Five-Year Plans Soviet industry had grown to a formidable size, but there were many weak spots and its capacity to supply a modern army was questionable. The Red Army was large, but its fighting powers were uncertain; it had been disorganized by the Great Terror and it had some difficulty in beating the tiny Finnish army in 1939-40.

If Hitler had known what all the world now knows about Russia's latent strength, he would hardly have risked attacking the Soviet Union on June 22, 1941. But the Soviet security authorities had hidden so successfully what was going on in the Soviet Union that many otherwise well-informed people supposed Russia to be far weaker than she proved. Excessive security had defeated its own purpose.

From about February 1941 it was obvious even to the present writer, who had no access to top-secret information, that the Germans were planning to attack Russia. The Kremlin, so often oversuspicious, was for once overconfident. Allied warnings were taken for "provocation," and the Red Army was not even at action stations when the Germans attacked. In the years that followed one might hear Russians speak of treachery on that night, but it seems that the first Russian defeats were due to a mere lack of preparation.

The Red Army had been reorganized since the Finnish war, but it took time to learn how to fight a modern war. Throughout that first summer the German panzer divisions advanced with irresistible speed. Russian armies were surrounded and broken up, and military experts assured us that the divisions in question must have ceased to exist as fighting units, but somehow or other large numbers marched out of their encirclement and rejoined their units. Russia was saved by the power of spontaneous cooperation of her soldiers and by their capacity to improvise from the simplest elements.

At first the invaders roused mixed feelings. There were many ardent Soviet patriots, and foreign attack rallied the loyalty of many waverers, but there remained many others who did not know whether to welcome the Germans as liberators or to resist them as invaders. If Hitler had treated the Russians with a little humanity or a little consideration, he might have had many on his side, particularly in the Ukraine and in other border lands where the sense of being Russian was weak or absent. But slowly it was borne in on ordinary Russians that the Nazis were their worst enemies. An old woman met in a village on the middle Volga in August 1942 expressed the feeling of many. "They (meaning the Bolsheviks) are devils, but he (Hitler) is worse." In the same spirit a young guerrilla who had lost his parents in the collectivization said "he could manage somehow with the party and the government but he could not stomach the Germans" (Borodin, *One Man in His Time*). Throughout 1941, however, many remained in doubt which was the worst.

By October the Germans were at the gates of Moscow. For a few days there was nothing on the Russian side to stop them from taking the capital, but the Germans had outrun their communications and were forced to wait for supplies. Factories and government departments were evacuated. There was general confusion in Moscow and morale was near to breaking. People spoke their thoughts without much concern for the secret police, those who could get onto trains fled, some absconded with cash entrusted to them, while others remained in Moscow to loot the rooms of those who had gone. The Volga Germans in Moscow (descendants of settlers originally brought to Russia by Catherine) exulted almost openly at the approach of their national liberators. But this was not for long. New divisions of Siberians arrived just in time to turn the tide. The front settled down for the winter some way from Moscow, Russia got her second wind, and Allied aid began to arrive.

The famous "scorched earth" policy ensured so far as possible the ruthless destruction of everything likely to be useful to the enemy. Factory buildings were destroyed. Machinery was dismantled and evacuated with the skilled workers who operated it. At the cost of infinite pains and of great hardship to the workers and their families the machinery would be reassembled out of reach of the enemy in the Urals. Much effort was wasted, but the evacuation of industry made a substantial contribution to the war effort; and it accentuated the eastward shift of Russia's industrial center of gravity.

By now the resolute way in which the government faced the war was rallying people to its side. Evidently this was a real Russian government capable of defending Russian soil. So, many who would have been called class enemies only a short time before now showed themselves to be Soviet patriots ready for any sacrifice in the Great War for the Fatherland, as the Second World War came to be called.

A shrewd observer who was in Moscow at the time has told me that one of the first results of Hitler's attack was a gigantic feeling of relief. Now, people felt, the secret police had something more important to do than to manufacture trouble for the innocent. The bond of patriotism made people more open with each other. A poetess, writing in the comparative freedom of 1956 before the Hungarian revolt, described 1941 as a "pure year" because "in that year of camouflage and blackout, chicanery crumbled like plaster and we saw our neighbors without masks." (Julia Neumann in *Literaturnaya Moskva*, Vol. 2.) In *Dr. Zhivago* Pasternak says the same thing in a different way: "When the war broke out, its real horrors, its real dangers, its menace of real death, were a blessing compared with the inhuman power of the lie, a relief because it broke the spell of the dead letter."

Pride in the exploits of the Red Army flowed together with old-fashioned patriotism, and the greater part of the people were carried away by national feeling. The army fought with traditional Russian stubbornness and self-sacrifice, and did wonders with insufficient equipment. Those who remembered the cynicism and corruption of the home front in the war against the Kaiser remarked that this time the home front seemed all of a piece with the fighting front. Everything was sacrificed for the war. Passenger trains might wait for weeks, but supply trains reached the front. Every factory was turned over to war production. Things that were not directly useful for the war were not made. So if you broke your teapot in July 1941, you might have to wait some years to get a new one. The peasants generally had enough to eat, but many of them sat in the dark after sunset because there was no kerosene for their lamps. In the cities people were hungry to the verge of starvation. Compulsory levies from the collective farms were never enough to feed the towns, and now the peasants did not bring anything extra into market, for there was nothing to buy in exchange. In winter the townspeople were as cold as they were hungry; the supply of fuel to the towns was not one of the Kremlin's priorities. These hardships were borne with quiet courage in the belief that they were necessary for the survival of Russia.

Guerrilla warfare behind the enemies' lines was developed systematically, and the support which these heroic bands of "partisans" received from the population showed the general loyalty of the people. This loyalty was more Russian than Soviet. When the Germans reached districts where the population was not Russian, they often received support from the people. It was to be expected that the Germans of the Volga would welcome their compatriots but this would not account for the disloyalty of the Crimean Tartars and of various North Caucasian tribes or of the nomadic Kalmucks, all of whom were punished for their disaffection by transport *en masse* to distant parts of the Soviet Union.* If the battle of Stalingrad had gone the other way or if the Germans had been able to break into Transcaucasia, there is reason to think that the disaffection would have spread. I have myself heard Russian complaints that in Central Asia the Uzbeks wished to transfer their allegiance to the British Empire. This was ridiculous but the mere fact that Central Asian disaffection could take this form was enough to arouse the Kremlin's suspicions of its allies. On a journey through Transcaucasia in 1944 I observed that the local Soviet propaganda conveyed the impression that the Soviet Government was in close and friendly relations with the Western Allies. In general, Soviet propaganda played down the role of America and Britain but in the Caucasus it was important to discourage the local peoples from thinking that the West would support them against Moscow. In a word, everything goes to show that the chief force behind the national resistance was not so much anything specifically Soviet as Great Russian patriotism, a patriotism that now embraced the October Revolution in a queer

* Many of these peoples have been "rehabilitated" after a long delay. It suits Soviet policy at this stage to play down past disloyalty. No doubt loyalties were divided among the non-Russian nationalities, so that in both condemnation and rehabilitation the innocent and the guilty were lumped together.

irrational way. Like it or hate it, the Revolution was something stupendous that only Russians could have made.

The Kremlin might well have been surprised at the readiness with which traditional sentiments were transferred to the Soviet cause. The traditions of the tsarist army were invoked, regimental spirit was encouraged, and General Ignatiev, formerly an officer of the tsarist army, was given the task of inculcating at the places where cadets were trained the standards of behavior and manners required of an officer and a gentleman. Necessity compelled the use of such means of strengthening morale, but it was dangerous to allow the growth of *esprit de corps* and professional solidarity in the army. Any alternative focus of corporate feeling was a threat to the Communist Party.

That, indeed, was one of the reasons why the Church was suspect to the Kremlin, but now under the spur of necessity the government reviewed its relations with the Church. The Russian Church had in the past been patriotic to a fault, as most churches have been throughout history; but the Soviet Government accepted the Marxist argument that, since the priests were class enemies by definition, they were certain to support the enemies of the Soviet Union. Yet when the test came, the Russian priests and their bishops showed themselves to be patriotic citizens. Indeed, they brought over to the Soviet cause many who would not have paid heed to other exhortations. And the Red Army found to its surprise that a believer generally made a better soldier. So by degrees the bond of national peril led to better relations between the government and the national Church.

The first indication to the outside world that changes were on the way came in 1942, when the wartime curfew was relaxed to allow the traditional celebration of Easter in Moscow. For many years past there had been no official contact between the Russian Church and foreign representatives. Some observers supposed that the Church leaders who were not in prison had purchased their immunity by becoming willing or unwilling agents of the Kremlin. The isolation of the Russian Church from all foreign contact was so complete that one guess was as good as another. I was at that time press attaché at the British Embassy in Kuibyshev, the temporary capital of the Soviet Union. Russian visitors to the embassy were exceedingly rare. On September 16, 1942, an elderly bearded Russian, describing himself as the Metropolitan of Kiev, presented himself at the door, asking to see the

Ambassador. The Ambassador was in Moscow and I was instructed to receive the unexpected guest. He looked for all
the world like an old-fashioned Russian *moujik,* but he carried in his hand a curious sort of hatbox. From this he took
the robes and mitre of a metropolitan archbishop of the Orthodox Church and in two seconds his appearance was transformed.

Our visitor was the Metropolitan Nicholas Yarushevich,
who soon became the right-hand man of succeeding patriarchs of Moscow. He had come to demonstrate the freedom of religion in the Soviet Union and gave us a book to
prove his point. He had no doubt made his call on instructions from his government and there were large gaps, to say
the least, in the information which he gave us, but there was
no mistaking the friendliness of his intentions or the significance of his visit. From that time on there has been a steady
development of relations between the Church in Russia and
in other countries. In the long run these interchanges are
likely to have a profound influence both on Russia and on
the rest of the world.

A few months later I had to call on the Metropolitan of
Moscow, who was then acting Patriarch, in connection with
the Archbishop of York's proposed visit to Russia which took
place in 1943. The acting Patriarch was lodged in a log cabin
on a dirt road on the outskirts of Moscow. His staff seemed
to consist of one chaplain and he was looked after by two or
three old women dressed in black, whom I took to be nuns.
There was one good icon in the principal room, but no other
sign of prosperity. There was no place to keep any but the
most elementary records. I concluded that the administration of patriarchal affairs must be extremely simple, and
mainly conducted by word of mouth, much as one supposes
the affairs of the Church to have been conducted in the second and third centuries A.D. Shortly after this, those bishops
of the Russian Orthodox Church who were still at liberty
were allowed to meet in synod and to elect the Metropolitan
of Moscow to be Patriarch. Thereupon he moved from his
log cabin to the former German Embassy, which became
henceforth the Moscow Patriarchate.

In *Conversations With Stalin,* page 47, Milovan Djilas, at
that time Tito's right-hand man, describes the way in which
the war forced state and Church to work together; but he
says there were occasions when "both sides were unable to
conceal their mutual intolerance even though they were in

the presence of foreigners, and though each in his way was
fighting against the Germans. I had previously learned from
Soviet officials that as soon as the war broke out, the Russian
Patriarch began, without asking the Government, to distrib-
ute mimeographed encyclicals against the German invaders,
and that they enjoyed a response which went far beyond his
subordinate clergy. These appeals were also attractive in
form: against the monotony of Soviet propaganda they shone
out with the freshness of their ancient and religious patriotism. The Soviet Government quickly adapted itself and
began to look to the Church, too, for support, despite the
fact that they continued to regard it as a remnant of the old
order. In the misfortunes of war, religion was revived and
made headway, and the chief of the Soviet Mission in Yugo-
slavia, General Korneyev, said that many people—and very
responsible people at that—considered turning to Orthodoxy,
in a moment of mortal danger from the Germans, as a more
permanent ideological motive force. 'We would have saved
Russia even through Orthodoxy if that were unavoidable!' he
explained."

Neither the Church nor the Communist Party had renounced their ultimate objectives, but circumstances had
made them allies for a particular purpose. The association
outlasted the war. The state continues to teach that there is
no God and tries to get rid of religion by pressure which begins when children go to school and follows them through
their lives. If, for instance, a child goes through school still
retaining some religious beliefs and then joins the Young
Communist League, as most do, he or she will be told firmly
by leaders of his own age that religion is a harmful superstition and that everything is now explained by science. If the
boy or girl does not then leave off going to church, he or she
may be expelled from the Komsomol. Thereafter, the avenues
of promotion and education are likely to be blocked. Probably a family of workers or peasants with no ambition to
rise could go to church without fear of bad consequences,
but even at the best times it might still be dangerous to take
a lead in the congregation.

If a couple are married in church, they may be forcefully
reminded by the party that their happiness "depends on
themselves and requires no heavenly blessing." Public lec-

tures on science are used regularly as an indirect means of
weakening religion. The lecturer gives what purports to be
a complete account of the universe in terms of nineteenth-
century materialism. There is no mention of modern scientific
theories which suggest that the universe had a beginning in
time or that the constitution of space and matter is in any
way mysterious. Jesus Christ is always referred to as "the
mythical Christ." Those churches which are open are full to
overflowing on Sundays and feast days and the congregations
hear sermons expounding the Christian faith. Apart from this
there is little opportunity to answer the propaganda of the
athesists, but this propaganda does not always go down well.
The Soviet press complains of the inefficiency and dreariness
of those who carry out antireligious propaganda, and from
time to time particulars are given of cases in which even the
younger generation is touched by faith. As early as 1954
Christians were found even among graduates of the Evening
University of Marxist-Leninism in Leningrad, and one of
these was a party member (*Literaturnaya Gazeta,* October 14,
1954). In the 1970s such things have become commonplace.

John Noble, an American who spent some years at the terrible concentration camp at Vorkuta in the Arctic, tells a significant story: Bibles were confiscated from the prisoners, but
not destroyed. John Noble found where they were kept and
asked for one. He was refused because it would be too risky.
The OGPU, he was told, "know exactly how many Bibles
they have got. They come in here at night sometimes and
read them when they think no outsiders are looking." (*I
Found God in Soviet Russia,* by John Noble.) Occasional
other indications point in the same direction. It is likely that
secret Christians were rare during and immediately after the
war, but now they are legion.

The war against Hitler caused suffering and destruction
such as no imagination can grasp. I have seen villages and
even towns which showed at first sight no signs that they had
ever been inhabited. The fields had gone back to nature, the
wooden houses were burned and overgrown with weeds, and
the people had disappeared. Some were evacuated and others
were carried off by the Germans into a Babylonian captivity.
If one looked closer one could generally see the remains of
brick-built stoves, and perhaps after a time a few old women

would come out of cellars. Moreover, the Russians were not sustained, as the British and Americans were, by a belief that they could never be beaten. Memories of the wars against the Kaiser and the Japanese were too green for that. Like all resolute men, the Russians put a brave face on their misgivings, but during the battle of Stalingrad I have heard Russians give away their expectation that the Germans would soon take all the Caucasus and advance to the middle Volga. If that had happened, the back of the Soviet Union would have been broken.

The Russians were not certain of victory, but many of them believed that if they did win, then they could count on better times, and they looked forward not only to greater plenty but to more freedom. An intangible change in atmosphere, which answered to the new-found national unity and was exemplified by the change in the position of the Church, seemed to be an earnest of greater relaxation, while better relations with the Western Allies encouraged many to hope that after the war Russia would come out of her isolation. Such dreams were vague enough and they were not shared by all, but many people were buoyed up by hope for a change which they might not have been able to define. The end of the war did indeed bring changes, but not such changes as the sanguine had hoped.

2. The Cold War

Russia entered the war with a doubtful standing among the nations. She emerged as the second power in the world. For a short time it seemed, to some at least, that she might begin to settle down with the other great powers and that if her relations with the West would be colored by suspicions on both sides, these suspicions might be kept under control and might even grow less. But soon things took a fatal turn for the worse. This is not the place to analyze what happened, to attribute blame or to consider whether the Kremlin did not bring upon itself most of the hostility which it incurred. In this book we are only concerned with the effect of the cold war on Russia's growth. For our purpose the most important fact is that the fear of a clash with the Western powers led by America greatly increased the inclination of the Soviet rulers to withdraw into their shell.

In 1945 the Red Army advanced to Berlin and Vienna, where it remained as an army of occupation, while millions of Russian "displaced persons" saw more of the West in their captivity than all their ancestors had seen. The Kremlin foresaw that these men and women might return with ideas which would be difficult to digest. Soldiers who served outside the borders of the Soviet Union were kept under strict discipline and prevented so far as was possible from having contact with the local people. Often the D.P.s resisted repatriation but the Allies sent many of them home by force. They, together with returning prisoners of war, were sent to concentration camps for long periods before being allowed to return to ordinary life. Many were given long sentences of forced labor or shot for real or imaginary collaboration with the enemy.

At home all the nation's resources were turned to restoring the damage of the war and to developing the basic industries as fast as possible. With seven million dead and her fairest provinces utterly devastated, merely to restore what had been destroyed would have taken up all Russia's resources, but even when that was done the Soviet Union would not have caught up with the gigantic industry of America.

Stalin could not feel safe until his power equaled that of his greatest potential enemy. So relaxing nothing from the tempo of the first Five-Year Plan, he spurred his people on to efforts beyond their strength. Not for the first time, the whole structure of Russian life was deformed by a burden of defense that was too heavy to be borne. Seeing themselves surrounded by real or fancied enemies, the Russian rulers discouraged all contact with the outer world. Inside the Soviet Union, personal relations with foreigners, which had never been easy, diminished to vanishing point. Sooner or later any Soviet citizen who had foreign contacts was almost certain to have trouble with the secret police, and few took the risk. The concentration camps had become almost as full as they had been in the Great Terror.

The patriotism of the Great Russians was given full rein, even to the point of chauvinism. The lesser peoples of the Soviet Union now found that they must eliminate from history the memory of anything unfavorable to Russia. There was indeed much to be proud of in the Russian past, and it is likely that the West had overlooked the Russian share in some discoveries, but the Soviet Union made itself ridiculous by claiming for Russia a universal pre-eminence in almost every art, science or virtue. All this was supposed to culminate in the glories of the October Revolution which found their fulfillment in Stalinism and the victories of the Great War for the Fatherland. These inflated claims made every failure seem the worse and sometimes even diverted attention from real achievements.

The Stalinist era had produced some very good technicians and generals, but not very many good writers or theoretical scientists of the first rank. The elements of modern culture had been communicated to many millions of people whose fathers had lived on the verge of the Middle Ages, but it was noticeable that many, perhaps most, of the leading writers and scientists were people who had been educated under the tsars. So to some extent the Soviet Union was still living on tsarist intellectual capital. Russian thought had ceased to grow with the times and had drifted out of touch with the developing life of other countries. Now once more, as in the first Five-Year Plan, all Russia's resources were concentrated upon heavy industry, and writers were expected to play their part in the Kremlin's plans along with soldiers and engineers. On the literary and artistic fronts, strict control led to a deadly conformity and a deep provincialism. It was dangerous to be original. A character in Ehrenburg's *Thaw* put the position of creative artists in a nutshell. "They don't pay for ideas. All you can get from ideas is to break your neck. In a book you need ideology." (*Znamya*, 1954 [5].) Those words were published in the slight relaxation that came in the first two years after Stalin's death. While he was alive, it would have been unthinkable to say such things in public.

In 1945 the war was barely over and in 1946 the harvest failed. Thus 1947 began as a year of great hunger and even starvation, but the harvest was good and after that life became easier. The devastated regions of the West were restored with energy, but during the war the balance of Soviet industry had shifted from European Russia towards the Urals and Siberia, and now great efforts were made to develop industry still faster in regions that were comparatively safe from enemies. Once more present consumption was sacrificed to the increase of basic production. Russia was now less poor in technical skill, and in the techniques of planning and administration. The hardships of the postwar drive are not to be compared with the hardships of the first Five-Year Plan and much was accomplished, but once again Russia was being driven too fast. Frustrations and distortions of the kind associated with the first Five-Year Plan still took a toll of happiness and efficiency. Grandiloquent plans often diverted attention from humble necessities. Stalin's "plans for changing nature" capture the imagination. The Don and the Volga are joined by a canal, the desert is irrigated, an enormous new lake was created near Kuibyshev on the middle Volga, and plans were made to divert the mighty river Ob from the Arctic Ocean to the desert of Central Asia and to pour the river Oxus into the Caspian Sea. Such schemes can bring much good and some of them have been completed, but one must wonder if the same energy would not have been more effective if it had been put into something less spectacular, into making cart tracks into country roads, into building 100,000 small bridges, or bringing piped water to 200,000 villages.

Soviet planners are not close enough to the villages and workshops where their plans are carried out, and their methods of planning can still be very crude. Factories making metal beams or sheet metal still find that it pays them best under the conditions laid down by the Five-Year Plans to make fewer but heavier articles, though lighter beams and thinner metal sheets would be more useful to the nation. *Pravda* gives the reason: "The plan knows only one thing—the ton." And *Pravda* draws the conclusion: "If you want to be considered a leader, take the easier shapes; don't introduce new ones but follow the rule of 'worse but more.' " (*Pravda*, July 1, 1956). An objective study of the working of the Soviet economy carried out by competent economists would reveal the dimensions of hidden waste from this and other causes. This would make it possible to use Soviet resources with far greater efficiency, but Soviet economists are trained to make a priori deductions from theory rather than to do sound research into the actual working of socialist and capitalist economies as they exist today.

One of the cleverest of the Soviet leaders, Mr. Mikoyan, speaking at the twentieth party congress in 1956 said: "Our economists in their study of the economy of the Soviet Union . . . frequently skim the surface, fail to reach the depths, produce no serious analysis or conclusions." In Stalin's day it was not safe to undertake thorough research. The conclusions might be unwelcome. Moreover all serious public discussion of economic statistics risked the accusation of disclosing secret information. Even if Stalin's successors are more alive to the need for objective research, it is taking time to train the research workers and they are not yet convinced that it is safe to reach unpalatable conclusions. In the meantime the Soviet planners and administrators lack much of the information which their work requires. Yet there is already the beginning of objective research into such matters as industrial psychology and the remuneration of labor. Changes in economic practice are coming, but so far they are not coming fast.

3. The Contradictions of Stalinism

No man who has risen by Stalin's means can grow old in tranquillity. His subordinates had reason to fear their chief, and he in turn knew that this fear might tempt one of them to raise his hand against his master. Stalin was seventy in 1949. About the turn of 1952-53 there were ominous signs that a new terror might be beginning. Jews were arrested in many places on various charges. Then in the middle of January *Pravda* announced that a group of nine doctors, six of them Jews, had been arrested for plotting to kill some prominent members of the government. The motives behind these events are still obscure, but the improbability of the "doctors' plot" made it the more ominous, and memories of the 1930s suggested that, unless something happened, there would be other victims besides the Jews. Then on March 2, 1953, something did happen. It was announced that Stalin had had a stroke. He never regained consciousness and three days later his death was announced.

Under him Russia had become the second power in the world, but she had not found inner stability. The very rigidity of the framework which he had fitted to Russian life was an indication of unresolved conflicts. Stalin had concentrated all power and influence in a few hands with himself at the center. He had done this because he could not trust his subordinates to be loyal and efficient, but too much centralization had led to inefficiency and corruption, as well as to remoteness and inhumanity. Stalin failed where the tsars had failed, by getting out of touch with the thoughts and needs of ordinary people. In theory the Communist Party kept its ear close to the ground, and a chain of reports from the humblest level up kept the Kremlin informed of what people thought and said. But those whose reports were unpalatable risked punishment. It is more than likely that the reports which reached Stalin's desk often failed to tell him those things which he most needed to know. The only cure for the evils of centralization is to trust subordinates even if they are not perfectly trustworthy.

National security as conceived by Stalin involved a sacrifice of present consumption in favor of faster development, but a sufficient incentive to greater output could only be given if consumption was increased. The peasantry had been organized into collective farms in order that they might be subjected to stricter discipline and produce more to feed the towns, but the collective farms did not produce enough because strict discipline was defeating its own purpose. The towns could not expect to get more food unless the peasants were given a chance to buy more in the shops. That could only be done if industry was turned to making the things that the peasants wanted, which in turn would have involved slowing down the production of armaments. Stalin judged that he could not risk that. Such were the contradictions of Stalinist Marxism.

During his life we knew much of what Stalin did but little of what he was. Peter the Great and Lenin lived in controversy surrounded by hatred and admiration. We know what they seemed to their friends, to their enemies and to themselves. Peter's greatness and weakness, Lenin's greatness and narrowness are as clear as if we had known them ourselves. With Stalin it was otherwise. He was hardly known until he became unapproachable. When he had overcome his rivals he became the hero of a myth, the effective symbol of every feeling and aspiration which belonged to the Bolshevik Party. Henceforth he allowed nothing to be published that did not minister to the ritual picture of himself as the repository of infallible practical wisdom, the wise father of the Soviet peoples.

Now that Stalin is cold in his grave, his daughter has given us an unforgettable picture of him as a father, "the bad father of a bad daughter," yet a father. "No man is a hero to his valet," yet Stalin inspired a deep and lasting devotion in his domestic servants. He remains an enigma, a monster but now a human monster. We shall never know what lines of human experience were hidden by that mustache, what suffering or what self-questioning went to make Stalin what he was.

CHAPTER XXIV

after Stalin

1. The Pattern of Power and the Social Structure

Stalin's daughter, Svetlana, has now made it clear that her father's death was natural, but at the time it was widely suspected that he had been murdered or at least that bulletins about the progress of his illness were broadcast after he had died, so that his successors might have time to prepare a smooth transfer of power into their own hands. Such suspicions, though now shown to be unfounded, indicate the tense atmosphere of those days and hours when the old tyrant lay dying. The fear of civil strife was clearly implied in an official announcement referring to the need for "the greatest degree of unity of leadership and the prevention of any kind of disarray or panic." In the event Stalin's power passed peacefully to a group of those who were next in line, but trouble lay ahead.

It was clear that the power held by Beria as head of the OGPU was a threat to all his colleagues. Yet if he gave up any substantial part of this power, that would give an opening to his many enemies. His only hope was to crush his rivals and gain supreme control. So it was no surprise, when in June 1953 he was suddenly dismissed from office, expelled from the party and accused of "aiming at seizing power" by "attempting to put the USSR ministry of internal affairs before the party and the government and by using MVD organs in the central and local bodies against the party and its leadership and against the government of the USSR by selecting workers for the USSR Ministry of Internal Affairs of personal loyalty to himself." This part of the accusation rings true, even if the other charges were invented. Beria was shot before the end of the year.

After Beria's fall, the OGPU remained a most formidable weapon of repression in the hands of the government, but it was no longer an independent force, and with the passage of time its subjection to the government became increasingly clear. At the same time the government itself was becoming distinctly less ferocious. In the summer of 1953, strikes and riots broke out in a number of concentration camps extending over a wide area. In Stalin's day any such movement would have been suppressed at once by unstinted use of the machine gun, but now the prisoners sensed that things had changed. The camp authorities seemed uncertain of themselves. Sometimes they parleyed with the strikers and sometimes they used their guns. After that there were other strikes and riots in concentration camps, and the treatment of the prisoners was improved. The great majority of the political prisoners were released and efforts were made to get free labor to take their place. Moreover, many of those who remain in exile are now allowed to live outside barbed wire, and in some cases to have their families with them. Much hardship and much injustice remain, but at least an effort is being made to turn the penal settlements of the Arctic into places where free men will be willing to live and to do the work which has hitherto been done by convicts. It is not possible to say whether the changes were a result of the strikes or whether they would have happened in any case. Conditions in Soviet concentration camps have always reflected conditions outside.

The new rulers inherited Stalin's problems; but they were not bound by all his past. His death roused momentary fears that there would be war now that the guiding hand was gone. The death of so extraordinary man caused conflicting emotions, but the greater part of the Russian people received the news with apathy or even with satisfaction. The new rulers must have known the people's true feelings, so it is significant that Stalin's photographs were removed from public offices and that for many months his name was not often seen in print. A partial amnesty was decreed, and promises were made that there would soon be more to eat and more to buy in the shops. Writers were encouraged to say some of those things which everyone knew to be true, but which no one had dared to say. So a few works of fiction were published, cautiously attacking some of the abuses described in the preceding chapters, but those authors who went too far were reprimanded and it became clear that writers must still be careful if they wished to avoid trouble. The Kremlin could not afford to allow evils to be exposed unless it was ready to tackle them.

Stalin's position rested upon the triple support of the party, the army and the OGPU. In theory the Communist Party was the chief instrument of policy, and the army and the political police were servants of the party. But in practice the party, the OGPU and the armed forces were intertwined in such a way that any general with political ambitions would at once come up against devoted Communists who were in the inner councils of every command and every regiment. Likewise, an ambitious OGPU chief would have to reckon with men on his staff who reported directly to Stalin, and every political leader knew that all his steps were watched by the OGPU. Marshal Bulganin, who became prime minister in 1955, illustrated these arrangements in his own person. A member of the Communist Party and a marshal of the Soviet Union, he had also worked for the OGPU and it is safe to assume that he maintained his contact with them. The threads of power ran intricately in and out of the army, the party and the police, but the ends of all the threads were in Stalin's hands. After his death it did not seem that anyone held all the threads.

The key posts in every walk of life are still held by members of the Communist Party, who in 1977 number sixteen million out of a population of two hundred and fifty-six million. In that respect there is no change since Stalin died, but the members of the party are not all of the same kind and the differences have become more important. Broadly one can distinguish four types of Russian Communist, but the groups overlap. First there is the steadily diminishing hard core of disciplined men and women who accept communism as a way of life. They have mastered the Marxist way of looking at life as a whole and their communism is sincere, but they lack the breadth and subtlety of Lenin's generation. Such people give wholehearted devotion to the task in hand and undeviating loyalty to the party line, but it would be surprising to find that they were a majority of the party at any time since 1945. Next comes the large army of self-seekers who have joined the party for the sake of their careers. Not all of them are completely cynical, but they can be relied on

to support the winning cause. Then, among the older generation, there are the disillusioned Communists, men and women
who joined the party through an idealistic belief which they
have now lost. Under Stalin to resign from the Communist
Party was equivalent to declaring oneself a traitor; so these
"lapsed" Communists remained members of the party. But
they made the minimum exertion necessary to keep out of
trouble and have often held jobs below the level of their
abilities. They watch the struggles of others with a sardonic
or compassionate eye, but for themselves they try to keep out
of the melée. Tragic and ineffective figures, these Communists
who have lost their faith live in a spiritual vacuum. Perhaps
the greater part of the Communist Party at this time consisted
of an outer circle of plain decent men and women who accepted communism because it was the accepted thing, but
had never thought deeply about Marxism. They had studied
the *Short History of the Communist Party of the Soviet
Union*, which has now been revised to reflect the partial de-
valuation of Stalin. They had read some of the works of
Stalin and a little Lenin and Marx, but they had not grasped
Marxism as a system and they held many traditional ideas of
right and wrong. Such men and women may often be able,
zealous and patriotic, but they are not a secure foundation
for building a Communist society. That is the meaning of
the complaints in the Soviet press about the "low level of
political consciousness" among the rank and file of the party.
Little remains of the revolutionary comradeship which once
bound party members in a close fellowship. Nowadays the
Communist Party hardly even pretends "to be a party of
heroic individual endeavors and fanatical consciences; the
cult of the Communist saint and martyr is found in fiction,
but the author usually seems to be saying that the Communist spirit has fled from the party and resides in an invisible
Church of true believers." (H. T. Willetts in *Soviet Survey*,
No. 35, p. 75.)

The key positions in industry and in the army are held by
members of the party, but important positions of the second
rank are often held by nonparty technicians. Some of these
are active sympathizers with the regime and are hardly distinguishable from hard-core Communists. Nearly all of them accept socialism and are proud of Soviet achievements; but
only a few of them think as Marxists. Many of such people
are secretly disgusted with Stalinism. Since the twentieth

party congress in February 1956 they have been able, in private at least, to express some of their feelings, but they have no means of exerting pressure on the government so long as all the key posts are held by hard-core Communists.

Stalin had been able to do much as he liked because he started with a clean slate. The old ruling classes were gone, the peasants were still as powerless as they had been under the tsars, and the workers had no influence apart from the Communist Party which Stalin himself controlled. So he was free to make a new society with new men, but in doing so he created a new class, the Soviet elite of managers, technicians, army officers and teachers who may one day cast his work into another mold.

From the earliest days of the Revolution down to 1956, the gap between the elite and the masses grew until the difference in outward appearance and way of life became almost as great as in a capitalist country. However the membership of the elite has not become fixed. In an expanding economy there is always more room at the top, so the Soviet elite is continually receiving fresh recruits from the poorer classes. As in Victorian England, so in Russia today it is interesting to observe how far newcomers to polished society have taken on the color of their new surroundings. With every year that passes, the upper ranks of Soviet society become more assimilated into the traditional ways of civilized life, and with ways of life they absorb ways of thought. The hard core of the Communist Party forms a part of this society, but only a part. Its members are still supreme in the state, but they are continually subjected to a sort of social attrition. Every year some of the older Communists die off, while others succumb to the social embrace of a society which they have created but to which they do not altogether belong. The party may take in new members every year, but these do not effectively take the place of the older generation.

Inside Russia the sophisticated Marxism of the 1920s had now already become very rare. Its place was taken by the simplified "utility" Marxism which grew up under Stalin and bears the same relation to the Marxism of Lenin or Trotsky or Bukharin as the simpler kind of muscular Christianity bears to the teaching of Augustine or Aquinas or Calvin. Moreover, contemporary Russian society is ill adapted to producing the Stalinist or Leninist breeds of Communist, for the stern standards of behavior which are put forward by the ruling group of the Communist Party do not fit well with the easygoing ways of most of the Soviet elite and of most of the talented young people who aspire to join them.

Professor Carr has observed that both Soviet Russia and Victorian England show "the same simple, unsophisticated eagerness to reward energy with success and to punish sloth with disgrace. Both inculcate the same virtues of industry and application in work and of respectability and restraint in living. These are the virtues which the ruling group in any rising industrial society will want to inculcate in the rank and file of its people." (*The Listener*, August 4, 1955.) These are indeed virtues which are advocated by the ruling group in the Soviet Union, but it may be doubted whether they have permeated the upper ranks of Soviet society as thoroughly as they permeated Victorian England. In England power and influence were widely diffused and the current morality reflected the attitude of the upper and middle classes as a whole, but in Russia power has been concentrated in a small group which has tried to enforce its own morality on a recalcitrant society.

Moreover, in Soviet Russia, even more than in Victorian England, to follow the dominant morality is not always the best way to succeed. Russia has her prosperous *spivs* and "artful dodgers" who live on the edge of the law. These intelligent villains flaunt themselves in the center of Moscow. Their leaders are said to be Georgians. Certainly the elegant hooked noses and the sallow skin of those who hang about the lounges of certain well-known Moscow hotels, talking furtively, indicate that they are Caucasians. Their *outré* clothes contrast oddly with the general Soviet shabbiness. Whenever one of them is caught the press denounces them for the skill with which they exploit the artificialities of the Soviet market. The *tolkach* or pusher is a little more respectable. No sizable undertaking can exist without at least one of them. The *tolkach* is a contact man whose job is to secure the supply of materials needed by the firm for which he works, and he is not expected to be particular in his choice of means (see, e.g., *Novy Mir*, 1955, No. 7, p. 34). Hitherto it has scarcely been possible even for respectable members of society to get through life without some questionable use of *blat*, a word which covers every shade of legal and illegal influence and back scratching.

But as shortages became less stringent, it had become a

little easier to live without *blat*. Changing conditions of production are already producing changes in the structure of society, as, indeed, the Marxists said they would. In the first stages of industrialization the rewards for success at work and the penalties for failure were fixed high in order to increase the incentive to work hard. But the Soviet Union, like the United Kingdom, has now reached the stage when there is a shortage of labor for the worst-paid jobs. So the lowest wage rates have been increased and the tendency is to reduce "differentials." The consummation which is held out for the not too distant future is the final transition from socialism to communism, that is, to a state of affairs where people will no longer be paid according to their work but according to their need. That, at least, is the theory, but it would not be far out to say that communism means for most Soviet citizens merely an affluent society based on socialist principles.

The government's attitude to Stalin's memory remained inscrutable. Would there be a revival of a modified Stalinism or would the Kremlin slowly allow Stalin's name to be forgotten? Either seemed possible until the last day of the twentieth party congress in Moscow during February 1956. On that day, February 25, Nikita Khrushchev, the "first secretary" of the Communist Party and in that capacity the heir to Stalin, speaking to a private meeting of the delegates, laid bare some of Stalin's iniquities. The substance of what he said was already known to all well-informed people both inside and outside the Soviet Union, but it struck the delegates like a thunderbolt. It was now officially admitted that Stalin had personally ordered the death and torture of many party members and officers of the Red Army, and that the OGPU acting on Stalin's orders had systematically extorted confessions which they knew to be false. As Khrushchev came to speak of the later phase of Stalin's rule a bitter hatred seemed to overcome him, and he blamed his former master in scathing language, not only for his cruelty and his contempt for those who worked with him, but also for mistakes in policy and for personal failings. He painted a disgusting picture of Stalin's all-consuming vanity, but it did not escape his hearers that his strictures on Stalin's policy often concerned matters in which he himself was involved. Indeed, the party leaders make no bones about it. At the session of the Central Committee of the Communist Party in June 1957 which expelled Molotov and his associates, Khrushchev, pointing at Molotov and Kaganovich, exclaimed: "Your hands are stained with the blood of our party leaders and of innumerable innocent Bolsheviks!" "So are yours!" Molotov and Kaganovich shouted back at him. "Yes, so are mine," Khrushchev replied. "I admit this. But during the Great Purges I only carried out your orders. I was not then a member of the Politbureau and I am not responsible for its decisions. You were." When Mikoyan later reported the incident to the Komsomol in Moscow, he was asked why the accomplices of Stalin's crimes were not tried in court. "We cannot try them," Mikoyan is said to have answered, "because if we start putting such people in the dock there is no knowing where we should be able to stop. We have all had some share in conducting the purges." (Deutscher, *The Prophet Unarmed*, p. viii.)

Khrushchev was ready to denounce Stalin, but he was not ready to publish to the broad masses the speech in which he did so. So the text was not made public, but throughout the country there were held special meetings at which the speech or "letter" as it was sometimes called, was read to all party members and all members of the Young Communist League and to nearly all intellectuals. Officially the general public still knew nothing, but it was impossible to prevent people talking. Delegates returning home and those who had heard the speech at special meetings soon spread the news. And to discuss the speech was to discuss everything that had happened in the Soviet Union for thirty years. Millions of tongues were loosened and have not been silenced.

Feelings which had been repressed for thirty years were suddenly released. The immediate effect was startling. The ultimate effect is not yet visible. Youth rediscovered the thrill of political aspiration and students began to express the boldest dissent quite openly. Some were arrested, but not enough to stop young people from talking. Nothing but a complete return to Stalinist repression would be effective now; and among the victims there would need to be sons and daughters of the most highly placed people in Soviet society.

At the time of the 1956 revolutions in Poland and Hungary Soviet discontent found new expression. The Soviet press admitted publicly that under communism in Poland and Hungary conditions were so bad that the workers were justified in protesting. The Russian workers concluded that what may happen in Poland and Hungary under communism may happen in Russia too, and there were a few sit-down strikes, the first strikes in thirty years.

Not all of Stalin's work was disowned. His general

policy was still upheld up to the time of Kirov's murder (see p. 281), and in particular the brutalities which accompanied the collectivization and the first Five-Year Plan were not denounced. The implication is that Stalin's crime was not that he oppressed the Soviet peoples, but that he oppressed the members of the Communist Party. The cry is "Back to Lenin," but Lenin was no more inclined than Stalin to respect the liberty of those who opposed the Bolsheviks. He was more sagacious in his methods, but he was not more accommodating to opponents. Yet there is a real change and, in spite of periodic attempts to put the clock back, the fact of change slowly became unmistakable.

The party, the OGPU and the new technocracy, these are the characters who hold the stage. Others remain in the wings, exercising no direct influence but yet potentially important. The peasants are unorganized, but their passive resistance is to be reckoned with and their active cooperation would make any government stable. The working classes are apathetic about politics but they are sensitive to anything that affects them directly, such as a change in norms of work or wage rates. The Russian Orthodox Church, likewise, has no political power, but no Russian government can altogether ignore it.

2. Faith and Freedom

Soviet policy toward religion has passed through various phases but at all times the Kremlin has kept the Church under tight control, and in theory still looks to the eventual dying out of religion. At times there has been savage persecution. At other times the desecration of churches and the tearing down of icons have been discouraged. At yet other times churches have been closed through a mixture of force and fraud, and not infrequently closure has been accompanied by destruction. At all times there is a steady pressure against religion by means of lectures, articles in the press and, above all, by teaching in the schools; most of this is dreary stuff but, in the short run at least, it has had a certain amount of success.

Soviet citizens are told that "not miracle-working icons but discoveries such as those of the collective farm socialist, T. S. Maltsev, are performing true miracles on the fields of our collective and state farms" (*Trud,* October 27, 1954). Or again, in secondary school No. 20 at Stalinabad, in the spring of 1955, chemistry instructor Vera Alekseyevna Korneyeva regularly gave "interesting talks on the reactionary essence of religion, on the way the clergy abroad attempt to help the Anglo-American imperialists and others to unleash a new war," and "told the schoolchildren how churchmen, making use of the reaction of peroxide and white lead, had spread in their time the legends of restored icons" (*Kommunist Tadzhikistana,* April 28, 1955).

Most children in the towns, though perhaps not in the villages, leave school with no church connections, but when they grow up and marry, they may well have their children baptized and taught to say their prayers. Quite often the parents find their way back into the Church. Many a Russian who lives without the Church wants, when he comes to die, to be buried with a cross over his grave. A Church marriage, a Church burial, and the great feasts of the Church have, as in other countries, a strong appeal to many but their celebration leads to awkward questions from the Party. On the whole, however, the growth of industry is probably a greater threat to religion than Marxism.

Inherited Christian standards still govern Russian ideas of right and wrong. The Communist morality founded on class hatred, merciless collectivity and respect for public property has not caught on. Scrounging and misappropriation of public property are general and shameless; that is one consequence of the pressures of Stalinism and it is viewed indulgently by public opinion. On the other hand, Russians generally fail to hate those who are held up to them from time to time as their class enemies. Even the German invaders in Hitler's war were not personally generally hated. This was strikingly shown toward the end of the war when a procession of German prisoners was made to march through Moscow as a sight for the populace. I mixed with the dense crowds who had come to watch and I heard hardly a word of reproach but many words of pity such as "Poor men, how hard for them to be so far from home," and "How they must miss their mothers." This picture is confirmed by Germans who have returned from capitivity in Russia.

Besides the residual Christianity of the majority there is a burning faith to be found in a large minority. Religious statistics should always be used with caution, but an unofficial estimate from good sources indicates that there are between twenty-five and thirty-five million regular adult worshippers in the Russian Orthodox Church alone. The figure is credible, indeed it may be too small. Even if a large discount is made, it remains clear that there are more believing Christians than convinced Communists in Russia.

After its long isolation the Russian Church is able to speak to modern intellectuals on equal terms. Until the fall of Khrushchev, the chief strength of the Church was still among the simple-minded. Russian popular religion has surprised the Communists by its vitality, and Russian unbelievers are naturally shocked by the superstition which is so intertwined with spirituality that even a sympathetic observer is hard put to it to disentangle one from the other. At one time, for instance, a large number of "holy springs" made their appearance. In one case "an analysis of the water carried out by the Health Resort Institute established that it possessed no curative properties whatever. However, believers continue to use this spring, expecting to be cured of their ills. . . . And all this because there is still too little explanatory work done among the believers." (*Overcoming Religious Survivals in the U.S.S.R.*, S. N. Khudyakov, printed in an edition of 100,000 at Moscow in 1958.)

Russian popular religion is often dismissed as superstitious, but in fact it is highly intelligent. Russian peasants can see the difficulties of Christian belief without the help of university professors and often they have thought long and deeply about the mysteries of faith. They used to discuss those things among themselves—and probably still do so— as well as going for council to trusted *startsy*, such as St. Seraphim and his successors. It is not possible to understand the renaissance of Christianity among the Russian intelligentsia since the fall of Khrushchev unless one realizes the depth of thought, as well as of feeling, that has gone into making the Russian religious tradition.

The discovery that these things are so caught the anti-religious propagandists off their guard. The pamphleteer quoted above observes that "a quite unexpected feature in the history of the church is that the clergy have begun to talk about their 'mistakes' in their fight with the people who think differently." Evidently this was his way of referring to a modern intellectual approach, and it alarmed the authorities. A review of some anti-religious films in the periodical *Literature and Life* for April 9, 1961, described "Father Dmitry, a priest of the ultramodern type," as "perhaps the most frightening figure" in the four films reviewed. However, until about 1965 most of the intellectuals remained still untouched by religion. *Dr. Zhivago* was an exception, albeit a very significant exception.

However, since the end of the war a sustained effort has been made to give the clergy a thorough intellectual training in the theological colleges which the Orthodox Church was allowed to establish. These colleges give teaching in Scripture, Church history, doctrine and pastoralia, but philosophy and social teaching are excluded. To permit a specifically Christian study of philosophy and the development of a contemporary Christian teaching about the nature of society would suggest dangerous questions about the Soviet system. The staffs of these colleges lack some of the learning which would be expected of them in the West, but academic standards are taken seriously. Spiritually and intellectually the best of the younger Church leaders are very good. This is specially important because those who were trained before the Revolution have come to the end of their time. The middle generation, consisting of those who sought ordination in the time of persecution, contains some heroes of the faith but generally they have not had a systematic theological training. Therefore intellectual leadership fell increasingly on the very young generation who received their theological education since the war. These are men whose minds were formed under Soviet rule. At their best they combine what is eternal in the Orthodox tradition with a realistic view of modern man. At their worst they have a pliability and lack of experience that make them a ready instrument for Communist control and infiltration of the Church. Moreover it must be said that the best and more independent-minded of the younger generation are seldom allowed to hold positions of responsibility, still less to meet foreigners. On the other hand some of those appointed by the Party to keep the Church under control have been influenced by what they have learned of the Christian faith and were even suspected, in some cases, of having become secret believers. In this, as in other areas, it is becoming increasingly difficult to know where the ultimate loyalty of anyone holding a public position really lies.

From about 1943 to 1958 the Kremlin's policy was to accept religious people as loyal citizens but to confine religion within the four walls of the church buildings and to prevent believers from holding positions of social responsibility, in the belief that if the faith can be isolated from society it will gradually die away. Therefore no Sunday schools were allowed. According to the letter of a law, which is not always observed, parents are allowed to give their own children religious instruction or invite a priest to their house, but if they invite their neighbors' children to join a class, they risk serious trouble. On the same principle the Church is not allowed to do social work and no organized evangelism is permitted. It is, however, impossible to prevent people telling each other privately about their beliefs and a great deal of personal evangelism goes on.

On the other hand atheist propaganda is officially organized; but atheist propagandists have an uphill task. In schools a sort of "anti-chaplain" is appointed with the task of ideological instruction, which includes atheism. This means that atheism is connected with the most boring part of the curriculum, and the ignorance of some of the atheist writers must help to make them ineffective; a writer already quoted makes much of the disagreements between faiths: "The Christians consider that the God of Sabaoth is the only God. . . . The followers of the Jewish faith consider that the principal God is Jehovah." (S. N. Khudyakov in *Will Religion Exist Forever*, Moscow 1958). After the war, atheist lecturers were told to preach their creed without personal attacks on believers. Some of them asked how they could "fight against religion without simultaneously fighting the clergy and without taking action against the servants of the church" (Khudyakov, *Overcoming Religious Survivals in the U.S.S.R.*). Finding no practical answer, they became slack in their work, and the government took alarm at "the increased activity on the part of churchmen and sectarian preachers."

About 1955 younger people began to go to church in greater numbers. In 1958 a new wave of anti-religious propaganda began and reached a peak of intensity in the early 1960s. At this time about half the already too few churches and over half the theological colleges were closed by the government. Sometimes force was used but more commonly the Party's methods were underhanded. If the authorities wanted to close a church, they would find some pretext for withdrawing the priest's license to officiate. The church would then be closed temporarily until a new priest was appointed. For this purpose a meeting had to be called first, and the churchwarden would apply for permission to hold one. He would have to wait all day for many days, losing working time and pay, before he could see the requisite official. Then he would be told he had come to the wrong place. The waiting for an interview would then begin again and lead to the same result. And so on for as long as might be necessary. No letters would be answered and nothing would be put in writing. But after six months it would be said that the congregation were obviously unable to keep the church going and it would be closed permanently. Concurrently with the closing of churches, priests and bishops have been arrested on trumped-up charges. There have been vicious attacks on certain Church personalities, and renegade priests and ministers have been encouraged to attack the Church. No one who knows the Soviet Union would be greatly surprised if the authors of these attacks were themselves party agents who insinuated themselves into the Church on instructions and now leave again under instructions. It would seem, however, that at least in some cases this propaganda overreached itself with the suspicious Soviet public.

Early in 1964 there were indications that the Kremlin intended to launch a full-scale campaign for the utter and final destruction of religion in the next few years. However, the Party drew back at almost the last minute and soon afterwards Khrushchev fell from power. The pressure on believers remained very severe but the churches had at least the possibility of continued existence as organized communities. Yet the circumscribed liberty which is now given to religion is precarious. It might not be easy for the State to take back the whole of what it has given since 1943; religion is too strong to be extinguished by force, and a new persecution might drive the people to the underground church," where it would be harder to control them; yet an unscrupulous government has many weapons that fall short of open persecution. The new policy was to restrict the Church's activity to the absolute minimum by the closing of churches and by making it difficult for ordinands to get a proper theological training. It is no longer likely that religious leaders will have to face a firing squad, but a priest or bishop who is too zealous in his duties might well receive a long prison sentence for something he has not done, or for doing something that he was bound to do by his duty as a Christian minister. To recommend a young man to a theological college can be represented as doing illegal religious propaganda among youth. Short of imprisonment a priest may be expelled from his parish for some imaginary offense and then prevented from taking any other work. His wife and children will suffer and he will have to watch their dire poverty in idleness, knowing that if he renounces the Church and speaks against religion, he and his family will be richly rewarded. Some parents who bring their children up to be religious have been deprived of parental rights on the ground that they are "crippling the minds" of their children who are then sent to boarding schools and may be lost forever to their families.

The new style of martyrdom is not a martyrdom of blood, but it can be no less cruel. It remains to be seen whether these devious methods will be more effective than the open persecution of the first twenty years of Soviet rule.

The renewed persecution has produced some unexpected side effects. In 1961 the pressure on the Baptists was such that their headquarters felt obliged to send a confidential circular to the Senior Presbyters in charge of Baptist affairs in the provinces, which contains the following sentence: "The Senior Presbyter must remember that at present the main task of divine services is not the enlistment of new members." When this leaked out, the cry of "Apostasy!" went up. If the Church does not evangelize, she is not true to Christ. On this issue a substantial number of believers left the Baptist Church and formed a rival group known as the Initsiativniki. These were the object of unremitting attacks in the Soviet press and unremitting pressure from the authorities; yet they built up a nationwide connection, publishing literature, sending appeals to the Soviet authorities and to the outside world, and even holding secret congresses. This was the first time for more than a generation that any dissident and illegal group had been able to maintain on such a scale any semblance of organized life. The rise of the Initsiativniki marks an epoch in Soviet evolution. They have shown great courage and ability and now this has been rewarded. A number of their churches have been given legal recognition. It is remarkable that the Kremlin should back down even to this extent, but the persecution continues. Details are known of many who have received long sentences of prison or exile and of one who was tortured to death. Such brave people win one's sympathy, but it would be foolish to take sides with them against the other branch of the Baptists which continues to maintain a legal existence. We do not know the precise circumstances in which the offending circular was sent, nor can we tell how it would have been understood in the varying circumstances of different Soviet localities, nor what may have been gained by an accommodation with the state at a difficult moment. Moreover the attentive reader will have noticed that nothing is said about evangelism outside the church services.

The truth is complex and, no doubt, most people remain outside the influence of religion. It would be wrong to assume that therefore they are Marxist. Up to the end of the war it was easy for a young idealist to excuse everything in the present for the sake of a glorious future, but after 1945 young people expected to see tangible results from nearly thirty years of labor. Already in 1945 some university teachers were alarmed by the free thinking of their pupils, and in subsequent years the concentration camps received a considerable number of recruits from idealistic youth at the universities. These new revolutionaries have no wish to imitate Western societies but they are very interested in new developments in other Communist countries of Eastern Europe. Such movements indicate some of the frustrations of that part of Soviet society which is still prepared to suffer for an ideal.

Every year something like a quarter of a million young men and women leave the Soviet universities and other places of higher education. Some of them will hold leading positions in Soviet life. Soviet students can be more interested in art than in politics and more interested in money than in art. They have a polish and sophistication which mark them off from the bright-eyed, tousleheaded boys and girls who filled Russian universities thirty years ago. The spoiled child of prosperous parents is the butt of Russia's comic paper, *Krokodil*, but there is good stuff in the younger generation. Experience has made a great part of Soviet society cynical but idealistic youth is reacting against its surroundings.

There is little doubt that most of the young are loyal Soviet citizens, but it would be wrong to assume that they believe everything that they read in the Soviet newspapers or that they take their ideals ready made. It might be equally wrong to suppose that their public statements necessarily reflect their true thoughts. *Komsomolskaya Pravda* for March

24, 1961, complained that a young man who distinguishes himself in public by his keen and orthodox Marxism may in private apologize for his sharp criticism of a comrade with words such as "Don't be offended. This is what has to be done." For such people orthodox "views are a kind of umbrella—something that is needed when it rains but that can be tucked out of sight when the sun comes out." (*Ibid.*) One particularly successful student of Marxism said, "The study of social-economic subjects does not place any moral obligations on me." (*Ibid.*) It is not the way of the Soviet press to admit such facts unless they are widespread; similar incidents come the way of any close observer of the Soviet scene. Such systematic concealment can be corrupting, but the best Soviet youth maintains an inner integrity in spite of all. "If you have written a lying article or exhibited a dreary picture painted according to the rules of socialist realism, no one will reproach you, because you may have on your studio walls a hundred magnificent canvasses which no hanging committee would accept. But if you take it into your head to boast about your fake you won't be forgiven." (David Burg in *Soviet Survey*, Oct.-Dec. 1958.)

3. Land and Food

The extremes of Stalinism were a product of hard times. Trotsky put this in a nutshell. "The basis of bureaucratic rule is . . . poverty . . . with the resulting struggle of each against all. When there are enough goods in a store the purchasers can come whenever they want to. When there are a few goods the purchasers are compelled to stand in line. When the lines are very long, it is necessary to appoint a policeman to keep order. Such is the starting point of the Soviet bureaucracy. It knows who is to get something and who has to wait." (Trotsky, *The Revolution Betrayed*, p. 110.) But now the progress of the Soviet economy is overcoming shortages and the new situation demands greater flexibility. Heavyhanded regimentation is a possible means of turning a backward country into an industrial state, even if it is not the most efficient or humane means of doing so, but when a complex industrial economy has come into being, it is no longer practicable to use Stalin's methods. In general Soviet industrial efficiency still lags far behind North America, but there are now enough skilled men and women to operate an increasingly complex economy. In 1945 it seemed that Russia's demand for more skills of every kind was insatiable, but now her whole system of education is geared to ensure that the schools produce enough manual workers as well as enough technicians. Nothing could show more clearly how far the Soviet Union has come since the first Five-Year Plan. Russia's problems are now those of a developed economy.

In Stalin's heyday if Russia was short of skill she had at least an abundance of unskilled labor. Men and women were therefore expendable. Now there is a shortage of labor. Therefore people have become more valuable. The Soviet regime has already taken the easy profits of the first development of what was almost a virgin continent. Not for nothing had Blok called Russia "the new America." Further development depends upon a more careful use of resources both in men and in materials. At the same time the demand for more food and better housing is becoming irresistible. This can only be met by diverting resources from other forms of development. The needs of a modern economy are steadily driving the Soviet Union toward greater flexibility and a more humane and imaginative attitude to workers and their families. There is still a long way to go.

So far there has been no fundamental questioning of the received notions of Soviet economics, but discussions of what may seem to be purely technical questions of economics reveal some of the stresses that Soviet society is undergoing. A long-drawn-out argument about whether "the law of value" has any relevance in the Soviet Union shows this. If prices are to have a part in regulating production under socialism, what becomes of the Soviet system of planning? If not, how is it to be decided what operations are profitable and what are unprofitable? The problem seems to be beyond the capacity of Soviet economists to solve. The difficulty is best seen in a concrete instance. While machines were scarce and labor plentiful, it was worth using any machine whose wheels would still revolve. There was no need to consider obsolescence. Now the machines are more plentiful and labor is becoming scarcer. So Soviet economists need a method of determining at what point a machine should be scrapped. It is difficult to see how this can be done without introducing cost accounting, as understood in the West, and other aspects of "the law of value." But this goes against received Marxist theory, which is supported at this point by the Russian attitude to money. The Russian peasants are avaricious enough but the townspeople, who set the tone, have always lacked bourgeois forethought and calculation. In tsarist Russia nobles, workers and intelligentsia alike treated money as dross, spending freely and lending without hope of return when they had money and borrowing without meaning to repay when they had none. Russia never went through Europe's long training in the realities of money. To us their attitude to money seems adolescent; to them our attitude seems ignoble.

The Soviet economy was long held back by a scanty and unreliable food supply. In some respects Russian farming a generation after the Revolution produced even less than before. For instance in 1916, according to figures given by Khrushchev himself, there were in all Russia 58,400,000 cattle of which 28,800,000 were cows, whereas in 1953 there were 56,600,000 cattle, of which only 24,300,000 were cows. That is to say, the number of cows had gone down by four and a half million. Stalin exerted enormous will power to get the peasants into collective farms and to keep them there, and he issued much propaganda about various methods of agriculture. Large numbers of tractors were brought into use and certain large schemes of irrigation were carried out. But apart from this he was reluctant to put money into the countryside. In his speech to the twentieth party congress Khrushchev asserted that Stalin had never once visited a village since January 1928. "He knew the country and agriculture only from films. And these films had dressed up and beautified the existing situation in agriculture. Many films so pictured collective farm life that the tables were bending from the weight of turkeys and geese. Evidently Stalin thought that it was actually so."

Khrushchev did at least make a serious and sustained effort to produce more food. The most spectacular aspect of the new policy was the plowing up of 75 million acres of virgin soil in southern Siberia and the adjoining parts of Central Asia. There was no adequate preparation before this vast operation was launched, but the land is fertile, though prone to drought, and, taking good years with bad, there would be a good chance of a fair return on the effort put into the "new lands" if they were well farmed, but this is the sort of land where bad farming makes dust bowls; and Soviet farming is very unequal. So the result was unequal, but in the end the new lands settled down and became one more agricultural province of Russia.

Russia cannot be fed from the "new lands" alone and it remains necessary to improve Russian food production throughout. Russian farming needs three interconnected things: firstly, more capital; secondly, an understanding of the peasants' point of view on the part of those who make policy; and lastly, educated leadership. It should be obvious that no agricultural policy is likely to give good results without the cooperation of the peasantry, but "the type of official who is sure that the collective farm economy can be developed by using administrative pressure is still alive" (*Kommunist* for November 1955). Capital is needed not so much for grandiose undertakings such as the reclamation of virgin lands, but for a very large number of small projects such as the construction of bridges over streams. It is things such as this which will in the end make the Russian villages into places where educated people will be willing to live and bring up their children.

Those villages which lie within ten or twenty miles of a big town are favorite places of relaxation for town-dwelling Russians and they are often fairly prosperous, being in the nature of things near a market; but they are not typical. Most Russian villages lie outside this magic circle. If one may judge from complaints in the Soviet press, even those party officials who are charged with the supervision of the country do not for the most part penetrate to the real "bears' corners." For educated people, country life in Russia had hardly become more attractive since Peter the Great. For many Russians the hardest deprivation of village life is the lack of educated companionship, which is itself a result of poverty and bad roads. An educated man will not live in a place where all his neighbors are poor, or in a place that he cannot get away from. The country roads are little more than cart tracks with wooden bridges over the streams. These were more or less adequate in the days of horses and carts, but now they are used by tractors and trucks which cut up the ground and break down the bridges. In the Soviet countryside a broken bridge may remain unmended for many months or even years. In the long run the food supply of Russia's towns depends on the amenities of her villages. And until recently villages were emptying at an alarming rate.

Khrushchev made concessions to the peasants which made it a little more worthwhile for them to work hard and show some enterprise, but the resulting rise in food prices caused great discontent in the towns and in 1962 there was something like an armed uprising in Novocherkassk. The disastrous failure of the harvest in 1963 was due to untimely frost followed by very severe and widespread drought, but the subsequent course of events has made it clear that any improvement in farming up to the fall of Khrushchev was merely relative to the previous gross inefficiency.

4. Gradual Relaxation

For three years after Stalin's death the strain of Soviet life was gradually relaxed, but so slowly that it was not possible to speak of a decisive change. The government did not fulfill its promise of a greatly increased production of consumer goods, but nonetheless there was a little more to buy in the shops. Relations with Western countries remained bad but became less explosive. The OGPU remained sinister and powerful, but it was no longer ubiquitous. Exchanges of technical and cultural delegations became an established feature of Soviet policy. Soviet delegations to foreign countries began to be chosen from those with the best technical qualifications rather than from those with the best Stalinist record, and the members of delegations were sometimes encouraged to meet foreigners with a freedom that had long been unknown. In this way Soviet technicians and men of learning were able to learn at first hand of the advances that had been made in the West during Russia's long isolation. In return for this, foreign delegations visiting the Soviet Union were shown the latest Soviet achievements with a freedom that would have been unthinkable while Stalin was alive.

More contact with foreigners reflects a lessening of fear and distrust among the Russians themselves. The machinery of thought control was not dismantled but it became less effective as the memory of Stalin receded. The Kremlin's problem is how to make concessions to pressure from below without letting it get out of hand. The difficulty is illustrated

by the case of Soviet satire. At the end of Stalin's life Soviet
writers had ceased to criticize any aspect of Soviet reality.
By 1952 empty theaters showed that the public would not pay
to see a varnished and prettified version of their own lives.
The party therefore demanded satire in the tradition of Gogol
and other great writers of the past, but even after Stalin's
death few writers dared to accept this challenge. Those who
did were immediately denounced for distortion of Soviet
reality. It is one of the rules of Soviet writing that typical
characters and situations must be depicted. But how could a
satirical writer use his gifts on a "typical" situation fifty years
after the October Revolution without implying that the characters and situations involved are produced by the Soviet
regime? It is idle for *Pravda* to say that "the satire of Gogol
. . . was directed toward shaking the foundations of the social
order which existed at that time . . . the purpose of our satire
is to *assert* the Soviet system through a criticism of short-
comings." The dilemma remains unresolved, but it is now at
least possible to discuss such subjects without the fear that
one may be shot for being on the wrong side in the argument.

After the events of the autumn of 1956 in Hungary and
Poland the Soviet government took back some of the liberty
which it had given to writers earlier in the year; but even so
writers remained freer than in previous years and after 1957
there was a very gradual further relaxation. Freedom of
speech in private conversation was not greatly affected by
the Hungarian Revolt. Ordinary Russians had been feeling
their way cautiously forward and at first found it hard to believe that they could speak openly about politics without
danger, but with each year that passed they spoke more freely.
Indeed the change was such that the younger generation
could find it impossible to understand the moral situation of
their parents before 1953. This is touchingly shown in a novel
by a young writer, Nina Ivange, published in *Novy Mir* for
August and September 1959. The hero is a young boy who
is overcome with shame by the discovery that his father did
nothing to defend his best friend when he was accused in one
of the purges, and even tried to conceal that he had ever
known him. The boy seems unable to take in that if his father
had said one word for his friend "the whole family would
have suffered." (See article by Vera Alexandrova in *Sotsiali-
stichesky Vestnik* for October 1959).

At the twentieth party congress (in 1956) it was laid down
that Soviet law was in the future to be better respected. So

far, very few Russians understand what is involved in the rule of law, but Soviet law and its administration are now receiving closer attention and there are signs of a slow growth of a sense of law among the Russian people and their rulers.

By the second half of the 1960s it had become just possible to speak of an opposition, albeit a fundamentally loyal opposition; and this opposition has been demanding its legal rights. We are told that since the death of Stalin "inner party democracy" has been restored. This should mean that the members of the Communist Party are to have more freedom of discussion among themselves, but there is little sign that posts of influence inside the party are being filled by genuine election. Still less is there any indication of an intention to extend to others the very limited freedom which is given to the members of the party. Yet the machinery of thought control is gradually breaking down.

In October 1964, Khrushchev fell from power. His fall was sudden and the reaction of Soviet public opinion was unexpected. He was never so popular as the West supposed, but two or three years before the Russians had been saying "It is all right under Khrushchev," though they would shake their heads and add ominously, "We do not know who will follow him." In 1964 his fall was greeted with widespread pleasure. The Russians had ceased—too soon, perhaps—to fear a reversion to Stalinism and Khrushchev had become in their eyes a hindrance to further progress. Moreover, the failures of his agricultural policy were for all to see and some of his international clowning made Russians feel uncomfortable. Yet this did not make his successors popular. Their methods had been conspiratorial and they failed to produce in public respectable reasons for overthrowing their former chief. Jamming of foreign broadcasts had ceased earlier in the year and the Soviet public found themselves relying on foreign stations for news of what was happening in their own country. This was galling to the intense national pride of the Russians. It might well have been expected that the Russian people would have grown accustomed to their Government doing things over their heads, but times had been changing and they had come to expect their Government to treat them as the patriotic and responsible people that they are. The loyalest of Soviet citizens could be heard to say "I no longer understand anything." To some extent Russia's rulers had lost caste with their people. Principle and ideology were seen to count for little. The pragmatic element in Soviet statecraft had been strengthened.

CHAPTER XXV

Russia on the move

πάντα ρεῖ

All things are in flux

Heraclitus

1. Ideals and Ideology

Khrushchev's successors took over at a moment when the official ideology had lost its credibility. The machine continued to turn out the usual slogans and commonplaces but most of those who wrote them neither believed what they wrote nor expected their readers to believe it. Principled Marxist Leninists still existed but were not many and they were aging. At the same time unofficial public opinion was finding expression through a vast underground literature known as *samizdat* or self-publishing. Poems, books and articles were typed and circulated widely among educated people.

Officially the jubilee of the Bolshevik revolution celebrated at the end of 1967 commemorated a generation and a half of solid achievement and was intended to consolidate its basis in Marxist ideology. Some of the achievements were indeed great, and the Russians felt a thrill of pride as they looked back on them. But the celebrations came at a delicate point in Russia's evolution, when for the first time in nearly fifty years public opinion was becoming vocal in its criticism of what is, if not yet articulate in aspirations for what might be.

By tradition the Russian writers are the guardians of Russia's conscience (See Chapter XIII, last page). In recent years some probing books have been published but the sharpest criticism is in *samizdat*. An enquiry into the moral state of the nation is now carried on openly among the intelligentsia, and almost amounts to a national inquest on what has happened to Russia since 1917. Those writers who are too bold may still become martyrs, but there is as good a chance of survival as in nineteenth-century Russia. Literary nonconformists do indeed run the risk of losing their livelihood, and they may suffer incarceration in prison, concentration camp, or lunatic asylum, but the days of Stalin's Siberian *oubliettes* are past. It takes courage to speak out, but those who do have the courage are respected. This can make poetry recitals popular for some of the same reasons as dangerous sport.

Pride in their country's achievement and disillusionment with the Marxist ideology, which is supposed to underlie it, are mixed together in Russian minds. This mixture of pride and cynicism is not new. What is new is that fundamental questions are now openly discussed, even if the most damaging criticism is not yet published except by way of *samizdat*.

Socialism as a form of economic organization is hardly in question. But Marxism-Leninism as a system of thought no longer commands serious interest, though certain elements of Lenin's thinking have no doubt entered the bloodstream of Russians. In Max Hayward's phrase, so far as the Soviet Union is concerned, and whatever may be the case elsewhere, "Marxism is a dinosaur that has died," choked by Stalin through lack of air. The governmental structure is still immensely strong, but the ideology has become like a very thin crust over a very large pie.

The non-God of Marxism-Leninism is dead and everyone can see it. The non-ideology of diluted Stalinism hardly gives a veil of respectability to the power of the state. Gulash Communism, or a welfare society organized under Communist leadership with a minimum of ideology, fills the stomach, but that is all it does. And the Russians are not the people to settle down to a spiritual or ideological vacuum. What then are the living elements in Russian thought and feeling which will affect the formation of guiding ideas in the next stage of Russian history?

The concept of a plural society, now in vogue in the West, is not understood and has no particular attraction for the Russians. Liberal neo-Marxism has a following in other countries but hardly in Russia. In theory a devotion to the early Marx and his concept of alienation could take the place of a more rigid ideology, but there is no indication of this. After an overdose of one kind of Marxism the Russians are more attracted by things that are entirely different. Some Soviet dissidents still claim that they are Marxist in some residual sense but—to me at least—this claim has no meaning.

Russian nationalism has always been a powerful ideological force, though a hidden one in the early years of the Revolution, but that card is a dangerous one for the Soviet government to play. Greater reliance on Russian nationalism would alienate the non-Russian nationalities who are already restless at the dominance of their Russian elder brother. However, Russian nationalism could lead beyond itself, for it is bound up with Russian history, and when the Russians look into their own past, they come up against the Russian Orthodox Church at every step. Here there has been a radical change of perspective. In 1965 there was a barely perceptible turning towards religion among educated people, but now the intelligentsia, which turned against religion over a hundred years ago, is becoming intensely interested in the religious answers to ultimate questions. In general the concern is for the values of Russian Orthodoxy, not for the structures of the Church, which are sometimes considered compromised by association with the régime. The Bible and commentaries on it are avidly studied, when they can be obtained. Often it is the less orthodox writers, such as Berdyaev, who have the greatest following, but religious books of all kinds command the highest prices on the blackmarket.

Moreover the Church and the intelligentsia meet in *samizdat*. There is now a sort of unofficial opposition within the Orthodox Church which publishes a stream of underground literature documenting in great detail the harassing and persecution of the Church and criticizing the Moscow Patriarch for not resisting it more. This type of *samizdat* puts forward demands that have a family resemblance to those of the writers. In particular both are now demanding honest and impartial application of the law in matters that concern them. The Baptists, too, demand legality, and there is some evidence of cross-fertilization of ideas between them and the Orthodox. The Baptists are thought, wrongly, to be a manifestation of an un-Russian activity, and few of them have been able to get an education such as would enable them to join the intelligentsia; they are therefore little known and widely misunderstood among educated people, but this is changing as educated people become converted to the Baptist faith.

It is too early to speak of an alliance or even an understanding between the Church and the intelligentsia, but the two bodies are on converging courses. So far, the Kremlin studiously ignores the signs of ferment or plays them down. If, however, at some future date it were decided to take more elements from the Russian past into a renewed ideology, there might be a sinister alliance between Russian chauvinism and the national Church. This, however, would be resented by the non-Russian nationalities for the same reason as other manifestations of Pan-Slavism. The ideas of Russian Orthodoxy could not become an effective element in a new ideology for the Soviet Union as a whole unless the Russian Orthodox Church were to grow beyond its sometimes narrow Russianness. The first indication that this may be happening is that since the second half of the 1960s Orthodoxy has an altogether new attraction for many Russian Jews, though not, of course, for all of them.

At the moment nationalism and the Orthodox tradition are the two ideological forces which have shown the most staying power. No doubt hindsight will eventually show that other powerful ideas and ideals are at work, but so far they are not clearly visible. Hitherto "nationalism" in the Soviet Union has meant above all Russian nationalism but this is changing. The astonishing revival of Jewish national consciousness has been fully reported in the West. It is less known that this is a particular instance of a general phenomenon. The national consciousness of other minorities has been similarly heightened. Ukrainians, Georgians, Armenians, Lithuanians, Latvians, Esthonians, Uzbeks (and other Moslem peoples), have all become intensely conscious of themselves as distinct from the dominant Great Russians. And the list should be lengthened to include those who have lost their national territory, such as the Soviet Germans, the Crimean Tartars and small tribes such as the Meskhi, the Biblical Meshech, who are not allowed to return to their mountainous home in the Caucasus. It is impossible to foresee the consequences of this for the future evolution of the Soviet empire, but already it has produced a strong reaction from the Great Russians, who resent being made the scapegoats for every calamity of the Soviet peoples.

Traditional feelings that had been forbidden expression under Lenin, Stalin and Khrushchev have erupted forcibly. And some of the controversies of the nineteenth century are resurrected in a new form. Today once more there are Westernizers and Slavophiles. Is Russia to follow the path of the West or has Providence marked out a special path for her? Should she continue to emulate the material and scientific progress of the West, albeit in a socialist form? And should she approximate increasingly to the free institutions which gave birth to western progress? Or has she a special destiny to build something fresh on her own traditions, at the heart of which lies the Russian Orthodox Church? This last is the view of those whom one must call Neo-Slavophiles. There are many gradations of both views and they sometimes fade into each other. Broadly, academician Sakharov is a Westernizer and Solzhenitsyn is a Neo-Slavophile, though an idiosyncratic one. Both tendencies are represented equally in the Soviet establishment and among its critics. The collapse of serious belief in ideology has opened the way for the expression of a wide variety of beliefs in private conversation and in underground literature, though not yet in print. Party members may have to be more careful how they express themselves, but the same variety of opinion is found among them as among the rest of the population. For instance, a party member could not openly practice a religion without risking expulsion. Yet there are many crypto-Christians among them and, I do not doubt, crypto-Jews, crypto-Muslims and crypto-Buddhists.

The forces working below the surface are various and they will have their consequences, but it should be emphasized that so far the Soviet government and the Communist Party show no intention whatever of abdicating their power or abating their ideological monopoly. They are conducting a stubborn rearguard action, but governments are not always able to calculate how much freedom they will permit. Elemental forces are in action. Since 1956 Russia has been visibly on the move; and very slowly but unmistakably she is gaining momentum. There will be setbacks, but it is hard to see how at this stage the direction in which Russia is moving could be permanently reversed.

If the West were for several years in such confusion that the Kremlin felt it could ignore the free world, this might greatly delay the internal evolution of Russia, but even that would not turn the tide back.

2. Vacillation

Faced with such evident dangers, Khrushchev's successors began to restore the network of internal espionage, which had been partly dismantled by Khrushchev. The KGB, as the secret police were now called, did not recover all the powers they had formerly held but they became once more nearly all pervasive. The government was nervous but it did not feel able to strike at dissent with Stalinist vigor.

At the beginning of 1968 a new Communist leadership overthrew the Stalinists in Czechoslovakia and began to give the people their head. The Kremlin showed its nervousness by trying to prevent its people from hearing much about what was happening in Prague, but the Soviet leaders vacillated until after the middle of August, letting slip all the relatively opportune moments for decisive intervention. Eventually, with the willing or enforced cooperation of five other satellite countries, the Soviet forces occupied Czechoslovakia without warning during the night of August 20th–21st. The military planning and execution were superb, but the political plan proved to be a miscalculation. The Soviet authorities showed that they were totally unprepared for the passive resistance and national solidarity which they encountered. They hesitated to overthrow the Czechoslovak leadership and impose a puppet government; this might have caused a national uprising, and they could not be sure that the Soviet troops would fire on fellow Slavs, and socialists at that. Yet they could not withdraw without a humiliating loss of face and without reinstating liberal forces which endangered the power of the present Soviet leadership. If the Czechs and Slovaks were to have freedom under Communism, the demand for freedom in the Soviet Union itself would be impossible to resist. Above all, freedom to publish the full truth about the immediate past was dangerous. So foreign broadcasts were jammed once more and foreign newspapers, including Communist papers, ceased to arrive at the Intourist hotels. This made it clear to all that the rest of the world, including the foreign Communist parties, was solid in condemnation of the Soviet action. This in turn stimulated the bush telegraph to more than usual activity. People became, indeed, very cautious about what they said and to whom they said it, but reasonably accurate information was spread with surprising rapidity.

Soon after the invasion the Soviet press began to publish detailed reports of the difficulties surrounding the Soviet forces in Czechoslovakia. These reports were ostensibly denouncing Czechoslovak and western "counter-revolutionary" forces but in fact they gave, to anyone who read between the lines, a not unsympathetic account of the Czech and Slovak resistance. I happened to be in Russia for six weeks over this period, living among Russians and seldom seeing the foreign journalists or embassies, and I soon began to suspect that some of the Soviet journalists in Czechoslovakia were engaged in a subtle sabotage of the Kremlin's policy. They reported the story of the resistance, as they had to, as a case of wrongheaded opposition to the forces of good, but in doing so they conveyed pretty clearly what was really happening. It soon became clear from many sources that a large part of the Soviet public had drawn conclusions that were unwelcome to the Kremlin.

Working-class people were from the start openly incredulous of the official story that the forces of the Soviet Union and its allies had been invited in by the Czechoslovaks, but they did not appear to be concerned about the morality of the matter. For them Czechoslovakia was a distant country of which they knew little. On the other hand the intelligentsia were greatly disturbed by "the Czech events," though they were careful what they said. Some of them were deeply concerned for the honor of their country. Nearly all of them understood that, if the Czechs and Slovaks lost their freedom, it would be harder for the Soviet peoples to gain theirs. The trials of writers and Ukrainian nationalists, and the increasingly oppressive control of the churches were an indication that the relative liberality of Khrushchev's policies was at an end. Evidently the Soviet rulers felt that freedom of expression was already going too far for their own safety. A number of them had begun their rise to power in the great terror of thirty years before and had secrets that must be kept at all costs. But in twenty years, and probably in ten, the present generation of leaders will have retired or been pushed out. Their successors will not be tied in the same way by what happened before 1953.

Nonetheless the slow evolution of a freer society in the Soviet Union was not noticeably set back by "the Czech events." In fact, the Soviet Union now needs the West. The easy profits of the first stages of industrialization of a country ripe for development have been taken. The next stages depend on a more advanced technology, and the "technological gap" between Russia and the West is growing. It is impossible for any country to keep up with the advanced countries unless its scientists and technologists can travel freely, meeting their colleagues at international conferences and having easy access to scientific writing, wherever it is published. But to allow this would destroy the system of thought control on which the Soviet system is based. Yet détente is the only possible foreign policy for the Soviet government. The quarrel between Russia and China goes deep and it is not practicable to have a foreign policy of hostility to your neighbors on all frontiers. The contradiction cannot be resolved. And this is the explanation of the vacillations and contradictions of Soviet policy.

The new rulers have some substantial achievements to their credit. In agriculture the terms of trade have at last been changed in favor of the peasants, and there is a new rural prosperity. Country roads are still extremely bad, and often hardly deserve the name of roads, but when the peasants can get to town, they come with money which they spend freely. If not yet universal, this relative prosperity is widespread. The peasants are even beginning to overcome their sense of social inferiority and to make their way into smart restaurants, to the astonishment of town dwellers. At the same time there is among all classes a new appreciation of country life and of life in some of the smaller towns. That is made possible by the vastly improved supplies now available in villages and in provincial shops. This marks an important change in the balance of Soviet life. There are now those who actually prefer to live in small towns and villages.

In the towns housing and clothing are greatly improved. It is the ambition of all Soviet citizens to dress in foreign clothes. In the big cities most of them seem to have succeeded in this by one means or another, sometimes legally and sometimes not. At the same time the design of home-produced clothes is so greatly improved that it often provides an acceptable substitute. Food is ample in bulk but sometimes lacks variety. An excessive reliance on carbohydrates shows itself in widespread corpulence. Foreign tourists now come in large numbers. Some of them are mere gapers but those who are sufficiently enterprising now have opportunities to meet Soviet citizens informally. Every year substantial numbers of Soviet citizens are permitted or compelled to emigrate. This "third emigration" is drawn from the intelligentsia and it is by no means exclusively Jewish. The process of emigration is accompanied by much hardship and injustice, but those who go maintain close links with those who stay by letters, telephone or message. The repression of dissidents remains cruel and sly but it is sporadic; and it is often deflected by the pressure of foreign public opinion.

The road is long and the going is heavy. Change comes so slowly that those who spend two or three years in the Soviet Union may not notice it, but over the decades the slow erosion of Stalinism continues ineluctably. Some of Russia's inheritance has gone forever, but in many fields Russian tradition is asserting itself with a vitality that no one expected.

A historian is not a prophet and I make no prediction beyond what may be inferred from my analysis of the forces at work. But I observe that in the last thirty years the Soviet Union has become a gerontocracy. It is ruled by septuagenarians. When they go, they will be succeeded by men who made their careers after the death of Stalin and are not prisoners of the Stalinist past. The Tsarist régime lost full confidence in itself more than a generation before its end. In India the British Raj began to lose its confidence after 1919. Analogies are never precise but the Soviet rulers are losing confidence in their ultimate aims and they have already lost belief in their absolute right to impose their will by unlimited coercion.

CHAPTER XXVI

a new beginning

*Let but society be rightly constituted—by victorious
analysis. The stomach that is empty shall be filled, the
throat that is dry shall be wetted with wine. Labor itself
shall be all one as rest; not grievous but joyous. Wheat
fields, one would think, cannot come to grow untilled,
no man made clayey or made weary thereby; unless
indeed machinery will do it? Gratuitous Tailors and
Restaurateurs may start up, at fit intervals, one as yet
sees not how. But if each will, according to the rule of
Benevolence, have a care for all, then surely—no one
will be uncared for.*

Thomas Carlyle,
The French Revolution *(first published in 1937)*

The rule of old men grew ever more ineffective. By the
mid-1970s it was clear to those who had eyes to see that the
Soviet Union had reached an impasse. Mercenary men and
women were at the top of every tree, living in comparative
luxury, as Eastern Europe measures luxury. High and low, most
people did no more than they were obliged. The common saying
was: "We pretend to work and the government pretends to pay
us." The gap between the Soviet Union's best efforts and the
West grew continually. Reform in Russia generally starts from
the top. It could not be long before there was a reforming Tsar,
as indeed I foresaw in an article published in the London *Times*
(January 3, 1978). But I did not foresee what my reforming
Tsar would do, nor the breathtaking pace at which events would
move. Finally, in March 1985 Mikhail Sergeyevich Gorbachev
succeeded to what was in effect supreme power. He meant to
make Communism work more as it was intended, not to substitute another system. Previously, incompetents had been promoted purely on the basis of party loyalty. So every branch of
science and technology fell behind. Moreover, the Soviet Union
has missed out on the "Second Industrial Revolution" and on
many other scientific discoveries, if not in theory, then in practice. To take a concrete example, Soviet medicine made great
strides up to the Second World War. The foundations of a

free health service had been laid and the best health care was comparable to the best in the West. But now doctors and nurses had to be given money or favors for their services, otherwise the patient got shoddy treatment. And there was a general shortage of modern drugs. I happen to suffer from bronchitis, and on a visit to the Soviet Union quite recently I was subjected to the eighteenth century remedy of cupping.

Gorbachev is a remarkable man. He inherited a situation that required action—urgently. Some preliminary thinking had been done but not enough. It was necessary to speed up reformation but this could not be accomplished without changes in structure and more openness. No state can stand on a basis of make believe. And Soviet power was based on a great deal of pretence. So Gorbachev decided at once that there must be "no more gaps" in Soviet history. He has implemented the policy of *glasnost* with a breathtaking intrepidity, but he is lacking in ideas about how to reform the Soviet Union in other respects. The iniquities of Stalin can now be discussed with objectivity; until recently Lenin alone remained taboo. But the fact is that Stalinism was built on a foundation that had been laid by Lenin, and in the course of 1990 Leninism collapsed irredeemably. It is symbolic that Leningrad has become St. Petersburg once more. It was not foreseen that *glasnost* would entail as a consequence the collapse of Communism particularly in Eastern Europe, where the Communist system had been imposed on unwilling peoples.

Gorbachev, like Alexander II, had the intelligentsia on his side to begin with. He was the first Soviet leader who had had a full university education, and he preferred, if he could, to work by consensus instead of fear. In all this he was distinguished from his Communist predecessors. He was wonderfully dexterous in managing the Communist system, but that was the system which he intended to make work. In other words, he remained an *apparatchik,* though a particularly gifted one. He had initiative combined with a natural gift for acting which was cultivated on the amateur stage when he was a student in Moscow. This impressed the West more than it impressed Soviet citizens, who were conscious of the grim realities of Soviet life, which got worse every month. Gorbachev's experience had been entirely among Russians. He had little experience or understanding of the other nationalities who inhabit the Russian empire. He had to learn about their problems the hard way. And his treatment of domestic affairs was hesitating and half-hearted. All in all, he had great qualities and it was hard to see how much of his work could be undone now that it had progressed so far.

But the queues grew ever longer and everything was in short supply for all but the favored few. Villages were emptying, not perhaps so drastically as in the days of Ivan the Terrible, but emptying all the same, and those who remained were mostly elderly. People preferred to live in the big cities, where hitherto there had generally been something to be had at the end of one's wait in a queue.

If *glasnost* succeeded, *perestroika* failed. What went wrong? The Communist system, with all its glaring faults, had a coherence, and once one part had been reformed the next part needed urgent attention. Gorbachev pulled down a system that worked after a fashion but failed to put anything in its place. Under Communism the local first secretary's word went. If there was delay on the railway, he alone could resolve it. Now there was a vacuum of power, and with every month that passed the situation became more desperate. Under the old system everything depended on the *nomenklatura,* the tried party hands who had risen to the top, or near the top, of the Communist system, a few hundred thousand persons in all. These had access to special shops where everything could be bought, and those at the top had special privileges such as theater tickets, vacations, and above all, foreign travel (when they returned they got rich from selling scarce goods on the black mai ket). They controlled all branches of industry, agriculture, science, and the arts. The *nomenklatura* could ensure that their families had the best education, while others had to take their chances. They had the best medicine, culminating in the famous Kremlin hospital, and access to the latest drugs. It was not surprising that when the population at last became free to express their opinions they were disgusted with this new form of feudalism. Every month they learned of new crimes committed by Stalin. Where were they to turn if not to the best elements among the Communists? But almost everywhere those who had benefitted from the old system were in power and were understandably reluctant to give up their privileges.

So it was a case of "too little, too late," almost at every point. It is at present obscure, and may always remain so, whether Gorbachev was hindered by Communist conservatives from doing what he saw was necessary, or whether he did not realize that urgent reforms were necessary and that these would involve in effect scrapping the whole Communist system.

Corruption has deep roots in Russian society, and in the So-

viet period it has produced a "mafia" as disgraceful as any in
the world. As always in thoroughly corrupt countries, the highest ranks of the *nomenklatura* can be the most greedy for bribes.
yet the *nomenklatura,* like the ruling classes of many other corrupt governments, besides including plenty of rascals and time
servers, contains some competent and honorable people. Gorbachev tried to promote the best of them, in hopes that in
time, the Soviet Union would no doubt have a better form of
government—if only there were time.

There were few outside the Communist Party who had any
conception of the manifold problems of governing a large country, and it takes time to train the hundreds of thousands of
competent engineers, technicians, and, above all, accountants
who are now needed. But time is what there was not.

It is all very well to proclaim a wish that every enterprise
should pay its way, but what does this mean? How can the value
of any enterprise be decided without accountants? It sounds fine
to authorize cooperatives, but what if these new cooperatives
charged what the market will bear and, in the general shortage
of everything, that meant that they charged too much? And
what if, as many believe, those who made a business of stealing
food from the state shops and bribing officials to turn a blind
eye had now gone into the cooperative movement? Perhaps it
is not surprising that the cooperatives became very unpopular.

It sounds equally good to allow the peasants to lease some
land for a relatively short term and grow on it what they like.
But a man will not take on the long-term investment of the
cultivation of land unless he can leave it to his children. Yet
what is now given may be taken away later, as had often happened before in the Soviet Union.

Where is the vast amount of capital needed for this purpose
to come from, or indeed for any other purpose? There are very
few roads in the vast bulk of Russia; horses were slaughtered
in the collectivization fifty or sixty years ago; and land is useless
without implements to cultivate it. Tractors or horses, ploughs,
and other implements must be obtained from somewhere. Soviet bureaucracy was as niggardly as ever in supplying these
necessary items. It was easier from their point of view to deal
with large collective farms than with hundreds of thousands of
peasants. Moreover there was much disgust among the chair-
men of collective farms in particular and among the *nomenklatura* in general at Gorbachev's reforms. So many, perhaps most,
were unwilling to cooperate with them—and were quietly sabo-
taging them.

No one knew how long it would be before the people lost patience and began to help themselves from the privileged shops. The East German people had already sacked the Stasi headquarters. What would happen if the citizens of Moscow did the same to the Lubyanka?

The problems of switching from an authoritarian to a free society were gravely underestimated (if indeed it was ever intended), and it would have taken much time for *perestroika* to give results. Some of the worst aspects of a Marxist economy were apparent before its potential benefits. In the meantime there might be anarchy; there certainly was great hardship. The Soviet Union began to come apart. Local nationalists underestimated the real difficulties of the Kremlin in untangling countries that had been together for at least a generation, in some cases for two hundred years or more, and whose population was often hopelessly mixed. But in the words of a recent visitor from the Soviet Union, "nationalists, all over the world, see only one thing, their nationalism".

There was no doubt most of the Islamic territories would go their own way. These included Azerbaijan and Russian Turkistan. It was already becoming disagreeable not only for Armenians but also for Russians and Ukrainians to live there. The Azeris are Shiite and may gravitate to Iran, but most of the Moslems in the Soviet Union are Sunnis and not fundamentalists. Indeed in Tsarist times they were notably liberal, and the emancipation of women has now become very marked. The Moslems of the Soviet Union numbered about 60,000,000. Their secession would increase the Slav element in Russia, but Russia would remain a hotch-potch of many peoples, albeit with a Slavonic predominance.

Provided that the Slavonic territories, Great Russia, the Ukraine, and Byelo-Russia, can stay together *in the end,* Russia will still cover a great part of the earth's surface. In the course of 1990 practically all the constituent republics of the Soviet Union declared their "independence" from Moscow, but it was not at all clear what this meant in practice.

It is sometimes said that the Russians are incapable of governing themselves. I believe that the Russians are as capable of good government as other people. The traditional Russian *mir,* the pre-revolutionary *Zemstvos,* and the *Dumas* had great potential, as did the cooperative movement before the revolution. And the phenomenal growth of a system of law between 1860 and the revolution was encouraging.

In contrast to *perestroika, glasnost* surpassed all expectations.

Soviet citizens could now discuss public affairs freely, and the churches were among the chief beneficiaries of *glasnost.* Believers were no longer regarded as second-class citizens, and in October 1990 a law was passed which gave believers most of the rights they had long demanded.

By a happy coincidence the year 1988 was exactly a thousand years after the "Christening of Rus," when Vladimir, the Grand-Prince of Kiev, turned from paganism to Christianity. It was obvious from the preliminaries that this was intended to be a great public relations exercise. But it turned out to be much more. The religious revival in Russia had reached a crucial stage and, with the help of *glasnost,* it became very hard to stop. In recent years very many people had chosen the Christian way. It is impossible to say exactly how many, but it is enough to leaven the whole lump. It was already planned to restore the Danilov monastery in Moscow, with its extensive grounds, to the Orthodox Church. This is now a suitable center for the Patriarch. It had previously been a center for the waifs and strays orphaned by Stalin's purges and other atrocities, and its buildings were in a disgraceful state. Now its churches have been restored, a center for visiting church dignitaries has been built, and, most important of all, the monastic life has been reinstated. A magnificent gateway in the seventeenth-century style was erected. Those who took part in all this extensive work might never have been in a church, but when they found that they were treated with consideration instead of in the offhand way, or worse, of other Soviet institutions, they stayed to worship.

A part of the famous monastery of the Caves at Kiev was given back to the Church, an event of great symbolic importance. At the same time the Orthodox Church and some other churches were allowed for the first time to open more seminaries for the training of priests and pastors. Church representatives were allowed to undertake some charitable work, notably by visiting hospitals, and a start was made in rehabilitation of alcoholics and drug addicts and in prison visiting. In one labor camp a church was already built. A few pioneers were already visiting western countries to learn from example—after a seventy-year gap it is understandable that no one knew how charitable work is to be done. (The improvement was indeed remarkable, but there was still a long way to go.)

Outside Moscow and the chief cities there was great reluctance to cooperate with the reforms. Soviet bureaucracy could still create difficulties: At least a thousand Orthodox congregations were known to be struggling in vain for permission to open a place of worship, though sometimes it was simply a question of repairing an existing church. The prisoners of conscience in concentration camps and psychiatric establishments were fewer, but in 1990 there were still some left, some of them prisoners or psychiatric patients merely for their religious beliefs. And there have been some ominous murders of prominent priests.

So far as was known religious believers were still excluded from positions of power, in particular in the teaching profession. The believers constituted a vast reserve of various talents, who are for the most part incorruptible and would be at the service of the regime and could take the place of many in the *nomenklatura*. The Soviet Union was hopping on one leg, when it needed to run on two.

Yet the revolution in progress was even more far reaching than that of 1917, which in the long run merely substituted one tyranny for another (and a worse one at that). But Tsarism, with all its faults, was capable of growth. Leninism was not.

By the spring of 1991 Russia had reached an impasse. As *perestroika* was increasingly seen to fail, Gorbachev's position was threatened and his decisions were increasingly disregarded. He had turned more and more to old style party comrades, who were colorless and convinced nobody. The Communist system had failed and was deeply unpopular, but what could take its place? Boris Yeltsin in contrast was a rising star, and he was backed by good advisers, some of them from Gorbachev's original entourage. He and Gorbachev needed to work together, but for one reason or another they found this difficult. The base of Yeltsin's popularity was Russia proper, much the largest component of the Soviet Union. Russia now had a parliament separate from the Supreme Soviet of the Soviet Union. He had submitted himself to a popular election and was now President of Russia. Gorbachev on the other had had never submitted himself to a popular election. Then Yeltsin declared Russia an independent state. What this amounted to in practice was far from clear. Moscow had a reforming city council but the Kremlin still claimed supremacy over it. Russia defied the Kremlin and the Kremlin defied Russia. Meanwhile the economic state of the country was catastrophic, and living conditions were intolerable.

But no one could do anything. The military was very strong on the face of it, but it remained uncertain if their troops would follow them if they tried to suppress popular discontent. The

KGB was powerful but had no solution for the problems of the Soviet Union. The Supreme Soviet of the USSR had a majority of the Communist Party but no solution and no leaders, and the Democrats were a minority and could not agree with each other. The Russian Parliament had a strong component of Democrats but was still short of a majority (and even had they had a majority, they would still have been unlikely to muster enough agreement to act). Yeltsin could theoretically have called free elections, but in practice this was out of the question because the Communists, who were well organized, would surely have won against the Democrats, who were not. This ridiculous state of affairs continued until the second half of August when it received a totally unexpected solution. But that is anticipating the end of the story.

As the summer progressed events followed each other swiftly, but nothing was quite as it seemed. Yeltsin forbade Communist Party activity in any workplace, but would the ruling be effective? Yeltsin and Gorbachev seemed at last to have realized that they needed each other, but their alliance was fragile. Yeltsin had charisma and Gorbachev had shown himself sure-footed in managing the Party. At a Central Committee meeting in July he appeared to disengage the Party from its Communist past. His hardliner opponents voted for all his measures including a mixed economy, private property, religious freedom (even for Party members), and freedom of writers and thinkers from "ideological and administrative dictatorship". The Communist Idea would be "a beacon for all mankind, but could not be attained in a foreseeable future". The hardliners did not dare oppose Gorbachev on this occasion, but they hoped later to bring in wrecking amendments. The Western powers promised much aid in "know how" but little cash.

The Party was increasingly unpopular—but so was Gorbachev. There were farcical as well as tragic elements in what was happening: It would take the combined genius of Aeschylus and Aristophanes to do justice to the confusion that reigned in the Soviet Union.

Quite suddenly, in the second half of August, a group of Gorbachev's associates tried to seize power for themselves while he was on holiday in the Crimea. For a brief moment it looked as if they might succeed in restoring the Communist Party to its former preeminence. But this bumbling gaggle of eight grey-haired and grey-suited nonentities made one mistake after another.

At this point, Boris Yeltsin, as President of Russia, stepped forth heroically. He demanded President Gorbachev's return and made it very clear that he stood for democratic reform and constitutional rights. Being warned just in time, he went to Russia's own Parliament in Moscow, which remained in continuous session for three days. He boarded one of the tanks which came to surround the Russian Parliament, shook hands with its commander and called on the army to resist the coup. A small contingent of elite troops went over to Yeltsin's side. Thousands of citizens gathered to defend their Parliament. The Patriarch of Moscow sided with Yeltsin, and a goodly number of the defenders of Parliament made their communions and vowed to shed their blood for freedom. On the second night of the confrontation an attack with overwhelming force was expected hourly. But seeing that they could not hope to prevail without bloodshed, the eight began to fall out among themselves, and the Soviet high command got cold feet. They said they backed the coup, but not with arms, which was the only way to make it prevail. In three days it was all over. Gorbachev was back in office, but there had been a revolution in public opinion.

Appearing for the first time in public he thanked the Russian people and Boris Yeltsin, but evidently he did not realize that public opinion had completely changed. He promised to purge the Communist Party but failed to denounce its complicity in the plot and said he was still a Communist. Evidently he meant to continue working through its organs. He was now back in position—but hardly in power. The eight were in prison awaiting trial. One of them committed suicide as did several less important plotters as well.

Gorbachev had been saved by Yeltsin and had to do what Yeltsin wanted. They appeared jointly in the Russian Parliament. Gorbachev was humiliated and compelled to a far more drastic purge of the Party than he had intended. He had already nominated on the previous day persons to succeed to the Ministry of Defence, the KGB, and the Ministry of the Interior. Now Yeltsin compelled him to cancel these appointments and to appoint trusted reformers in their place. At subsequent meetings Gorbachev showed himself as sure-footed as ever; he had at last made his decision to break with the Party—but too late.

The Party headquarters in Moscow and Leningrad were sealed to prevent the destruction of incriminating documents, and perhaps most significant of all, the statue of Feliks Dzherzhinsky, founder of the KGB, was ignominiously toppled from its resting place outside the Lubyanka. Yeltsin forbade Communist Party cells in the armed forces or the KGB (they had been forbidden in workplaces already). Then on August 24, 1991, Gorbachev bowed to the inevitable. He resigned from his position as General Secretary of the Party and decreed its dissolution. All the vast property of the Party was to be handed over to the civil authorities in each district. Communism and the Russian Empire were finished in one day. A new chapter was beginning with all its fearful dangers and glorious potentialities.

A Peek at the Future

This is a history book and I have been careful to refrain from speculating about the future, but on other occasions I have been free from this inhibition. I have recently been reminded of some words that I used twenty years ago in a lecture at St. Antony's College, Oxford: "Communism will one day collapse like a house of cards, and I shall live to see the day. Beyond the lust for power, there is no substance to it." Once upon a time, Communism was inspired by ideals, but they have gone the way of all flesh. I have had to live more than ten years beyond the allotted span to see these words of mine come true, but in the course of 1989 and 1990 Communism had indeed collapsed throughout central and eastern Europe, and only a tattered remnant remained in the Soviet Union. Russia is now entering on a new time of troubles, a *smutnoye vremya*.

I repeat what I have said before, that Russian human nature abhors a vacuum. If one ideology fails then they will search for something better. It is now clear that the Russian Orthodox Church in one form or another will be at the center of Russian life in the next century. It has learnt much from its tribulation over the past seventy years—how much will now become clear. It is greatly to be hoped that in the future Russia will be subject to the rule of law, but traces of Leninism may remain.

I did not foresee that the collapse of Communism would coincide with the end of the eighteenth-century Enlightenment in the rest of the world. This is not so obvious or so spectacular as the collapse of Communism, but the signs are there. The Enlightenment, which has dominated the world for nearly three centuries, gave us many good things—in particular, science. But science now has to justify itself by results, notably in ecology but also in other aspects of human well-being. We are now more prepared to listen to what other cultures and other peoples may have to each us. We have learned much, but may we not also have unlearned as much since man was "primitive"?

The eastern variety of materialism is now discredited, but the western variety of materialism is also now on trial. The damages of unrestrained capitalism are becoming daily more apparent. In the new age that is now dawning, there will be many dangers. The eminent philosopher Alfred North Whitehead said, "It is the business of the future to be dangerous".

Laplace, the great eighteenth-century astronomer, said to Napoleon, "God is a hypothesis that I do not find necessary." Scientists are becoming increasingly unsure, as evidence accumulates that the universe has to be finely tuned in order to make life possible.

A hundred years ago on a day of full tide at Dover Beach, Matthew Arnold wrote:

> The sea of faith
> Was once, too, at the full. . . . . . .
> But now I only hear
> Its melancholy, long, withdrawing roar.

But now the tide may well be on the turn. And the\people of Rus will play their full part in this turning of the tide.

Postscript

This book was revised just in time for Christmas 1991. But owing to the vagaries of publishing in a depression it will not reach the public until the middle of 1993. In the meantime the disintegration of the Soviet Union has continued. Yeltsin is faced with the impossible task of getting results in a short time. He has initially lost popularity in consequence. Moreover he is faced with a Congress in which his supporters are outnumbered by his critics. He has lost some ground but his critics have next to nothing to put in the place of his reforms; the West looks on benevolently but not altogether helpfully.

Yeltsin has great qualities and does not lose hope. In this situation the media almost inevitably concentrate on the difficulties, and less news is given of the grains of mustard seed which are scattered over the face of the former Soviet Union.

A.D.

A.D.

1914 Outbreak of First World War.

1917 February Revolution. March to November, Kerensky regime. Oct. 25th, O.S./Nov. 7th, N.S., October Revolution.

1918 March, Treaty of Brest-Litovsk. November, victory of Allies over Germany.

1918-22 Civil war followed by German, and afterward Allied, intervention.

1921 NEP (New Economic Policy).

1921-22 Famine.

1924 Death of Lenin.

1927 Expulsion of Trotsky from Communist Party.

1928 Beginning of first Five-Year Plan and of collectivization.

1933 Beginning of second Five-Year Plan.

1936-38 Moscow trials and the Great Terror.

1938 Third Five-Year Plan.

1939 Ribbentrop-Molotov agreement. Soviet Union occupies eastern Poland and secures bases in Esthonia, Latvia and Lithuania.

1939-40 Soviet-Finnish War.

1940 Lithuania, Latvia, Esthonia and Bessarabia incorporated into Soviet Union.

1919 Treaty of Versailles.

1923 Failure of Communist rising in Germany.

1926 General strike in Great Britain.

1927 Kuomintang turns against Chinese Communists.

1929 Beginning of world economic crisis.

1931 Japanese seize Manchuria.

1933 Nazi revolution in Germany.

1935 Abyssinian crisis and war.

1936-39 Spanish Civil War.

1937 Beginning of Sino-Japanese War.

1938 Munich crisis.

1939-45 Second World War.

1940 Collapse of France.

1941 Pearl Harbor.

1945 Death of Roosevelt. VE Day. Hiroshima. VJ Day.

1947 Independence of India and Pakistan.

1948 Communist victory in China and Tito breaks

1941   Hitler invades Soviet Union, June 22.
1943   Sergius becomes Patriarch.
1945   Victory over Germany.
1946   Bad harvest.
1947   Beginning of cold war.
1953   March, Stalin dies. August, Soviet Union explodes hydrogen bomb.
1956   Twentieth party congress (*"dethronement of Stalin"*).
1957   Khrushchev supreme.
1964   Fall of Khrushchev.
1975   Soviet Union and other powers sign Helsinki agreement.
1985   Gorbachev becomes First Secretary of the Party.
1991   Yeltsin elected President of Russia. Russian Empire collapses.

       with Cominform.
1952   America explodes hydrogen bomb.
1956   Gomulka becomes first secretary of party in Poland.
       Hungarian revolt.
1959   Khrushchev visits USA.
1968   January, Stalinist leaders ousted in Czechoslovakia.
       August, Warsaw-Pact powers led by Soviet Union invade Czechoslovakia.
1991   Communism collapses.

suggestions
for further reading

NOTE.—Where an author is referred to in the text of this book by name without further details, the reference is to the book listed below under his name.

GENERAL HISTORIES OF RUSSIA
B. H. Sumner, *Survey of Russian History*, 1944.
Brilliant but rather confusing. Tells the story backward.
D. S. Mirsky, *Russia, a Social History*, 1931.
Stimulating; semi-Marxist.
S. F. Platonov, *History of Russia*, 1925.
Good standard history; goes down to 1881.
V. O. Klyuchevsky, *A History of Russia*. 5 vols.
The greatest work of Russia's greatest historian.
Michael T. Florinsky, *Russia, A History and an Interpretation*, 1953.
John Lawrence, *Soviet Russia*, 1967.
A richly illustrated historical and geographical sketch. Differs from the present work in treating the history of Russia in its context as part of the history of the Soviet Union as a whole.

STUDIES OF SPECIAL ASPECTS, PERIODS OR SUBJECTS
Sir Donald Mackenzie Wallace, *Russia*. 2 vols., 1905.
A classical account of Russia at the end of the last century.
A. Leroy Beaulieu, *L'Empire des Tsars*. 3 vols.
Quite as good as Mackenzie Wallace, but more detailed.
N. Berdyaev, *The Origin of Russian Communism*, 1937.
A penetrating account of the spiritual origins of Bolshevism by a Marxist turned Christian.
Sir Bernard Pares, *Russia, The Fall of the Russian Monarchy*, and many other books
Sir Bernard Pares' *History of Russia* is a useful guide but it lacks some of the inspiration of his other books.

354

Sir John Maynard, *Russia in Flux*, 1941, and *The Russian Peasant*, 1942.
Very interesting studies of various aspects of Russian thought and society by a distinguished Indian civil servant.

Hugh Seton-Watson, *The Decline of Imperial Russia*, 1952.
A useful account of the last decades of tsarism.

W. E. D. Allen, *The Ukraine*, 1940.
An excellent short history.

B. H. Sumner, *Peter the Great and the Emergence of Russia*, 1950.
Short and illuminating.

George Kennan, *Siberia and the Exile System*, 1891.
A classical account of the exile system as it was in the 1880s.

Camilla Gray, *The Great Experiment, Russian Art 1863–1922*, 1962.
A pioneering work on the great age of modern Russian art. First class.

Eugene Schuyler, *Life of Peter the Great*, 2 vols., 1884.
A good, standard Victorian biography by an American diplomatist.

Maurice Baring, *An Outline of Russian Literature*, 1914, and *Landmarks in Russian Literature*, 1910, and other books.
Wise and sympathetic observations of Russia before the revolution.

W. Weidlé, *Russia Absent and Present*, 1952.
Perceptive, well-informed, discerning and well-written ruminations on Russian history.

Hans Kohn, *The Mind of Modern Russia*, 1955.
Admirably chosen extracts from Russian thinkers with a useful introduction to each section.

Voltaire, *Charles XII*.
A classical picture of the confrontation of Charles XII and Peter the Great.

Edward Crankshaw, *The Shadow of the Winter Palace*, 1976.
A brilliant account of the drift to revolution from 1825 to 1917. Very critical of Russia, but sympathgetic to Russians. One of the few books that does justice to the reformers who worked within the system.

THE SOVIET UNION

E. H. Carr, *The Bolshevik Revolution*.
Eight vols, have appeared so far.
An immensely able account of the early years of the Bolshevik regime.

I. Deutscher, *Stalin,* 1949, *The Prophet Armed, Trotsky: 1897–1921,* 1954 and *The Prophet Unarmed, Trotsky: 1921–1929,* 1959.
These famous biographies deserve their reputation.

L. Schapiro, *The Origin of the Communist Autocracy, Political Opposition in the Soviet State, 1917–22,* 1955.
Scholarly, well written and full of moral penetration. Corrects Carr and Deutscher on some important points. Readers who are in a hurry will get the gist of the argument by reading the first few pages and the last few pages of every chapter.

L. Schapiro, *The Communist Party of the Soviet Union.*
A history of the party from its origins to 1959. Scholarly and illuminating but not always easy reading.

Sir Robert Bruce-Lockhart, *Memoirs of a British Agent.*
A real-life thriller about the Bolshevik revolution.

N. Sukhanov, *The Russian Revolution, 1917,* 1955.
A firsthand account of the period between the two revolutions of 1917 by an active left-wing socialist who was not a Communist. Assumes much detailed knowledge but could be skimmed with profit by any intelligent reader.

John Scott, *Behind the Urals,* 1942.
A firsthand account of Magnitogorsk in construction.

Littlepage and Bess, *In Search of Soviet Gold,* 1939.
Memoirs of an American mining engineer who worked in the Soviet Union. Valuable for its firsthand observation and lack of political *parti pris.*

Beck and Godin, *Russian Purge,* 1951.
An objective account of the Great Terror by two of its victims.

Alex Novre, *The Soviet Economy: An Introduction,* 1961.
Short, clear, well-informed and realistic.

Donald W. Treadgold, *The West in Russia and China, Vol. 1, Russia 1472–1917,* 1973.
An invaluable account of secular and religious thought. Learned, original, and judicious.

Axkady Vaksberg, *The Soviet Mafia,* 1991.
A brilliant and brave account by a Soviet journalist. Shows how corruption leads to the very top of the system. Makes your hair stand on end.

RELIGION

G. P. Fedotov, *A Treasury of Russian Spirituality,* 1950.
Contains translations of Russian spiritual classics including the "Autobiography of the Archpriest Avvakum," "The Way

of a Pilgrim" and biographical notes about St. Seraphim of Sarov.

W. H. Frere, *Some Links in the Chain of Russian Church History*, 1918.

By the late Bishop of Truro. First class.

Nicholas Zernov, *St. Sergius*, 1939, *The Russians and their Church*, 1945, and *The Russian Religious Renaissance of the Twentieth Century*, 1963.

J. Birkbeck, *Russia and the English Church*, 1895.

Birkbeck and the Russian Church. Ed. Riley, 1917.

Paul B. Anderson, *People, Church and State in Modern Russia,* 1944.

Michael Bourdeaux, *Opium of the People*, 1965.

The best up-to-date account of religion in Russia since 1917 available so far.

Walter Kolarz, *Religion in the Soviet Union*, 1961.

A work of careful, pioneering scholarship. Especially good on the Protestants.

C. P. Fedotov, *The Russian Religious Mind*. 2 vols., 1946 and 1966.

The best general account of Russian religion from the beginning. Combines scholarship with originality of interpretation. Has elements of greatness.

The Unknown Homeland, 1978.

The moving story of an Orthodox priest from Tsarism to Stalin, written by his niece. Likely to become a classic. Beautifully written and translated by Marite Sapiets.

Michael Bourdeaux, *Gorbachev, Glasnost and the Gospel*, 1990.

A brilliant account of the Developments in Christianity up to 1990. An American edition published by Stephanie House under the title of *The Triumph of Christianity over Communism* brings the story up to date to the middle of 1991.

Victor Borovsky, *Chalyapin*, 1988.

More than a biography—casts light on Russian life, high and low, and history, as well as the arts of the turn of the century.

THE RUSSIAN CLASSICS

Russian classical literature contains much sound history. Pushkin had a strong historical sense. The opera *Boris Godunov* follows closely a play by Pushkin, which is modeled on Shakespeare's historical plays, and *The Captain's Daughter* is a long short story about the revolt of Pugachev in the reign of Catherine the Great. Merezhovski's *Peter and Alexis* is a first-class historical novel about Peter the Great which makes extensive and skillful use of original documents. Alexis Tolstoy's *Peter I* is a panoramic picture of Peter's age; the evident wish to find indirect justification for Stalin does not spoil its value as much as might be expected.

The work of the Russian novelists of the nineteenth century constitutes a sort of collective history of the period; it is scarcely possible to make a rational selection from such a rich field. No one is likely to miss *War and Peace* or Tolstoy's stories about the siege of Sevastopol. Gorgol's *Dead Souls* and Turgenev's *Sportman's Sketches* describe the Russian countryside before the liberation of the serfs. Turgenev's *Fathers and Sons* describes the Nihilist movement at the moment of its birth (Turgenev invented the name "Nihilist"). Leskov, who is not as well known outside Russia as he should be, describes every aspect of Russian Church life. His *Cathedral Folk* is the story of a Russian Barchester, but it is even better than Trollope. Gorki's autobiographical works are a panorama of Russian working-class life toward the turn of the century.

Doctor Zhivago by Boris Pasternak is a poetical novel that gives a true and perceptive account of the Revolution as seen by the liberal intelligentsia. Until his death in 1960 Pasternak was probably the greatest Russian poet alive. The unvarnished realities of life in the Russian countryside are well described in Abramov's *The New Life* (tr. by George Reavey, 1963) and in "Matryona's House" by Solzhenitsyn. Such works give flesh and blood to some facts which otherwise would only be inferred from obscure hints and silences. Solzhenitsyn's *One Day in the Life of Ivan Denisovich* is a description of life in a concentration camp which stands in the great tradition of Russian realism; it is now followed by *First Circle* and *Cancer Ward,* which have not been published in the Soviet Union but establish Solzhenitsyn as a great writer. His subject is Stalinism; and Stalinism will probably be remembered in Solzhenitsyn's picture of it, as the life of exiles under tsarism is remembered in the picture given by Dostoyevski in *Letters from the House of One Dead.* Solzhemitsyn's *The Gulag Archipelago* must now be added to the incomparable history of Russia left us by the great Russian writers.

index

THE MAKING OF AMERICAN HISTORY

☐ **LEE AND GRANT by Gene Smith.** One was the great personification of the Southern beau ideal; the other was a graceless, small-town Midwesterner. Both reached their summits of glory in a war that filled them with horror and each had to build a new life in the war's aftermath. In this book—as in life—they illumine and define each other's greatness, and give human meaning to the conflict that the struggle between them decided. (010004—$11.95)

☐ **ABRAHAM LINCOLN: The Man Behind the Myths by Stephen B. Oates.** He has been called the Great Emancipator and a white racist, a devotee of democracy and an incipient tyrant. His life has been cloaked in the mists of time and distorted by both the devotion and the enmity that he inspired. With his pioneering research Oates offers us a picture of Lincoln as he really was. (009391—$10.00)

☐ **WITNESS TO GETTYSBURG by Richard Wheeler.** An eyewitness history of the bloodiest battle in America's Civil War. From the courageous fighting men and officers to the men and women watching as the conflict raged through their towns, from the reporters riding with the regiments to the children excited or terrified by the titanic drama unfolding before them—each account stems from personal experience and blends with the whole to create a startlingly vivid tapestry of war. (009847—$9.00)

☐ **CRAZY HORSE AND CUSTER by Stephen E. Ambrose.** Crazy Horse, leader of the Oglala Sioux, and General George Armstrong Custer. Both were men of aggression and supreme courage, and became leaders in their societies at very early ages. Their parallel lives would pave the way, in a manner unknown to either, for an inevitable clash between two nations—one red, one white—fighting for possession of the open prairie. "Movingly told and well written."—*Library Journal* (009340—$15.00)

Prices slightly higher in Canada.

Buy them at your local bookstore or use this convenient coupon for ordering.

NEW AMERICAN LIBRARY
P.O. Box 999, Dept. #17109
Bergenfield, New Jersey 07621

Please send me the books I have checked above.
I am enclosing $_____ (please add $2.00 to cover postage and handling).
Send check or money order (no cash or C.O.D.'s) or charge by Mastercard or VISA (with a $15.00 minimum). Prices and numbers are subject to change without notice.

Card # _____ Exp. Date _____
Signature _____
Name _____
Address _____
City _____ State _____ Zip Code _____

For faster service when ordering by credit card call **1-800-253-6476**

Allow a minimum of 4-6 weeks for delivery. This offer is subject to change without notice